A FAMILY OF NO PROMINENCE

The Descendants of Pak Tŏkhwa
and the Birth of Modern Korea

Eugene Y. Park

Stanford University Press
Stanford, California

Stanford University Press
Stanford, California

Printed in the United States of America on acid-free, archival-quality paper

Library of Congress Cataloging-in-Publication Data

Park, Eugene Y., author.
  A family of no prominence : the descendants of Pak Tŏkhwa and the birth of
modern Korea / Eugene Y. Park.
      pages   cm
  Includes bibliographical references and index.
  ISBN 978-0-8047-8876-2 (cloth : alk. paper)
  1. Pak family. 2. Korea—Genealogy. 3. Social status—Korea—History. 4. Korea—
History—Choson dynasty, 1392–1910. 5. Korea—History—Japanese occupation,
1910–1945. I. Title.
CS1339.P37 2014
929.209519—dc23
                                                                2013033797

In memory of Edward W. Wagner

Contents

Acknowledgments

IN RESEARCHING AND WRITING THIS BOOK, I HAVE LEARNED MUCH from mentors and colleagues over the years. First and foremost, my deepest gratitude goes to Edward W. Wagner at Harvard. It was he who led me to study the social history of Korea through a wide range of sources rarely used for such purposes, especially written genealogies (*chokpo*). Sadly, he succumbed to illness and passed away in 2001, but his influence on my research continues and I dedicate this book to his memory. Many other colleagues and scholars have shared their insights on various aspects of this project, and I would especially like to thank An Jong Chol, Donald L. Baker, Frank L. Chance, Chu Chin-Oh, Frederick R. Dickinson, John B. Duncan, Todd A. Henry, Kyung Moon Hwang, Kim In-Geol, Kyu Hyun Kim, Kirk W. Larsen, James B. Lewis, Mizuno Naoki, Park Tae-Gyun, Mark A. Peterson, Kathryn A. Ragsdale, Kenneth R. Robinson, Song Hyeon-Kang, Ronald P. Toby, Anne Walthall, Yang Jin-Suk, and Yi Tae-Jin, as well as three anonymous reviewers.

This book would not have been feasible without the innumerable testimonies that supplement the written sources. For this, I would especially like to thank Chu Ja Cho, Kim Yosuk, Pak Kŭndong, Pak Pyŏnghae, Pak Yŏngil, Pang Kijun, and Brian Park. Before I completed the book, Chu Ja Cho passed away in 2011; of the remaining group the youngest is eighty. Interviewing the elderly has taught me the importance of oral history and of tapping into their wisdom and knowledge before it is too late.

This book project has received funding from various sources. Though I began the original research in 2004, a 2007–08 Seoul National University Kyujanggak Institute for Korean Studies Fellowship allowed me to take a giant step forward. Conducting research at the institute was an enviable experience from any scholar's vantage point in that I had unlimited access to a huge archive of primary sources—including many unavailable anywhere else in the world. For this support, I thank Kim Young Shik and Cho Eun-su, then the directors of, respectively, the Kyujanggak Institute for Korean Studies and the International Center for Korean Studies. Thereafter, a Weiler Fellowship from the University of Pennsylvania School of Arts and Sciences (spring term of 2013) provided research funding and release from teaching obligations so that I could focus on revising my book manuscript. Since the inception of the project, I have also received smaller research grants from the Humanities Center and the International Center for Writing and Translation, both at the University of California, Irvine, as well as the Penn Center for East Asian Studies.

Of course, a historian's craft would be impossible without the support of librarians, and in this regard I would like to thank Ying Zhang and Alban Kojima. As the East Asian Studies Librarian of UC Irvine's Langson Library, Ying was both capable and tenacious in acquiring microfilm copies of the Korean household registration records of 1896–1907 presently possessed by the Kyoto University Museum, an important primary source for this project. Alban is now happily retired, but in his former role as East Asian studies librarian at Penn's Van Pelt Library, he ably arranged the purchase of and subscription to electronic Korean journal databases. Thanks to his work, I have been able to consult the necessary secondary sources for my research more readily.

Throughout the writing and revision stages, I received much help with manuscript preparation. Frank L. Chance and Holly J. Stephens copyedited the presubmission text; An Gwang Ho, John S. Lee, Lee Youjin, and Wai Kit Tse suggested additional source citations; Jae Won Kim designed maps and genealogical charts; and Seok Lee assisted with obtaining permissions for illustrations.

More than anyone else, my wife, Seri, has been my rock of support. Almost as soon as my previous book was published in 2007, Seri let me go to South Korea to conduct the field research necessary for this project, even though this meant that she had to take care of our young daughter, Lauren, alone while working full-time. For Lauren too, it was hard to not see her father for so long. Born in 2009, my son, Harry, is still too young to have noticed much of my book-writing odyssey, although I look forward to sharing the detail of this most personal research project with him and Lauren in time. Not only does this book tell the story of the Paks over 350 years; writing it has come to help me further appreciate my own family as they continue to build their own history.

Illustrations

Maps

Figures

Photographs

Tables

Conventions

MEASURING TIME FROM A GLOBALLY ACCEPTED REFERENCE point is a relatively recent phenomenon in human history, and this is all too evident in the story of Korea's transition to modernity. The East Asian lunar calendar was the standard in Korea until the Chosŏn government went solar on the seventeenth day of the eleventh lunar month of 1895, or New Year's Day of 1896 according to the Gregorian calendar. To distinguish between the two date types, my primary source citations use the format of "January 1, 1800," for Gregorian dates and "1800.1.1" for the East Asian lunar calendar. This is not the only example of cultural differences in recording time. On a more personal level, the customary Korean age count regards a person to be of one *se* in age at birth, subsequently gaining a year on every New Year's Day. This means that one's age in *se* is either one or two years greater than one's age according to Western practice.

A large number of non-English terms appear in this book, and this reflects the relative youth of the field of Korean history in the West. Compared to Chinese and Japanese terms, widely accepted English translations are unavailable for the majority of Korean terms. Accordingly, I provide the romanized Korean in parentheses for almost every English translation of a Korean term, though in some rare cases I found romanized Korean terms preferable to translations. For example, in the bibliography, I leave the somewhat antiquated term "Hanmal" (or "Kuhanmal") untranslated, as the literal translation "at the end of old Korea" is awkward. Wherever necessary, I give the English meaning inside parentheses following these romanized Korean terms.

This book generally employs Pinyin, Revised Hepburn, and McCune-Reischauer systems for the romanization of, respectively, Chinese, Japanese, and Korean terms. Exceptions include alternative spellings such as "Seoul" that have become widely known. Likewise, for the sake of practicality and recognition, I render colonial Korea's local place names in Korean pronunciation, even though the official language at the time was Japanese.

I translate the administrative units of place names as follows (in descending order of size):

Province (*to*) → county (*kun, hyŏn*) → district (*myŏn*) → subdistrict (*i*)
Post-1914 urban center (*si, pu*) → district (*ku*) → subdistrict (*tong, chŏng*)

The pre-1914 administrative hierarchy of Seoul (Hansŏng, Kyŏngsŏng) had more levels. Instead of translating these I employ romanized Korean originals for such localities, but they follow the descending order of size as follows: *pu, sŏ* → *pang* → *kye* → *tong*. The text omits the administrative label for given locales if it is clear from context.

Besides places, how this book refers to individuals will be unfamiliar to many readers, and this is especially true for females. Until the late twentieth century, written genealogies (*chokpo*) rarely recorded the given names of females. Instead, it typically noted the wife of a subject descent group's male member by her patrilineal ancestral seat (*pon'gwan*) and surname, for example, "Kimhae Kim," while recording a daughter only by the full name of her husband. A corollary to this custom is that a genealogy omits a daughter who died without marrying. When discussed in the text, I precede a woman's ancestral seat and surname with "Madam," roughly an English equivalent of the Korean term referring to a man's wife as "*puin*." Even if just implied in the text, the Character List supplies the surname of a person listed. Also, on genealogical charts, only those mentioned in the text appear with names.

Conversion rates for Korean measures and currency are as follows:

Measures of distance, area, and volume

chŏk	approximately 0.3 meters
kan	approximately 1.8 meters
i	approximately 0.4 kilometers

p'yŏng   3.3058 square meters
sŏk   90 to 120 liters

Relative value of currency

p'un   worth approximately 0.18 liters of rice in the nineteenth century
chŏn   10 *p'un*
yang   10 *chŏn*
wŏn   10 *yang*

CHINA

Manchuria

RUSSIA

Tumen R.

Paektu M. ▲

Yalu R.

Hamgyŏng P.

P'yŏngan P.

Yŏnghŭng

P'yŏngyang

Taedong R.

Kŭmgang M.

Hwanghae P.

Kangwŏn P.

•Haeju

Sŏrak M.

East Sea

Kyŏnggi P.

Hansŏng (Seoul)

Han R.

•Wŏnju

Yellow Sea

Ch'ungch'ŏng P.

Kyŏngsang P.

Kŭm R.

Kongju

Naktong R.

Chŏnju

Tŏgyu M. ▲

Taegu

Chŏlla P.

▲ *Chiri M.*

Korea Strait

Tsushima I.

N

Cheju I.

▲ *Halla M.*

0 ▬▬▬ 100km

JAPAN

MAP 1 Chosŏn Korea as of 1864. Provincial boundaries and seats, major rivers and mountains, and neighboring countries are shown. Abbreviations: I. (Island), *M.* (Mountain), P. (Province), *R.* (River). Source: a digitized map provided by Research Institute of Korean Studies, Korea University. Revised with permission.

MAP 2 Kyŏnggi province as of 1864. For a county shown on the map, a dashed line indicates its administrative boundary, within which subcounty-level administrative units, if mentioned in the text, also are shown. Abbreviations: F. (Fortress), *M.* (Mountain), P. (Province), *R.* (River). Source: a digitized map provided by Research Institute of Korean Studies, Korea University. Revised with permission.

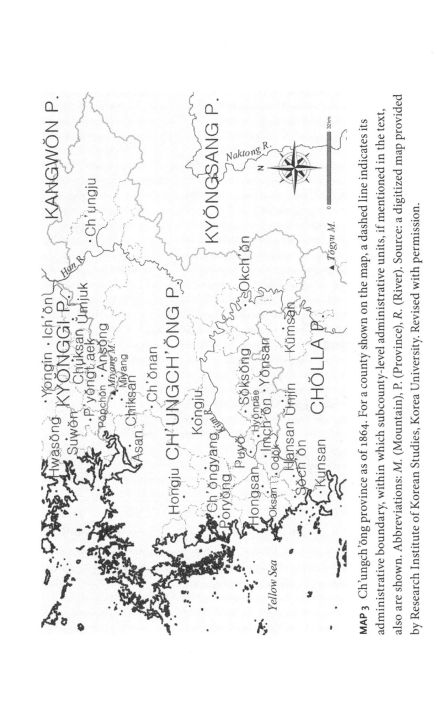

MAP 3 Ch'ungch'ŏng province as of 1864. For a county shown on the map, a dashed line indicates its administrative boundary, within which subcounty-level administrative units, if mentioned in the text, also are shown. Abbreviations: M. (Mountain), P. (Province), R. (River). Source: a digitized map provided by Research Institute of Korean Studies, Korea University. Revised with permission.

A FAMILY OF NO PROMINENCE

Prologue

ANY IN MODERN KOREA REMAIN CONCERNED NOT SO MUCH with their actual ancestors as with their supposedly inherited ancestral status. By the early twentieth century, every Korean had a surname and an ancestral seat (*pon'gwan*) designation.[1] As a genealogical identifier, the combination ostensibly designated the individual as a member of a descent group with a history informed by a master narrative emphasizing descent from royals or aristocrats (*yangban*).[2] Unlike communist North Korea, where the notion of a descent group as a discrete historical entity has more or less vanished,[3] in the South it has become so institutionalized that even as recently as a decade ago civil law prohibited a man and a woman of ostensibly the same descent group from marrying each other.[4] Despite this strict attention to genealogy, today an ordinary South Korean would be hard-pressed to name all four grandparents or explain the whereabouts of ancestors before the twentieth century.[5] In fact, most do not know their immediate ancestors' roles, if any, during such nationally celebrated historical events as the March First Movement of 1919, when millions of Koreans protested Japanese colonial rule.[6]

How did so many Korean families lose the memory of their past? What was the process by which people shed old identities and took on new ones? What does the series of changes in how families think about their past tell us about Korea's transition from a largely agrarian, rigidly status-bound society to a modernizing nation-state to a Japanese colony to a land governed by an industrialized democracy in the south and a totalitarian regime in the north?

My book explores these issues through the story of a Miryang Pak family of "middle people," or *chungin*, social standing by the end of the early modern era (ca. 1500–ca. 1880).[7] During the period, the family's social status improved from that of commoners to *chungin*, state-employed specialists in various areas, by careful investment of their increasing cultural and economic capital. From roughly 1880 to 1904, during the period of Korea's adjustment to the world of imperialism, they, like so many other *chungin*, achieved prominence in politics, business, and culture. My study of the Paks suggests that the *chungin* as a distinct status group encompassed a greater variety of specialist families and took longer to take shape in early modern Korea than has been hitherto recognized. Existing studies highlight certain famous *chungin* who "collaborated" with the Japanese, but many Paks were bitter about the Japanese annexation of Korea as it deprived them of newfound leadership roles in Imperial Korea (1897–1910).[8] Even more importantly, colonial modernity produced a sense of dislocation and a suspicion of history among the Paks and other Koreans of *chungin* descent.[9]

The story of the *chungin* Paks reveals an apparent contradiction. It was the increased prominence and success of the Paks and other *chungin* during Korea's transition to modernity that led to their exclusion from modern Korea's hegemonic discourse on descent. In general, as the demise of rigid status hierarchy accelerated in the nineteenth century, *chungin* responses varied in accord with the phases that modern Korean society underwent vis-à-vis perceptions of status and memory. Although *chungin* kept their own genealogical records (*chokpo*), in the modern era they and their descendants displayed increasing ambivalence toward genealogies. While some chose to invent traditions through genealogical maneuvers popular among families of commoner or low-born descent, and others preserved genealogies out of custom, most rejected the old culture by ceasing to participate in genealogy compilations. In fact, how the *chungin* responded to the emerging master narratives as the rigid status hierarchy broke down suggests phases of general social change and the broadening of the base of actors represented in historical narratives.[10]

Telling the story of the Paks is not only an inquiry into social change but also my own effort to recover memories of personal significance. The Paks are my patrilineal ancestors, whose stories I have come to know only in the last few years. As an elementary school student in 1970s South Korea, I liked history, which, as everyone was taught at the time, could not be merely interesting but had to inspire. Thus on New Year's Day and Autumn Harvest Day (*Ch'usŏk*) of each year, family members near and far were supposed to come together to perform ancestor worship rituals and share stories about forebears who had distinguished themselves as loyal subjects, filial sons, or chaste widows. Neither I nor most of my friends, however, were aware that we had any such ancestors. My father, grandmother (my grandfather had died twenty-three years before I was born), uncles, and aunts were not much more knowledgeable, although as is true for every Korean they knew our ancestral seat as Paks. I had some friends who mentioned the voluminous genealogical records their families possessed as well as the generational characters in their given names, but no one in my family knew about such things. In the 1980s, as an undergraduate at UCLA, where the library's East Asian–language section had books on Korean genealogy, I concluded that tracing my patrilineal ancestry without determining the branch (*p'a*) affiliation or the generational characters was perhaps impossible. During my graduate study in the 1990s at Harvard, thanks to the large collection of dusty, often moldy, old Korean genealogies in the Harvard-Yenching Library, I learned a great deal about my mother's amazingly well documented ancestors, who were mostly landed local aristocrats, but could find nothing about my paternal side. I subsequently completed my dissertation in 1999 and became a tenure-stream academic doing research and teaching while my more personal search continued.

It was during my research on military examination graduates that the breakthrough came on April 14, 2004—my birthday, as if my patrilineal great-grandfather's spirit had chosen the day to reveal itself. After years of wondering who he was, I found him in a late nineteenth-century record of palace guard duty officers. What he, his kinsmen, and his associates did during the Open Port Period (1876–1910) showed that my great-grandfather was from a Seoul *chungin* family, apparently a line descended from an illegitimate (*sŏŏl*) son. Some of my great-grandfather's associates were already known to historians, as conventional studies and references mention them in conjunction with their involvement in various events or organizations during the period of the Korean Empire. Such works, however, while providing details about these individuals' activities, make no mention of their seemingly unknown family backgrounds.[11]

During the months of further research, I realized that the minutiae about my ancestors, their time, and their world, as well as how I uncovered them, were laden with implications. By examining the fate of *chungin* in the modern era in connection with master narratives on ancestry, we can begin to understand how old status anxieties under the Chosŏn dynasty (1392–1910), the impact of Western institutions and ideas, Japanese colonial rule, and varied Korean responses to all these things have contributed to the construction of a usable past while obscuring diverse human experiences. The descent group narratives that crystallized in early modern Korea have framed popular discussions of ancestry in a way that allows little room for real family stories. Also, historical practice has compounded this preclusion. As is true now among historians everywhere, Korea historians have begun to pay attention to the historical agency of marginalized groups, but narratives on nonelite families spanning generations across the modern-premodern divide are rare.[12]

The *chungin* and their descendants, sometimes by their own doing, have not made their family histories an easy subject of inquiry. Unlike the aristocracy, for whom genealogies record most members and their descendants to the present, the majority of *chungin* and their descendants have not participated in genealogy compilations since the late nineteenth century, and the editions published since then record descendants for fewer than a quarter of those who had been recorded in the genealogy as of the midnineteenth century.[13] Moreover, as is true for others who were not of the aristocracy, the *chungin* are vastly underrepresented in comparison to the aristocracy in primary sources such as court histories, local gazetteers, literary collections, and other private documents.

Overrepresentation of the elite in sources certainly is not a problem unique to Korea, but misperceptions, often invidious, about *chungin* have long exacerbated the situation. Consider, for example, detailed Korean genealogical encyclopedia entries on individual descent groups—all stressing royals and aristocrats among their antecedents. One such entry states that in the Chosŏn period, members of an ostensibly aristocratic lineage avoided living at the county seat "swarming with *chungin*," that is, hereditary local functionaries (hyangni).[14] Even a dean of Korean history declares in his popular Korean history survey that, lacking the strong self-esteem of aristocrats, status-seeking *chungin* ultimately not only welcomed Western culture but also produced many pro-Japanese collaborators.[15]

More careful studies examining the *chungin* from various angles began to appear in the 1980s, and we can divide their approaches into four groups. One group of studies seeks a better understanding of the capital *chungin* of Seoul through institutional histories.[16] Highly empirical in approach, these works shed light on the formation of Seoul *chungin* as a status category with an emphasis on technical specialists, their career patterns, and their struggles against the aristocracy's denigration of their expertise and their exclusion from the most important positions in officialdom. Although laying a good foundation for further research on *chungin*, many among these studies lack a narrative with more vivid human faces.

A new group of studies examining *chungin* families or individuals eventually emerged.[17] Mostly article-length publications, these generally highlight renowned technical specialist *chungin*—particularly those who played a prominent role during the Open Port Period. These studies tend to be microscopic in that their analyses and observations focused on narrow, period-specific issues rather than viewing the *chungin* within the larger historical context of Korea's transition to modernity.

The third group of studies exploring *chungin* culture and examining its literature reveals that by the nineteenth century, many Seoul *chungin* not only were maintaining lively literary circles of their own but were even interacting with the aristocracy.[18] A major weakness of these studies is that they tend to overemphasize the extent to which the *chungin* rubbed shoulders with aristocrats, even though in reality the former, even if duly performing specialized duties for the state and its aristocratic proprietors, were frustrated with the glass ceiling blocking their advancement.

Looking at prominent *chungin* of the modern era during the Open Port and colonial periods, a fourth group of studies highlights their roles in politics, culture, and business.[19] These works present *chungin* as harbingers of Korea's modernity as they welcomed Western institutions and ideas while accommodating Japanese colonial rule. Many tend to overestimate *chungin* wealth, influence, and pro-Japanese collaboration—ultimately regarding them as the prototype for the new elite flourishing in postcolonial South Korea.

Overall, even though explaining who the *chungin* were and what prominent *chungin* did, previous studies have not situated them within the social changes of early modern and modern Korea. The larger meaning of the lives of more rank-and-file *chungin* and their descendants during the colonial and postcolonial eras in relation to the macrohistory of Korea remains to be elaborated. Accordingly, studying the history of the Paks can help us not only better understand *chungin* status in early modern Korea but also reflect on master narratives and historical agency in modern Korea.

This book employs several strategies. Above all, it consults a wide range of previously underused primary sources, as well as oral history, to reconstruct a multigenerational history of the sort of ordinary, nonelite family that historians often neglect.[20] Second, in pursuit of the larger issue of social change, it involves the Paks to a significant extent in each chapter to offer a stronger narrative thread and to give the account an essential element of human interest. Third, this study seeks to identify patterns of self-representation of *chungin* through their genealogies, a project that requires addressing issues of accuracy and reliability in Korean genealogy in general. Fourth, it endeavors to map the varied responses of *chungin* and their descendants to the demise of a rigid late Chosŏn (ca. 1724–1910) status hierarchy. Although many *chungin* descendants, as noted, sought to distance themselves from genealogy compilation, a small number of *chungin*-descent families did continue to participate in genealogy compilation—a pattern that seems to correlate with education or influence.[21]

Each chapter of this book comprises two sections, together intended to keep the story of the Paks closer to the broader story while furnishing necessary context. The first section explains the general historical setting and how the *chungin* evolved within it. Since part of this discussion derives from my own genealogical inquiry, in this section I also challenge the standard assumptions of other historians. I introduce the next section—on the Pak story—by explaining the specific problems of research and the kind of information on which I had to rely. Though it is essentially an exercise in showing how one family's history interacted with larger events, even more importantly the second section is a model of inquiry. It takes the reader, step by step, showing my evidence and explaining my logic, through a process of discovery—a kind of detective story.

Chapter 1 maintains a dialogue between the story of the Paks' obscure origins and the social history of Korea. What we know about *chungin* status formation, the spreading interest in genealogy compilation, and the popularity of such state-sanctioned status markers as examination degrees, court ranks, and government offices sheds some light on the first four generations of Paks. In these early years, they indeed were commoners without distinction.

A much greater body of extant documents allows Chapter 2 to paint a more interesting and complex portrait of the family during the eighteenth century. Contrary to the common assumption that the specialist *chungin* status category crystallized in the seventeenth century,[22] the chapter shows that the Paks, as a family of lower-level army officers, found marriage partners not only among others like themselves but also from merchant families and even illegitimate-son offshoots of the aristocracy. At the same time, the Paks accumulated wealth as managers (*tojang*) of royal estates in Kyŏnggi province surrounding Seoul. Moreover, they began to acquire profitable ramie fields further south in Ch'ungch'ŏng province.

By the early nineteenth century, the wealthy Paks were unequivocally specialist capital *chungin* in social status, and Chapter 3 explores the meaning of this elevation. From 1800 to 1897, the Paks not only were pursuing careers in technical specialties in addition to military tracks but also were forming marriage ties to technical specialist families. In fact, available sources point to a range of choices wider than commonly assumed for military *chungin* fathers contemplating marriage partners for their daughters. Decisions regarding potential sons-in-law reflect the Paks' pursuit of a broader spectrum of activities as Korea began engaging and adjusting to the new world of imperialism.

Chapter 4 brings the Paks even more closely to the forefront of documented history as they thrived in the new Korean Empire. None achieved the kind of prominence needed to win them recognition among historians specializing in this period, not to mention a place in a standard biographical dictionary, yet the Paks' successful adjustment to more Western-style ideas, institutions, and practices before the Japanese takeover in 1905 allows new insights into the lives and aspirations of rank-and-file *chungin*.

In Chapter 5, the hitherto Pak-centered narrative shifts its focus to their in-laws, the military *chungin* Tanyang U family, whose story both mirrors and outshines that of the Paks. The U family and their associates were active as civic movement leaders, modern businessmen, and children's education advocates who were ahead of their time in their vision for Korea's future. Their activism during the Korean Empire and its abrupt end in Japan's dominance run counter to the common perception that most reform advocates of Imperial Korea ultimately saw accepting Japanese tutelage as the only viable option for Korea's future.[23]

Shifting focus back to the Paks, Chapter 6 shows how more ordinary people fared under Japanese colonial rule. With their connections to the palace, king, and aristocracy, as well as to their large mansion in urban Seoul, now fading memories, some Paks expressed resentment toward the colonial state, and others served it dutifully, while the majority struggled for survival. In particular, the contrast between a schoolteacher, constantly expressing his frustrations with the Japanese, and his cousin, who became a colonial police chief, illustrates the range of possible life trajectories of educated Koreans who remained in Korea. At the same time, issues such as modern education for daughters, the coexistence of old and new marriage practices, and what meaning Christianity gave to the vagaries of life are common themes in the story of the Paks.

As a conclusion, my epilogue reflects on post-1945 developments and their significance vis-à-vis historical research. It examines varying attitudes of the descendants of specialist *chungin* toward genealogy compilation in post-1945 Korea, and extrapolating on them, I end the book with some thoughts on historical agency.

1 From the Mists of Time

FOLLOWING THE COURSE OF THE PAKS' EMERGENCE FROM OBSCU-
rity requires an understanding of currently recognized Korean
descent groups and their master narratives. Pak is one of some 280 surnames
documented in South Korea, each with its own mantle of history. Pak, moreover, is one of the five most commonly used surnames, which together account
for half of all South Koreans.[1] Though no statistics are available, the number
of surnames in North Korea, with a population roughly half of the South's,
should be about the same, since the most common South Korean surnames
seem to be just as common among North Koreans.

With the number of surnames so small, a surname, especially a very common one such as Pak, can function as a historically meaningful identifier only
when combined with an ancestral seat designation. Currently in South Korea,
more than forty-one hundred ancestral seat–surname combinations are in
use, each ostensibly denoting a descent group with a master narrative that
honors a common patrilineal male ancestor and stresses descent from royals or aristocrats of the Silla (n.d.–935), the Koryŏ (918–1392), or the Chosŏn
period.[2] We can surmise that roughly the same number of ancestral seat–surname combinations must have been in use in the North as of the 1945 division of Korea by the U.S. and Soviet occupation forces, though the communist
state since then has discouraged its citizens from thinking about such a vestige of feudal culture to the extent that most younger North Koreans today
reportedly do not know their families' ancestral seats.[3]

Modern Korean genealogies are full of claims that logic and fact easily contradict. If, for example, we were to take the claims of all descent group master narratives at face value, then roughly a quarter of Koreans today would descend patrilineally from just four males who lived in the tenth century.[4] Second, in spite of master narratives that clearly explain the origins and history of every ancestral seat–surname entity (or descent group), no more than a quarter of Koreans can actually find themselves or their patrilineal kinsmen in genealogies.[5] Third, fewer than half of such pedigreed Koreans appear in older-edition genealogies published in the first part of the twentieth century or earlier.[6] And, finally, the Y chromosome DNA mutation analysis that can determine roughly how many generations ago the common patrilineal ancestor of two given individuals lived (the analysis that has shown, for example, that more than 80 percent of the Cohens, Jews of priestly tradition, share an apex figure who lived around the time of the Exodus) discerns no particular genetic marker distinguishing Koreans from their neighbors, not to mention distinguishing descent groups among Koreans.[7]

Although the empirical veracity of the process is in doubt, the cultural imperative is strong and of long standing. As is well acknowledged among social historians, widespread pursuit of status across class boundaries was a postmedieval trend as early as the fifteenth century, depending on region.[8] Rather than a component of some sort of colonial modernity sparked by Western imperialism in the nineteenth century, early modern Korean understandings of kinship identity took shape long before any gunboat arrived on the shores of the "Hermit Kingdom." One needs to go farther back in time in a search for the historical origins of institutionalized Korean descent groups, both real and imagined.

Descent and Kinship in Medieval and Early Modern Korea

We can begin the search with the medieval period (ca. 850–ca. 1500), when the notions of a surname and an ancestral seat spread among the elite and a central aristocracy took shape. Unifying the Korean Peninsula in 936, the Koryŏ dynasty granted surnames to local strongmen who gradually evolved into hereditary functionaries performing day-to-day administrative work for the fledgling central government in Kaesŏng. Besides surnames, the state also extended other incentives, including eligibility for entering officialdom through the government service examination established in 958.[9] Such official families formed the central aristocracy whose members, even after moving to Kaesŏng, kept a house in the countryside while identifying themselves by the ancestral locales where their forebears had served as local functionaries.[10] Increasingly, patrilineal principles shaped how the Korean aristocracy understood descent and kinship. Although matrilineal connections continued to influence how Koreans divided inheritance and determined residence, the strengthening notion of an ancestral seat contributed to a more strictly patrilineal conception.[11]

In late medieval Korea (ca. 1270–ca. 1500), the aristocracy became a closed status category. In the thirteenth century, when the local social order experienced instability, displaced functionaries began flocking to Kaesŏng in search for new opportunities, and the scale of influx was such that in the fourteenth century the central government sought to force them back to their ancestral locales to perform their original duties.[12] The scholar-officials supplanting the Koryŏ with the new Chosŏn dynasty in 1392 effectively barred local functionaries, hitherto the main supply pool of new families for the aristocracy, from officialdom and increasingly applied neo-Confucian ideals of family structure to define familial status ever more narrowly.[13] Rejecting the custom of polygamy among the Koryŏ aristocracy, according to which a man legally could have up to four wives, the Chosŏn state and its elite proprietors took measures to identify concubines (ch'ŏp) and illegitimate children as such and legally discriminate against them, whereby they lost prerogatives as bona fide members of the aristocracy, including the right to sit for government service examinations.[14] All this began in the fifteenth century when the Chosŏn elite began to insist on a "monogamy" that allowed a man just one legal wife, though it left him free to maintain concubines. A law first enacted in the early fifteenth century distinguished illegitimate children mothered by a concubine from children of a legal wife. A series of new legislations followed, culminating in 1469 with the State Administrative Code (Kyŏngguk taejŏn), which formally banned illegitimate sons from the civil service examinations.

Prior customs did not vanish immediately, however, and the oldest known genealogical record of a descent group, the 1476 Andong Kwŏn genealogy, is revealing.[15] Recording about nine thousand individuals descended from a twelfth-century aristocrat who, in turn, was a descendant of the eponymous tenth-century ancestor of the Andong Kwŏn, the genealogy reflects a not-yet-fully-patrilineal notion of kinship. Only about 30 percent of the descendants in the genealogy are patrilineal descendants of the twelfth-century ancestor; the rest are affines, though the presumably nonaristocratic lines that had branched off before him are not shown. As evidenced by the genealogy, the Korean elite at the time was rather homogeneous: 901 out of 1,794 (51 percent) government civil examination (*munkwa*) passers from 1393 to 1481 appear. The genealogy, additionally, unlike later ones, respects birth order rather than listing all sons before daughters, and though it does not record a daughter's name, it does record the son-in-law's name as that of the daughter's husband (*yŏbu*) rather than treating it as the name of the daughter. The genealogy even records a daughter's second marriage—a phenomenon that would become unthinkable in late Chosŏn Korea, when chaste widowhood was idealized. There also are no adopted sons recorded under heirless males, as adoption was not the societal norm it would become in late Chosŏn. And although it is unclear whether a strict legitimate-illegitimate distinction had become the custom in distinguishing the status of children, the genealogy records not a single child as illegitimate.

Published eighty-nine years later, the 1565 Munhwa Yu genealogy recording about forty-two thousand descendants of a tenth-century founding ancestor reflects many of the new social trends of early modern Korea.[16] Characteristics that it shares with the 1476 Andong Kwŏn genealogy include coverage of all direct descendants of the eponymous tenth-century founding ancestor's first famous descendant but exclusion of the presumably nonaristocratic lines that had branched off during the intervening generations; a high percentage of examination graduates and prominent statesmen; respect for the actual birth order in recording children; indication of daughters' multiple marriages; and lack of the designation "illegitimate" (*sŏ*) for any children, though again it is unclear whether the parents did not make the distinction to begin with or illegitimate children simply were not recorded. At the same time, the 1565 genealogy shows that the notion of a male heir had assumed greater importance. First of all, the "son-in-law" (*sŏ*) notation has replaced the "daughter's husband" label for a daughter. Second, some heirless men are shown to have adopted an heir, though the genealogy records only seven cases. Significantly, even such adopted sons appear under their natural fathers—with a mention of the name of the adoptive father. This marks the beginning of the early modern practice of aristocratic Korean men without a legitimate son (*chŏkcha*) adopting within their respective descent groups.[17]

For ancestral seat–surname entries, a seventeenth-century genealogy, the *Origins of Descent Groups* (*Ssijok wŏllyu*), tends to leave recorded descent lines unconnected to a putative noble ancestor. Unlike later Korean genealogies that generally sought to demonstrate that all descent lines of any one ancestral seat and surname pair descended from a common founding ancestor, the work demonstrates that the seventeenth-century Korean elite reckoned descent groups as more microscopic patrilineal kinship units, each descended from a documented, traceable ancestor. Also, the work duly notes local functionary origins and even conflicting pedigree information, again in general contrast to modern genealogies. In the cases of an Ŭisŏng Kim descent group segment and a Ch'angnyŏng Cho descent group segment, for example, the author includes two versions of their pre-Chosŏn pedigrees and rightly suggests that the one showing most of the individuals as holding local functionary posts is probably more accurate.[18]

In the eighteenth and nineteenth centuries in Korea, genealogies compiled by the aristocracy became more expansive and detailed. The driving force behind these changes was an emerging new cultural identity. The Manchu (Qing) conquest of China in the seventeenth century spurred neo-Confucian Korean aristocrats to view their kingdom as "Little China" (*So Chunghwa*). As preservers of the Way (that is, civilization), the aristocracy's emphasis on correct rituals entailed conceptualizing kinship and descent in more strictly patrilineal terms and making appropriate status distinctions even among children of the same parents.[19] Looking beyond a narrowly defined lineage or a descent group segment, genealogies covered even entire descent groups sharing a common surname, ancestral seat, and descent from a putative ancestor. In constructing such large-scale genealogies, compilers brought together family pedigree records that in the medieval period typically had been kept by individual households. As the printed genealogy started recording all members rather than just the aristocratic ones, it also began recording adoptions of male heirs of the same social status as the heirless father.[20]

As status distinctions mattered, nonelites of means increasingly adopted a surname or, if already in possession of one, claimed a widely known ancestral seat to go with it.[21] Household registers, examination rosters, and other documents of the time record individuals claiming affiliation with a historically long recognized descent group although their names do not appear in the genealogies compiled by the aristocracy. Already well represented at the time were modern Korea's most common ancestral seat–surname combinations, such as the Kimhae Kim and the Miryang Pak.[22]

For a given descent line, determining the beginning point of its reliable genealogy sheds light on the family's social status at the time. Whereas for the early modern aristocracy a single-line succession for generations was a pattern applicable only to genealogies of their ancestors of the earlier medieval period, this was still true in the early modern era for many sub-*chungin* families in genealogies.[23] As of the early modern period, aristocratic descent groups resource-rich enough, since the medieval period, to boast a large number of members descended from a medieval-era common ancestor, before whom the available record had information only on his direct patrilineal ancestors. In contrast, those of lower social status were able to organize themselves into sizable descent groups as such only in the early modern era or later. Also, descent lines of sub-*chungin* status, as recorded in genealogies, tend to leave out daughters until the nineteenth century or so.[24] In contrast, during the early modern era, bona fide aristocrat and *chungin* genealogies scrupulously recorded daughters by their husbands' names—providing information on their ancestral seats and, if applicable, degrees, court ranks, and offices, as well as including even the names of their fathers and sons.[25] After all, indicating the prominence of the son-in-law's family was as important as showing that of the father-in-law.

The *Chungin* in Medieval and Early Modern Korea

The importance of genealogy as a record of a descent group's social standing raises questions about the nature of *chungin* as a status category below the aristocracy but above commoners. How did the *chungin* status group emerge? Did *chungin* families attain their status by rising from below, or falling from above? What was the extent to which various groups that were neither aristocrat nor commoner viewed one another as a social cohort?

To answer these questions, we must begin with the history of *chungin* status in the late medieval period, with the definition becoming quite complex. When the term *chungin* began gaining currency in the early Chosŏn period (1392–ca. 1567), it referred to those whose social standing was of middle level in terms of wealth or other attributes. The *History of Koryŏ* (*Koryŏsa*), completed in 1451, and other sources on the earlier Koryŏ dynasty recognize only the aristocracy, commoners, and low-born as ascriptive status categories.

Although an intermediate social stratum clearly neither aristocrat nor commoner existed, at the time it evidently did not constitute an ascriptive *chungin* status category per se.[26]

Another fifteenth-century source, the *Veritable Records of King Sejong* (*Sejong sillok*) of 1454, makes it clear that *chungin* was not yet in place as an unequivocally recognized social status category. The geographical treatise (*chiriji*) section of the source lists each administrative locale's indigenous surnames, but most of the ancestral seat–surname combinations that would become uniquely *chungin* family identifiers by the seventeenth century are missing.[27] This suggests that most of early modern Korea's *chungin* descent groups with distinct ancestral seat–surname combinations had come to regard as their "ancestral seats" the places where they had been residing sometime after the Koryŏ dynasty's institutionalization of the indigenous surnames system for local functionaries in the tenth century. Certainly more research is necessary on the origins of such *chungin* families, but the *chungin* families bearing identifiers unique to them included the dislocated local functionaries of late Koryŏ who had managed to stay in Kaesŏng as well as others arriving in Seoul from elsewhere after the 1392 dynastic change.

At the beginning of the early modern era, the term *chungin* began to refer to technical specialists and others of social status below the aristocracy but above commoners. According to *A Brief Study on the History of Chung-in* (*Chungin naeryŏk chi yakko*) by Hyŏn Ŭn (1860–n.d.), a foreign language interpreter, anyone browsing through *chungin* genealogies should notice that *chungin* families had been serving as government technical specialists for no more than ten generations or so—showing that such families had arisen in the sixteenth century when court factionalism began to take on a more hereditary character. Expressing his pride as a member of a prominent *chungin* lineage, Hyŏn contended that among the scholar-officials politically marginalized owing to factionalism the well-to-do of moral probity pursuing practical studies became known as "*chungin*." He acknowledged, however, that the circumstances wherein they acquired the label were not known in detail, and he mentioned that according to some the designation referred to those occupying the position between scholar-officials and common folks.[28]

Overall, the status of *chungin* as a whole became distinct as that of administrators serving the aristocratic proprietors of the early modern state. While entrusting productive labor to low-born slaves and burdening the *chungin* with potentially unpopular administrative duties dealing directly with the population, the aristocracy could indulge in literate culture in the name of assisting the ruler to pursue the "kingly way" (*wangdo*). In order to secure service by the *chungin* as administrative staff, the aristocracy locked them into an ascriptive status category subject to institutional and cultural discrimination. For their part, *chungin* prospered by using the power of the early modern state to exploit the population of lower social status. As administrative staff personnel, *chungin* reputedly were sophisticated in word and deed, tidy in daily habits, and good at interpersonal relations. *Chungin* also had their own way of preparing documents as well as of composing essays and poems.[29]

In the early modern era, "*chungin*" as an ascriptive status label designated not just technical specialists but all groups that were neither aristocrat nor commoner. In his "Position Diagram of Families" (*Kajwap'yo*), Chŏng Yagyong (pen name Tasan, 1762–1836), a Practical Learning (*Sirhak*) scholar who wrote on a vast range of subjects, put the status labeled the "middle" (*chung*) below the "local" (*hyang*), the locally based aristocratic families, but above the "good" (*yang*), that is, commoners he described as those who were lowly but not "low-born" (*ch'ŏn*).[30] In *On the Equal Service Regulations* (*Kyunyŏk samok*), Tasan noted that well-to-do commoners enrolled as county school students (*kyosaeng*) or working as select military officers (*Sŏnmu kun'gwan*) styled themselves *chungin*.[31] Such incidental *chungin* receive an extensive treatment in the *Ecological Guide to Korea* (*T'aengniji*), written by Yi Chunghwan (pen name Ch'ŏngdam, 1690–1756) and the *Memoir of Maech'ŏn* (*Maech'ŏn yarok*) by Hwang Hyŏn (pen name Maech'ŏn, 1855–1910). According to these works, the *chungin* were composed of not just technical specialists but also other groups of intermediate social status, such as illegitimate children of aristocratic fathers, yamen clerks, local functionaries, certain lower-ranking military officers, and unemployed individuals of means.[32] In other words, some *chungin* were those who had dropped out of the aristocracy; other *chungin* had risen from below.

Diverse living and working conditions characterized the broadly defined *chungin*. Although the top *chungin* enjoyed a lifestyle and social status comparable to the aristocracy, at the bottom were those whose lot in life was similar to that of the low-born. The primary reason for this variation was that the broadly defined *chungin* included members of a broad spectrum of occupations. In early modern Korea, ascriptive status largely determined the range of occupations available to an individual, but at the same time the occupation could also influence social standing within the ascriptive status category.[33]

In terms of prestige, no occupation could match that of a central government official in Chosŏn society, though officialdom itself comprised distinct categories. Many were unsalaried officials (*murokkwan*) as distinct from salaried officials (*nokkwan*). Constituting the latter were temporary position holders—those receiving a stipend post (*ch'eajik*), which entailed no formal duties while still entitling its holder to a stipend—and regular position (*chŏngjik*) holders. The salaried officials, in turn, were made up of "actual post" (*silchik*) and sinecure (*sanjik*) holders.[34]

Not only did specific restrictions on promotion in court rank determine the type of office that one could receive, they also illustrate variation among the members of the broadly defined *chungin* class. Government-employed technical specialists could advance as far as the lower (*tangha*) senior third rank, northern indigenous officers (*t'ogwan*) to the senior fifth rank, and yamen clerks to the senior seventh rank. In contrast, local functionaries, post station attendants, and deliverymen (*uri*) held no ranks, though in terms of perceived social standing local functionaries were comparable to northern indigenous officers.[35]

Each of these broadly defined *chungin* strata consisted of sublayers. Among the office-holding technical specialists, interpreters, physicians, jurists, and accountants could advance to the lower senior third rank whereas the senior seventh rank was the limit for astronomers, geomancers, and painters; other technical specialists could receive only "miscellaneous posts" (*chapchik*) that were not part of civil or military officialdom, and these posts were available even to the low-born.[36] Occasionally, some government technical specialists rose into the stratosphere above the lower senior third rank or received an enfeoffment title—both of which were honors generally reserved for aristocratic officials—but of course these were rare cases.

Among local functionaries too, there were distinct tiers. Township headmen (*hojang*) advised the centrally appointed magistrate (*suryŏng*), who most likely was an aristocrat, while the "Six Chambers" (*Yukpang*) functionaries divided among themselves the administrative work concerning the six matters of personnel, rituals, taxation, the military, punishment, and public works. Other local functionaries performed more day-to-day administrative chores. The overall arrangement was more or less a continuation of the earlier Koryŏ practice of maintaining three tiers of local functionaries: one, the township headmen holding senior fourth (*taesang*), junior sixth (*chwayun*), or junior ninth (*chungyun*) local government ranks; two, the township administrative staff (*kigwan*), namely security chiefs (*pyŏngjŏng*), supply chiefs (*ch'angjŏng*), and jail chiefs (*okchŏng*); and three, the township assistants (*sa*) who performed various petty chores. The aristocracy regarded the duties of the lowest-tier local functionaries as work befitting the low-born, but to commoners and the low-born even such functionaries were their social superiors.[37]

We likewise can recognize different substrata of *chungin* among local military officers (*changgyo*) and yamen clerks. In the Koryŏ period, township headman-level functionaries had served in the provincial military corps (*chuhyŏn'gun*) as subcolonels (*pyŏlchang*), while administrative staff-level functionaries served as lieutenants (*kyowi*) and sublieutenants (*taejŏng*). The Chosŏn state turned Koryŏ provincial military corps commandants (*toryŏng*), deputy commandants (*pyŏlchŏng*), and lieutenants into regular military officers. Thus it seems likely that the local military officer stratum of Chosŏn had two substrata: true central-government military officeholders and those who were not. As for the yamen clerks, there were chief clerk (*noksa*) and common clerk (*sŏri*) sublayers. Whereas the chief clerk positions went even to protection or "shadow privilege" appointees (*ŭmsŏ*) among aristocrats and thus enjoyed some prestige, common clerks were low-level petty functionaries. Although yamen clerks resembled local functionaries in that neither group was part of the central officialdom, the former were better off in that they could still receive a court rank.[38] The story of the Paks as told here nicely illustrates various dimensions of the world of *chungin*.

The Origins of the *Chungin* Line
Descended from Pak Tŏkhwa

Although it is relatively easy to trace the developing contours of the specialist Seoul *chungin* status group, the process by which individual families, such as the Paks, became members of the group is complex, variegated, and drawn out. In developing an account of that process, it is difficult even to find a starting point. Evidently, the majority of such *chungin* descended from men who had risen from commoner status. The *Records of Surname Origins* (*Sŏngwŏllok*), which is a late nineteenth-century genealogy recording prominent capital *chungin* lines, leaves the majority of the listed families untraced beyond the fifteenth century. Since the first few generations of such a listing often show no rank or officeholder, it would seem that these families arose from a lower social status. Typically, the genealogy of a descent group using the same surname and ancestral seat designation as those of a specialist Seoul *chungin* line either leaves out such a line or records it with a problematic link embodying chronological and other discrepancies.

Addressing such issues of origin is unavoidable when telling the story of the Paks because in the early modern era they too put efforts into elaborating a genealogy for the family. Most certainly by the early nineteenth century if not earlier, the *chungin* Pak family was identifying itself as Miryang Pak.[39] According to the master narrative that emerged during the early modern era, the Miryang Pak descended from the eldest of the nine sons of King Kyŏngmyŏng (Pak Sŭngyŏng, r. 917–924) of Silla, Pak Ŏnch'im, enfeoffed as the Grand Prince of Milsŏng (Milsŏng Taegun). Milsŏng is an alternative name for Miryang, located about 90 kilometers to the southwest of Silla's capital in southeastern Korea, Kyŏngju. The king is said to have enfeoffed Ŏnch'im and his brothers, allocating them land from various locales in central and southern Korea.[40] In 2000 in South Korea, some three million Miryang Pak accounted for 6.6 percent of the country's population of forty-seven million.[41] With the Paks of other ancestral seats, the Paks together make up about 8 percent of the South Korean population.[42]

Such understanding of the origins of the Miryang Pak took root sometime between the early seventeenth and early nineteenth centuries. The oldest known sources mentioning the Grand Prince of Milsŏng, along with his eight younger brothers, as sons of a Silla king are a Miryang Pak genealogy compiled in 1620 (*Miryang Pak-ssi sebo*) and *A Genealogy of Various Surnames* (*Chesŏngbo*) compiled by Chŏng Sisul (n.d.) during King Hyŏnjong's reign (1659–74).[43] In contrast, the oldest extant record of select aristocratic descent lines, the *Origins of Descent Groups*, which was compiled in the middle or late seventeenth century, does not connect any Miryang Pak descent line to the most recent Pak-surnamed Silla kings (early tenth century).[44] Clearly, the notion that the Miryang Pak descended from a particular Silla king was not widely accepted even at the time, whereas by the nineteenth century it would become so.

Alleged descent from the tenth-century Silla prince being highly suspect, a credible account of our *chungin* Pak history begins in the early modern era with a certain Pak Tŏkhwa (1590–n.d.). Some editions of the Miryang Pak genealogies published since the nineteenth century record him as the youngest of the four sons of a junior sixth-rank county magistrate (*Hyŏn'gam*), Pak Chu (1540–81?) who, if the recorded sixty-year

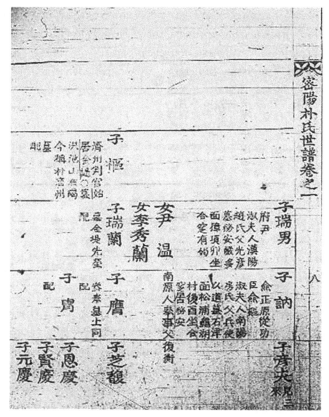

FIGURE 1.1 1873 Miryang Pak genealogy recording only three
sons under Pak Chu. Source: *Miryang Pak-ssi sebo*, 1.8b.

cyclical death year of *sinsa* is correct, either died in 1581, nine years before
Tŏkhwa's recorded birth year, or lived to the age of 102 *se* until 1641 (Figures 1.1 and 1.2).[45] Even if we were to assume that Chu lived so long, we
have other reasons to doubt that Tŏkhwa was his son. The name Tŏkhwa
deviates from the pattern of the names of his three alleged elder brothers,
Ŭn'gyŏng, Hyŏn'gyŏng, and Wŏn'gyŏng, all sharing a generational character, *kyŏng* (Ch. *qing*, "to celebrate").[46] Also, the gravesites of Tŏkhwa,
his wife, his immediate descendants, and their spouses in Chiksan county
of Ch'ungch'ŏng province (at a location known today as Pŏpchŏn subdistrict, Miyang district in Ansŏng, Kyŏnggi province) are far from those of
the three alleged brothers and their later Chosŏn-period descendants in
Chŏlla and Kyŏngsang provinces.[47]

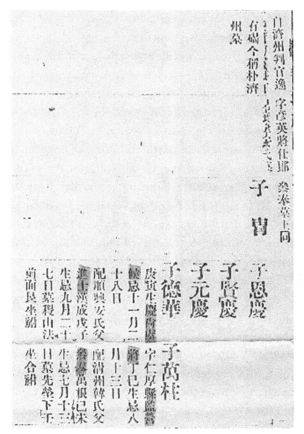

FIGURE 1.2 1924 Miryang Pak genealogy recording a fourth son, Pak Tŏkhwa. Source: *Miryang Pak-ssi Kyujŏnggong-p'a sebo*, 1.65a.

With no document specifically mentioning their residence, we can only assume that the Paks lived in or close to Chiksan. Late Chosŏn burial customs generally located graves in the same county or vicinity as the deceased's residence.[48] The first four generations of the Paks and their wives rest in graves set on a low-lying hill, Miyang Mountain, overlooking a village in an open field. The setting is idyllic, especially at dusk in autumn, when the radiant sun sets over the golden sea of rice stalks awaiting harvest. In spite of all the modern buildings and facilities dotting the landscape, as well as the Seoul-Pusan Expressway nearby, a stroll in the area even today can be a calm, peaceful experience. More than just enjoying their tranquil surroundings, the Paks most likely were profiting from good harvests. Chiksan was—and still remains—a part of a major rice-producing region centered in Ich'ŏn in south-eastern Kyŏnggi province. Also, as will be discussed below, the earliest indications of the Paks' growing wealth and influence in the eighteenth century were that they and their fathers-in-law obtained court-rank titles and offices as well as the area's royal estate managerships (*tojang*).

Before enjoying this prosperity, however, the Paks had to overcome chaos and desolation in the area. Centuries before, in Tŏkhwa's lifetime, Chiksan and its neighboring counties in northern Ch'ungch'ŏng province and much of Kyŏnggi province were a scene of bloody battles that also turned some soldiers into social climbers. Under Manchu siege in 1637, King Injo (r. 1623–49) and his court, holed up inside Namhan Fortress in central Kyŏnggi, to the south of Seoul, saw their hopes fade as one small Korean detachment after another, seeking to lift the siege, suffered annihilation by the vast Manchu Qing dynasty (1616–1911, renamed from Later Jin in 1636) armies occupying the area. Injo granted thousands of manumitted-slave soldiers, who mostly were from the area and made up the majority of the troops manning the fortress, the right to compete in a military examination (*mukwa*), which was an institution that in principle made the passers eligible for military positions in central officialdom.[49] Administered later in the year after the court's capitulation to the Qing, this particular competition awarded degrees to 5,536 men, the all-time highest figure in the history of the Chosŏn military examinations from 1402 to 1894.[50]

At this point one would expect Tŏkhwa to appear as a genealogical presence, though an investigator has to rely on inference in the absence of hard evidence. Even though his name is not on the examination roster, passing the 1637 examination is what could possibly have allowed Tŏkhwa, as a soldier, to lay the foundation for his descendants to achieve higher social status. To begin with, the fact that the roster is missing thirty passers leaves room for entertaining this hypothesis. Besides Tŏkhwa and his immediate descendants' likely residence in the region of battles during the Manchu invasion and the eighteenth-century descendants' occupations as commoner military men (as discussed in Chapter 2), the post that the genealogy attributes to him suggests a military connection.[51] The office he allegedly held, that of Kyŏngsang provincial troop commander's aide (*Uhu*), was either a junior third-rank or senior fourth-rank military post depending on whether his superior commanded an army or marines (*sugun*). Regardless, it was a high-level "actual post" (*silchik*) with formal duties, generally held by members of aristocracy.

Most likely, Tŏkhwa did not hold this particular post, but the claim made by the Pak genealogy reflects his military service.

The obscure background of his wife, too, suggests that Tŏkhwa's social status was, at most, that of a commoner. Two *se* older than her husband and buried together with him in Chiksan, she was the daughter of a certain An Hansŏng (n.d.), allegedly a literary licentiate (*chinsa*; Figure 1.3).[52] The Pak genealogy records him as a Sunhŭng An, but he does not appear in any ostensibly comprehensive Sunhŭng An genealogy set.[53] Considering that genealogies generally include even the illegitimate children of aristocratic men and record their lines for at least a generation or two, it seems that Tŏkhwa's wife came from a family that could not claim even such a modest place in a Sunhŭng An genealogy. Also, An Hansŏng does not appear in any of the extant licentiate (*sama*) rosters that account for 40,649 out of all 47,997 Chosŏn licentiates (84.7 percent).[54] If he was indeed a licentiate as claimed by the Paks, then all we can surmise is that, in spite of the attainment, his social status was such that somehow he was omitted from the Sunhŭng An genealogy. He almost certainly was not a bona fide aristocrat. And nothing else is known about the life of his daughter, Tŏkhwa's wife.

Assessing information about the couple's only recorded child and son, Pak Manju (1617–n.d.), also requires speculation as well as skepticism. Reportedly a junior sixth-rank county magistrate (*Hyŏn'gam*) and a provincial troop garrison commander (*Yŏngjang*), he does not appear in any of the standard dynastic histories or court records of this period such as the *Veritable Records* (*Sillok*), the *Daily Records of the Royal Secretariat* (*Sŭngjŏngwŏn ilgi*), and the *Certified Records of the Border Defense Command* (*Pibyŏnsa tŭngnok*).[55] Since not all magistrates and provincial garrison commanders rate mention in these sources, we cannot dismiss the genealogy's claim of these offices for Manju outright. Also, it is true that a local magistrate indeed held the two posts concurrently. All we can conclude, then, is that Manju either held these two positions or the Paks recording the information were familiar with the local administrative system of Manju's time. Considering, though, that until the end of the Chosŏn era the majority of local magistrates were of aristocratic background, it is unlikely that Manju actually attained these offices.

Available information on his marriage does not shed much light on the family's status either, and again we turn to conjecture. Manju's wife was a Ch'ŏngju Han woman (1619–n.d.), the daughter of Royal Tomb Manager (*Ch'ambong*) Han Man'gŭn (n.d.).[56] At the time, the court filled these lowly

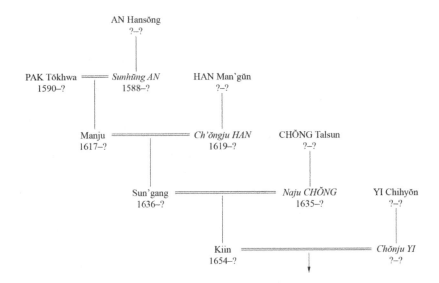

FIGURE 1.3 Genealogy of the Paks: the first four generations.

junior ninth-rank civil offices with individuals of diverse backgrounds, though they still tended to be from the aristocracy. As is true for Manju's own matrilineal ancestors, Madam Ch'ŏngju Han and her father do not appear in any edition of Ch'ŏngju Han genealogies that I have consulted.[57] It seems that, as his father most likely had done, Manju married a woman from a family of subaristocratic credentials. They were buried together in Chiksan.[58]

Our suspicion that the Paks were not of social distinction gets stronger with the evidence regarding Manju and Madam Ch'ŏngju Han's only child and son, Pak Sun'gang (1636–n.d.), and his father-in-law. Sun'gang evidently did not hold a court rank or an office, as the genealogy mentions none. Considering that Chosŏn period genealogies customarily record only the court ranks or offices that were part of the nine-rank central bureaucracy, divided into civil and military branches, it is perfectly possible that Sun'gang served as a military officer without ever achieving such trappings of status. He married a Naju Chŏng (1635–n.d.) woman whose father, Chŏng Talsun (n.d.), also did not appear to have held any court rank or office.[59] In addition, as is true for the fathers-in-law of Sun'gang and grandfather, Chŏng Talsun does not appear in the genealogy of the descent group to which he supposedly belonged. Unlike the two previous in-laws, though, we have some leads on his ancestry. The

Naju Chŏng descent group's ostensibly comprehensive genealogy records a branch that had members buried in counties of Kyŏnggi province neighboring Chiksan. Offering only a spotty coverage of the branch, though, the record also reveals many irreconcilable chronological discrepancies, patently false genealogical claims, cases of brothers not sharing a generational character, and names that are obviously of commoners.[60] All this strongly suggests the family's obscure origins—as is true for the Paks. Along with the two previous generations of Paks and their respective wives, Sun'gang and Madam Naju Chŏng were buried together in the by then well-established family gravesite in Chiksan.[61]

After three generations of men and women about whom we know precious little, we have somewhat more concrete, interesting pieces of information on the fourth generation. To begin with, the genealogy records Sun'gang and Madam Naju Chŏng's only child and son, Pak Kiin (1654–n.d.), with a posthumously granted civil post of junior third rank: rector (Chŏng) of the Quartermaster Bureau (Kunjagam).[62] A man of the same name appears on a late seventeenth-century document as a runner (saryŏng) working for the Directorate of Construction (Sŏn'gonggam) as of 1699,[63] but so far I am unable to confirm whether this is the same person. The posthumous honor (ch'ujŭng), though, makes sense in that it seems to have been part of the honor that his son would later receive from the state for military service in the quelling of a rebellion, to be discussed in Chapter 2. Kiin himself married a Chŏnju Yi woman (n.d.), the daughter of Yi Chihyŏn (n.d.), about whose background we can at least entertain a hypothesis.[64] I have come across a proto-chungin Chŏnju Yi line that produced Seoul-resident contemporaries using given names ending with the same Chinese ideograph, hyŏn (Ch. xian, bright, worthy), as that used in Yi Chihyŏn's name.[65] Moreover, during the same period, an individual with the same name is known to have held some military posts.[66] If this is the same person as Pak Kiin's father-in-law and he hailed from the Yi family in question, then the Pak-Yi marriage joined two families that were both on their way to achieving bona fide chungin status, though the Yis were to shift from a military orientation to technical services. Interestingly, generations later, in the eighteenth century, a member of the same Chŏnju Yi line that produced the military-man namesake would marry one of the descendants of Pak Kiin, to be discussed in Chapter 3.

Besides the absence of the fathers-in-law from their respective descent group genealogies, other characteristics of the recorded Pak genealogy for the period reveal the family's lower social status. The fact that the Pak genealogy for this period does not record a single daughter indicates the family's sub-*chungin* social status. Unless the Pak men somehow did not have any daughters for four generations, the lack of any mention of a son-in-law in the genealogy suggests that the family had none of distinction. Also, unless for four generations in a row the father had only one son, the single-line succession for four generations likely indicates that the Paks did not yet constitute an organized, extended lineage, as discussed above.

A large body of extant documents concerning Chiksan public school (*hyanggyo*) also implies that the social status of Paks and their in-laws was well below the aristocracy. From 1543, local aristocrats began favoring the rapidly increasing number of private academies (*sŏwŏn*), even shunning local schools. Surviving documents on the Chiksan public school include "Confucian rosters" (*yusaengan*), the community compact (*hyangyak*), edifice renovation records (*chungsugi*), and slave rosters. Reflecting the low prestige of local schools among aristocrats, none of the scores of native sons who are known to have passed the licentiate examination appear in the Confucian rosters of Chiksan public school. Still, the Paks and their in-laws are missing.[67] They were not significant enough even for the schools that higher classes rejected.

Overall, it seems that the Paks' social status was no higher than that of commoners performing military duties and attaining military offices at the end of their service, if not posthumously. We can rest on this conclusion so long as no new documents surface to shed more light on the family's first four generations. But if we can presume that they were not of high social status, how do we determine just how low their social status was? Could they have been slaves, or descendants of recently manumitted slaves?

Available evidence suggests that they probably were not at the very bottom of the social hierarchy. A recently discovered register reportedly recording 3,878 Ch'ungch'ŏng province *sogo* army soldiers of the late seventeenth and early eighteenth centuries does not record any of the Paks or their in-laws.[68] Dating back to 1594, the *sogo* army generally comprised commoners who could not buy their way out of military obligation, illegitimate sons serving on the promise of winning eligibility for government service examinations, public slaves to be manumitted after completion of their duties, and private slaves serving as substitutes for their owners.[69] Unless the Paks and their in-laws were living in locales within neighboring Kyŏnggi province rather than Ch'ungch'ŏng province's Chiksan (where the Paks were buried for four generations), it seems that their lot in life was better than the register's Ch'ungch'ŏng *sogo* soldiers. According to the document, the average *sogo* soldier's recorded height was just 4 *ch'ŏk*, and 18 percent were noticeably pockmarked.[70] The low height figure seems puzzling, but the record seems to reflect general hardship in their lives, suggesting that they were either commoners or low-born.

Conclusion

In light of state-sanctioned status markers and *chungin* status, it is clear that the bare bones narrative of single-line succession for four generations of Paks is about a family on the rise. When stripped of the clearly questionable claim of descent from a Silla prince, the real Pak family history begins with the birth of its obscure founding ancestor in 1590—nicely in line with the early modern beginnings of most specialist *chungin* families of Korea. The fact that all four generations of Pak men married women from families just as obscure reflects the Pak family's own position: we can only surmise that they were most likely commoner military officers living and working in, or near, the county of Chiksan, at the time a part of Ch'ungch'ŏng province bordering Kyŏnggi province immediately to the north. The locale was a part of a region where thousands of slaves won manumission for military service during the 1637 Manchu invasion. It is unclear whether the founding Pak was one of them, but regardless, it seems that he and his descendants were in a position to pursue status with success. Aristocratic patronage was important for social climbers, and Chiksan was in the crescent of early modern Korea's central political power, made up of Seoul, the entire Kyŏnggi province, northern Ch'ungch'ŏng province, western Kangwŏn province, and southeastern Hwanghae province—together constituting home to more than half of all central officials.[71] The early Paks were well positioned for seeking court ranks and offices, be it in life or posthumously. What the next century had in store for them was a world of status ambiguity and new socioeconomic opportunities.

2 Living with Status Ambiguity
Guardsmen, Merchants, and Illegitimate Children

I N EIGHTEENTH-CENTURY KOREA, EXPANDING COMMERCE AND
urbanization of Seoul allowed social upstarts to accumulate wealth
and join the society's middle ranks, that is, those who were neither artisto-
crats nor commoners. Commercialization and urbanization in Korea were
limited in comparison to China and Japan but nonetheless expanding, for a
number of reasons. Manufacturing catered to the largest urban center, Seoul.[1]
The Uniform Land Tax Law (*Taedongpŏp*), in effect throughout the country by
1708, proved a further factor in accelerating economic transformation.[2] Under
the law, tribute merchants (or tribute contractors) selling various products to
the government had to obtain them in the first place through purchase or
self-maintained handicraft workshops. Many maintained warehouses to store
items for delivery, thus creating a base for the eventual evolution of a more
complex distribution system.

Expanding intra-Korea commerce as well as trade with China accompanied a rapid increase in the population of Seoul and vicinity, which in turn
increased demand for essential goods. In particular, licensed rice merchants
in and around Seoul prospered. Among them, the "upper Seoul rice shops"
(*sang mijŏn*) covered the city to the west of T'ongun Bridge, the "lower Seoul
rice shops" (*ha mijŏn*) served an area to the east of the bridge, the "Western River rice shops" (*Sŏgang mijŏn*) supplied the areas between the city wall
and the Han River, and the "outside-the-gate rice shops" (*munoe mijŏn*),
including that of Pak Taedŭk mentioned below, did their business in the

immediate vicinity of Seoul beyond the city walls, outside the Lesser West Gate (Sŏso-mun).

Booming commerce in the capital and its vicinity stimulated provincial markets too. In the mid-eighteenth century, there were approximately one thousand periodic, local markets throughout Korea, which opened once every five days. As Korea at the time comprised some three hundred counties with a total population of roughly twelve million, we can estimate that the average population per county was about sixty thousand. Since, on average, each county had five markets, one market served approximately twelve thousand residents. In comparison, both China and Japan at the time maintained about one market per forty-five hundred to eight thousand residents. Moreover, in Korea, rice and cloth still functioned as the main means of transaction, and the same media made up a large portion of the state tax revenue. In fact, throughout the eighteenth century, court officials' relatively limited knowledge of currency and its circulation often produced both inflation and deflation.

At the same time, the number of unlicensed private merchants increased, and by 1800 they were handling nearly half of all commercial transactions. Finding it more sensible to legalize private commercial activities and tax them, in 1790 the government discarded the official rosters of approved buyers and permitted artisans to sell their goods to anyone they wished, so long as they paid the taxes in kind or in cash. Then, in the following year, the government's Joint Sales Action (*T'onggong*) abolished licensed monopolies except in some key industries and began collecting a new merchant tax. Although now liberated from government control, many artisans lacked sufficient capital and marketing skills. Accordingly, they remained financially dependent on big merchants. A typical arrangement was for such a merchant to first provide raw material and an advance before an artisan could deliver the goods. Nonetheless, in the eighteenth century, the variety of handcraft productions financed by big merchants expanded, including farming tools, kitchenware, pottery, processed food, wine, ginseng, paper, and shipbuilding.[3] These changes influenced the development of the *chungin* by creating a conducive environment for upward socioeconomic mobility.

Pursuit of Status: Potentials and Limits

Those capable of doing so pursued status through obtaining ranks and offices. To upwardly mobile nonelite families, including big merchants who wanted to enhance their social status, various resources such as the court ranks and offices were available.[4] Generally these were titular in character, without involving actual appointment or incumbency, and the government even maintained guidelines for pricing and other requirements. The state awarded ranks and offices to generous aristocrats for their contributions to the state and the people in difficult times. In contrast, nonaristocratic grain donors pursued ranks and offices as trappings of state-sanctioned social status.[5]

These distinctions did not turn commoners into aristocrats, and this is not surprising, especially since even the *chungin* who passed the civil examination could not join the aristocracy. Although most *chungin* examination graduates held either a technical or a military examination degree, a small number went further to compete successfully in the licentiate or the civil examination. A case in point is Chŏng Ch'ungŏn (1720–n.d.) who, hailing from a prominent Hadong Chŏng *chungin* lineage, passed both the literary licentiate (1740) and civil (1747) examinations. Apparently held back by his *chungin* status, though, the most prominent office that the genealogy credits him with is a county magistracy. Including his son, Chŏng Sinmin (1739–n.d.), who was a classics licentiate (1780), Ch'ungŏn's direct descendants had neither technical specialist careers nor meaningful careers as civil officials.[6] It appears that for a *chungin* from a specialist family, passing the licentiate or the civil examination earned social respect but left him and his descendants stuck in a world of status ambiguity. Although unable to gain membership in the aristocracy, perhaps pursuing or "reverting to" technical specialties was not a desirable option. Presumably, such an individual preferred to lead the life of an erudite private scholar if his financial circumstances allowed.

In fact, nothing could turn nonaristocratic families into bona fide aristocrats. For sure, nonelite families increasingly invented traditions so that by the end of the eighteenth century, genealogies tended to trace a descent group segment further back in time.[7] For instance, in explaining their origins, northern Korea's local elite Miryang Pak lineages invented traditions according to which they were scions of the capital or southern local aristocracy. Although unable to present supporting documents, they claimed descent from early Chosŏn scholar-officials, generally portrayed as the victims of fifteenth- or sixteenth-century literati purges who had allegedly been banished to the north. All the same, chronological discrepancies in northern genealogies are such that any close analysis by a genealogist can readily catch them.

Not surprisingly, the descent group genealogies published in Seoul or in the south often did not find northern lines to be credible members for inclusion.[8]

Such status anxiety vis-à-vis genealogies was widespread even among bona fide aristocrats who were not part of the central political process.[9] For example, the Namp'yŏng Cho family of Kimhae, descended from Minister of Personnel (*Ijo P'ansŏ*) Cho Yuin (1370–1434), a civil examination passer (1396), was a leading aristocratic lineage of the locale, but it too resorted to new genealogical assertions.[10] Sometime in the eighteenth century, the lineage members changed their ancestral seat name from Namp'yŏng to Ch'angnyŏng—a move they justified on the ground that the Namp'yŏng Cho had originally branched off from the Ch'angnyŏng Cho, the latter by then a much more populous group that, more importantly, included politically powerful central official lines.[11] It seems that regardless of the historicity of the claim or the sincerity of members' belief in the connection, such an adoption of a new ancestral seat name may also have been a pragmatic strategy by politically marginalized local aristocrats.

Increasingly, in the eighteenth century many Korean descent groups claimed origins in China, from which the Korean elite traced the origin of their country as a whole as "Little China," and the throne affirmed such claims. In 1794, for example, when King Chŏngjo (r. 1776–1800) learned that two men with the surname of Kong, the family name of Confucius (trad. 551–trad. 479 BCE), had passed the latest civil and military examinations, he expressed joy and declared that the descendants of Confucius had come to Korea and passed the government service examinations.[12] Regardless of whether Chŏngjo's statement reflected sincere belief or political rhetoric, it is germane to our discussion to consider that the fifteenth-century geographical treatise section of the *Veritable Records of King Sejong* lists almost all known Korean surnames at the time as indigenous to Korea—including Kong.[13]

While honoring the families that it recognized as descended from Chinese émigrés, Chŏngjo's court also monitored genealogic forgeries. Censorate officials' memorials submitted to the throne in 1787 and 1788 observed that an exemption from the military duties required of commoners was an important motivator for forging genealogies.[14] At the time, Chŏng Yagyong, a prominent Practical Learning advocate and a favorite of Chŏngjo, concluded that a desire to avoid military duty fueled genealogy forgery.[15]

The Paks: From Obscurity to Opportunity

The story of the eighteenth-century Paks suggests that various larger developments, which previous studies on the late Chosŏn have either overemphasized or dismissed, were at work simultaneously within the society. The known members of the Pak family were more numerous after a century of single-line descent, and, fortunately, various sources other than the genealogy, such as court histories, royal protocol manuals (*ŭigwe*), meritorious subject (*kongsin*) rosters, and land transaction documents, allow us a better understanding of their professions, status, and wealth. Also, more information becomes available on their wives' families, though the Pak genealogy still does not record any daughters—an indication not so much of the actual lack of female offspring as of noteworthy sons-in-law.

The eighteenth century is a crucial part of the Pak story, as it was then that they emerged from obscurity, accumulated wealth, made powerful connections, and enhanced their social standing. Most continued to serve as military officers and soldiers, but a fifth-generation Pak's role during the government's suppression of the Yi Injwa Rebellion (1728), and his subsequent enrollment as a "minor meritorious subject" (*wŏnjong kongsin*), paved the way for the family's attainment of specialist Seoul *chungin* status by the early nineteenth century.[16] Obtaining high-level court ranks and offices that were honorary in nature but nonetheless prestigious, the Paks also acquired land. As was true for other royal estate managers at the time in Korea, the Paks were de facto owners of these tax-exempt lands subject to minimum obligations to the state and thus were entitled to much of the harvest. Moreover, the Paks formed marriage ties to the likes of a great Han River merchant and an illegitimate-son scion of an aristocratic family belonging to the ruling Patriarch (*Noron*) faction.

The militarily meritorious Pak of the fifth generation is Pak Kiin's only recorded son, Pak Myŏngŏp (1675–n.d.), a Royal Division soldier (*Ŏyŏnggun*). For his service, the court enrolled him as one of some 7,200 minor meritorious subjects, among whom were 867 (12 percent) *chungin*, 2,134 (30 percent) commoners, 163 (2 percent) *sillyang yŏkch'ŏn*, that is, legal commoners performing duties socially perceived as those of the low-born, and 437 (6 percent) slaves.[17] Though short in duration, at least in terms of the size of its forces and the regions affected the rebellion was the largest the three-century-old Chosŏn dynasty had experienced to that point. For two weeks, rebels engaged government troops in four provinces, as the Disciple (*Soron*)- and Southerner (*Namin*)-faction extremists who rejected the legitimacy of the new king, Yŏngjo (r. 1724–76), rallied a diverse group of disaffected elements, including many local aristocrats from politically marginalized Kyŏngsang province.[18] The remarkable number of nonelites recognized as minor meritorious subjects indicates how desperately the state and the aristocratic proprietors belonging to the ruling Patriarch faction needed the support of military officers, soldiers, retainers, household slaves, and others of varying shades of social status. Not only was Pak Myŏngŏp among them, the fact that the genealogy records him with a posthumous honor, an upper senior third-rank civil post as the third minister of public works (*Kongjo Ch'amŭi*), suggests that the state was either further recognizing his service or responding to a descendant's request for such an honor.[19] As we saw in Chapter 1, the government apparently also bestowed on his father Kiin a posthumous honor, a junior third-rank civil post as the rector of the Quartermaster Bureau. The practice of posthumous recognition continued to expand, and the state's motivation in granting it was to satisfy status aspiration of an expanding base of educated and wealthy population.

Myŏngŏp's marriage, too, reflects the family's rising fortune. His wife, Madam Kimhae Kim (1677–n.d.), was two years younger than her husband and the daughter of a certain Kim Sŏngji (n.d.). As with the fathers-in-law of the previous four generations of Paks, so far I have not been able to find him in the genealogy of the descent group from which he ostensibly hailed. Unlike the previous fathers-in-law, however, he held a high court rank title, *Chŏlch'ung changgun* ("enemy chariot repelling general"), an upper third military rank.[20]

Also reflecting the Pak family's rising fortune is the fact that Myŏngŏp and his household evidently relocated to the capital, a move marking a new chapter in the Paks' increasingly complex story. He was the first member of the family to be buried just outside Seoul, in what was then Yangju county.[21] Located to the northeast of the capital's city walls, the new location in Yangju, unlike the previous family gravesites in Chiksan, was higher up in the mountains screening Seoul.

From many scenic spots, one can get a good view of the city while appreciating the changing colors of autumn foliage. As was true for the Buddhist temple near the family's graves back in Chiksan, the nearby Buddhist temple, Puram-sa, in Yangju must have welcomed visits by the devout from members of the family, most likely women and children, to offer prayers for the family's wellbeing. On a breezy day, walking by fields of waving reeds in the neighborhood could have reminded them of life's transience.

For some reason, the Paks did not use this location for Madam Kimhae Kim's burial; her grave is located in Ansŏng county, at a site not too far from the former Pak family graves in Chiksan.[22] It seems she married Myŏngŏp before his relocation to Seoul, and her natal home was probably in the Ansŏng-Chiksan area. The fact that they were not buried together suggests, then, in accordance with what we know about late Chosŏn burial practices, that she died either before or not long after the Pak family's establishment of its regular residence in Seoul.

Significantly, the couple was the first in the Pak family to record more than one child (Figure 2.1). The genealogy indicates four, all sons: Tongsu (1702–n.d.), Isu (ca. 1704–n.d.), Samsu (n.d.), and Sasu (ca. 1720–n.d.).[23] Except for the eldest, they bear names indicating their birth order in all-too-literal a fashion: "I" for two, "Sam" for three, and "Sa" for four. These names are not the kinds that aristocratic adult brothers would have used as formal names. They may reflect the family's less-than-aristocratic social status, unless those with numeric names indicate that all three were illegitimate sons. The latter is a distinct possibility, given that even the 1998 edition of the family genealogy does not record Isu, Samsu, and Sasu's descendants beyond their sons' generation.[24] Early modern genealogies tend to stop covering an illegitimate-son descent line after one or two generations beyond the illegitimate son himself.[25] The illegitimacy of the three younger sons of Myŏngŏp, if true, would also explain why their descendants were so obscure. In fact, Isu's descendants, whose story is the main subject of Chapter 5, were not able to marry members of families as distinguished as the more prominent *chungin* lines that provided spouses for the descendants of Tongsu. Limited genealogical data on Isu's nineteenth-century descendants suggest their marriage kin and associates were descendants of illegitimate sons of specialist *chungin*.

The Challenges of Tracing Descent Lines

From this point on, the main story of the Paks centers around two descent lines: one, a senior line comprising direct descendants of Tongsu's son Chisŏng (1725–n.d.); and the second, a junior line most likely descending from Chisŏng's younger full brother, Chibŏn (ca. 1727–n.d.), adopted by Isu.[26] At least since the early twentieth century, if not before, the members of the

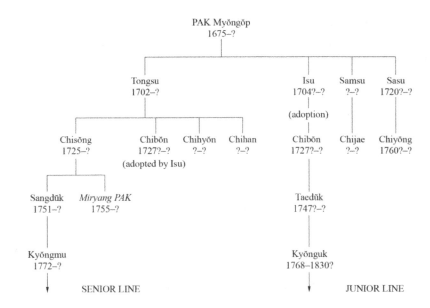

FIGURE 2.1 Pak Myŏngŏp and his known direct male descendants: the senior and junior lines.

latter line—along with the descendants, if any, of Chisŏng's other brothers and cousins—seem not to have participated in genealogy compilation; so far I have not come across any edition recording them, though again illegitimacy may have been the main reason.

Besides various documents, interviews with descendants who were not even aware of their pre-nineteenth-century ancestry strongly suggest that the junior line most likely is descended from Isu's adopted son, Chibŏn. Above all, the recorded male descendants of Chisŏng and those evidently descended from Chibŏn shared common generational characters in their names until the mid-nineteenth century.[27] Second, both lines continued to produce military officers while forming marriage ties to ever more prominent families, and by the nineteenth century the members of both lines were marrying those from specialist capital *chungin* families.[28] Third, by the nineteenth century, both lines owned land in Koyang county to the northwest of Seoul and Puyŏ county in southwestern Ch'ungch'ŏng province.[29] And lastly, according to the oldest of the surviving unrecorded descendants today, her paternal grandfather was of the fourth or fifth generation in the descent line to be the only son—meaning that his closest Pak kinsmen were fourth or fifth cousins.[30] In other words, the cousins had to trace back five or six generations for a common ancestor, who then must have lived in the late seventeenth or early eighteenth century. In nineteenth-century Korea, the members of a lineage, in a socially meaningful sense, of aristocratic or specialist Seoul *chungin* status tended to be descended from a common male ancestor who lived in the sixteenth or seventeenth century.[31] None of the more than a dozen other known Miryang Pak descent lines of specialist capital *chungin* status satisfies all of these conditions, whereas the line descended from Chisŏng is a perfect match.[32]

Given that my interviewee's grandfather, born in 1855, was the fourth or fifth in his descent line to be born the only son, his ancestor must have been one of Chisŏng's brothers or cousins. We can readily eliminate Chisŏng himself as a possibility, since the extant genealogies give a detailed, seemingly complete, coverage of his descendants, and my interviewees' family is not among them.[33] Among Chisŏng's brothers and cousins, that is, grandsons of Myŏngŏp, we can also eliminate the latter's fourth son Sasu's only son, Chiyŏng (ca. 1760–n.d.), as a possibility, since the generational character in the name of the interviewees' grandfather places him five generations after the *chi*-character (Ch. *zhi*, a branch, to branch off) generation—with the average generation being just nineteen years.[34] In fact, Chiyŏng's known daughter was born in 1811, her adopted son in 1849.[35] By the same logic, Myŏngŏp's third son Samsu's only son, Chijae (n.d.), born sometime between 1726 and 1760—probably closer to the latter—is an unlikely candidate as well.[36]

So we are left with Myŏngŏp's eldest son Tongsu's three younger sons, one of whom, a full brother, was adopted by Tongsu's younger brother Isu. Among the three, Pak Chihan (n.d.) is the least likely candidate in that his birth year sometime between 1728 and 1760 produces an average generation of just 19 to 25.4 years between him and the interviewees' grandfather— that is, five generations. Two remaining candidates, Pak Chibŏn and Pak Chihyŏn (n.d.), most likely were close in age, and the average generation figures are also close (25.8 versus 25.6 years).[37] Since nothing is known about Chihyŏn, whereas both Chibŏn and his only known son Taedŭk were wealthy military officers, as was my interviewee's grandfather (discussed in Chapter 3), Chibŏn probably is the ancestor of the unrecorded junior line to which my interviewees belong.

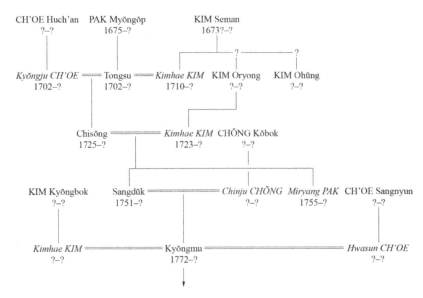

FIGURE 2.2 The senior line.

The Senior Line

Tongsu, the ancestor of the senior line, possessed more family wealth than his father Myŏngŏp did (Figure 2.2). The genealogy records the junior-second civil court rank of *Kasŏn taebu* ("magnate admirable and good"), which an individual in late Chosŏn could achieve (held alone or concurrently with an actual office) after a long career in central officialdom or through grain submission.[38] Since Tongsu clearly did not have a career as a regular member of officialdom, it is almost certain that he purchased the rank. This particular distinction is one of the proliferating indications that the Paks were accumulating wealth and satisfying their status aspirations more successfully, with their residence now firmly established in the capital. Reflecting this, Tongsu and his two wives were all buried in Yangju, just below Myŏngŏp's grave mound.[39]

What we know about Tongsu's two fathers-in-law also suggests that the senior-line Paks commanded significant wealth. Tongsu's first wife, Madam Kyŏngju Ch'oe (1702–n.d.), who apparently died no more than a few years into the marriage, was the daughter of an upper senior third-rank military officeholder, Fifth Minister-without-Portfolio (*Ch'ŏmji Chungch'ubusa*) Ch'oe Huch'an (n.d.).[40] Unfortunately, we know nothing else about him, as he appears in none of the editions of the genealogy purportedly recording all members of the Kyŏngju Ch'oe descent group.[41] Nor does the *Record of Surname Origins* show a Kyŏngju Ch'oe line with a member using the same name or one similar to it during his lifetime.[42] Nonetheless, it is significant that unlike any of the previous generations of Pak men's fathers-in-law, Ch'oe actually held a high-ranking sinecure (*sanjik*). If he purchased it through grain submission, then this is a clear sign of wealth, perhaps greater than that of any of the fathers-in-law of previous generations of Pak males. His sinecure would have required submitting several hundred *sŏk* of rice, certainly a fortune, to the government.[43]

Tongsu's second marriage adds a new dimension to the story of the Paks, with his new father-in-law typifying the great merchants who thrived in a more commercialized economy driven by agricultural surplus and markets. Emerging in the late seventeenth century, especially prominent among them were the "capital-[Han] River" (*kyŏnggang*) merchants who operated in the booming markets along the southwestern city walls of Seoul, driven by the demands of the capital's growing population.[44] According to the marriage customs of the time, the fact that the new wife, Madam Kimhae Kim (1710–n.d.), was eight years younger indicates not only a marriage between a widower and a first-time bride but also a mutually recognized difference in social standing between the two families.[45] A commoner living in Map'o, a Han River port in southwestern Seoul, the wife's father, Kim Seman (1673?–n.d.), transported grain between the capital and the seaports of neighboring regions.[46] Sometime in or before 1719, on surviving a shipwreck, he expressed his gratitude to the local garrison soldiers who saved his life. Declaring that he was now living a second life, Kim donated to the garrison commander what he recovered from the 100 *sŏk* of rice he had been transporting.[47] Typical of countless wealthy individuals who donated grain to the government, he received a senior-third military rank of *Chŏlch'ung changgun* ("enemy chariot repelling general").[48] It is uncertain whether this Kim Seman is the same person as his namesake from Hwangju, Hwanghae province born in 1673, who was the son of a commoner military support taxpayer (*poin*) and a special cavalryman (*Pyŏlmadae*) when he passed the military examination in 1710—a feat unsurprising in that special cavalrymen were Hwanghae province recruits who served rotation duties in Seoul.[49] What is clear is that for thirty-five years after the 1719 shipwreck, Tongsu's father-in-law of the same name was active as a shipping merchant, royal estate manager (*tojang*), and coastal trade broker. His operational network included ports as far away as the shores of Hwanghae and Ch'ungch'ŏng provinces, where merchants relied on his financial backing and even his hospitality when visiting Seoul.[50]

In an economy where markets and commerce were assuming greater importance, Chisŏng, the eldest son of Tongsu, and married to a woman possibly a granddaughter of Kim Seman, made further advances.[51] Chisŏng probably was Tongsu's "successor to the legitimate line" (*sŭngjŏk*), a Chosŏn kinship designation for an illegitimate son continuing a legitimate line as its heir. After all, Chisŏng's full brother Chibŏn was adopted by Isu, who likely was an illegitimate son, and customs at the time would not have allowed him to adopt a nephew born a legitimate son of a legitimate son. Chisŏng married Madam Kimhae Kim (1723–n.d.), who was the daughter of a certain Kim Oryong (n.d.), a contemporary of Kim Ohŭng (n.d.). The latter was a shipping merchant based on the Han River banks to the southwest of Seoul who also enjoyed a legendary reputation as a "traveling fighter" (*yuhyŏp*), always willing to intervene on behalf of anyone in danger—reportedly capable even of overcoming a tiger with his bare hands.[52] Since both men shared in their given names the ideograph *o* (Ch. *wu*, five), it is plausible that they were brothers or cousins, that is, the sons of the earlier Han River merchant Kim Seman. If this speculation holds true, then the latter must have been the father of Chisŏng's stepmother; otherwise, it would mean that Chisŏng married his natural mother's niece—a conjugal tie not allowed by the marriage customs of the time. Of course, if Chisŏng's wife was indeed from the family of Kim Seman, then the marriage must have reinforced the Paks' ties to the capital region merchants and even facilitated the expansion of whatever commercial activity they were pursuing with greater vigor. Available circumstantial evidence makes the ties both likely and sensible, though they must remain conjectures.

From this point on, we have firmer evidence since the family's growing economic clout under Chisŏng is evident in his government-sanctioned status markers and economic activity. Holding not only the *Kasŏn taebu* ("magnate admirable and good") court rank that he most likely purchased, as his father had, Chisŏng also received the junior second rank sinecure of fourth minister-without-portfolio (*Tongji Chungch'ubusa*).[53] Though this too was one of the high-ranking offices that the state sold, the distinction surpassed what the Paks had previously achieved. Aside from such lofty status trappings, Chisŏng could have been any one of a number of individuals of the same name recorded in various sources: an unemployed military examination candidate (*hallyang*; 1746, 1756), a patrol officer (*sulla pijang*; 1751), a former port commander (*Manho*, junior fourth rank; 1757), an "enemy chariot repelling general" rank holder (1762), or an unemployed military examination candidate of illegitimate son status or descent (*ŏbyu*) living in eastern Seoul (1773).[54] What is certain is that in 1759 Chisŏng acquired the managership (*tojang*) of a royal estate of Princess Myŏnghye (*Myŏnghye Kongjubang*) in Ŭmjuk county in Kyŏnggi province.[55] The extant transaction document shows that he was a commoner, as implied by the lack of the respectful title reserved for aristocratic buyers and any mention of low-born status.[56] The transaction amounted to de facto ownership of the land, because it was tax-exempt and the portion of the harvest that he had to send the government was small. As was true for other such estate managers at the time, Chisŏng almost certainly lived in Seoul—most likely the eastern quarters inside the city wall. Such estate managers benefited from the patronage of powerful aristocrats.[57] In fact, from 1731 to 1736, the brother-in-law of his cousin Chiyŏng's wife's grandfather, Min Chino (1684–1753)—who was an illegitimate son of a powerful Patriarch-faction aristocratic official, Min Yujung (1630–87) and also a minor meritorious subject for a role in quelling the 1728 Yi Injwa Rebellion—had served there as the magistrate.[58] As discussed further below, this seemingly remote kinship connection nonetheless reveals a new dimension to the Paks' rising fortunes. With the family now solidly established in the capital, both Chisŏng and Madam Kimhae Kim were buried, together, near his parents' and grandparents' graves in Yangju.[59]

As a commoner with some wealth and influence, their only son, Pak Sangdŭk (1751–n.d.), expressed a new kind of status aspiration. The genealogy records a court rank title of *T'ongdŏngnang* ("companion thorough and virtuous"), a senior-fifth civil court rank. Since 1623 the state had begun granting this as the highest-level rank to, among others, aristocrats with no prospect of having a career in the central government.[60] By the late eighteenth century, it had become a devalued credential, though one still attracting social newcomers aware that it once carried prestige among the elite.[61] In various sources, the same name "Pak Sangdŭk" is borne by a Royal Division soldier passing a royal archery test (*chungsun*; 1775), a military-owned hillside property ranger (*sanjik*) in Ch'ungnyŏng Mountain in Kap'yŏng county in Kyŏnggi province (1794), and a soldier in the Concurrent Stable (*Kyŏmsabok*;

1807) that formed one of the three elite royal guard units (*Naesamch'ŏng*).[62] If one or more of them is a member of our subject family, which seems highly likely, then we can see that Sangdŭk's lot in life resembled those of his immediate forefathers, though the Pak genealogy does not record any court rank or office for Chŏng Kŏbok (n.d.), father of Sangdŭk's wife Madam Chinju Chŏng (n.d.). Both Sangdŭk and his wife were buried at the Pak family gravesite in Yangju, making it the resting place for four generations.[63]

As readers must have noticed by now, extant sources are frustratingly silent on the lives of women in the family. By then in Korea, women had no place in a genealogy unless they were the wife of a patrilineage male member or of a son-in-law.[64] Even for those females who are recorded we do not know given names, as they are unrecorded.[65] As is true for most families of sub-*chungin* status, the genealogy of the Pak family does not record any daughters before the family achieved solid *chungin* status in the early nineteenth century. Thanks to a mention in the *Daily Records of the Royal Secretariat*, however, one Pak woman of the pre-*chungin* phase of the family history, unrecorded in the Pak genealogy, is known, specifically Chisŏng's daughter, born in 1755 and unmarried as of 1773.[66] If somehow she never married, then of course she would not have been included in her patrilineal kin group's genealogy.

The Junior Line

The story of the next generation of senior-line Paks belongs in Chapter 3, so we now turn to the junior line, most likely descended from Sangdŭk's great-uncle Isu (Figure 2.3). We know almost nothing about Isu other than that he married Madam Kimhae Kim (n.d.), the daughter of a certain Kim Ch'angyun (n.d.), and that the couple adopted one of Tongsu's sons, Chibŏn, who must have been an illegitimate son if Isu himself was indeed an illegitimate son.[67] This is the fourth time we encounter a Kimhae Kim as a Pak male's wife. Considering that both the Miryang Pak and Kimhae Kim were the most commonly represented descent group identifiers among the socially diverse late Chosŏn military examination passers and among the post-1948 South Korean population, the high frequency of the Kimhae Kim among the wives of Pak men suggests the popularity of the Kimhae Kim descent group identifier among the general population of early modern Korea as more people acquired genealogies, real or otherwise.[68]

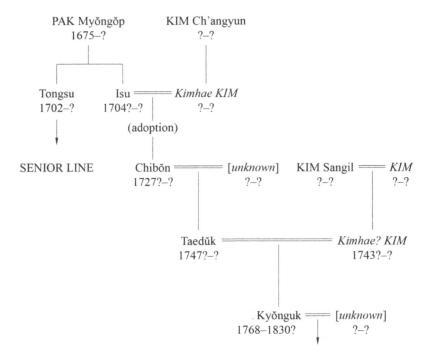

FIGURE 2.3 The junior line.

Isu and Madam Kimhae Kim's adopted son Chibŏn further enhanced the junior line's socioeconomic standing. Individuals with the same name appear in various sources, including a military examination candidate advancing to the palace examination stage (1756), a Royal Division soldier (1764), a Concurrent Royal Stables soldier (1764), a palace guardsman (1766, 1769, 1774), and a paper-product shop merchant (*chisangjŏn*; 1777).[69] In light of the nature of these occupations and the history of his family, Chibŏn could have been any one of them, and we may surmise that he served as a military officer for some time before attaining a court rank. All the same, the paper-product merchant in particular is interesting in that if he is the same person as the namesake of our subject family, then what we have at hand is the earliest evidence of a junior-line member engaging in commerce in the capital. Regardless of whether or not this was the Chibŏn of our inquiry and he was engaged in the paper business, the verifiable documented land transactions of Chibŏn and his relatives in Kyŏnggi province imply significant wealth. As of 1759, he had plots in Ŭmjuk county in southwestern Kyŏnggi.[70] Moreover, between

1744 and 1761, Chibŏn possessed land just outside southwestern Seoul in Ansan county, where earlier his brother Chihan's father-in-law, a certain Yi T'aegyŏng (n.d.), had purchased land.[71]

Chibŏn's son, Pak Taedŭk (ca. 1747–n.d.), had just as much at his disposal. Married to Madam Kim (n.d.)—whose ancestral seat I have not been able to determine—in 1777, he inherited some land from his father-in-law, Kim Sangil (n.d.) and held on to it at least until 1791 (Figure 2.4).[72] Since his father's lifetime, if not earlier, this branch of the Pak family had maintained an economic presence in the part of Kyŏnggi province where they capitalized on ties to Ŭmjuk Magistrate Min Chino and his aristocratic kinsmen, as discussed below. Moreover, in 1778 Taedŭk assumed an estate managership entailing the right to develop abandoned royal land in the area; the extant transaction document implies that he was a commoner.[73] It is not certain whether this transaction was related to the aforementioned one of 1759 involving his uncle. Considering that royal estate managers generally resided in Seoul and hired caretakers to manage the actual holdings, Taedŭk most likely lived in the city, as his father did.[74] As an absentee estate manager, Taedŭk had the harvest at his disposal except for a certain portion, or its cash equivalent, that he had to present to the government agency that officially owned the land. Since the required remittance for such a piece of land was small, Taedŭk enjoyed de facto ownership as well as tax exemption.

Even more significantly, Taedŭk had enough surplus harvest to seek profits as a licensed rice merchant, a coveted status for an enterprising individual at the time. In the eighth lunar month of 1777, when he and forty-three others submitted a memorial to the throne, the court recorded them as the capital rice merchants licensed to perform transactions outside the city wall, beyond the Lesser West Gate.[75] As a licensed capital rice merchant, Taedŭk and others like him enjoyed a large share of the market, ever expanding thanks to the burgeoning population of Seoul.[76]

Although the Paks' economic foundation had become secure by the late eighteenth century, they could not rest complacent within a protected market. As discussed above, toward the end of the century the government legalized and taxed private commercial activities, by then accounting for nearly half of all commercial transactions, and also abolished licensed monopolies except in some key industries. Of course, the immediate impact of a more liberalized economy and growth of private mercantilism was greater competition for licensed merchants such as Taedŭk.[77] How the succeeding

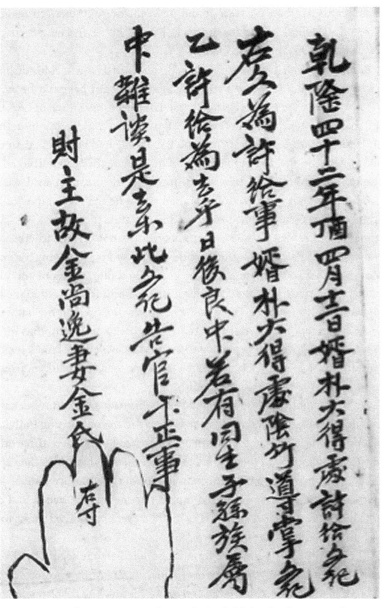

FIGURE 2.4 A document recording Pak Taedŭk's land inheritance from his mother-in-law, Madam Kim (1777). Source: *Kyŏnggi-do Ŭmjuk-kun sojae changt'o: Chang Sŏkkyu chech'ul tosŏ munjŏk ryu*, Kyujanggak-assigned document number 3 (1777). Reprinted with the permission of Kyujanggak Institute for Korean Studies, Seoul National University.

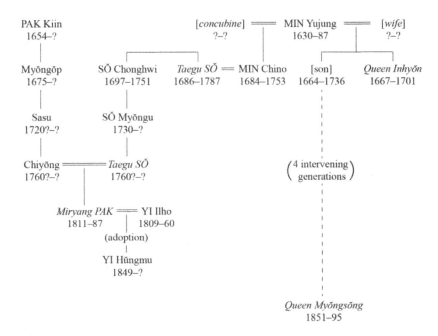

FIGURE 2.5 Marriage ties between the Paks and the illegitimate-son lines of aristocratic Taegu Sŏ and Yŏhŭng Min descent groups.

generations of Paks fared shows that they made adjustments and found ways to capitalize on new developments.

Compared to Taedŭk and the junior line's rising prosperity, the history of Taedŭk's grandfather Isu's younger brothers Samsu and Sasu, both probably illegitimate sons as was Isu, and their descendants is far less clear. It is uncertain whether Samsu's line became extinct or the genealogy omitted his descendants, as was common among genealogies vis-à-vis coverage of the descendants of illegitimate sons beyond one or two generations. The coverage of Samsu's line stops with a single son, Chijae.[78] Apart from the given name itself comprising two ideographs, the entry provides no other information.

Samsu's younger brother Sasu is also obscure. So far, I have not uncovered any information on his line of work. Also, we know nothing about his wife, Madam Chinju Kang (n.d.).[79] What is clear is that Sasu's descendants are known at least to the nineteenth century.[80]

Available information on Sasu's only known son, a Five Guards (*Owi*) director of the upright (*Sajŏng*) Pak Chiyŏng, again allows us a glimpse of a world of status ambiguities among nonelites (Figure 2.5).[81] Several individuals bearing the same name appear in various documents, and the one most likely to be the relevant person is an Anti-Manchu Division Command (*Ch'ongyungch'ŏng*) soldier with a military examination degree (as of 1798).[82] What makes Chiyŏng particularly interesting in light of the future of the family is his marriage connection. He married Madam Taegu Sŏ (ca. 1760–n.d.), whose father, Sŏ Myŏngu (1730–n.d.), was the son of a military examination passer, Sŏ Chonghwi (1697–1751), an illegitimate son of an aristocrat from a prominent Patriarch-faction lineage.[83] Chonghwi's sister, herself an illegitimate daughter (*sŏnyŏ*), married Min Chino, who was an illegitimate son from a prominent Patriarch-faction branch of the Yŏhŭng Min and a minor meritorious subject for a role in assisting the government in quelling the 1728 Yi Injwa Rebellion.[84] Among Chino's other siblings who were legitimate children were high-ranking civil officials and Queen Inhyŏn (1667–1701), the wife of King Sukchong (r. 1674–1720).[85] As will be discussed in Chapter 3, a descendant of one of Chino's brothers was Queen Myŏngsŏng (also known as "Queen Min," 1851–95), whose murder by the Japanese involved a later Pak's remote affinal kin, while Chiyŏng's Pak line itself continued through his daughter, who married a technical specialist *chungin*.

Conclusion

By the early part of the century, the Paks had relocated from a sleepy rural locale to bustling Seoul, though they continued to maintain an economic presence in the region of their origin in southeastern Kyŏnggi province. It is not entirely clear why they moved, but the fact that the first member to be buried just outside Seoul, Myŏngŏp, was a Royal Division soldier and a minor meritorious subject for aiding the government in suppressing the Yi Injwa Rebellion suggests that serving in capital army units and the patronage of some powerful aristocrats were deciding factors. Predominantly military men, the Paks also obtained high-level, largely honorary court ranks and offices, acquired royal estate managerships, engaged in paper-product and rice businesses, and formed marriage ties not only with commoner families of means like themselves, including the famed Han River merchant Kim Seman, but also with an illegitimate-son offshoot of a powerful aristocratic lineage belonging to the Patriarch faction. Still dwelling in the world of status ambiguities, rising to a higher social realm—that of *chungin* just below the aristocracy—was what the nineteenth century had in store for them.

3 As a Middle People

Military Officers, Jurists, and Calligraphers

WELL BEFORE THE IMPERIALIST POWERS' MOUNTING DEMANDS for diplomatic and commercial relations, Chosŏn Korea coped with intensifying internal socioeconomic problems. While a dozen or so Patriarch faction aristocratic families of Seoul dominated court politics, in southern counties local aristocrats faced challenges from increasingly wealthy, influential social newcomers.[1] In the north, members of a regional elite of significant wealth and cultural sophistication not recognized as social equals by the capital and southern aristocracy played roles that ranged from working within the system to fomenting the Hong Kyŏngnae Rebellion of 1812.[2]

Various practices led to greater social unrest. Continuing the policy of the previous century, the state ensured that some three hundred magistrates worked closely with local functionaries and wealthy commoners, even bypassing the old local elite.[3] As those who had acquired magistracies through bribing aristocratic power holders at court sought dividends, spreading administrative corruption aroused the enmity of those of little means, especially the overtaxed peasantry.[4] Moreover, centuries of overcultivation and deforestation, driven by late medieval technological advances in agriculture, progressively denuded mountains as well as causing frequent flooding and silting irrigation facilities. Resulting failed harvests, widespread starvation, and deadly epidemics contributed to a population decrease while fueling social discontent among the living—including the 1862 riots that swept across scores of southern and central counties.[5]

Of particular significance for tracing the story of the rise of the *chungin*, the old aristocracy-dominated social order reached its limit in terms of ability to contain the pressures of upwardly mobile nonelites.[6] As more social newcomers commanded influence and resources, by the time of Sunjo's reign (1800–34) the state virtually ceased its effort to combat the production and circulation of forged genealogies.[7] By then, Korean genealogies of questionable provenance had come to embody many problems that must have been evident to any bona fide aristocrat: (1) chronological discrepancies or anachronistic information; (2) conflicting pedigrees for the same individual in various editions of the genealogy published by those claiming him as their ancestor or kinsman; (3) claims to high ranks and offices that other sources do not substantiate; and (4) hiding nonaristocratic origins by omitting or forging the career data of certain ancestors or grafting the entire family onto an obscure line.[8] By resorting to one or more of these maneuvers, less prominent, numerically small descent groups assumed better-known ancestral seat names and asserted that they shared common ancestry with those already using the designations.[9]

Upwardly mobile nonelites sought such genealogical legitimacy even as they assumed more active political, cultural, and business roles. Having accumulated much cultural and economic capital in the early modern era— thanks to expanding interstate trade, frequent foreign travels, lively intellectual exchanges with aristocrats, and pleasant poetry gatherings—the Seoul *chungin*, along with local functionaries and the illegitimate sons of aristocrats, gradually also gained the right to hold even the most prestigious civil offices, previously reserved for those from prominent aristocratic families.[10] It is significant that they now were in a position to acquire these rights by demand. In 1851, for example, some sixteen hundred *chungin* signed a memorial petitioning the throne for their eligibility for recommendations to Office of Diplomatic Correspondence (*Sŭngmunwŏn*) positions for civil examination passers, herald (*Sŏnjŏn'gwan*) posts for military examination passers, and magistracies for protection appointees—all coveted distinctions even among aristocrats.[11] Gradually, more *chungin* assumed ever higher, more prestigious sinecures and even "actual positions" (*silchik*), including magistracies—the mother lode for enrichment through corruption in the form of tax gouging.[12]

During the nineteenth century, the activities of the members of capital specialist *chungin* families came to extend beyond strictly technical specializations. The famous *chungin* Indong Chang lineage, known for producing a large number of interpreters, for example, by the nineteenth century had come to be known more for military officials.[13] The shift was in part an adjustment in response to the reduced supply of silver from Japan since 1694 and to Chosŏn Korea's declining trade with Qing China, as both developments deprived interpreters of the lucrative trading opportunities they had enjoyed during their official diplomatic missions.[14] Overall, Korea's trade tied to diplomatic missions to China and Japan further declined with the opening of three ports in 1882, and the *chungin* interpreters began turning to other careers and activities.[15]

Likely aided by exclusive networking, the dominance of a small number of most successful *chungin* descent lines vis-à-vis technical careers—especially as interpreters—became more pronounced.[16] In the seventeenth century, 124 descent groups (each identified by a combination of surname and ancestral seat) produced interpreters, but during the reign of Kojong (1864–1907; Kwangmu emperor from 1897) the number was just 87. Also, the percentage of interpreters hailing from the 20 most successful descent groups increased from 48.7 percent during the reign of Kwanghaegun (1608–23) to 60.4 percent during Kojong's reign.[17] The same change affected the technical examinations as a whole. In the sixteenth and seventeenth centuries, the majority of the 413 descent groups producing technical examination passers could each claim a single passer, but in the eighteenth and nineteenth centuries there were just 28 one-passer-only descent groups.[18] Moreover, by the nineteenth century both a technical examination passer and his father were highly likely to be married to wives from one of the three most successful descent groups vis-à-vis technical examinations.[19]

Some Prominent *Chungin* on the Eve of Modern Korea

In the nineteenth century, the economic clout of the affluent Seoul *chungin* families too seems to have reached its apex. On his death, O Ŭnghyŏn (1810–77), who had a successful career as an interpreter, was able to pass down to his eldest son, the famous O Kyŏngsŏk (pen name Yŏngmae, 1831–79), an asset worth about two thousand *sŏk* of rice as well as two houses.[20] Even if we were to assume that the four younger sons of Ŭnghyŏn each got considerably less, there can be no doubt about the impressive wealth of the father. Whereas the O family commanded wealth on the basis of generations of service as interpreters profiting from official trade during visits to China or Japan, many physician *chungin* became rich by serving as inspectors of local medicinal herbs presented to the court. During terms of local postings ranging from five to twenty-four months, a physician typically received gifts and bribes from competing local herb merchants.[21]

Chungin families with ample resources continued to pursue various forms of cultural activity, ranging from artistic connoisseur to erudite antiquarian to versatile literatus to social critic. Frustrated with the glass ceiling in spite of their education, learning, and scholarship, the specialist *chungin* explored various cultural realms. Some turned to such radically new practices as Catholicism, which the establishment condemned as a "false teaching" (*sahak*). For example, Hyŏn Sŏngmun (baptism name Carlo, 1799–1846), who was from a prominent specialist *chungin* lineage, welcomed French priests, led a gathering of Catholics in Seoul, and authored a biographical collection of martyrs on the request of his bishop, before being apprehended by the authorities and himself attaining martyrdom in 1846.[22]

A more typical course for the specialist *chungin* was that illustrated by O Kyŏngsŏk's experience. One of his tutors, Yi Sangjŏk (pen name Usŏn, 1804–65), a most renowned poet and literatus at the time, exerted a strong influence, and O developed an early passion for epigraphy, calligraphy, and painting. Overall, through home tutoring, O studied and inherited the teachings of the famous Practical Learning (*Sirhak*) scholar Pak Chega (pen name Ch'ojŏng, 1750–1805).[23] Since O occupies a special place in the history of modernizing Korea in general and the specialist *chungin* in particular for reasons that will be evident below, the evolution of his outlook on the world and subsequent activity deserve particular attention.[24]

Along with Pak Kyusu (pen name Hwanjae, 1807–77) and Yu Honggi (pen name Taech'i, 1831–84?), O Kyŏngsŏk became a key figure in the emergence of Enlightenment Thought (*Kaehwa sasang*) in Korea. Although the thought's manifest goal was not Westernization per se, in practice it generally meant imitation of the West, especially the ideas and institutions that made the West superior, in any way, to the rest of the world. For O, the turning point in his outlook on the world came during his stay in Beijing from the fourth lunar month of 1853 to the third lunar month of the following year, when he became more familiar with Western culture and interacted with many intellectuals from Southeast China. At the time, Qing China was coping with the aftermath of the Opium War (1840–42), the humiliating Treaty of Nanjing (August 1842), which entailed paying indemnity and yielding Hong Kong to

Britain as well as opening five ports for trade with Britain and other Western powers. Chosŏn Korea's longtime suzerain was being forced into semicolonial status amid Western powers scrambling to carve up the empire through gunboat diplomacy and unequal treaties. Moreover, during O's stay in Beijing, the Qing government was preoccupied with the Taiping Rebellion (1851–64)—even borrowing British troops to battle the rebels in the south. During this and subsequent visits to Beijing (1856–57, 1857–58), O befriended some sixty young intellectuals from Southeast China, and they maintained intense discussion on world affairs. Mostly "recommended men" (*juren*) who were studying in Beijing in preparation for the "presented scholar" (*jinshi*) examination, O and his friends freely debated China's various problems and how to address them through reforms.

In the meantime, O Kyŏngsŏk and other *chungin* traveled abroad, agonized over the future of their country, and formulated the ideas that eventually constituted Enlightenment Thought.[25] Besides discussions with Chinese friends, O also acquired and read various books to enhance his knowledge of the world beyond East Asia. In 1860, he was shocked by the joint British-French occupation of Beijing, and in explaining his thoughts and giving new books to Yu Honggi, his close friend and a teacher of his son O Sech'ang (1864–1953), O urged Yu to study ways to save Korea from imminent Western threats. He likewise influenced the formation of Enlightenment Thought by Pak Kyusu, who had returned from his 1861 diplomatic mission to China with a strong sense of crisis.[26]

O played an important role as a progressive intellectual and a formulator of Korean foreign policy vis-à-vis the Western powers and Japan, though unfolding events did not allow him to realize his vision. In 1866, while visiting China, he learned that the French fleet in Asia was preparing to attack Korea in retaliation for the execution of French priests during the anti-Catholic persecution led by the de facto regent Hŭngsŏn Taewŏn'gun (1820–98). After consulting various Chinese officials and intellectuals, he urged the court to confront the logistically constrained French, though noting that if forced to trade, Korea must sell goods for French gold and silver rather than the opposite. Persuaded, the Taewŏn'gun ordered his generals to engage the invaders advancing toward Seoul; after losing two battles, the French withdrew. Spurred on by this event and other Western incursions, at the end of 1869 or early 1870, with the support of Pak Kyusu, O and Yu Honggi began teaching Enlightenment Thought to bright youngsters from prominent aristocratic families of Seoul.

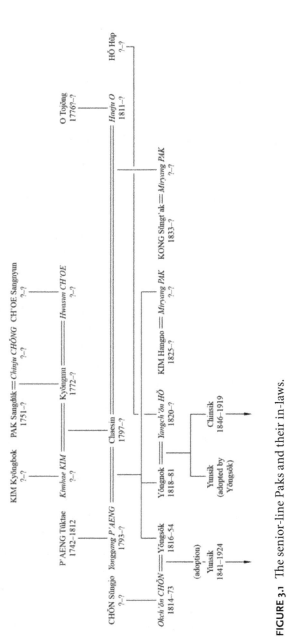

FIGURE 3.1 The senior-line Paks and their in-laws.

Seeking greater support from Japan and the West, they would eventually form the Enlightenment Party (*Kaehwa-dang*), engineering the abortive 1884 Kapsin Coup, but O insisted on an independent course of modernizing reform.[27] In 1871 the United States dispatched a fleet to press for relations and trade, and this time O recommended accommodation; but the Taewŏn'gun refused. After the Americans won all the battles and withdrew, in the following year O joined the mission (headed by Pak Kyusu) that the court dispatched to Beijing to tie up diplomatic loose ends vis-à-vis the United States. In 1876, when Japan sent a fleet to impose an unequal treaty, he concluded that the post-Taewŏn'gun leadership, under Kojong's personal rule and the influence of Queen Myŏngsŏng, was not committed to resisting the Japanese. Thus he focused on softening the Japanese demands. Shortly after the Japanese fleet withdrew, O died after collapsing from fatigue and stress.

The Senior Line

O Kyŏngsŏk's career raises questions pertinent to the story of the Paks. At the time, how representative was O of other specialist *chungin* of Seoul? How readily did his ideas influence his social peers—not to mention those of other status categories? In particular, were those, such as the Paks, who were undergoing a status transition from commoner to *chungin* more likely to invest their resources in the establishment of agents of change such as the Enlightenment Party? To answer these questions, we need to go back in time.

Continuing to climb the social ladder, the Paks had attained specialist *chungin* status by the late eighteenth century. The standard bearer was Pak Kyŏngmu (1772–n.d.) of the senior line, the only son of Sangdŭk (Figure 3.1).[28] Kyŏngmu received the senior-third military rank of *Chŏlch'ung changgun* ("enemy chariot repelling general"), though the highest office that he ever attained was a junior fourth-rank temporary stipend post (*ch'eajik*), the deputy protector (*Puhogun*) of the Dragon Prancing Guards (*Yongyangwi*).[29] In the nineteenth century, common recipients of such temporary stipend posts included former or incumbent officeholders, that is, government technical specialists such as interpreters, physicians, jurors, astronomers, accountants, calligraphers, painters, and musicians, as well as military officers from (or married to wives from) specialist *chungin* families.[30] Accordingly, we can surmise that Kyŏngmu either received a technical post or held an actual office prior to his deputy protector position.

The evidence of the social standing of Kyŏngmu's two known brides, however, suggests that the Paks' *chungin* status may not yet have been on a truly solid footing by the early nineteenth century. His first wife was Madam Kimhae Kim (n.d.), the daughter of Kim Kyŏngbok (n.d.), about whose family background or career we know nothing.[31] The second wife, Madam Hwasun Ch'oe (n.d.), was the daughter of the junior-second civil *Kasŏn taebu* ("magnate admirable and good") court rank holder, Ch'oe Sangnyun (n.d.), who does not appear in the Hwasun Ch'oe genealogy; nonetheless it records a segment that may be his.[32] Not only were the recorded members of the segment buried in Koyang county to the northwest of Seoul, but an entire generation of members used the same *sang* (Ch. *shang*, to beg, still, further) character to begin the given name, and some were contemporaries of Sangnyun.[33] Unrecorded Sangnyun may have been a descendant of an illegitimate son belonging to this segment.

Though it is uncertain whether the Paks had attained any technical specialist positions in the government or were secure in their *chungin* status, Kyŏngmu is evidence that the senior line was doing well economically. Between 1809 and 1810 in southwestern Ch'ungch'ŏng province, he acquired some land in Ŭnjin and Hongsan counties, both known for ramie production.[34] As discussed in Chapter 6, family members and associates would continue to capitalize on the production of ramie until at least the late nineteenth century. While expanding the family land holdings in the provinces, Kyŏngmu maintained a residence in the capital. Considering that he and both of his wives were all buried in the Pak family gravesite in Yangju, just to the northeast of Seoul (in the present-day Nowŏn district of Seoul), their residence most likely was in the Great East Gate (Tongdae-mun) area where soldiers and lower-level officers tended to reside.[35]

Like his father, Kyŏngmu had just one son, Pak Chaesin (1797–n.d.), who is the first member of the family definitely known to have held a technical specialist position in the government. Without a relevant source available, we can only speculate that as its socioeconomic capital accumulated since relocation to Seoul, an earlier family member, if not Chaesin himself, landed a job as an administrative functionary. Perhaps it was a yamen clerkship through which his calligraphy stood out; Chaesin is known to have been a state-employed calligrapher. As such, he also held temporary stipend posts that *chungin* specialists customarily received, including the Five Guards director of the trusty (*Sagwa*, senior sixth rank) and the Dragon Prancing

Guards director of the straight (*Sajik*, senior fifth rank).[36] Chaesin married Madam Yonggang P'aeng (1793–n.d.), from a specialist *chungin* family known for calligraphers, including her father P'aeng Tŭktae (1742–1812).[37] In contrast, Chaesin's second wife, Madam Haeju O (1811–n.d.), who was fourteen years younger than he, came from a family in which several members were military men, notably her father O Tojŏng (ca. 1776–n.d.), a Royal Retinue Office (*Howich'ŏng*) military officer (*kun'gwan*).[38] Considering that the father married his daughter to a widower fourteen years her senior, we suspect that something about the Paks made them superior to the O family, be it wealth or the generally coveted attainment of a technical specialist position in the government. After all, using a marriage tie to improve a family's social standing was nothing new, and in this context it is not surprising that the father of a young unmarried daughter considered marrying her to a much older but socioeconomically well-endowed widower. In fact, a Pak male would act in a similar manner in the late nineteenth century, as discussed in Chapter 5.

Chaesin, Madam Yonggang P'aeng, and Madam Haeju O's grave locations also indicate the Pak family's improved socioeconomic standing. Rather than the traditional family gravesites in Yangju, both Chaesin and Madam Yonggang P'aeng were buried in Puyŏ, where the Paks by then owned much land, including the plots famous for ramie, and possibly maintained a residence.[39] Madam Haeju O, however, was buried in a then-Koyang county location to the east of Seoul, not too far from older Pak family graves in Yangju.[40] Without any additional information, we can only speculate on the separate burial. A few years younger than her, perhaps the two stepsons, mothered by Madam Yonggang P'aeng, had mixed feelings toward Madam Haeju O. Alternatively, if not at the same time, the Paks may have had logistical reasons for locating her grave separately.

After three generations of fathers producing just one son each, the size of the senior-line population suddenly began to swell. Chaesin had two sons and two daughters, all of whom survived to adulthood. His first wife, Madam Yonggang P'aeng, gave birth to both sons and at least one of the daughters, whereas the second daughter's mother might have been Madam Haeju O.[41] In fact, from this point on we begin to learn more about the Pak women, albeit still primarily as wives of the Pak family sons-in-law.

The life of Chaesin's eldest child and son, Pak Yŏngsŏk (1816–54), evidently was not as fulfilling as one would expect in light of his father's success.

Perhaps in part because Yŏngsŏk was only thirty-nine *se* when he died, the genealogy records a Five Guards senior ninth-rank military officer post, the director of the brave (*Sayong*), as his only career accomplishment, though this temporary stipend post suggests, given his family's social status, an early stage of a technical service career.[42] He married Madam Okch'ŏn Chŏn (1814–73), the daughter of a *Kasŏn taebu* ("magnate admirable and good") court rank holder, Chŏn Sŭngjo (n.d.), from a technical specialist *chungin* lineage.[43] Having one daughter but no son, the couple adopted one of Yŏngsŏk's nephews. Whereas Yŏngsŏk was buried in the old family gravesite in Yangju, his wife was buried in Sŏch'ŏn, a county neighboring Puyŏ, in southwestern Ch'ungch'ŏng province. Since the wife outlived the husband by almost two decades, we can surmise that sometime in or after 1854 the Pak family began to bury their dead in Ch'ungch'ŏng. In fact, Yŏngsŏk's father, Chaesin, probably outlived him, since the father's grave was in nearby Puyŏ.[44]

The life of Chaesin's second son and Yŏngsŏk's younger brother, Pak Yŏngnok (1818–81), was longer but more or less mirrored the elder brother's in terms of career, marriage, and residence patterns. The genealogy records Yŏngnok with only the same temporary stipend post his elder brother held, but compared to the latter, Yŏngnok married a woman from a more prominent specialist *chungin* family.[45] His wife, Madam Yangch'ŏn Hŏ (1820–n.d.), was the daughter of a Five Guards director of the upright (*Sajŏng*), Hŏ Hŭp (n.d.), of a *chungin* family especially known for government-employed painters (*hwawŏn*).[46] The couple had two sons and a daughter, from among whom sonless Yŏngsŏk adopted. Though the couple must have resided in Seoul, both the husband and the wife were buried in the Paks' new family gravesites in Puyŏ in southwestern Ch'ungch'ŏng province.[47]

Chaesin's third child and elder daughter (n.d.) married Kim Hangno (1825–n.d.), a union reflecting the Paks' newly achieved *chungin* status. The son of a Royal Genealogies Office (*Chongbusi*) paymaster (*nangch'ŏng*), Kim Chŏnghyŏn (n.d.), who was a member of a specialist-*chungin* Kimhae Kim lineage, Hangno passed the jurist examination (*yulkwa*) in 1846 before serving as a sixth-rank statute officer (*Yulhak Pyŏlche*) and a junior fifth-rank secretary (*Tosa*).[48] Considering that Korea's first group of modern judiciary officers tended to be of broadly defined *chungin* backgrounds including statute specialists, it is likely that Hangno either failed to make the transition or died before the era began.[49] So far I have not found a record of his holding any new-style office during the Open Port Period, when King Kojong established the overarching Office for Extraordinary State Affairs (*T'ongni Kimu Amun*) in 1880 in an effort to make the government machinery more effective in dealing with Western countries and with Westernizing Japan.

In contrast, Chaesin's younger daughter (n.d.) married a professional who typified the *chungin* playing an important role in the modernization of Korea. Hailing from a *chungin* Ch'angwŏn Kong lineage, the husband, Kong Sŭngt'ak (1833–n.d.), whose four immediate patrilineal ancestors were all jurist examination graduates, passed the same examination himself in 1859, and from 1887 to at least 1889 he served as the county magistrate's judicial aide (*Kŏmnyul*), a junior ninth-rank position responsible for handling day-to-day judicial matters and education.[50] Among the various documents that I have examined, Kong reappears, after a gap of a few years in career data, as a stock-taker (*Sap'an wiwŏn*) successively posted in Kongju (1895, 1896, 1899) in Ch'ungch'ŏng province, P'yŏngt'aek (1896–98) in Kyŏnggi province, and Yŏnsan (1897), again in Ch'ungch'ŏng.[51] Between 1895 and 1899, when the Ministry of the Royal Household (*Kungnae-bu*) assumed the management of most palace and government office land holdings throughout Korea, the stock-taker dispatched to each parcel of land appointed lower-level on-site managers (*kamgwan, marŭm*) as well as setting the amount of harvest to be submitted as rent by the cultivators.[52]

As previously mentioned, the senior line of the Pak family, represented by Chaesin, continued through the elder son Yŏngsŏk's adopted son, Pak Yunsik (1841–1924), with whom the family fortune evidently declined. Rather surprisingly, given the family's upward social mobility during the previous generations, the genealogy records no degree, court rank, or office for Yunsik.[53] This is puzzling, especially in light of the fact that contemporaneous individuals with the same name appear in various documents, including a fourth minister-without-portfolio (1887), Five Guards director of the trusty (*Sagwa*, senior sixth rank; 1891), a sixth-rank holder receiving a senior third court rank of *T'ongjŏng taebu* ("magnate thorough and regulatory") (1902), a Secretariat Court (*Pisŏwŏn*) amanuensis (*Sŭng*) concurrently a Bureau of Slave Administration (*Changnyewŏn*) official (*Changnye*) (1903), and a clerk (*Chusa*) in the Telephone Section (*Chŏnhwa-kwa*) of the Communication Office (*T'ongsinsa*; 1903).[54] Without additional information, though, we cannot be certain that any one of them is the Pak individual in question.

Given that the genealogy mentions no court rank or office in spite of the family's social status, available information on Yunsik's residence and burial location suggests that at some point he moved from Seoul to Ch'ungch'ŏng province. Actually, a source records an individual with the same name as a capital resident, as of 1878, of Sumundong-gye, Chŏngsŏn-bang, Chung-bu, located at the northern edge of Seoul's heavily *chungin* area, the "Middle Village" (Chung-ch'on).[55] Both Yunsik and his second wife, Madam Ch'angnyŏng Sŏng (n.d.), who appears not in the 1924 edition but in the 1998 edition of the genealogy, were buried in Hongsan district in Puyŏ, whereas the first wife, Madam Kimhae Kim (1842–76), the daughter of Kim Sŏnghan (n.d.), was buried at Tŏgyu Mountain in Anŭi county in southern Kyŏngsang province, bordering Chŏlla province, for reasons I cannot yet ascertain.[56]

We know little about Yunsik's natural younger brother, Pak Chinsik (1846–1919)—the heir to their father Yŏngnok owing to Yunsik's adoption by his uncle—other than that he too moved to Ch'ungch'ŏng province. Again, the genealogy records no degree, court rank, or office for Chinsik.[57] Even the background of his first wife, Madam Ch'ŏngp'ung Kim (1846–n.d.), is obscure. Her father, judging from his name, Kim Tonggwan (n.d.), may have been a member of the famous *chungin* Haeju Kim family, which sometime between 1885 and 1907 changed their ancestral seat designation to the more aristocratic-sounding Ch'ŏngp'ung and made their way into the Ch'ŏngp'ung Kim genealogy, as discussed in Chapter 4.[58] The Ch'ŏngp'ung Kim genealogy, which offers a highly incomplete coverage of the original Haeju Kim members, does not record Tonggwan.[59] Available information on Chinsik's second wife, Madam Nŭngsŏng Ku (1860–1910), does not shed any more light on Chinsik's life either, since the genealogy omits her father's name. Interestingly, whereas both Chinsik and Madam Ch'ŏngp'ung Kim were buried in Puyŏ, Madam Nŭngsŏng Ku was buried in Poryŏng (present Oksan district in Puyŏ), a coastal county adjacent to western Puyŏ.[60] Unfortunately we can only speculate: Madam Nŭngsŏng Ku probably hailed from a family of lower social standing than that of Chinsik, and perhaps the children of his first wife did not want their stepmother to be buried alongside their parents.

The Junior Line

Unlike the senior line of Paks whose fortunes declined in the nineteenth century, the position of the less populous junior line, descended from the aforementioned Pak Taedŭk, further improved (Figure 3.2). Although the feeble

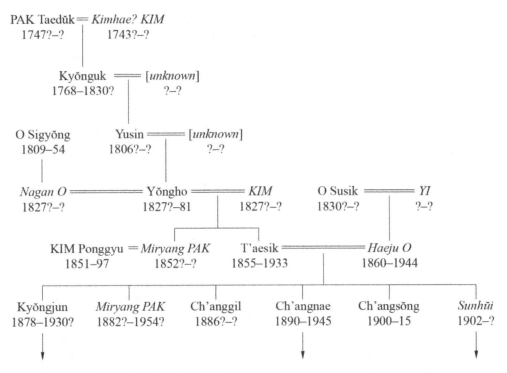

PAK Taedŭk = *Kimhae? KIM*
1747?–?   1743?–?

Kyŏnguk = *[unknown]*
1768–1830?   ?–?

O Sigyŏng   Yusin = *[unknown]*
1809–54   1806?–?   ?–?

Nagan O = Yŏngho = *KIM*   O Susik = *YI*
1827?–?   1827?–81   1827?–?   1830?–?   ?–?

KIM Ponggyu = *Miryang PAK*   T'aesik = *Haeju O*
1851–97   1852?–?   1855–1933   1860–1944

Kyŏngjun   *Miryang PAK*   Ch'anggil   Ch'angnae   Ch'angsŏng   *Sunhŭi*
1878–1930?   1882?–1954?   1886?–?   1890–1945   1900–15   1902–?

FIGURE 3.2 The junior-line Paks and their in-laws.

genealogical evidence suggests the senior line's decline, we can only conjecture why its members seem to have been "failures." In the late Chosŏn context, typical reasons for such falls had to do with inability to obtain an examination degree, a court rank, or an office; in contrast, we see a steady improvement in this regard for the junior line. Unfortunately, extant editions of the Pak genealogy cease coverage of the junior line with Taedŭk's father, Chibŏn. In reconstructing the single-line succession between Taedŭk and his known great-grandson, Pak Yŏngho (ca. 1827–81), I had to search various primary sources for Pak-surnamed individuals who had the right generational characters in their names, were active during the period in question, and held the kind of occupations sensible in light of those of the Pak generations that preceded and followed him.

On the basis of my research so far, Pak Kyŏnguk (pen name Oso, 1768–1830?), a well-documented military officer and physician from Seoul, is the man most likely to be the only son of Taedŭk. The given name contains the same ideograph, *kyŏng* (Ch. *jing*, a light, rays), as does the name of his contemporary and presumed cousin Kyŏngmu of the senior line. In terms of social status, we know from the available sources that Kyŏnguk was a specialist *chungin*, a commoner, or somewhere in between—thus mirroring the status of the members of the senior line. Also, the *Record of Surname Origins* does not record him or any other contemporaneous *chungin* Miryang Pak using a given name starting with the same *kyŏng* character; what this means is that he hailed from a *chungin* Miryang Pak line unrecorded in this work—including our subject family.

Indeed, Kyŏnguk's early career mirrors the military orientations of his hypothetical kinsmen. As of 1794–99, Kyŏnguk was a special martial arts officer (*Muye pyŏlgam*).[61] He and others of the same assignment formed a special unit of the Military Training Administration (*Hullyŏn Togam*) responsible for the royal household security at close quarters.[62] At the time, special martial arts officers often escorted the royal party, and thus Kyŏnguk could easily be one of the scores of such officers depicted in a painting of a 1795 royal procession.[63] For good performance during royal archery tests (1797, 1799), he received permission to advance to the palace examination stage of the military examination in 1799 at the age of thirty-two *se*.[64] Since he is missing from the extant military examination rosters, which account for merely a fifth of the roughly 160,000 Chosŏn military examination graduates, we can only surmise that he earned his degree through one of the two palace examinations that were held immediately afterward, in the ninth month of 1799 and the fourth month of 1800. Considering that the 1799 competition selected just 13 men through a "royal visitation examination" (*alsŏngsi*) typically targeting those from elite families whereas the 1800 competition granted degrees to 928 men, most of whom were active-duty soldiers and officers who had bypassed one or more of the earlier stages of the examination and thus were not included in the extant roster recording those who had passed all stages, Kyŏnguk most likely passed the latter military exam.[65]

We know nothing about Kyŏnguk's subsequent career until 1811, when, at forty-three *se*, he is known to have been a physician concurrently holding a temporary stipend post in the Five Guards.[66] Before or while serving as a military officer, Kyŏnguk acquired expertise in medicine—an impressive accomplishment in light of the fact that he did not hail from a technical specialist *chungin* family. After all, throughout the early modern era from the seventeenth to the late nineteenth century, specialist *chungin* families of Seoul monopolized technical specialist positions in central officialdom through intensive training of their sons from an early age, a well-established network of mentors providing the appropriate curriculum, dominating technical examinations, and perpetuating generations of intermarriages among specialist *chungin* families.[67]

Although not from such a background, Kyǒnguk got a chance to visit Japan, thanks to his expertise in medicine, and indeed he is the only documented member of the Pak family to have traveled abroad before the twentieth century. From the twelfth lunar month of 1810 to the seventh lunar month of 1811, as a physician and the deputy director of the brave (*Pusayong*, junior ninth military rank), Kyǒnguk was a member of Chosǒn Korea's last diplomatic mission to Tokugawa Japan.[68] Unlike previous Chosǒn missions that visited Edo, this one proceeded only as far as Tsushima.[69] The main reason for scaling back the endeavor is that the grandiose missions cost both sides too much financially, and as of the nineteenth century neither had the resources for the display.[70] In spite of the abbreviated nature of the mission, the Chosǒn court duly rewarded all members of the returning delegation, including Pak Kyǒnguk, who received a promotion in military rank (1811).[71]

Subsequently, Kyǒnguk held other military posts and played a role in another historic event, this time within Korea. When the Hong Kyǒngnae Rebellion erupted in the twelfth lunar month of 1811 (January 1812), the government dispatched troops from the Military Training Administration; among them Kyǒnguk served as a cavalryman (*mabyǒng*).[72] After crushing the rebellion in the sixth lunar month of 1812, the government announced the rewards for military personnel: Kyǒnguk received rice and hemp cloth and also was recommissioned to serve in one of the Five Military Divisions.[73] Afterward, he is known to have been, concurrently, a junior eighth-rank civil official (*Pongsa*) of the Military Training Agency (*Hullyǒnwǒn*) and a sacrificial ritual assistant (*Ch'anin*; 1814).[74]

If Kyǒnguk was indeed the only son of Taedǔk, then the latter's only known grandson, Pak Yusin (ca. 1806–n.d.), had a career quite different from that of his presumed father. In 1821, the Military Training Administration enlisted Yusin as a reservist (*taenyǒn'gun*) working as a cart driver (*ch'abu*).[75] Sixteen *se* or less in age at the time, he and other reservists like him were responsible for covering for fathers or near kinsmen in the event of their failure to continue their active duties.[76] Since in 1830 Yusin was promoted as a regular soldier of the Military Training Administration, it is likely that his father, Kyǒnguk, died then.[77] Maintaining his active duty status, Yusin eventually began working as a cartwright (*ch'ajang*) and continued to do so at least until 1856.[78]

Although it may appear he declined in status, as an army cartwright Yusin most likely accumulated wealth and solidified the socioeconomic foundation for his descendants' prominence later in the century. It is known that during the Hwasŏng city wall construction project (1794–96) launched by King Chŏngjo, the government employed just ten Seoul-resident cartwrights for construction projects in the city: four palace artisans (*kungjang*) actually working for the Military Training Administration and the Royal Division, and six private artisans (*sajang*). During the construction, a cartwright received a daily pay of four *chŏn* and two *p'un*, an impressive remuneration comparable to what government project painters and sculptors received.[79] While meeting their production quotas, Yusin and other cartwrights enjoyed a virtual monopoly in cart manufacturing that brought them huge profits.

By the time Yusin's only son, Pak Yŏngho (ca. 1827–81), reached adulthood, it is probable that the junior line was both deeply engaged in commerce and commanding wealth. Yŏngho's only documented occupation is that of a soldier in the Winged Forest Guards (*Urimwi*), and this information is revealing.[80] Originally created by the court in 1492 to accommodate unemployed yet martially endowed illegitimate sons of aristocrats, it is almost certain that by the eighteenth century the Winged Forest Guardsmen, as was true for most capital regiment soldiers in general, had come to perform their duties on a rotational basis.[81] When not on duty, they pursued commercial activity. This was especially true for the Winged Forest Guards, as they tended to be commoners.[82] Not much is known about the nature of this unit in the early modern era, and it is possible that Yŏngho's assignment to the Winged Forest Guards may reflect his descent from an illegitimate son. While serving as a guardsman in 1857, Yŏngho participated in a royal archery contest during which he hit the target's rim once while missing the target entirely in two other attempts—a performance that still won him a royally bestowed arrow from King Ch'ŏlchong (r. 1849–64).[83]

So far in my research, Yŏngho stands as the first member of the junior line to have married someone from an unequivocally technical specialist *chungin* family. His first wife was the daughter—probably an illegitimate child, given Yŏngho's own background—of O Sigyŏng (1809–54), who attained a junior fifth-rank civil post in the Bureau of Translators (*Sayŏgwŏn*). As was typical for a specialist Seoul *chungin* family, Sigyŏng's kinsmen included many technical specialists, especially interpreters, as well as military officers.[84] Yŏngho's Nagan O brother-in-law had daughters who married men fitting these patterns. One of them, Yi Hakkyun (n.d.), would become a pro-Russia military officer and supporter of monarchy-centered modernization reform in Imperial Korea before fleeing to China on the eve of the Russo-Japanese War.[85] The other, Kim Chinhwan (n.d.), in 1912 founded the modern printing company Pojinjae, which is currently owned by his great-grandson.[86]

Maintaining its military-mercantile orientation, the Pak junior line continued not through Madam Nagan O but instead another woman, Madam Kim, about whom nothing other than grave location is known.[87] Whereas somehow Madam Nagan O's gravesite is unknown, Yŏngho and Madam Kim were buried together in or near Taejang subdistrict in Chido district of Koyang county, bordering western Seoul.[88] Given that her sister was married to an Onyang Pang descended from an illegitimate son of a royal physician, and that the Pangs had been residing in Taejang as well as nearby Paeksŏk subdistrict in Chung district for generations, it is possible that Madam Kim was from a local *chungin* Nagan Kim family descended from an illegitimate son.[89] These locations also suggest that the junior-line Pak's residence was in western Seoul. In fact as of 1890, the couple's only son, Pak T'aesik (1855–1933), who had begun his career as a military officer, was living inside the Great West Gate (Sŏdae-mun) in what is now northern Sŏsomun subdistrict.[90] Compared to the senior line's eastern Seoul neighborhood, where nonaristocratic military officers and soldiers tended to live, T'aesik's neighborhood somehow had residents of various occupations, among them nonaristocratic administrative functionaries, military officers, and merchants.[91]

In his world, aristocratic patronage mattered, and T'aesik had ties to King Kojong's in-laws, the Mins, or others such as the Military Guard Agency commanders (*Muwi Tot'ongsa*) who were close to the throne (Table 3.1). In 1874, Kojong created the Military Guard Agency (*Muwiso*) as part of an effort to enhance royal power, on commencing his personal rule (1873) with the retirement of his father, the Hŭngsŏn Taewŏn'gun, and among the military personnel the agency officers received preferential treatment.[92] For example, in 1878 Kojong approved the agency's recommendation that its special military officers (*Pyŏlmusa*), along with overseers (*Chigugwan*) and instructors (*Kyoryŏn'gwan*), be promoted after forty-five months of service.[93] In the twelfth lunar month of 1880, when T'aesik was an unemployed military examination candidate (*hallyang*) twenty-six *se* in age, the Military Guard Agency recruited him as a special military officer, stipulating that later he would be promoted to an actual post (*silchik*).[94] The agency assigned him as extra-quota assistant (*kach'ul*) in the Palace Guard Division (*Kŭmwiyŏng*) among the Five Military Divisions.[95] Apparently, the assignment reflects his residence in northern Sŏsomun subdistrict to the south of Kyŏngun Palace (present Tŏksu Palace). The neighborhood was a part of the region regularly patrolled by the Palace Guard Division, while the Royal Division and the Military Training Administration were responsible for other segments of the city wall.[96]

Extant documents on T'aesik's subsequent activity until 1882 allow us a glimpse of the life of a nonaristocratic military officer who served on a stand-by basis. During the eighteen-month period of his service from the twelfth lunar month of 1880 to the sixth lunar month of 1882, the Military Guard Agency had him on duty for just twenty-one days, meaning the average interval between two duty days was about twenty-four days, with the interval ranging from one to 119 days.[97] We know that T'aesik returned to his duty fifteen days after his father Yŏngho's death in the fourth lunar month of 1881.[98] This was more or less in line with the fact that government regulations granted a paid ten-day leave for a special military officer such as T'aesik mourning for a parent near his service location.[99]

At least while on duty, T'aesik was a military man, pure and simple. The fact that the king's crack troops, the Military Guard Agency, hired him as a special military officer shows that he possessed at least respectable archery and horse riding skills, both prerequisites for his position.[100] Regardless, in the third month of 1882, fifteen months after his employment, T'aesik passed the military examination that, along with a companion civil examination, the government held in celebration of Queen Myŏngsŏng's recovery from measles.[101] On the fifth day of the fourth lunar month of 1882, when the ceremony for the examination passers to thank the king took place at Hŭijŏng Hall of Ch'angdŏk Palace, all twenty-three civil examination passers and five out of some twenty-six hundred military examination passers, including T'aesik, had the privilege of acknowledging his majesty's grace in close proximity while the rest of the military examination graduates stood outside the Sŏnhwa Gate at the edge of the courtyard.[102]

After T'aesik's service as a special military officer ended in 1882 upon the Imo Military Revolt, all we know about his official career is that by 1894 he had

TABLE 3.1 Military Guard Agency commanders (*Muwi Tot'ongsa*), 1874–82

Tenure	Commander	Birth and Death Years	Highest Degree	Notes
1874.7–1875.8	Cho Yŏngha	1845–84	Civil	Son of Kojong's adoptive mother's first cousin
1875.8–1876.7	Min Kyuho	1836–78	Civil	Royal in-law Min
1876.7–1877.4	Sin Hŏn	1810–88	Military	Well rounded, moderate reformist
1877.4–1877.12	Kim Kisŏk	n.d.	Military	Trusted by both the Taewŏn'gun and Queen Myŏngsŏng
1877.12–1878.6	Yi Kyŏngha	1811–91	Military	Trusted by both the Taewŏn'gun and Queen Myŏngsŏng
1878.6–1879.3	Kim Pyŏngsi	1832–98	Civil	Moderate conservative opposed to reform
1879.3–1880.4	Min Kyŏmho	1838–82	Civil	Royal in-law Min
1880.4–1881.9	Yi Kyŏngha	(As mentioned)	(As mentioned)	(As mentioned)
1881.9–1881.12	Min T'aeho	1834–84	Civil	Royal in-law Min
1881.12–1882.6	Yi Kyŏngha	(As mentioned)	(As mentioned)	(As mentioned)

Source: *Sŭngjŏngwŏn ilgi.*

attained the senior-third grade post of Five Guards general (*Owijang*).[103] The post was a distinction of social significance and has not received adequate scholarly attention. Law codes, personnel records, and known activities of the generals of the Five Guards, which over the centuries had devolved from a large capital army to a small security force, suggest that the state used the appointment to recognize good service by someone without any realistic prospect of achieving one of the important, high-level offices reserved for aristocrats. The generals tended to be members of social groups neither aristocrat nor commoner in status, as well as elderly aristocrats of scholarly distinction. Although many appointees saw the post purely as an honor and simply resigned after a brief tenure, sometimes as short as a day, those of a military background, such as T'aesik, often performed capital patrol duties. Thus the generalship was more than the sort of devalued rank or office that the Chosŏn state had been selling since the seventeenth century. It seems that by the late nineteenth century, intermediate status groups such as the government specialist *chungin* had accrued cultural and economic capital to the extent that the state, which needed their resources and services, could not fool them with empty honors. At the same time, the aristocratic proprietors of the state had a vested interest in maintaining some gradation of honors so that they could ensure the integrity of the existing social hierarchy.[104]

In T'aesik's case, the government seems to have granted him the Five Guards general post in recognition of either good military service or a financial contribution in the 1880s or 1890s. That he obtained the post is certain on several grounds. Above all, the genealogy of the family of the man that T'aesik's second daughter married into records him with the post.[105] Also, one of T'aesik's grandsons, who grew up in Puyŏ in the 1930s, recalls the villagers referring to his grandfather as "Five Guards General Pak" (Pak *Owijang*).[106] Moreover, in October 1902, when T'aesik received a promotion from the senior third to the junior second rank, the lower rank apparently reflected the rank of his last official appointment as a Five Guards general.[107]

T'aesik's activities within the evolving political context of the time remain unknown, though one can use various sources of evidence to deduce possibilities. It is certain that he was not deeply involved in the most dramatic events of the era: the Imo Military Revolt (1882), the Kapsin Coup (1884), and the Tonghak ("Eastern Learning") uprisings (1894–95), even though these all involved capital troops.[108] Also, at the time, Military Guard Agency soldiers such as T'aesik were enjoying preferential treatment in comparison to the mutinying Military Training Administration troops.[109] When analyzing the cause of the mutiny, Chief State Councilor (*Yŏnguijŏng*) Hong Sunmok (1816–84), a senior official of integrity and good reputation, noted that whereas the Military Guard Agency soldiers were receiving fully filled bags of grain as salaries, the mutinying Military Training Administration soldiers were not.[110] Furthermore, since T'aesik probably was able to join the favored Military Guard Agency troops thanks to some kind of tie to the royal in-law Mins or their affiliates supporting the throne at the time, he would have had little reason to take part in the Imo Military Revolt or the Kapsin Coup, which targeted the Mins and their political allies. In the case of the Kapsin Coup, Qing China again intervened and, in the end, punished those perpetrators who could not flee.[111] Known participants tended to be aristocrats or commoners rather than *chungin*.[112] Finally, if the Tonghak uprisings involved T'aesik at all, it would have been on the side of the government as either an officer or a financial sponsor, though the lack of any documentation suggests he probably was not involved to the extent that he earned a mention in any of the extant government documents I have examined.[113]

What he actually did during this period cannot be established, but available evidence strongly suggests he was at least sympathetic toward, even if he did not associate with, reform advocates. The military examination that he passed in 1882 was a companion competition to the civil examination passed by none other than Sŏ Chaep'il (American name Philip Jaisohn, 1861–1951), eventually famous as one of the Enlightenment Party leaders.[114] In Chosŏn society, the graduates of the same examination maintained a lifelong relationship, if not close friendship.[115] Also, T'aesik lived in a neighborhood (what is now northern Sŏsomun subdistrict) where Western presence was strong in many ways, and he was a Christian by 1905 if not earlier, as will be discussed in Chapters 4 and 6. Moreover, he not only sent a son to one of Korea's earliest governmental institutions of higher learning, Seoul Normal School (Hansŏng Sabŏm Hakkyo, now Seoul National University's College of Education) in 1906; his surviving granddaughters recall growing up in a family that was decidedly more Westernized than Confucian in worldview, customs, and education.[116] All the same, it is telling that T'aesik was not involved deeply enough in the Independence Club (Tongnip Hyŏphoe, 1896–98) and other reformist movements at the time to leave behind any documentation, as did his marriage kin, highlighted in Chapter 5. Perhaps he was not by nature a political person or an activist. Also, if some kind of tie to the royal in-law Mins or their associates was what dissuaded T'aesik from involvement in the earlier Imo Military Revolt and the Kapsin Coup, then it could easily have distanced him from the various groups that were at odds with the monarch and royal in-law Mins, even though T'aesik seems to have associated with or had ties to monarchist reform advocates.

We know more about T'aesik's personal life. His wife, Madam Haeju O (1860–1944), likely was from a family of comparable or lower social standing for at least two reasons. First, she was five years his junior, which was more typical of a man's second wife than his first, who generally was close in age or slightly older than the husband. If she was his second wife, then apparently his first wife died without mothering any child.[117] Also, since Madam Haeju O's parents, O Susik (ca. 1830–n.d.) and Madam Yi (n.d.), had died early in their daughter's life, and thus deprived her of parents to vouch for the bride's social status, Madam O's brother's wife reportedly arranged her marriage to T'aesik.[118] Madam O's brother had a career in the government, but so far I have not been able to verify his name or any details of his career.[119] Madam Haeju O and T'aesik had six children: the eldest son, Kyŏngjun (1878–ca. 1930); an elder daughter whose name remains unknown (ca. 1882–ca. 1954); the second son, Ch'anggil (ca. 1886–n.d.); the third son, Ch'angnae

(1890–1945); the fourth son, Ch'angsŏng (1900–15); and younger daughter Sunhŭi (1902–n.d.).[120]

Perhaps reflecting increased kinship distance, the names of T'aesik's sons no longer share a generational character with those of their closest cousins, the sons of T'aesik's fifth cousins, Yunsik and Chinsik. If a documented petition requesting permission for a name change from "Pak Myŏnghwan" to "Pak Ŭijun" concerns (and this is perfectly possible) the Pak lineage heir (*chongson*) whose name as given in the genealogy is Myŏnghwan, then we can surmise that T'aesik named his eldest son, Kyŏngjun, so that his given name's second character, *chun* (Ch. *jun*, excellent, lofty), was the same as the one used in the new name of the lineage heir.[121] Other than that, the only commonality between the names of T'aesik's younger sons, all beginning with the ideograph *ch'ang* (Ch. *chang*, flourishing, growing), and the names of their sixth cousins, all ending with the ideograph *hwan* (Ch. *huan*, flame, shining), is that both relate to Fire, which follows Wood in the Five Phases.[122] After all, the ideograph of *sik* (Ch. *zhi*, to plant) in Yunsik, Chinsik, and T'aesik's names contains the wood radical.

The surviving children of T'aesik's son Ch'angnae have provided much oral history material for this book. Their accounts suggest that T'aesik commanded wealth while serving as a military officer. It is uncertain whether the source of wealth was a state-authorized monopoly, as with his grandfather, Pak Yusin. We do know that in what is now northern Sŏsomun subdistrict, T'aesik lived in a house of such size, measured in scores of *k'an*, that his wife, Madam Haeju O, deemed it too large and decided move to a smaller one.[123] At the time, mean sizes of thatched-roof and tile-roof homes inside the city walls were, respectively, 7.37 *k'an* and 16.55 *k'an*.[124] Also, at the least, T'aesik owned land in both Puyŏ and Koyang, including the plot around the graves of his parents, Yŏngho and Madam Kim.[125] Even after the family's fortunes were ruined at the outbreak of the Russo-Japanese War (1904–05), as discussed below, the holding in Puyŏ was about ten thousand *p'yŏng* in area (about eight acres).[126]

T'aesik was a generous bon vivant. Late into the night he enjoyed drinking and gambling. After a few drinks, he often merrily shelled out his cash to those present—on some occasions even 100 *yang* at a time.[127] For the first birthday of his third son, Ch'angnae, in 1891, T'aesik put on a lavish celebration by entertaining the guests in the main hall (*taech'ŏng*) of his mansion, replete with a troupe of *kisaeng* female entertainers. As the mistress of the inner sphere, his wife had to take the blame for this extravagance: T'aesik's elder sister found the whole affair excessive and scolded her sister-in-law, Madam O.[128]

It seems that T'aesik's sister was a concubine of a Kim-surnamed man who is said to have served as a magistrate in several counties in the countryside, including Okch'ŏn.[129] In late Chosŏn Korea, office-holding aristocrats and *chungin* were more likely to have concubines than non-office-holding aristocrats and the rest of the male population.[130] What this shows is that the society perceived office holding as a premium vis-à-vis social standing and that fathers were willing to let their daughters become concubines of officeholders rather than wives of other men. The information revealing that T'aesik's sister was a concubine of an officeholder is that in her old age, the members of the Pak family referred to her as "Okch'ŏn *mama.*"[131] Given the usage of the term of address "*mama*" in the late nineteenth and early twentieth centuries, the testimony more or less confirms that she was a concubine of a government official.[132] Also, the fact that none of the Okch'ŏn magistrates from the era was a nonaristocrat like the Paks or had a Miryang Pak as a wife suggests that the woman in question was a concubine of a male of higher social status.[133]

According to the Pak family oral history, she was a woman of strong character as well as a helpful companion to the magistrate, and their story offers us a glimpse into the world of concubinage among Korean elites at the time. On the coldest winter day, the two would go hunting. Afterward, they would retire into a hut of thick, matted coverings with a bonfire. Like his "brother-in-law," T'aesik, the magistrate was fond of drinking. When too hung over to perform his duty on the following day, T'aesik's sister sometimes substituted for her husband—even presiding over legal disputes, as unbelievable as this may seem. Apparently the magistrate cared deeply for her as well as her family. Learning while in Kangwŏn province that his brother-in-law, T'aesik, was ill, he dispatched to Seoul a boiling pot of potent herbal stew with a servant fanning it to control the temperature throughout the transport. The couple apparently had no child of their own, though the magistrate seems to have had sons by other women. The magistrate's sons were killed during a riot, reportedly by a "violent mob" (*p'okto*)—a term that seems analogous to the "brigands" (*pido, piryu*) so well documented in primary sources from the period.[134]

The historical personality who comes closest to matching the descriptions of the magistrate as given by the Pak family oral history is Kim Ponggyu (formerly Kim Hŭigyun, 1851–97). Born into the powerful royal-in law Andong Kim lineage, he passed the licentiate examination (1873) and performed a series of rotation duties in the Office of Crown Prince Guards (*Seja Igwisa*) before holding magistrate or comparable positions in five locales in four different provinces.[135] His last posting was in Okch'ŏn, from the third to the seventh lunar month of 1894 when, at one point, the Tonghak militants attacked those they deemed corrupt and in effect paralyzed local administration.[136] This seems to be the event during which Kim was attacked by "brigands" who then killed his sons.

Unlike the relationship between T'aesik's sister and the magistrate that embodied an obvious status difference, the members of a third Pak line formed marriage ties similar to those of the senior line. T'aesik's fifth-generation ancestor's first cousin, Chiyŏng, whose in-laws were aristocratic offshoots through illegitimate children, married his daughter (1811–87) to a man from the technical specialist Chŏnju Yi family, Yi Ilho (1809–60).[137] The couple adopted a son, Yi Hŭngmu (alternate name Yi Namsu, 1849–n.d.), who passed the interpreter examination in 1882.[138] By the seventeenth century, this particular Chŏnju Yi line had established itself as a specialist *chungin* family.[139] They may have been the descendants of the same Chŏnju Yi man discussed in Chapter 1, Yi Chihyŏn, who in the seventeenth century married his daughter to Pak Kiin, the great-grandfather of Chiyŏng.

Conclusion

We can conclude that in the first half of the nineteenth century, the Paks attained *chungin* status while remaining military officers engaged in commerce. Though continuing to serve in various capital army units, the Paks diversified their economic activity by acquiring land outside Kyŏnggi province as well as running state-approved monopoly businesses. In contrast to the status ambiguities raised by previous generations' marriages to women from wealthy families, many nineteenth-century Pak men chose daughters from established *chungin* lines. As for the Pak women, they either married *chungin* men such as jurists and calligraphers or became concubines of men of higher social status. This is a pattern newly evident thanks to the fact that from the early nineteenth century on, the genealogy of the up-and-coming Paks began to record daughters, albeit by the husband's name. The change was not so much about any significant improvement in the status of women as an indication that the Paks were acquiring socially presentable sons-in-law. Having gained a solid foothold in *chungin* society, the Paks would assume interesting new roles during the coming era of Korea's radical adjustments in the world of imperialism.

4   Long Live the Korean Empire

Hopes, Fulfillment, and Frustrations

O N OCTOBER 12, 1897, THE MONARCH NOW COMMONLY KNOWN in English as "King Kojong" assumed an imperial title and inaugurated the Korean Empire (Taehan Cheguk).[1] For at least a century, the prevalent view of modernizing Korea's situation at this time was that, amid the lingering strife between his father, the Hŭngsŏn Taewŏn'gun, and his own wife, Queen Myŏngsŏng, as well as the conflict among those of varying political shades, helpless Chosŏn Korea became a Japanese colony.[2] In the past two decades or so, however, an increasing number of historians have demonstrated that the outcome was not inevitable: the monarch played a critical, leading role in sustaining a reform effort designed to strengthen an emerging nation-state, much of which he even personally financed.[3] Even more importantly, the resulting reform culminated with an Imperial Korea aligned toward Russia.[4] The victory over Russia by a Japan determined not to allow Korea to become—from the Japanese imperialist perspective—a continental dagger pointed at its heart sealed Korea's fate.[5]

A key part of Imperial Korea's effort to meet the challenges of an imperialist-dominated world was tapping the talent of those with a sincere interest in and a good knowledge of Western institutions and ideas. This meant new opportunities, especially for the specialist *chungin*. The Kwangmu emperor— we henceforth shall refer to King Kojong by the era name that he adopted on assuming imperial title in 1897—tended to trust most those not from an aristocratic background who nonetheless were loyal and supportive of his initiatives.[6] The Seoul-based Patriarch-faction aristocratic families featured proud Confucian scholar-officials of predominantly "Little China" ideological orientation with strong opinions not necessarily in agreement with the emperor on all issues; by contrast, men from less distinguished families had a vested interest in the success of a monarchist reform effort geared toward more Western-style institutions and ideas. Possessing significant wealth that they could use to finance the kind of projects the emperor favored in building a modern nation-state, many *chungin* were in a position to assume prominent roles in Imperial Korea.

The Empire's New Capital

In this light, the emperor's effort to develop P'yŏngyang as Korea's secondary capital, designated "Western Capital" (Sŏgyŏng), is relevant to our consideration of the roles of *chungin* in modernizing Korea. The official justification of P'yŏngyang as the Korean Empire's Western Capital stressed historical precedents.[7] On May 1, 1902, the Ministry of the Royal Household's Special Entry Officer (*Tŭkchin'gwan*) Kim Kyuhong (1845–n.d.) submitted a memorial arguing that historical empires have had two capitals, including the Zhou (1045–256 BCE), the Han (202 BCE–220 CE), the Tang (618–907), and the Ming (1368–1644) dynasties of China, and that the practice culminated with the Ming system of Beijing ("Northern Capital") and Nanjing ("Southern Capital"). Kim used Nanjing as the case in point, and reference to the city would recur in subsequent discussions of the P'yŏngyang project—a rhetorical tactic more than sensible in light of the critical importance of the Ming in the still-influential Little China ideology among Imperial Korea's mainstream elite.[8] Stressing that P'yŏngyang's water virtue (*sudŏk*) and psychosomatic energy (*ki*) made it worthy to be a dynastic capital for "a myriad years," as well as the fact that it had been Korea's earliest cultural center, Kim reminded the emperor that the city had been the capital for the Old Chosŏn (n.d.–108 BCE), Koguryŏ (trad. 37 BCE–668 CE), and Koryŏ rulers. On reading the memorial, the emperor expressed his agreement as well as a desire to pursue the matter further.[9]

The Western Capital project had cultural and ideological significance, but it also addressed the strategic concerns of an Imperial Korea negotiating with the major powers in the region. A secondary capital situated almost 200 kilometers from Seoul would have given Korea a degree of breathing space from

Japanese encroachment. It would also avail opportunities to explore a closer partnership with Japan's main continental rival, Russia.[10]

The swiftness with which the monarch launched the project leaves little room for doubt that Kim's memorial was a coup de théâtre. The general tone of the memorial exudes the author's faith in the dignity of both empire and emperor, a position well in line with Kim's known anti–Independence Club stance. Only five days later, on May 6, the Kwangmu emperor professed he had been thinking about the project for a long time, articulating Chinese historical precedents as well as noting that of late, foreign countries too establish two capitals. He ordered that appropriate officials discuss constructing a new palace in the "Western Capital."[11] On May 10, the emperor appointed appropriate officials to manage the project, among them the governor of South P'yŏngan province, Min Yŏngch'ŏl (1864–n.d.), as the senior supervising official (*Kamdong tangsang*) of construction work.[12] To fund the project, the monarch, on May 14, released 500,000 *yang* of cash from the royal treasury fund (*naet'angjŏn*) and subsequently also assessed a series of extraordinary taxes on the residents of the province.[13]

Although there still was insufficient funding, materials, and manpower, the court undertook the project with organization and efficiency at a level previously unseen, even using the new rail transportation system.[14] The project officially began in June 1902 when the emperor approved the names of the palace's new edifices. In September, a procession of officials transported portraits of the emperor and the crown prince (future Yunghŭi emperor) to the city.[15] Then on October 5, the emperor gave an audience to the processional officials returning from P'yŏngyang and announced rewards for them, including promotions.[16] In the Korean cultural context at the time, the meaning of a royal portrait arguably was analogous to—if not inspired by—the iconization of the emperor's portrait in Japan.[17] Thus housing the emperor and the crown prince's "icons" in the Western Capital symbolically amounted to connecting the nation's new capital to the substance of the emperor as a being both physical and metaphysical.[18]

For this momentous project, the court mobilized individuals from diverse backgrounds, though status consciousness persisted. The court categorized the individuals involved in the project as follows: (1) government officials with specific duties, (2) soldiers (*kunbyŏng*) and policemen (*sun'gŏm*), and (3) master craftsmen (*changin*).[19] In terms of social status, the members of these three groups appear to have been, respectively, (1) predominantly aristocrats but also some *chungin*; (2) a mixture of broader-definition *chungin* and common-ers, and (3) mostly commoners. When rewarding the individuals who helped transport the royal portraits, the court again recognized three distinct tiers: (1) "escorting high officials" (*paejong taesin*), who were mostly incumbent aristocratic officials; (2) "escorting personnel" (*paejong inwŏn*), who were gen-erally court rank-holding *chungin*; and (3) policemen and "staff personnel" (*wŏnyŏk*), mostly commoners.[20]

In terms of larger social significance, the list of "escorting personnel" is particularly revealing. It suggests that in spite of a power structure still domi-nated by the aristocracy, the state had to honor even *chungin* men who appar-ently had never held politically meaningful posts. Name searches using the online *Daily Records of the Royal Secretariat* find none of these men among those who received high-level "actual posts" (*silchik*) during the period.[21] Somehow, then, they all won the court's attention and appreciation for par-ticular reasons—possibly financial contributions or other forms of service, if not direct or indirect ties to the emperor.

The Japanese ascendancy in Korea proved the death knell of the Western Capital project. Anticipating the Russo-Japanese War, the Korean government declared Korea's neutrality on January 21, 1904. Nonetheless, at the outbreak of the war on February 8, Japan moved swiftly to tighten its stranglehold on the Korean government and to occupy large portions of Korea.[22] By August, advancing Japanese forces had occupied most of the northwest, including P'yŏngyang, and the palace halls became makeshift barracks for the Japanese army.[23] Despite the circumstances, the state was keen on granting the West-ern Capital–related honors to as many individuals as possible for as long as feasible. For instance, up to May 1906, the court continued to appoint new managing officials (*Ch'amsŏgwan*) for P'unggyŏng Palace, but each appoin-tee's brief tenure—some as short as one day—clearly suggests these were hon-orary assignments.[24]

The Japanese deposed the recalcitrant Kwangmu emperor and enthroned the Yunghŭi emperor (temple name Sunjong, r. 1907–10) against his will. In August 1907, less than a month after his accession, the Japanese disbanded the Korean army, depriving P'yŏngyang of the Garri-son Army (*Chinwidae*) responsible for the security of P'unggyŏng Palace. In April 1908, the Korean government under Japanese control brought the royal portraits back to Seoul and abolished all official posts associated with the palace.

Inventing Tradition

The Western Capital project, even though abandoned in the end, did leave a legacy in that it further encouraged upwardly mobile nonelites to seek a long-time symbol of status assertion in the form of genealogies. Originally, many such records presented an ancestry not tracing back beyond the fifteenth or sixteenth century, the beginning of the early modern era.[25] Many *chungin* families resorted to modifying their genealogies.

Altering or even constructing depictions of the past to suit present needs of course was not a new practice in Korea. As discussed in Chapter 2, the Confucian aristocracy in seventeenth-century Korea, traumatized by the "barbarian" Manchu conquest of China, had begun to see itself as guardians of the Way. Maintaining an idealized kinship group documented through genealogy become crucial to this new status identity. Over time, genealogies evolved into a powerful medium for inventing new traditions transcending social boundaries. By the end of the early modern era, nonelites—including many *chungin* families—were actively inventing traditions. Crumbling of late Chosŏn social hierarchy could only facilitate the trend.

Recreation of tradition occurred as the majority of specialist Seoul *chungin* descent lines using unique ancestral seat labels let go of them in the modern era. In the *Record of Surname Origins* compiled in the nineteenth century, fifty out of some two hundred descent lines listed in its table of contents bear surname–ancestral seat combinations not found in the later *Comprehensive Genealogy of Ten Thousand Surnames* (*Mansŏng taedongbo*), a 1933 compilation recording the most eminent aristocratic descent lines.[26] And of those fifty listings in the *Record of Surname Origins*, at least thirty-one (62 percent) were no longer found in the 1985 South Korean census survey.[27] Among those still remaining, the 1985 population of each descent group ranged from scores to a few thousands, generally concentrated in Seoul or surrounding Kyŏnggi province.[28] Since a nineteenth-century capital *chungin* family typically descended from a founding figure who lived sometime in the fifteenth or sixteenth century, it produced ten to fifteen generations of direct male descendants that by the twentieth century could number in the thousands. Unless most of them somehow left what is now South Korea in the modern era, the only logical conclusion we can draw is that since the compilation of the *Record of Surname Origins* in the late nineteenth century, many *chungin*-only descent groups have changed their ancestral seat designation to that historically used for the

given surname to denote a more socially diverse, if not predominantly aristocratic, descent group.

The case of the specialist *chungin* Haeju Kim typifies this phenomenon.
Sometime between 1885 and 1907, family members changed their ancestral
seat designation from Haeju to Ch'ŏngp'ung, as well as recording themselves
as the descendants and kinsmen of prominent aristocratic scholar-officials in
the Ch'ŏngp'ung Kim genealogy.[29] The most famous member of the descent
group, the independence activist and statesman Kim Kyusik (1881–1950),
appears in all modern biographical references as a Ch'ŏngp'ung Kim. The
Haeju Kim chose to hide under the umbrella of a descent group known for
prestigious aristocratic lineages—including the capital line that produced
a queen consort in the seventeenth century, as well as Kim Kyuhong whose
memorial mentioned above urged the emperor to develop P'yŏngyang as the
Western Capital.[30]

Hiding *chungin* origin was easier for families already using a surname-
ancestral seat designation common across late Chosŏn status boundaries. In
early modern Korea, persons of all shades of social status claimed popular
combinations such as the Kimhae Kim and the Miryang Pak. The nonelites
using historically known ancestral seat–surname combinations included
aristocracy "dropouts," that is, those descended from illegitimate children of
aristocratic fathers. In genealogies, their entries are identifiable, because they
tend to have less detailed information than those for aristocratic members. In
fact, a genealogy often stops covering an illegitimate branch after one or two
generations beyond an illegitimate son. For example, the 1869 edition Miryang Pak genealogy recording the aforementioned Practical Learning scholar
Pak Chega, who was an illegitimate son of an aristocratic civil official, stops
the coverage of his descendants after two generations without mentioning
whether or not the line became extinct.[31] Besides such aristocratic offshoots,
the nonelites using a historically known ancestral seat–surname combination
in the early modern era also included the descendants of functionaries who
not only had failed to attain aristocratic status by joining central officialdom
during the medieval period but also sank into obscurity when unable to maintain even their status as functionaries.[32]

In the nineteenth century, for example, the specialist Seoul *chungin* Miryang Pak line descended from a certain Pak Chungsan (b. ca. 1460) latched
itself onto a member of a known aristocratic Miryang Pak family. One of
sixteen *chungin* Miryang Pak lines that the seventeenth-century *Record of
Surname Origins* leaves untraced beyond the early modern era, the family

descended from Chungsan evidently produced no officeholder during the first four generations, and the first degree holder passed a technical examination (ca. 1590).[33] Sometime between 1867 and 1873, the family made its way into a thirteen-volume genealogy recording a large Miryang Pak descent group segment traced to an aristocratic civil official, Pak Simmun (1408–56). Published in 1873, without an explanation, the genealogy replaces Chungsan with one of Simmun's sons, a literary licentiate with a different name.[34]

During this period, if not somewhat earlier, status insecurity spurred the subject family of this book, the descendants of Pak Tŏkhwa, to perform a genealogical maneuver and make itself, too, a descendant of Pak Simmun. The Tŏkhwa line does not appear in older editions of published Miryang Pak genealogies, though by the early nineteenth century its members evidently were using "Miryang" as their ancestral seat designation.[35] Then, apparently between 1873 and 1924, the family made its way into an officially recognized Miryang Pak genealogy.[36]

The fact that the name "Tŏkhwa" does not use the generational character shared among his alleged brothers requires a consideration of how upstart families made their way into the genealogies of other families. Recorded as the sons of a junior sixth-rank county magistrate, Pak Chu, the three brothers appear as Ŭn'gyŏng (ca. 1560–n.d.), Hyŏn'gyŏng (1571–98), and Wŏn'gyŏng (n.d.)—all sharing the "-gyŏng" given name pattern.[37] Ordinarily, someone representing the family that wanted to be recorded in the genealogy of a supposedly related family had to present supporting documents to someone from the latter charged with collecting and examining such documents. The degree to which the representative of the petitioned family scrutinized the veracity of a kinship claim varied widely depending on the circumstances surrounding the particular genealogy compilation, but overall in the early modern era it apparently became more difficult to be too stringent as most ostensibly comprehensive genealogies became increasingly voluminous—with kinsmen, real or not, residing throughout the country.

By the twentieth century, the nature of the target family was such that the representative of the Pak Tŏkhwa line perhaps saw no need to make Tŏkhwa's name conform to those of his alleged brothers. In the early modern era, the descendants of the three brothers were scattered throughout Korea and were of varying shades of social status. It is certain that the three brothers were indeed the sons of Pak Chu, a member of the Ch'ŏngjaegong subbranch of the Kyujŏnggong branch of the Miryang Pak, and the earliest known editions of the Kyujŏnggong branch genealogy and the subsequent editions all record them. Also, the various late Chosŏn editions continue to record the descendants of one or more of the three brothers. The problem is that as time went on, the descendants dispersed from what apparently was Pak Chu's residence locale, Kimje in Chŏlla province, and also descent lines of questionable membership began appearing in later editions. For example, as found in the genealogy, the recorded information on one of Tŏkhwa's alleged brothers, Hyŏn'gyŏng, whose alternate name is given as "Yŏngho" in some editions, seems to suggest that sometime in the early modern or modern era, a Pak family descended from Yŏngho, yet unable to trace its ancestry beyond him, simply identified him with an originally obscure, poorly documented individual, Hyŏn'gyŏng.[38] Thus by the time of the compilation of the 1924 edition, one can hardly regard the descendants of Ŭn'gyŏng, Hyŏn'gyŏng, Wŏn'gyŏng, and—for that matter Tŏkhwa—as constituting a tightly knit lineage of the kind where everyone knew one another.

Moreover, unless the ancestor of our *chungin* Paks somehow acquired this name during his lifetime, we can only wonder if his descendants used the name to replace an obviously slave- or commoner-sounding name. In early modern Korea, nonelites often used given names that stand out from the rest in extant primary sources.[39] If the upwardly mobile descendants indeed posthumously renamed their earliest known ancestor, then most likely they first changed his name in their records before managing to get their entire family included in a larger, official Miryang Pak genealogy.

Lastly, we also have to consider the real likelihood that "Tŏkhwa" was a name the descendants devised for the founding ancestor whose actual name they did not even know. The main ground for this suspicion is the fact that late Chosŏn household registration documents generally record the household head's patrilineal ancestors' names and occupation-service (*chigyŏk*) labels up to the great-grandfather. Given that the family's first member for whom more detailed genealogical and career information is available and who fathered more than one child is Myŏngŏp, recorded as Tŏkhwa's great-great-grandson in the genealogy, I suspect that the information on his father, grandfather, and great-grandfather derives from a household registration record showing Myŏngŏp as the household head. This is all that the family at the time (back in the early eighteenth century) had to go by in constructing a genealogy, as they were not yet making up a lineage in any meaningful sense after just a few generations of single-line succession.

Built around such recorded facts, fabricated family histories became invented traditions cherished by descendants. Since the eighteenth century, specialist *chungin* had been petitioning the court for greater access to the prestigious government positions previously monopolized by the aristocracy. Such petitions tended to stress that before the seventeenth century their ancestors had been aristocrats.[40] In the late nineteenth century, when many *chungin* families changed their ancestral seat designations to common ones or attached their previously untraceable ancestors to those already recorded in existing aristocratic genealogies, they often claimed that previous editions had somehow omitted them. When a genealogy records a previously unrepresented descent line, it sometimes includes an explanation by a representative of the long-lost kinsmen that earlier editions had somehow omitted one of the brothers (or cousins) and his descendants, if not just the descendants. When provided, such an explanation typically cites as the reason the descendants' residence at a faraway locale. In the case of the Haeju Kim, the 1907 Ch'ŏngp'ung Kim genealogy notes that according to the "kinsman" presenting the Haeju Kim segment record, his ancestors changed the ancestral seat designation from Ch'ŏngp'ung to Haeju after relocating to Haeju.[41] In contrast, the 1924 Miryang Pak genealogy recording the Pak Tŏkhwa line offers no such explanation.[42] Since a *chungin* document admitting to any forgery or fabrication will probably never surface, all we can conclude is that the pedigree justification used by the specialist *chungin* was an important part of their effort to argue their case for equal treatment alongside the aristocracy, as well as inventing a tradition for the family to embrace. As much as the maneuver may have served a purpose for them, it makes the historian's job more challenging.

Tracing the Stories of "Unimportant" Individuals

Previous studies, based on limited samples, have focused on only the most prominent *chungin* families and individuals of Imperial Korea. This narrow view can distort the general picture by presenting these groups on the whole as opportunists who welcomed both the birth of the Korean Empire and Japan's colonization of Korea. Allegedly, the *chungin* fared well through the early decades of the twentieth century and went on to attain elite status in

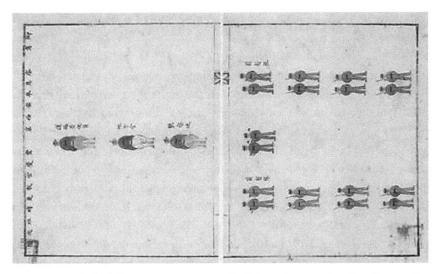

FIGURE 4.1 Head of the 1902 procession as depicted in the royal protocol manual. Source: *Kojong Ŏjin Tosa Togam ŭigwe*, pp. 351–52. Reprinted with the permission of Kyujanggak Institute for Korean Studies, Seoul National University.

post-1945 South Korea. Setting aside the issue of pro-Japanese collaboration until Chapter 6, suffice it for now to point out that some of the individuals discussed in that chapter—such as both U Pŏmsŏn (1857–1903) and P'aeng Hanju (1856–n.d.) from families related to the Paks—are known among historians, but additional research can shed more light on their family backgrounds, interpersonal relationships, and pre–Open Port Period careers, as well as offering stories of human interest. This chapter seeks to present a model for exploring additional dimensions of such stories by looking at the case of the Paks and their associates.

Unlike the earlier chapters examining all descent lines of the Paks, the family history as narrated in this chapter highlights Pak T'aesik. He took part in the ambitious Western Capital project, an event rich in symbolism for Korea. In September 1902, after two decades of a career that entailed military service and probably business too, he took part in the official procession that transported the imperial portrait to P'yŏngyang. T'aesik was a member of the "escorting personnel" (*paejong inwŏn*; Figures 4.1, 4.2). In October he received promotion from the senior third rank, which apparently reflected the rank of his former Five Guards general post, to the junior second rank with the civil court rank of *Kasŏn taebu* ("magnate admirable and good"), as mentioned in Chapter 3.[43]

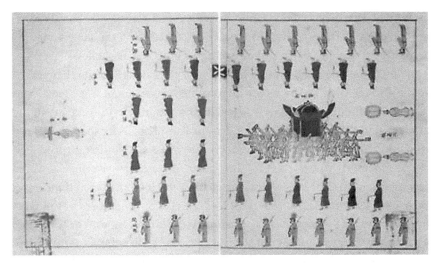

FIGURE 4.2 Procession personnel surrounding the imperial portrait. Source: *Kojong Ŏjin Tosa Togam ŭigwe*, pp. 343–44. Reprinted with the permission of Kyujanggak Institute for Korean Studies, Seoul National University.

A little over a year later, in early 1904, came the effective end of the new capital project, and the Korean Empire for that matter, and all that they had promised for *chungin* men on the rise such as T'aesik. Two of his grandchildren can remember hearing from their parents only that the ensuing chaos of the war ruined family fortunes and that the family fled Seoul for Puyŏ county in South Ch'ungch'ŏng province, where it had land.[44] Considering that T'aesik is not known to have held a politically influential position in officialdom, whether he was a political victim of Japanese ascendancy remains unclear, though it seems likely the Japanese took note of financial donors supporting imperial Korean enterprises such as the Western Capital project. What is certain is that when the Japanese took over much land in Seoul and artfully imposed a large debt on the Korean government by carrying out a currency reform (1905) that devalued the existing currency, the financial fortunes of T'aesik suffered.[45] He could no longer conduct normal business operations nor maintain his large household in Seoul.

T'aesik fled to Puyŏ with a cousin, a friend, and their respective households. The cousin was Pang Munyŏng (ca. 1874–1935), whose mother and T'aesik's mother were sisters; the friend was Yang Cheha (also known as Yang Chuha, ca. 1850–1922?).[46] Whereas Pang hailed from an illegitimate-son line of a prominent, specialist *chungin* family, I have yet to determine the family background of Yang, though several specialist *chungin* lines of the same Yang surname are known. More detailed discussion of both families follows.

Pang Munyŏng came from a *chungin* Onyang Pang lineage that placed scores of members in the technical and military branches of officialdom in the early modern era as well as producing prominent individuals in the modern period. Descended from a certain Pang Kyech'ang (ca. 1500–n.d.), who was the first family member to reside in Seoul, the Pangs produced at least forty-eight interpreters, thirty-four physicians, two jurists, three astronomers, and three accountants passing the technical examination in their respective fields. Moreover, at least thirty-four members of the family are known to have passed the military examination, and at least one, none other than the founder of the line, passed the licentiate examination. As was true for specialist Seoul *chungin* families in general, the *chungin* Onyang Pang lineage enjoyed no success in the civil examinations that the capital civil aristocracy dominated as the gateway to prestigious civil officialdom.[47] The most famous member of the lineage in the early modern era, Pang Ujŏng (1772–1820), the seventh cousin of Munyŏng's great-grandfather, participated as a military officer during the suppression of the 1812 Hong Kyŏngnae Rebellion—as did Pak T'aesik's likely great-grandfather, Pak Kyŏnguk.[48] Pang is also one of the very small number of military *chungin* men whose own writing is extant. His *Daily Records of the Western Expedition* (*Sŏjŏng ilgi*) gives a detailed account of his thoughts and actions during his service.[49] With the opening of Korea, many from the Pang family played a prominent role in the rapidly changing world as political, business, or cultural leaders. Especially noteworthy is the sixth cousin of Munyŏng's father, Pang Handŏk (1846–1913), who was one of the leaders of the Independence Club and arguably Korea's first joint-stock company, as discussed below in Chapter 5.[50] Celebrated today as a children's welfare activist, an even more famous kinsman is the son of Munyŏng's tenth cousin, Pang Chŏnghwan (pen name Sop'a, 1899–1931), whose patrilineal ancestors had been, for at least two generations, capital merchants rather than state-employed specialists.[51] To modern readers, these relationships must seem too distant to be significant, but in early modern Korea the members of a sociopolitically meaningful kin group, such as a lineage, tended to share a common patrilineal ancestor who had lived sometime between roughly 1500 and 1650.[52]

Munyŏng does not appear in Pang genealogies where coverage of his generation and beyond is spotty, but I am certain he was a sixth-generation descendant of an illegitimate son of Pang Chin'gi (1655–1729).[53] A royal physician rewarded with magistracies for exceptional service, Chin'gi fathered just one legitimate son, whose descendants enjoyed all the privileges of a prominent *chungin* family. The genealogy's coverage of the line of his illegitimate son, Pang Seyang (n.d.), however, stops two generations thereafter—reflecting its marginalized social status. Both the information provided in various editions of Pang genealogy and what is missing, as well as various details on Munyŏng that I have gathered through archival research and interviews with family members, leave little doubt that he indeed was a descendant of Seyang.

A kinsman's career may explain why Munyŏng and his cousin, Pak T'aesik, moved from Seoul to Puyŏ in 1904–05. Pang Hanch'ŏl (1834–87), who most likely was a fifth cousin of Munyŏng's father, had once served as Puyŏ county magistrate (*Hyŏn'gam*).[54] Given the tendencies of late Chosŏn magistrates, Hanch'ŏl probably acquired some land in the area. If so, this would have been something on which Munyŏng could fall back.

Moreover, the grave locations of Munyŏng's known close kinsmen and those of Chin'gi's recorded descendants match. Both the Pang genealogy and the Koyang city gazetteer record that the members of the branch of the *chungin* Onyang Pang family from which Munyŏng most likely hailed were buried in Paeksŏk subdistrict, Chung district, Koyang county (present Ilsan district, Koyang city).[55] One of Pak T'aesik's grandsons recalls spending a night at a Pang family household in the nearby Taejang subdistrict of Chido district whenever he and his mother visited his great-grandparents' graves.[56] Also, the grandson's recollection of how he and his mother got off a train at Nŭnggok station and walked roughly 10 *i* (approximately 4 kilometers) in the northwesterly direction, with the rail line on their left for some time, points to Taejang.[57] In addition, a grandson of Munyŏng states that before the latter's flight from Seoul, the ancestors were buried in Taejang and that his great-grandfather, that is Munyŏng's father, had a cousin living there.[58]

As was true for T'aesik, relocation from Seoul to Puyŏ amounted to a break from the past for Munyŏng. For sure, leaving the capital meant little vis-à-vis his career in the government, as the highest post that he is known for is Five Guards director of the trusty (*Sagwa*), merely a temporary stipend post of senior sixth military rank. Nonetheless, not only did his two brothers remain in Seoul, Munyŏng was also widowed while living in the capital. In fact, after settling in Puyŏ, he married a much younger woman, Yi Haesuk (1888–after 1932), a daughter of local resident Yi Suyong (n.d.), who reportedly was a twelfth-generation descendant of King Sŏnjo (r. 1567–1608).[59] Considering Munyŏng's status as a *chungin* and a widower, presumably it was a royal descent with an illegitimacy somewhere in the intervening generations, though the Yi family seem to have wielded considerable local influence, as discussed later in this chapter. Once settled in Puyŏ, the extent to which Munyŏng and his descendants were cut off from their kinsmen in Seoul was such that they do not even know where they belong in the Onyang Pang genealogy. As is true for many South Koreans today without a genealogy, Munyŏng's descendants recently acquired one presumably after negotiating with a local Onyang Pang lineage on continuing the line of an heirless lineage member and making a financial contribution.[60]

About Yang Cheha, the friend of Pang Munyŏng and Pak T'aesik, we know precious little. Other than that he was also known as Yang Chuha and that he once had been either the fifth minister-without-portfolio (*Ch'ŏmji Chungch'ubusa*) or the fourth secretary (*Ch'ŏmjŏng*), a junior fourth-rank civil official, I have yet to obtain any information on his career while living in Seoul.[61] So far, I have come across a Namwŏn Yang namesake (recorded as Yang Chuha) of the same era appearing as a son-in-law in a Kimhae Kim genealogy. Today the Kimhae Kim claiming descent from the ancient state of Kaya officially recognize an apparently Seoul-based line that can trace itself back, in terms of unbroken genealogy, only to an eighteenth-century literary licentiate. According to this genealogy, Yang Chuha's father in-law, Kim Munsik (1819–86), also once held the sinecure, the fifth minister-without-portfolio, and the latter's own father-in-law held a junior ninth-rank civil office of royal tomb manager (*Ch'ambong*).[62] If this Kimhae Kim family is indeed the one from which Cheha (or Chuha)'s wife came, then we can conclude that his own family too was most likely based in Seoul and of nonaristocratic descent, producing no politically significant officeholders.

Accepting Christ the Savior

Along with both Yang Cheha and Pang Munyŏng, Pak T'aesik would spend the last decades of his life as a Protestant Christian. Before the arrival of the three men in Ch'owang subdistrict, Yanghwa district in Puyŏ county, local villagers had already founded Wanggol (also known as Ch'owang) Church, which initially was affiliated with a nearby Baptist congregation. In 1899, the

American Baptist missionaries began to withdraw from the region on the death of their main sponsor, and in 1901 the departure of their on-site mission leader completed the end of the Baptist mission in the area. Wanggol Church and others in the area sought support and guidance from increasingly active Southern Presbyterian missionaries in the region, led by William F. Bull (Ko. Pu Wiryŏm, 1876–1941), who arrived in 1899 in the treaty port of Kunsan about 20 kilometers southwest of the village and in 1903 began visiting various isolated congregations such as Wanggol Church. During one such visit in July 1905, Bull baptized fifty-one members of the Wanggol congregation.[63] Apparently Pak T'aesik, Pang Munyŏng, and Yang Cheha were among the newly baptized.

Shortly thereafter, the three men moved to neighboring Odŏk subdistrict, where they and some local leaders established a new congregation, Odŏk (Such'im) Presbyterian Church. According to the commemorative stele that the church recently erected in celebration of the establishment of the congregation on April 15, 1906, Pang and Yang, along with Pang's brother-in-law Yi Haegon and two other leaders, held a service to celebrate the founding of their new church which, at the time, was a modest thatched roof house.[64] Somehow Pak T'aesik is missing from the list on the stele, although his descendants and those of Pang Munyŏng state that Pak was indeed one of the founders.[65] At this point, we do not know whether the omission is simply an error or is in deference to the unrecorded founder's desire to stay out of the limelight, but certainly until the 1980s one of his grandsons served as a presbyter at the church.[66]

In the late nineteenth and early twentieth centuries, status aspiration and a desire for security drove many in the South Ch'ungch'ŏng region, such as Pak T'aesik and his friends, to the new faith. What allowed greater room for mobility for such individuals was the region's relative freedom from strong Confucian traditions and powerful aristocratic lineages. In South Ch'ungch'ŏng, the power of local aristocrats had declined amid early modern social change, though the Seoul aristocracy continued to wield some influence through caretakers. In such a social milieu, the region's earliest converts to Protestantism tended to be open-minded aristocrats, former officeholders regardless of social status, and small-scale cultivators. Overall, they seem to have understood the role of Confucianism to be regulating individual morality rather than protecting civilization, as still upheld by the mainstream aristocracy. In fact, many former officeholders and some aristocrats accepted the

Enlightenment Thought, and they saw Protestantism as an integral component.[67] Such an attitude gradually spread among nonelites as well, but even though Protestantism increasingly reshaped the sociocultural norms of local communities, little detailed orientation to the teachings of the new religion or any intensive education seems to have accompanied conversion. Instruction at local bible schools that educated the converts tended to focus on explaining biblical passages and interpreting the biblical vocabulary from the church leadership's viewpoint.[68]

T'aesik's own conversion fits this profile fairly well. It seems that his background as a *chungin* with ties to the central government and the traumatic events in Seoul spurred him to find solace in the new faith. His career as a *chungin* military officer most likely included personal relationships that exposed him to Western ideas and made him more open to them than would have been possible for other Koreans. Well before fleeing Seoul, he probably had begun to empathize, if not associate, with pro-emperor reform advocates. Also, T'aesik's residence just inside the Great West Gate of the city wall was in a neighborhood that included Western legation compounds and the Saemunan Presbyterian Church. There can be no question that before leaving Seoul he had heard about or witnessed, if not actually been drawn into, many traumatic events, notably the Imo Military Revolt (1882), the Kapsin Coup (1884), the storming of the palace by the Japanese (1894) on the eve of the First Sino-Japanese War (1894–95), the Japanese murder of the queen (1895), and the Japanese takeover of various installations and strategic locations in Seoul at the outbreak of the Russo-Japanese War (1904). Even though he was a former military officer, perhaps it is telling that he never mentioned any kings, queens, palaces, military examinations, or armed combat to his grandchildren.

T'aesik's conversion to Christianity also seems to reflect the appeal of a religion preaching equality of all children of God to those Koreans coping with the rigid Chosŏn status hierarchy. The marriage partners of T'aesik's children show well the extent to which the Paks were still bound by their status. The first daughter became a concubine of a wealthy literary licentiate from a military Seoul *chungin* family (ca. 1900), as discussed further in Chapter 5 on the *chungin* Tanyang U. Her younger brother, T'aesik's first son, married a daughter of a technical specialist Seoul *chungin* (ca. 1904). T'aesik's second son became the first among the children to find a spouse in the greater Puyŏ area, marrying a local woman whose ancestry I have not yet been able to trace (ca. 1906). The third son married a daughter of a wealthy merchant in Kunsan, whose ancestors had been either local functionaries or commoners in status (1911). As for T'aesik's two youngest children, the fourth son, Ch'angsŏng, died when only sixteen *se* in age (1915), whereas the second daughter, Sunhŭi, became the second wife to a local Puyŏ widower (1919) descended from an illegitimate son of a sixteenth-century local aristocrat.[69] These marriage patterns as a whole suggest that even the rising fortunes of the family before the war could not overcome the old status distinctions.

Conclusion

Entering the Korean Empire period, the Paks were ready to assume a variety of new political, economic, and cultural roles, and this chapter focuses on the story of Pak T'aesik from the junior line. As a retired military officer, a former Five Guards general, and probably a successful merchant, in 1902 T'aesik served as a member of the personnel that transported royal portraits to P'yŏngyang, which the government was developing as the Western Capital (Sŏgyŏng). The Russo-Japanese War and Japanese ascendancy not only brought this project of symbolic and strategic significance for Imperial Korea to a halt but also ruined T'aesik's fortunes. Together with the households of Pang Munyŏng, a *chungin* man who was both a cousin and a friend, and another friend of subaristocratic status, Yang Cheha, in 1904 T'aesik and his family fled Seoul for Puyŏ where the Paks had some land.[70] Attracted to a new faith representing the Enlightenment Thought, preaching social equality, and promising salvation both personal and national, in 1905 T'aesik and forty-nine others received baptism by a Southern Presbyterian missionary.[71] Then in 1906, T'aesik and a few other local leaders began their own fellowship, Odŏk Presbyterian Church.[72]

In a world of new visions and activism, the old status anxiety nonetheless persisted. Spanning a generation from about 1890 to 1920, marriages of T'aesik's sons and daughters show that the Paks' *chungin* status remained relevant if not binding. During this period the Paks also claimed a place in a larger Miryang Pak genealogy—getting their founding ancestor, Tŏkhwa, recorded as a previously unknown sibling of three brothers who had been recorded in the genealogy for centuries. What the Paks accomplished was typical of invented traditions widespread among specialist *chungin* families at the time. Adapting to a new situation where the old status hierarchy was weakening and new opportunities were opening up, many changed their distinctly *chungin*-sounding ancestral seat designations and placed their previously untraceable founding ancestors as the kinsmen of aristocratic descent line members. Evidently a status trapping such as a genealogy still concerned many Seoul *chungin*, including the *chungin* Tanyang U family, which Pak T'aesik's elder daughter joined as a concubine. As discussed in the next chapter, during the same period the U family played new and even more active political, economic, and cultural roles.

5 Fortunes that Rose and Fell with Imperial Korea

The Tanyang U In-Laws

EVEN TODAY, MANY SOUTH KOREANS AND THOSE OF THE DIASPORA can be rather cautious when approaching the parents-in-law of their child. Propriety governs interactions with the *sadon*, as they are known in Korean, though with much at stake the two families strive to maintain a respectful distance. In fact, after the wedding ceremony late Chosŏn culture, which many, if not most, Koreans today assume to be the "tradition," stipulated no formal occasion or rite of passage requiring the presence of both sets of in-laws.[1]

Arguably in both early modern and modern Korea, an ideal marriage is a union of social equals, or at least two families that can somehow complement each other. Among various factors that determine a family's social status, economic resources are important. Consider, for example, that as of 2006, an amazing 27 percent of South Korean parents with children desired to financially support the latter until they get married.[2] With the lingering influence of early modern practice, according to which a new bride is to bring along a dowry befitting the status or accomplishments of the groom, making mutually agreeable financial arrangements between two families—often negotiated between the two mothers—can be stressful. Given this room for tension, even today in South Korea it is not unheard of for an aspiring couple to break up amid prenuptial, interfamilial politics.[3]

The Origins and Rise of the *Chungin* Tanyang U Family

It was a *sadon* relationship that tied Pak T'aesik to U Hangjŏng (1854–
1926), whose family mirrored the Paks in some ways and outshone them in
others (Figure 5.1). Hangjŏng was born into a *chungin* Tanyang U lineage that
had been producing military officers for generations. In the summer of 1873 if
not earlier, he married Madam Kimhae Kim (1855–1922), the daughter of Kim
Chungjin (also known as Kim Chungbyŏk, n.d.) who, judging from his given
name ending with the *chin* (Ch. *zhen*, to calm, to suppress) character and his
son-in-law's family background, most likely was from a specialist *chungin*
Kimhae Kim lineage with which the senior line of the Paks had twice formed
marriage ties in the nineteenth century. Hangjŏng also had a concubine, Cho
Un (1859–1924), the daughter of Cho Toro (n.d.) about whom we know nothing other than her ancestral seat, Paech'ŏn. As was common among wealthy
men with concubines at the time, Hangjŏng maintained a separate household
for Un. After the death of Madam Kimhae Kim, as an elderly man of seventy
se, in 1924 Hangjŏng formally married his concubine.[4] Besides such personal
details, we find that Hangjŏng and many other members of the family had
careers that are far better documented and more impressive than those of the
Paks. They are important for what they illustrate about the story of modernizing Korea, as discussed below.

The claimed kinship connection between the *chungin* U family and the aristocratic Tanyang U of the late medieval period as recorded in the genealogy
is suspect. The genealogies published since the late nineteenth century record
the U lineage as the descendants of a famous aristocratic military official, U
Maengsŏn (1475–1551), but the seventeenth-century aristocratic genealogy, the
Origins of Descent Groups, states that he had no heir.[5] In contrast, a Tanyang U
genealogy published in 1800 records sons under Maengsŏn; regarding the son
from which the *chungin* claimed descent, the genealogy explains—while indicating that his descendants are unknown—that although the earlier edition of
the genealogy did not record him, he appears in a collection of household registration documents (*changjŏk*).[6] Of course, without seeing the household registration documents, the statement is not verifiable. Another inconsistency is that
the members of the generation including Hangjŏng, whose earlier name was
Hangsŏn, all initially used a "-sŏn" naming pattern containing the ideograph
sŏn (Ch. *shan*, meaning good, virtuous, right, competent), used in their alleged
ancestor Maengsŏn's name. In general, aristocratic lineages in the early modern

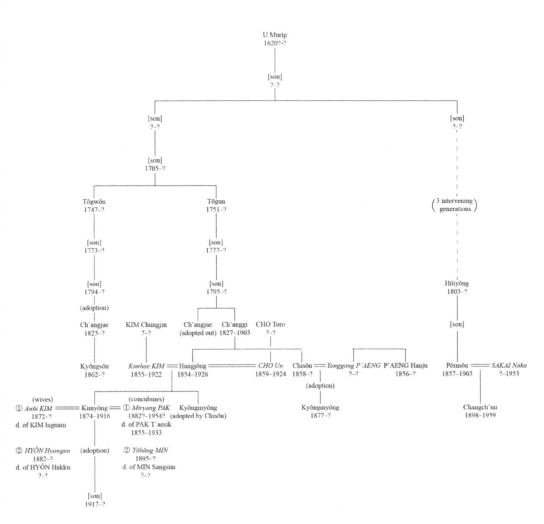

FIGURE 5.1 The *Chungin* U family.

era avoided choosing as a generational character an ideograph that had already been used in a direct ancestor's name. Given that between 1891 and 1900 the members of Hangjŏng's generation and the next all changed their naming patterns from, respectively, "-sŏn" to "-jŏng" and from "T'ae-" to "-myŏng" so that they were all using appropriate pan-Tanyang U generation characters, it seems to me that the *chungin* U line found their place in the larger Tanyang U genealogy sometime during that era.[7]

In addition, the history of the three intervening generations between Maengsŏn and the first U ancestor residing in Seoul is obscure. Maengsŏn either resided in or had ties to Hansan county in Ch'ungch'ŏng province, whereas his alleged descendants for three generations were buried in neighboring Imch'ŏn county. Other immediate descendants of Maengsŏn as recorded in the genealogy were buried in locales scattered throughout the province, including Imch'ŏn, as well as Chŏlla province's Man'gyŏng county near Hansan. It was not until the late seventeenth or even eighteenth century that U Murip (ca. 1620–n.d.), recorded as the fourth-generation descendant of Maengsŏn and the eighth-generation ancestor of Hangjŏng, became the first member of the line to be buried in Yangju county bordering northeastern Seoul—the same locale where many military *chungin* such as the Paks who resided in the eastern part of the capital were buried. Along with Murip, both his father and son were the only son recorded in the genealogy for their particular generations.[8] As explained in the discussion of the first four generations of the *chungin* Paks, in early modern Korea a single-line succession for multiple generations in a genealogy tends to indicate a nonelite family not yet having entered the organized extended lineage phase of its development as a cohesive, sizeable patrilineal kinship group.

Fortunes of the *chungin* U line began to improve noticeably in the early eighteenth century, the same era as when the Paks began their steady ascent to *chungin* status. If ninth-generation descendant U Pŏmsŏn's claim that he and his patrilineal ancestors had been military officers (*kun'gyo*) for ten consecutive generations is accurate, then Murip was the first in the family to serve as such.[9] This seems more than likely, considering that Murip evidently was the first person in the descent line to reside in Seoul and was buried in Yangju. The Tanyang U genealogy shows that after three generations of posthumous officeholders (Murip's father, Murip himself, and his son), family members began to hold honorary court ranks and offices beginning with Murip's two grandsons in the early eighteenth century. In the late eighteenth century, two great-great-grandsons of Murip, U Tŏgwŏn (1747–n.d.) and U Tŏgun (1751–n.d.), attained actual military offices, and the trend continued through the nineteenth century, when Tŏgun's great-grandson and Tŏgwŏn's great-grandson by adoption, U Ch'angjae (1825–n.d.), passed the military examination (1846) and rose all the way to become the Chuksan defense command magistrate (*Pusa*; 1887). Interestingly, the majority of the middle and late nineteenth-century occupants of this post were *chungin*, and each tenure was brief—less than a month in the case of Ch'angjae. The reasons for this are unclear, though it appears that in the early modern era, certain locales in Kyŏnggi and Ch'ungch'ŏng provinces had become common destinations for *chungin* recipients of magistrate posts. Ch'angjae's biological brother and Hangjŏng's father, U Ch'anggi (1827–1903), also passed the military examination (1846) and held various military posts before being appointed as a privy councilor (*Chungch'uwŏn Ŭigwan*, 1897).[10]

A Pioneer of His Time: U Hangjŏng

Hangjŏng's government career typifies those of his kinsmen in that in the late nineteenth century, military rank or office holding became less common among the U men. The posts that Hangjŏng held were largely honorary, including the deputy director of the brave (*Pusayong*, junior ninth military rank, 1887–n.d.), the director of the brave (*Sayong*, senior ninth military rank, by 1894), the sixth court rank (n.d.–1898), the third grade privy councilor (1898), the fifth court rank (1898), the senior third court rank (since 1898), the first grade privy councilor (1898), the auxiliary court chamberlain (*Pun Sijong*; 1899), and the supervising official (*Kamdonggwan*) of the Western Capital project (1902). What is particularly noteworthy is that most of his office tenures were less than a year long, with the chamberlain appointment lasting just ten days (November 15–25, 1899).[11]

The court's rewarding of Hangjŏng in the Western Capital and other royal house–related projects exemplifies how the state honored the *chungin* on the margins of the political establishment. For example, in December 1898, on the repair of Kyŏnghyo Hall, a structure the government built as the shrine housing Queen Myŏngsŏng's spirit tablet, he received a leaping promotion from the fifth to the senior third court rank.[12] In November 1899, when the court elevated the status of the Kyŏngmo Hall shrine of the spirit tablets of Crown Prince Sado and Crown Princess Hyegyŏng (the great-great-grandparents of the Kwangmu emperor), Hangjŏng again received a reward after serving as the auxiliary court chamberlain.[13]

While retaining ties to the central government, Hangjŏng actively participated in various civic movements emerging in the 1890s. He not only was a member of the Independence Club but also from time to time made donations, including four *wŏn* in 1898. These facts raise questions about the nature of the club leadership.[14] It comprised two distinct groups: one, primarily men of aristocratic backgrounds who advocated civic rights and pro-Japanese, pro-American, and pro-Western European policies; and the other, men of educated *chungin* and other nonaristocratic backgrounds who empathized with a modernization program centered around the emperor and who showed flexibility vis-à-vis foreign policy, even if they were not openly pro-Russian.[15] After the emperor ordered the club to disband amid rumors that it was advocating republicanism, Hangjŏng remained involved in various successor groups and other civic organizations, although the Japanese takeover of Korea as a protectorate made such activities seditious. In March 1907, for example, together with all five of his sons and both sons-in-law, he contributed five *wŏn* to the Repay the National Debt Movement (Kukch'ae Posang Undong).[16] As of June 1908, he was a member of the Korean Association (Taehan Hyŏphoe, 1907–10), the successor to the Korean Association for Self-Strengthening (Taehan Chaganghoe, 1906–07), which had in turn succeeded the Society for the Study of Constitutional Government (Hŏnjŏng Yŏn'guhoe, 1905).[17] Initially led by Namgung Ŏk (1863–1939), Yun Hyojŏng (1858–1939), and other nationalist activists, the Korean Association held a series of lectures intended to raise the popular awareness of the importance of education and industry before becoming more accommodating toward the Japanese and finally being disbanded.[18] And as of August 1908, Hangjŏng was a member of the assisting duty staff (*ch'anmuwŏn*) of the Kyŏnggi-Ch'ungch'ŏng Educational Association (Kiho Hŭnghakhoe).[19] His activism acquired him enemies. In June 1899, one of his sons found in the water drain just outside the family mansion a canister wrapped in oiled paper. He turned the object into the police, who confirmed that it was a bomb.[20]

What evidently financed his activism as a major figure in Korea's budding civil sphere was his remarkable wealth. A household registration record, dated 1903, shows the size of the mansion of Hangjŏng's father, Ch'anggi, as 62 *k'an*—comparable to those of the most affluent, high-ranking aristocratic officials at the time whose homes measured in scores of *k'an*.[21] In fact during a court trial in 1908, the judge described Hangjŏng—along with another prominent businessman of specialist *chungin* background and the co-founder of Seoul Electric Company (Hansŏng Chŏn'gi Hoesa), Yi Kŭnbae (1849–n.d.)—as the city's richest men.[22] Reflecting his growing wealth and social influence, Hangjŏng moved to a better, more prestigious neighborhood. By 1903 and until 1907, he was living in Mukchŏng-dong, which bordered both the Middle Village, the specialist *chungin* neighborhood, and the traditional military officer neighborhood of eastern Seoul.[23] Sometime after 1908, he was residing in Ipchŏng-dong near Ch'ŏnggye stream as well as in Kye-dong, which was located in the "North Village" (Puk-ch'on) just east of the Kyŏngbok Palace—a neighborhood traditionally known for the mansions of prominent aristocratic statesmen.[24] Recognizing his stature as one of the wealthiest men in Korea, in May 1906 the Seoul Chamber of Commerce (Kyŏngsŏng Sangŏp Hoeŭiso) honored him for donating 50 *wŏn* to help finance construction of its building.[25] And on at least ten newspaper-reported occasions from March 1908 to November 1909, Hangjŏng made gifts to various private schools.[26]

More than just as a wealthy man, Hangjŏng claims a place in the economic history of modern Korea for his roles in capitalistic ventures, especially Korean Ramie Spinning, Ltd. (Tae Chosŏn Chŏma Chesa Chusik Hoesa). In 1897 in Seoul, he and twenty-nine others launched the corporation, making it, along with Bank of Seoul (Hansŏng Ŭnhaeng), founded in the same year, one of Korea's earliest joint-stock companies. The management was made up of seven Koreans and three foreigners, notably Philip Jaisohn, who by then had become a naturalized American citizen (Table 5.1).[27] What is striking is that none of the seven Koreans in the management was a bona fide aristocrat. Instead, all seven were either of Seoul *chungin* or illegitimate son background.

What the company leaders envisioned was a business venture of a nature unprecedented in Korea at the time. In contrast to the government's economic policies geared toward mitigating Korea's economic servitude to foreign powers by domestically producing daily consumer goods, the leaders wanted Korean Ramie Spinning to be an exporter. In this vein, Hangjŏng and his colleagues worked to establish a joint-stock company to plait Korean hemp and ramie fabric thread together and export the resulting product to overseas weaving factories.[28] Hansan county near Puyŏ in particular was famous for lucrative ramie production, and along with Imch'ŏn the county was one of the Ch'ungch'ŏng locales to which the U family had historical ties, if not any business interests. In the early nineteenth century, the aforementioned Chŏng Yagyong, the famed Practical Learning scholar and an advocate of more commercialized farming, had already noted that ramie farming was ten times more profitable than cultivating the highest-grade rice paddy of the same size.[29]

Korean Ramie Spinning Ltd. got off to a promising start, though it would fold before entering the production stage. Hangjŏng and his co-founders were able to launch the company with sizable capital. With a total investment comprising 40,000 *wŏn* of foreign capital and 35,000 *wŏn* of Korean capital, the

TABLE 5.1 Management personnel of Korean Ramie Spinning, Ltd. (1897)

Name	Years	Position	Ancestral Seat	Social Background	Examination Degree
An Kyŏngsu	1853–1900	Chairman (*hoejang*), executive officer (*chumugwan*)	Chuksan	Illegitimate son?	Unknown
Yi Ch'aeyŏn	1861–1900	Vice chairman (*puhoejang*)	Kwangju	Descendant of an illegitimate son	Literary Licentiate (1894), civil (1894)
Yi Kŭnbae	1849–n.d.	Chief executive officer (*changmugwan*), executive officer	Suwŏn	Specialist *chungin*	Interpreter (1867)
Yun Kyusŏp	1847–n.d.	Chief executive officer, executive officer	P'ap'yŏng	Specialist *chungin*	Interpreter (1880)
Pang Handŏk	1846–1913	Secretary (*sŏgigwan*)	Onyang	Specialist *chungin*	Interpreter (1864)
Yun Hyojŏng	1858–1939	Secretary	P'ap'yŏng	Specialist *chungin*	Literary Licentiate (1894)
U Hangjŏng	1854–1926	Secretary	Tanyang	Specialist *chungin*	None
[unknown given name(s)] Johnson	n.d.	Executive officer	N/A	British	N/A
Walter D. Townsend	1856–1918	Executive officer	N/A	American	N/A
David W. Deshler	1872–1923	Executive officer	N/A	American	N/A
Philip Jaisohn (Sŏ Chaep'il)	1864–1951	Executive officer	Taegu	Aristocrat, American (naturalized)	Civil (1882)

Sources: *Tongnip sinmun*, June 12, 1897; Chu Chino, "19 segi huban Kaehwa kaehyŏngnon ŭi kujo wa chŏn'gae," pp. 237, 239, 242, 243; Yi Sŭngnyŏl, *Cheguk kwa sangin*, pp. 79–80; and *Han'guk minjok munhwa taebaekkwa sajŏn*.

subsequent public sale of company stock reportedly brought in some 17,000 *wŏn* in just one day. The leaders calculated that producing one ton of plaited ramie fabric threads would cost 500 *wŏn* but that they would be able to export it at a price of 1,400 *wŏn*. The new Korean-English bilingual newspaper *Tongnip sinmun* (*The Independent*), the official newspaper of the Independence Club and controlled more or less by the company leaders including Philip Jaisohn, published an editorial urging Koreans to invest in the company, arguing that ramie fabric manufacturing produced hundredfold profit, three hundred times greater than that from buying a top-quality rice paddy. The company proceeded to hire more than seventy employees, but the continuing political turmoil and social upheaval at the time did not allow it to actually build a factory.[30]

Hangjŏng was an active player in Korea's emerging banking industry too, though it is a sphere that also clearly shows his prominence beginning to fade after the Japanese annexation of Korea. From June 1906 to July 1918, he was a founding committee member and a major shareholder of Seoul Agro-Industrial Bank (Hansŏng Nonggong Ŭnhaeng) and its successor, Seoul-Ch'ungch'ŏng Agro-Industrial Bank (Hanho Nonggong Ŭnhaeng). On June 1, 1906, Hangjŏng and a few investors established the bank as a joint-stock company with capital of 200,000 *wŏn*; he was a founding committee member.[31] Then in June 1907 Seoul Agro-Industrial Bank merged with similar banks in Kongju in South Ch'ungch'ŏng province and Ch'ungju in North Ch'ungch'ŏng province to form Seoul-Ch'ungch'ŏng Agro-Industrial Bank, Ltd.[32] In May 1909, Hangjŏng even became a new major shareholder of the Ch'ŏnil Bank of Korea(Taehan Ch'ŏnil Ŭnhaeng), which, founded in January 1899 evidently as Korea's third joint-stock company, suffered relatively less than other Korean banks did from Korea's economic recession between 1906 and 1911, thanks to a large number of Japanese shareholders who were hardly affected by the recession.[33] In 1918, however, the Korea Industrial Bank (Chōsen Shokushan Ginkō), which along with the Bank of Korea (Chōsen Ginkō), dominated the world of finance in Korea, acquired Seoul-Ch'ungch'ŏng Agro-Industrial Bank in accordance with the Government-General of Korea's new Ordinance on the Korea Industrial Bank (June 1918).[34] By then, Hangjŏng's days of business success were numbered. I have yet to find a document suggesting he was a leading Korean businessman beyond the first decade of Japanese colonial rule. Scholars continue the complex debate on the origins of capitalism in Korea, but the Koreans who surmounted Japanese impingement, such as the famous families of Pak Sŭngjik (1864–1950) and Kim Sŏngsu (1891–1955), apparently did so by, among other strategies, diversifying early (hence weathering the 1905 currency reform) and working closely with the Japanese.[35] In the case of Hangjŏng, perhaps his involvement in various patriotic organizations during the final years of Imperial Korea reduced his appeal to the Japanese, who by then were calling the shots.

More Pioneers: U Hangjŏng's Cousins

Among Hangjŏng's several cousins who also played interesting roles during the Korean Empire period, U Kyŏngsŏn (1862–n.d.) stands out for a career that helped him get into the shipping business. Biologically Hangjŏng's first cousin and at once, due to adoption, a fourth cousin, Kyŏngsŏn began his career by holding various specialist positions concerning interactions with foreign countries. In the first lunar month of 1886, he was appointed as the clerk (*Sŏgigwan*) at the Office of the Inch'ŏn Maritime Customs Superintendent of Trade (*Haegwan Kamnisŏ*), concurrently with a temporary stipend post, the deputy director of the brave (*Pusayong*), a common post among *chungin*. Until the sixth lunar month of 1888, Kyŏngsŏn's assignment alternated between the Office of the Inch'ŏn Maritime Customs Superintendent of Trade and the Office for Extraordinary State Affairs in Seoul. Since 1883, Inch'ŏn had been Korea's third treaty port (after Pusan and Wŏnsan), and as a government officer entrusted with the more day-to-day affairs involving foreigners, Kyŏngsŏn undoubtedly sharpened his sense of the wider world in general and Western commercial practices in particular. His horizon continued to broaden as, later in 1888, he became a Transport Bureau (*Chŏnun-guk*) deputy (*wiwŏn*), as well as receiving promotion to the sixth court rank—a milestone achieved by only a small segment of the members of Chosŏn officialdom. After that, from the eleventh lunar month of 1890 to at least the fifth lunar month of 1892 he held various Transport Bureau posts as well as serving as the Inch'ŏn police magistrate (*Kyŏngch'algwan*).[36]

Kyŏngsŏn's long-term duty in Inch'ŏn helped him play a leading role in managing Korea's first modern shipping company, Iunsa. After helping launch the company in the twelfth lunar month of 1892, Kyŏngsŏn served as its secretary and collaborated with President Min Yŏnghwi (formerly Min Yŏngjun, 1852–1935), a prominent aristocratic statesman, and Vice-President Chŏng Pyŏngha (1849–96), an influential *chungin* official.[37] A 200,000-*yang* loan that the Transport Bureau had acquired from China further financed the company. Since other executives continued to hold their government posts elsewhere, Kyŏngsŏn, who concurrently served as the Inch'ŏn police magistrate, remained the de facto chief executive officer. Essentially a government-private joint corporation modeled after China Merchants Steamship Company (Zhaoshangju), Iunsa's primary business was to transport tax grain, though it also handled private goods and carried traveling passengers.[38] The company owned a 1,000-ton ship purchased from Germany; 709-ton, 536-ton, and 236-ton vessels acquired from the government; and five 30- to 100-ton ships imported from Japan and China.[39]

Despite the company's monopolization of the shipping lanes connecting various coastal ports and Han River landings, the Japanese ascendancy stymied Kyŏngsŏn. During the First Sino-Japanese War, the Japanese army used Iunsa ships to transport military supplies, and after the war Japan Mail Shipping Line (Nippon Yūsen Kabushiki Kaisha) continued to operate the ships. With expanding Russian influence checking the Japanese presence in Korea, in 1896 Iunsa got the ships back, but by then the government tax collection in cash (instead of grain), effected by the Kabo Reform (1894–96), had reduced the amount of grain transport so much that the company was not able to resume normal operation. Iunsa had to turn over the ships to another company to operate, and various private businesses took over the shipping business that Iunsa once monopolized.[40] Not giving up, Kyŏngsŏn persevered in his efforts in shipping business, getting a second chance through a new company, Kwangt'ongsa. Founded in 1897, the company maintained regular shipping lanes connecting Inch'ŏn, Kunsan, and Mokp'o. The company even served Cheju Island, though not regularly.[41]

As was true for many other members of the *chungin* Tanyang U family, Kyŏngsŏn was a man of wealth who pursued philanthropy until largely stopped by the Japanese takeover of Korea. Kyŏngsŏn's choice of beneficiaries suggests that ideals of national independence, civic spirit, and modern education inspired him.[42] As he was less interested in politics than Hangjŏng, Kyŏngsŏn made gifts more strictly among education circles.[43]

U Pŏmsŏn, a cousin of Kyŏngsŏn and Hangjŏng, is the best known among the *chungin* Tanyang U, though his precise genealogical position within the family remains unclear. As is true for most specialist *chungin* lines, in modern genealogies the coverage of the *chungin* Tanyang U stops in the late nineteenth century, and Pŏmsŏn is absent from the pages showing those who were born before the late nineteenth century and their ancestors. In fact, the first ostensibly comprehensive Tanyang U genealogy, published in 1966, records him and his famous son in a special section at the end of the six-volume set— without any information on his ancestors. For several reasons, however, it is certain that he was either a fourth or a sixth cousin of Hangjŏng (earlier name Hangsŏn) and Kyŏngsŏn. First, his given name conforms to the uniquely *chungin* Tanyang U naming pattern of "-sŏn" (before they changed to a "-jŏng" pattern). Second, the earlier given name of his famous son (Myŏngjŏn, later Changch'un) matches the pattern ("Myŏng-") used by some members of the next genealogical generation. Third, it is well known that he had a career as a *chungin* military officer, as was true for many other *chungin* Tanyang U with the "-sŏn" naming pattern. Fourth, his self-described family background matches what is known about the other *chungin* Tanyang U. And fifth, he is known to have resided in Seoul. Apparently Pŏmsŏn belonged to a collateral line, the coverage of which continues beyond U Hŭiyŏng (1803–n.d.)—most likely Pŏmsŏn's grandfather—with those who clearly are not true descendants in all the modern editions of Tanyang U genealogy published since the mid-nineteenth century.[44]

Winning promotions while serving in the modernizing Korean army, Pŏmsŏn stayed on a fast-track military career. Just nineteen *se* in age in the fourth lunar month of 1875, he was already a Military Guard Division (*Muwiyŏng*) steward (*Chipsa*) when he passed the military examination.[45] According to a close acquaintance, Yun Hyojŏng, who was a co-founder of the Korean Ramie Spinning Ltd. along with U Hangjŏng, and who, incidentally, also plotted Pŏmsŏn's death, King Kojong and Queen Myŏngsŏng were impressed by the young military examination graduate and often gave him gifts when he was on duty.[46] In 1876, the agency promoted him to special military officer (*Pyŏlmusa*), and by 1878 he was already an instructor (*Kyoryŏn'gwan*).[47] Between 1878 and 1883, Pŏmsŏn even held midlevel government offices—a distinction that Pak T'aesik, who was also a special military officer serving in the agency, never achieved. Instead of taking a traditional Chosŏn dynasty office, however, Pŏmsŏn was appointed as a field officer ranked major (*Ch'amnyŏnggwan*; 1881) in the newly created Special Skills Force (*Pyŏlgigun*), arguably Korea's first modern Western-style military unit. This appointment secured him a place in the slowly modernizing Korean army. In the following fourteen years until the end of his military career, he held positions such as the Royal Army's Left Division company commander (*Ch'in'gun Chwayŏng Ch'ogwan*; 1883); the Royal Army's

Robust Guard Division right battalion (*Ch'in'gun Changwiyŏng Udae*) colonel (*Chŏngnyŏnggwan*; 1894); member (*Wiwŏn*) of the Deliberative Council (*Kun'guk Kimuch'ŏ*; 1894); military attaché (*Sujong mugwan*) of the minister plenipotentiary to Japan (1894); and Drilled Troops (*Hullyŏndae*) second battalion commander (*Taedaejang*; 1895).[48]

Despite his success as a military officer, Pŏmsŏn seems to have wanted to achieve more important, decision-making-level positions in an officialdom that was dominated by the aristocracy. Of a tall stature that impressed many, he was willful—never afraid to clash even with social superiors. Especially during his tenure as a Special Skills Force officer, he expressed frustration over the less than fully respectful forms of address that his subordinates from aristocratic families used with him.[49] For a crime of which details are murky, in 1886 the government banished him to a county near P'yŏngyang; the punishment lasted six years, until his release. Interestingly, before recommending the sentence to the king, the Ministry of Punishments (*Hyŏngjo*) described Pŏmsŏn as an erratic character no longer normal in behavior.[50] Not only was the six-year banishment a conspicuous blemish on his career, it added at least that many years to the time required of him before he could attempt to receive a politically meaningful position in regular officialdom—a career threshold that typically came to aspirants in their forties.

Awareness of the delay in his prospects may have been a factor in the ambitious Pŏmsŏn's participation in the events of the early morning hours of October 8, 1895.[51] As the second battalion commander of the Drilled Troops, he led 250 to 300 troops alongside some 60 Japanese leading operatives and three Japanese battalion troops in an attack on Kyŏngbok Palace, where they overcame the resistance of 300 to 400 less well-armed Bodyguard (*Siwidae*) troops loyal to the king, and the Japanese then killed Queen Myŏngsŏng in cold blood. Pŏmsŏn evidently was not aware of the Japanese plan to kill the queen until his battalion had entered the city through the Great West Gate to join the Japanese troops, but he cooperated. After the Japanese had burned the queen's body, he threw the remains into the Hyangwŏn Pavilion pond, though a subordinate managed to retrieve and secretly hide them. According to Yun Hyojŏng, Pŏmsŏn had always desired to kill the queen. As a young military examination graduate with access to the king and the queen, Pŏmsŏn reportedly once claimed that he could see a large fox seated behind her, and that he became determined to kill the queen, the female fox, with his own hands.[52] The story may apocryphally reflect his growing frustration and anger toward the queen, widely regarded as the archenemy among many Korean reform advocates who were favorably inclined toward Japan, the United States, and western European countries rather than China or Russia—the powers that the queen herself preferred.

Regardless of the psychology of his attitude toward Queen Myŏngsŏng, the incident catalyzed a series of events that affected Korea in general as well as Pŏmsŏn in particular. King Kojong, after months of virtual house arrest under the watchful eyes of the Japanese, functioning as the rubber stamp for the new pro-Japanese cabinet, managed on February 11, 1896, to escape the palace and find sanctuary inside the Russian legation building, where he stayed for a year. With Russia now committed to protecting him and resisting Japanese designs, the pro-Japanese cabinet collapsed and Pŏmsŏn had to flee to Japan, where he took up residence in Tokyo. He traveled the country widely, presenting himself as the "legitimate lineage heir (*chŏk chongson*) of a military officer (*kun'gyo*) family for nine generations." Eventually he married a Japanese woman, Sakai Naka (n.d.–1953), and the couple had two boys, one of whom had a future ahead of him as a famous scientist. In December 1903, Ko Yŏnggŭn (n.d.), an assassin from Korea bent on punishing Pŏmsŏn for the crime, mortally shot him with Yun Hyojŏng's assistance.[53]

An Opportunist? P'aeng Hanju, a Marriage Kin

Among the kinsmen of the *chungin* Tanyang U by marriage, P'aeng Hanju stands out for his interactions with foreigners. Coming from the *chungin* Yonggang P'aeng family, which had been producing calligraphers, military officers, minor officials, and sinecure holders for generations, P'aeng's sister was married to U Hangjŏng's brother.[54] As is the case with many—such as the *chungin* U and the Paks—from specialist *chungin* families that had not produced technical examination passers and were thus not as well known, conventional biographical entries on P'aeng do not mention his birth year, death year, ancestral seat, early activity as a calligrapher in the Office of Diplomatic Correspondence, or membership in the Korean delegation to the 1887 Sino-Korean border clarification talks.[55] Instead, such sketches offer merely a brief description of his later career, beginning with his appointment as the Wŏnsan treaty port clerk (*Sŏgigwan*; 1888). After holding Foreign Office interpreter positions (1894–99), he served as, among other things, the superintendent of trade (*Kamni*), concurrently as magistrate (*Puyun*), of Tŏgwŏn (1898,

1899–1900, 1901), Sŏngjin (1899), Samhwa (1899), and P'yŏngyang (1900–03)—all locales of importance for foreign relations and trade.[56] Yun Ch'iho (pen name Chwaong, 1865–1945), who succeeded P'aeng as the Wŏnsan treaty port clerk, found him an avaricious, corrupt official.[57] During his service as the P'yŏngyang magistrate (*Kunsu*; 1903–04), he reportedly amassed a fund of 1.3 million *yang* through such unlawful means as an attempt to confiscate a local widow's significant wealth.[58] If true, such a bad reputation did not prevent him from having a successful career. A rich man wielding influence, by the 1900s he was maintaining multiple residences in and outside Seoul, including a separate household for a concubine.[59]

In fact neither a principled defender of Imperial Korea nor a faithful advocate of Japanese ascendancy, P'aeng was an opportunist sensitive to the changing political climate. In July 1896, when the Independence Club formed and strived to build the Independence Gate, the Independence Hall (*Tongnipkwan*), and the Independence Park, he served as a promoter (*palgiin*) and an assisting administrator (*kansawŏn*) for the club.[60] Later, while serving as the magistrate of P'yŏngyang when the Russo-Japanese War broke out, however, he welcomed the Japanese troops into the region and kept them well provisioned.[61] Indeed, when the court decided to dismiss him amid complaints about his corrupt administration in P'yŏngyang, the Japanese minister to Korea requested his retention on the ground that he rendered assistance when the Japanese troops moved into the northwest.[62] For his merit, the Japanese Residency-General of Korea awarded him in October 1904 the third-class Medal of the Order of the Rising Sun and in April 1908 the sixth-class Medal of the Order of the Rising Sun.[63] Nonetheless, as was true for most specialist *chungin* who had achieved prominence shortly before the Korean Empire period, P'aeng's government career effectively ended after the Russo-Japanese War, though we do find him attracting attention as an influential person in other ways. For example, in June 1920 he was the guest of honor at the inaugural meeting of the Inch'ŏn branch of the Labor Mutual Assistance (*Nodong Kongje*) group.[64]

The fading of P'aeng Hanju, as well as of the Pak and the U families, with the Japanese ascendancy in Korea also suggests that the members of the next generation had to adapt accordingly. Even more than their parents, the younger generation had to cope with a radically new set of challenges as Koreans in general found themselves with less control of their destiny than ever before. Setting aside for Chapter 6 the stories of the younger generation during the era of Japanese colonial rule, let us consider here two cases of U men of this generation that foreshadowed what was to come.

Unlike many other *chungin* at the time who desired government posts pertaining to foreign relations, U Hangjŏng's son and Pak T'aesik's son-in-law, U Kimyŏng (1874–1916) aimed for a distinction of more hallowed tradition. Known as U T'aewŏn before his name change, even as a youngster his writing talent won the attention of everyone around him. As an intern (*Isŭp*) of thirteen *se* at the Office of Diplomatic Correspondence, in the tenth month of 1886 he received appointment as a calligrapher (*sajagwan*) with a stipend military post (*ch'ea kunjik*).[65] Rather than staying on this course befitting a specialist *chungin*, however, in the second month of 1891 Kimyŏng passed the "third day task" (*samil che*), a composition test normally given on the third day of the third lunar month and geared toward those aspiring to pass the licentiate examination. His performance was so impressive that the court added his name at the end of the roster of those who passed the preliminary stage of the recent licentiate examination. He received special permission to advance to the next stage, the metropolitan examination held in the fifth month.[66] Passing it as well, in the following month he received his degree as a literary licentiate—at only eighteen *se* of age.[67] Interestingly, the licentiate examination passer roster recording him shows the occupation-service of his father Hangjŏng (Hangsŏn in the roster) as "private scholar" (*yuhak*)—traditionally an indicator of aristocratic status though by then devalued as a label claimed by nonaristocrats as well—even though he could have chosen to present himself as a "former deputy director of the brave" (*chŏn Pusayong*). Evidently the father saw more prestige in the status label by then not valued among many aristocrats than in a stipend post (*ch'eajik*) commonly held by *chungin*.

Kimyŏng's post-examination career and activity confirm that though he commanded wealth and influence, the overall power and prestige of the U family suffered from the Japanese ascendancy. At least from 1903 to March 1907, Kimyŏng was living with his father in Seoul's specialist *chungin* neighborhood, the Middle Village.[68] Sometime in or after 1907, he moved to Inch'ŏn, where his mansion in Hwasu subdistrict near the port would remain until at least 1945.[69] Not as impressive as his father's, Kimyŏng's governmental career included appointments as the clerk (*Chusa*) at the South Chŏlla Provincial Governor's Office (1900) and as privy councilor (*Chungch'uwŏn Ŭigwan*, 1901), as well as a promotion from the sixth to the senior third court rank (1905) for supervising the repair of a stele commemorating the Japanese battle victory in Haeju—all brief tenures or largely honorary distinctions.[70] Again, compared to his father, it is not clear to what extent Kimyŏng was involved in civic movements, though in March 1907, along with his father, he contributed one *wŏn* toward the Repay the National Debt Movement.[71] As was the case with his father, such an involvement in a patriotic organization during the final years of Korean Empire would not have put Kimyŏng in a good light as far as the Japanese were concerned.

Cut short by an illness and untimely death at just forty-three *se* in age, Kimyŏng's personal life features two marriages and multiple concubines. By his first wife, Madam Anŭi Kim (1872–n.d.), who was the daughter of Port Commander (*Ch'ŏmjŏlchesa*) Kim Ingnam (n.d.) from a Seoul *chungin* lineage, Kimyŏng had two daughters. Presumably after her death, Kimyŏng married Hyŏn Hyangun (1882–n.d.), a daughter of Hyŏn Hakku (n.d.), who was a member of the prominent *chungin* Ch'ŏllyŏng Hyŏn lineage. Kimyŏng also had concubines, notably young Madam Yŏhŭng Min (1895–n.d.), the daughter of a certain Min Sangsun (n.d.) whose name suggests that he most likely was not an aristocratic member of the royal in-law Yŏhŭng Min lineage.[72] Considering that a household registration document recording the deaths (1916, 1926) of both Kimyŏng and his father Hangjŏng records her, along with the two wives, but not Pak T'aesik's daughter, more than likely the latter was a concubine residing at his mansion in Inch'ŏn (meaning a separate household register I am yet to find recorded her)—and her concubine status, if true, implies that either she or one of her patrilineal ancestors was an illegitimate child.[73] All the same, Kimyŏng brought home many ladies for pleasure.[74] Since none bore his child and the household would eventually adopt a second cousin's son after Kimyŏng's death, it would seem that he was either sterile or impotent. During a period of mourning after a grandparent died, his sense of Confucian propriety was such that he smoked using a long pipe wrapped in white cloth.[75]

The activism of Kimyŏng's younger brother, U Kyŏngmyŏng (1877–n.d.), also did not outlive Imperial Korea. Adopted by his natural father Hangjŏng's younger brother, U Chisŏn (1858–n.d.), who seems to have died before his generation's use of the *chŏng* (Ch. *ding*, kettle, cauldron) character in the 1890s, Kyŏngmyŏng went through name changes as his kinsmen did, reflecting the status anxiety of a non-elite family on the rise. Sometime between 1891 and 1903 he changed his name from U T'aehyŏng to U Kyŏngmyŏng.[76] His known governmental career included serving as the clerk at the Office of the Tŏgwŏn Superintendent of Trade (1898–99) and a promotion from the sixth to the senior third court rank (1906).[77] Although it is not clear whether he ever lived with his adoptive father, if it was not a posthumous adoption, during the Korean Empire period Kyŏngmyŏng was living in the same household with the members of his natal family in Seoul, where they participated in various civic movements, including making a donation to the Repay the National Debt Movement (March 1907).[78] His career took an interesting turn when in late January 1907 he went to Tokyo to study.[79] In May, along with other members of the second graduating class of the T'aegŭk Educational Association (T'aegŭk Hakhoe), he donated 10 *chŏn* to the Repay the National Debt Movement.[80] Later in the year, he contributed two articles to the *T'aegŭk Educational Association Journal (T'aegŭk hakpo)*, titled "Purposes of Education" and "Raising a Child in the Household."[81] About his own children, though, we know little. Married to Madam Haeju O (1880–n.d.) whose family background remains unknown, Kyŏngmyŏng had at least one son, U Kŭmbong (1901–n.d.), whose given name as recorded in the household registration document is clearly a childhood name.[82] Without knowing his adult name, we cannot trace his activity.

Conclusion

The story of Pak T'aesik's in-laws, the *chungin* Tanyang U, suggests it was difficult for even the most influential, powerful *chungin* of Imperial Korea to keep their positions as the Japanese took control of Korea. In spite of a not particularly impressive government career, T'aesik's *sadon*, U Hangjŏng, was one of the wealthiest Koreans at the time and played an active role in, among other things, launching one of Korea's earliest joint-stock companies, Korean Ramie Spinning Ltd., and establishing the Independence Club; yet he faded with the passing of Korea. His cousin, U Kyŏngsŏn, was able to capitalize on his official duties at the treaty port of Inch'ŏn to become the de facto CEO of Korea's first modern shipping company, while supporting various modernization efforts in cultural spheres; but his philanthropy came to a halt with the Japanese ascendancy. The story was quite different for those who became actively pro-Japanese, in particular the distant cousin U Pŏmsŏn, infamous for his participation in the Japanese raid on the royal palace and the murder of Queen Myŏngsŏng.

The story was no different for the next-generation U lineage, even such prominent descendants as U Kimyŏng, to whom Pak T'aesik's elder daughter became a concubine, and a younger brother, U Kyŏngmyŏng. For both, governmental service and involvement in civic movements ended sometime after Korea became a Japanese protectorate. Younger members had no choice but to use their education, if they had received one, to make adjustments and find new professions in a system dominated by the Japanese.

6 Vignettes

Colonial Subjects of Imperial Japan

FOR MORE THAN A GENERATION, FROM 1910 TO 1945, JAPANESE colonial rule forced distinct choices on the people of what was formerly Imperial Korea. Some continued resisting the Japanese, others worked with the Japanese, and most struggled to survive. The decision could be more painful for those who had memories of Imperial Korea, but over time, active resistance became almost unthinkable among most Koreans, young and old alike. For the idealistic minority that was willing to risk all to fight for Korean independence, essentially only two options were viable: leave Korea (also leaving family and property behind) to join an independence movement, or stay in Korea and continue resisting Japanese colonial rule at the obvious risk of going to jail—a course of action limited, after 1919, to a small number of underground communists. To insist that any Korean who "collaborated" with the Japanese must be condemned effectively asserts that national independence should have been the ultimate goal for all Koreans, an unrealistic expectation in light of human nature and history.[1]

A more nuanced view of collaboration distinguishes between those who collaborated to make a living and those who went out of their way to suppress nationalism. According to this paradigm, police officers who brutally tortured the March First Movement protesters during interrogations clearly fit the latter category. More problematic are those who played a role that promoted Japanese interests over Korean ones, such as members of the educated elite who urged Koreans to support the Japanese war effort. This example of an educated elite serving as the propaganda tool of the colonial government raises a question: To what degree can a society's elite be who they are without working for, with, or within the system?

The plight of specialist *chungin* suggests that the paradigm recognizing reprehensible collaboration, understandable collaboration, and resistance overlooks the complexities of Korea's colonial experience.[2] As is true for historical studies on precolonial Korea, previous studies looking at the colonial era have considered largely the most famous, prominent *chungin*. In doing so, they have handed down a guilty verdict on *chungin* as a group for welcoming and collaborating with the colonizers. A claim that *chungin* were more likely than allegedly self-proud aristocrats to collaborate with the Japanese is not difficult to find in the discourse among ordinary Koreans as well as professional Korea historians.[3]

Rejecting the Hegemonic Discourse

Not only were many *chungin* and their descendants simply struggling to get through each day, they also stopped bothering with genealogies. In the post-nineteenth-century genealogies that record *chungin* lines, coverage of the majority of *chungin* members stops at the nineteenth century. Over the years, I have been able to determine how 80 out of some 200 Seoul *chungin* lines appearing in the *Record of Surname Origins* fit—at least ostensibly—into larger descent groups as recorded in modern genealogies, whereas the other 120 await future research. Significantly, 24 of the 80 do not appear in modern genealogies that otherwise claim to cover the entire descent group. As for the remaining 56, the genealogy's coverage stops by the nineteenth century in 31 cases, and even the pre-nineteenth-century coverage is spotty. Thus only in 25 cases do at least some post-nineteenth-century family members appear in a modern edition.

The low rate of representation in modern editions is evident even among the celebrated specialist *chungin* families, and the case of the Hanyang Yu suggests that many *chungin*-descent families do not care about their genealogies. Not only do modern genealogies fail to mention the activity of Yu Honggi, a prominent intellectual and a mentor to the young political leaders advocating Western-style reform for Korea, modern Yu genealogies such as the 1975 and 1994 editions stop the coverage of the *chungin* segment at the 1860s.[4] Of 129 *chungin* members who were born between 1800 and 1864, incredibly 110 have no twentieth-century descendants recorded (85 percent). Unlike older entries generally recording bare-bones information such as birth year, death year, and grave location, the final *chungin* entries provide only birth years—indicating that the descendants have not participated in post-1860s updates of the Yu genealogy.[5] Considering the universal acknowledgment of Yu Honggi's role as the teacher to the leaders of the abortive Kapsin Coup (1884) inspired by Meiji Japan's success, it is remarkable that modern Korean genealogies offer no tribute to his life.[6]

Even in many modern genealogies offering full documentation of *chungin* careers, the coverage of *chungin* segments stops at the nineteenth century, as illustrated by the case of the Ch'ŏllyŏng Hyŏn. The most recent, ostensibly comprehensive edition of the genealogy of the entire descent group records in detail the members' technical examination degrees, specialist positions in the government, and the court ranks and offices normally revealing *chungin* status—all this in addition to customary burial information. Yet, of 117 members who were born between 1800 and 1864, 53 have no twentieth-century descendant recorded (45 percent).[7] Compared to the Hanyang Yu, the Ch'ŏllyŏng Hyŏn produced an even greater number of individuals who played prominent roles in the late nineteenth and early twentieth centuries, but the descendants' enthusiasm for genealogies evidently was still limited.[8]

These patterns are striking, given that genealogy compilation was popular during the colonial era, when the old status consciousness and anxiety persisted without a state controlled by the aristocracy. Between 1920 and 1929 the colonial government granted more publishing permits to genealogies than to any other publications.[9] In the 1930s too, genealogies received a larger number of publishing permits than other print genres.[10] At the least, this phenomenon suggests a significant interest in producing genealogies, and perhaps the colonizer regarded the attitude as binding more Koreans to traditional social networks. Of course, some applicants may not have actually used the issued permits, but the statistics show that the appeal of genealogies remained strong. Even in 1949 in South Korea, a major daily newspaper, the *Tonga ilbo* (*The Dong-A Ilbo*), printed an article, "Still harping on genealogies: let us get rid of feudal customs," deploring widespread genealogy publication in a post-colonial nation that had just inaugurated a democratic government.[11]

Throughout the colonial period, the print media dominated by the overlapping categories of Western-style intellectuals, social reform advocates, Protestants, northwesterners, and specialist *chungin* expressed negative views on genealogies. For example in 1921, in criticizing what it regarded as a wide-spread competitive zeal for genealogies, an editorial in *Creation* (*Kaebyŏk*), an influential magazine dedicated to social reform based on Ch'ŏndogyo ("Religion of the Heavenly Way," the reorganized Tonghak), likened the phenomenon to living off of one's ancestors rather than one's own merit, as evidence, ultimately, of the lack of modern education in a changing world.[12] Reviewing what it regarded as the previous year's noteworthy events, the 1925 New Year's Day edition of *Creation* delightedly reported that in August 1924 in a rural county in the southwest, the local farmers' association (*nononghoe*) members had burnt their genealogies and ancestor worship spirit tablets in a drive to destroy "old superstitions" and "lineage consciousness."[13] Then in a 1926 editorial titled "Let Us First Reform Undesirable Customs (4): The Power of Genealogies and an Aristocratic Mind," the *Tonga ilbo* criticized the popularity of genealogy publication, even in what it viewed as the modern environment of Seoul, as a vestige of feudal practice elevating the aristocracy above everyone else. The editorial rhetorically asked what meaning there could be in boasting of an aristocratic ancestry when the Koreans had lost their nation-hood to the Japanese.[14] Reflecting this same attitude in 1928, the Kyemyŏng Club (Kyemyŏng Kurakpu), a social reform organization formed in 1918 by thirty-three intellectuals from diverse backgrounds including numerous *chungin*, urged Koreans not to waste their national energy on genealogy compilation, which it branded as a feudal practice.[15]

These criticisms against genealogy compilation suggest an explanation of why many specialist *chungin* and their descendants are missing from modern genealogies even though they had the means to maintain or forge one. It is well worth considering that by the late nineteenth century, the *chungin* families had become more receptive to Western-style world views, education, business, religion (Protestantism), and fashion than any other social group.[16] In this light, it seems reasonable to postulate that many *chungin* and their descendants turned their backs on the old discourse.

What they rejected arguably was a hegemonic discourse. The manner in which socially influential actors defend such self-aggrandizing practices as boasting of aristocratic descent can contribute to the reproduction of the existing power structure that they dominate. As such, hegemonic discourse favors the power holder, and the spread of genealogy compilation across status boundaries in early modern Korea attests to its vital importance for status consciousness at the time.[17] In the early nineteenth century, only a dozen or so aristocratic lineages based in Seoul dominated national politics, but birth was what enabled aristocratic families throughout the country to maintain their positions.[18] As we have seen, this social reality was especially vexing for the specialist *chungin*, a group that had become increasingly wealthy and culturally sophisticated in the early modern era while performing distinct functions that were critically important to the state yet held in low regard by the aristocracy.

Thus, the absence of many *chungin* and their descendants from modern genealogies seems to be more about rejecting an old mindset than embracing any status shame. Given the high level of education, urban background, and decidedly pro-Western orientation of Seoul *chungin* by the early twentieth century, it should come as no surprise that their descendants tend to be either unaware of their ancestors' *chungin* status per se (many no longer have a genealogy set in the household, even though their ancestors were recorded earlier) or, if aware, do not think much of it. Instead, they seem proud of their family's modern orientation and accomplishments during the late nineteenth and early twentieth centuries.[19] In fact, some descendants of *chungin* harbored pride in their families in a way that in the modern era they have actually desired to express through more objective genealogical records, as discussed in the Epilogue. For others of *chungin* status or descent, including many Paks, worrying about the past was a lower priority than making a living in a new socioeconomic environment dominated by the Japanese.

Varied Lives of the Paks

The economic stature of the Paks as a whole deteriorated. If during the Korean Empire period the Paks continued to control any palace land holdings in the vicinity of Seoul, then with the Japanese takeover they lost control of most of them. The colonial government replaced older palace land management arrangements throughout Korea with state-owned lands cultivated by tenant farmers. Also, the worldwide recession greatly devalued the Korean currency. The fates of Korea's wealthiest varied tremendously.[20] The Koch'ang Kims, for example, who went on to found the Kyŏngsŏng Textile Corporation (Kyŏngsŏng Pangjik Chusik Hoesa), were successful in making the transition to a modern economic system as they reinvested their landed wealth into a variety of lucrative enterprises, ranging from factories to corporations to schools, and their successes owed heavily to their cooperation with the Japanese as junior partners.[21] Others, including most of the highly touted Kaesŏng merchants, were not so successful. The Pak population of both the senior and junior lines began increasing rapidly in the late nineteenth century after generations of single-line succession, likewise with varying degrees of socioeconomic success.

The lineage heir Pak Myŏnghwan (1861–1936), the eldest son of the senior line's Pak Yunsik, maintained his forefathers' financial legacies, now limited to some land in South Ch'ungch'ŏng province (Figure 6.1). Unless he is the documented military examination passer (by 1885) of the same name, Myŏnghwan is not known to have had a governmental career; that he most likely resided in South Ch'ungch'ŏng province rather than Seoul is telling.[22] In fact, it is known that by 1908 he had submitted paperwork to the government showing a significant number of landholdings in what were then Ŭnjin and Hongsan counties, possibly as well as Yesan county, in the province.[23] As discussed in Chapter 3, his great-great-grandfather, Pak Kyŏngmu, had acquired this land in the early nineteenth century. Although the region was known for ramie production, it is not certain if Myŏnghwan in any way had committed himself to producing or marketing it for the company, Korean Ramie Spinning, Ltd., launched by his kinsman Pak T'aesik's in-law U Hangjŏng. Nor do we know anything about the family backgrounds, other than the fathers' names, of Myŏnghwan's two successive wives, Madam Ch'ŏngju Han (1862–88), who died not long after the wedding, and Madam Indong Chang (1871–1960), who was ten years his junior. Along with their husband, both women were buried in Puyŏ, where the Paks as a group seem to have taken refuge from Seoul and settled by the early twentieth century.[24]

Myŏnghwan's younger brother, Pak Kyuhwan (1865–n.d.), remained connected to other Seoul *chungin* families while maintaining residential and economic bases in Puyŏ. His tie to central officialdom was tenuous: when appointed as a clerk (*Chusa*) in the Communication Office's Telephone Section on July 1, 1904, he resigned on the following day—suggesting that the post was either honorary or onerous.[25] We do know that, as was true of his elder brother Kyuhwan, he also owned a significant amount of land. As of 1901, he had land in Hyŏnnae district in Puyŏ county.[26] Evidently his social capital was greater than that of his elder brother: Kyuhwan had at least one marriage tie, if not two, to prominent capital *chungin* families. His first wife, Madam Hamyŏl Namgung (1864–n.d.), was a daughter of Namgung Chin (n.d.), who attained a senior third court rank of *T'ongjŏng taebu*

FIGURE 6.1 The senior line: Pak Yunsik, Pak Chinsik, and their descendants.

("magnate thorough and regulatory"). Coming from a capital *chungin* family whose members were buried in Puyŏ for generations, Namgung Chin is known to have resided in nearby Sŏksŏng county (which later became part of Puyŏ) as well as Yangju county, bordering Seoul, while possessing much land in Hyŏnnae district; he also assisted the central government in suppressing the Tonghak.[27] The most famous member of the Namgung family is the grandson of Chin's eleventh cousin, Namgung Ŏk (1864–1939), best known for his involvement in civic movements, including the Independence Club and the Korean Association.[28] Kyuhwan's second wife, Madam Yu (1876–n.d.), appears in the 1924 Miryang Pak genealogy as a Kangnŭng Yu, but as indicated by the *yŏng* (Ch. *yong*, long, eternity) ideograph in the name of her father, Yu Yŏnghŭi (n.d.), most likely she was a member of the *chungin* Hanyang Yu linage. As is true for the majority of *chungin* lines, the modern Yu genealogy offers a spotty coverage of the members after the midnineteenth century, and Yu Yŏnghŭi too is missing. Along with Madam Namgung and their husband, Madam Yu was buried in Puyŏ.[29]

Although we know that Kyuhwan's younger brother was a landlord, of significance to the larger story of the role of *chungin* during the colonial period are the cases of their cousins, the sons of Pak Chinsik.[30] The little that we know about the two eldest sons, Pak Minhwan (1880–1962) and Pak Chonghwan (1886–1930), suggests that, no longer living in Seoul, the Paks tried to maintain their social standing through appropriate local marriage ties. I have not uncovered anything else about their lives other than their wives, fathers-in-law, and burial locations in Puyŏ, Poryŏng, and Kŭmsan counties, but this information shows that now the Paks were living in southwestern South Ch'ungch'ŏng province with widely scattered landholdings. Unlike Minhwan's three wives, about whose fathers I have not been able to confirm career-related information, the father of Chonghwan's only wife, Madam

Naju Kim (1882–1956), Kim Chonggu (n.d.), had a bureaucratic career culminating with the senior third civil court rank title of *T'ongjŏng taebu*
("magnate thorough and regulatory").[31] The Naju Kim genealogy records
Chonggu as a twelfth-generation descendant of a well-documented sixteenth-
century civil official, from Muan, southern Chŏlla region, with both licentiate
and civil examination degrees. Unlike his descendants in Muan who enjoyed
social status as members of a celebrated prominent local aristocratic lineage
in the early modern era, the descent lines based in various locales in southern Ch'ungch'ŏng region were not so privileged. In fact, considering that the
genealogy records Chonggu as a descendant of the civil official's son who had
relocated to Ch'ungch'ŏng and that Chonggu's daughter married into the
senior-line Paks, we can surmise that he was a descendant of an illegitimate
son somewhere in the intervening generations, if not a member of a family
making a false genealogical claim—as were the Paks.[32]

We know much more about Minhwan and Chonghwan's younger brother,
Chinsik's youngest son, Pak Changhwan (1891–1946), who had a successful
police career and resided in both the provinces and the capital. As of 1935, the
locality of his family's original household registration (*wŏnjŏk*) was Poryŏng
county in South Ch'ungch'ŏng province, a fact suggesting that certainly as of
1915, by which time the Japanese-mandated 1909 People's Registration Law
(*Minjŏkpŏp*) and its 1915 revision were in effect, he was a member of a household registered in Poryŏng.[33]

Though he was originally based in Poryŏng, his long career in the colonial police from 1912 to 1939 included postings mostly located in Seoul and
the surrounding Kyŏnggi province. He held a number of positions of increasing importance.[34] In fact, he was one of the rapidly growing number of colonial police personnel, which rose from 6,222 as of 1910 to 20,771 in 1922 to
more than 60,000 in 1941 (ultimately one policeman for every four hundred
Koreans).[35]

Changhwan was among a growing number of Koreans—not just police
personnel—recognized by the colonial government for good service to the
Japanese empire. On several occasions throughout his career, he received
rewards and commendations.[36] In particular, in 1935 he was one of 2,083
Koreans out of the total of 5,402 individuals commended on the occasion of
the twenty-five-year anniversary of the establishment of the Government-
General of Korea.[37] Then in 1938, he received the eighth-class Order of the
Sacred Treasure decoration.[38] An official report published in April 1940 to

recognize those who contributed to the Japanese war effort during the Second Sino-Japanese War (1937–45) acknowledges him for assisting with guarding and delivering military supplies.[39]

More than just a public servant on the payroll of the colonial government, Changhwan evidently was an individual of some wealth. In particular, he was active among business circles. In November 1912 and again in March 1915, for example, he received gold mining permits for joint ventures in Ch'ŏngyang and Hongju counties, both in South Ch'ungch'ŏng and thus not far from his home locale.[40]

His career won Changhwan the dubious distinction of an entry in the three-volume *Dictionary of Pro-Japanese Collaborators* (*Ch'inil inmyŏng sajŏn*; 2009).[41] Compiled by South Korea's Institute for Research on the Korean Nation (Minjok Munje Yŏn'guso), the compilation lists him among 4,776 entries though without any mention of whether after Korea's liberation he was charged with a crime against fellow Koreans. It seems, then, that he was simply a dutiful member of the colonial apparatus.[42]

Among Changhwan's contemporaries of the senior line Paks were the six sons and four daughters of his eldest cousin and lineage heir, Myŏnghwan, about whom I have been able to obtain only limited information. We have more information on what some of Myŏnghwan's sons did, and the eldest son and thus the new lineage heir, Pak Chun'gi (1891–1914), is noteworthy for his wealth even though he died when he was just twenty-four *se* of age.[43] In January 1914, the colonial government rewarded him as a private land-owner contributing his holding for road construction in April 1911 when he was just twenty-one. He reportedly had given 175 *p'yŏng* of land—an amount large enough to be the plot for a sizable Korean house with many rooms.[44] The "contribution" was voluntary, and presumably in service of a Japanese-sponsored infrastructure project. Chun'gi was married to Madam Naju Kim (1888–1964), who was a daughter of Secretary (*Tosa*) Kim Hakku (n.d.) and thus from an aforementioned southern Ch'ungch'ŏng region family either descended from an aristocrat through an illegitimate son or making a false claim of aristocratic descent. Chun'gi was buried in Puyŏ—again confirming that the Paks by then were living there rather than in the capital—whereas Madam Naju Kim, who long outlived him, was cremated.[45]

Chun'gi's younger brother and Myŏnghwan's second son, Pak Man'gi (1893–1950) enjoyed a more normal span of life, and he both possessed wealth and wielded local influence. He worked as an executive for at least two companies. Between 1923 and 1929, he is known to have been the auditor (*kamsa*) of South Ch'ungch'ŏng Ramie, Ltd. (Ch'ungnam Chŏp'o Chusik Hoesa). This suggests that he either had inherited the family's landholding producing ramie in southwestern South Ch'ungch'ŏng or had ties to such plots. Then between 1931 and 1935, Man'gi served as the auditor for Ch'ungnam Hŭngsan, Ltd. (Ch'ungnam Hŭngsan Chusik Hoesa), a company founded in August 1917 with headquarters in Hongsan district, Puyŏ.[46]

For what he illustrates about Christians during the colonial period and replacement of his identity based on status hierarchy with identity as a Christian, we return to the story of the junior line's sole heir, Pak T'aesik. By the 1920s, T'aesik and his wife, Madam Haeju O, were living with their third son, Ch'angnae, and daughter-in-law Yonghwa.[47] As was true for most nonelite girls of her generation or earlier, originally Yonghwa was "nameless" in the sense that she had only the informal given name by which she had been known from her childhood, and thus officially she was "Madam Kim." T'aesik bestowed a given name, "Yonghwa," literally meaning "countenance of harmony"; in 1930 he reported her new name in an update for the household registration document.[48] His naming of a daughter-in-law suggests that Christianity was playing a part in helping women achieve a more "modern" status at a time when the missionaries' perception of "modern womanhood" evolved through their encounters with Korean women, who were supposed to be premodern.[49]

In his later years, T'aesik himself was seeking harmony and peace through Christ.[50] Toward the end of his life in the early 1930s, when the household was living in Seoul again, he asked to be buried near Segŏmjŏng in the northern outskirts of the city so that he could rest in peace until Christ returned.[51] Predicting that his expectant daughter-in-law would give birth to a son, T'aesik chose for the baby the name Pyŏnggang, meaning "distinguishing with [the] peace [of Christ]." His grandson arrived three weeks after T'aesik's death, on October 17, 1933.[52]

The life of T'aesik's eldest son, Pak Kyŏngjun, reflects Korean culture in transition (Figure 6.2). Born in Seoul, Kyŏngjun was married to Madam Yangch'ŏn Hŏ (1885–n.d.), a daughter of Hŏ Chusŏng (also known as Hŏ Imsŏng, n.d.) who most likely was a member of a *chungin* line known for court painters, and the couple had at least one daughter.[53] Kyŏngjun did not achieve any degree, court rank, or office, unless a contemporary namesake who was palace key manager (*Sayak*) as of 1906 was him, but the post's senior

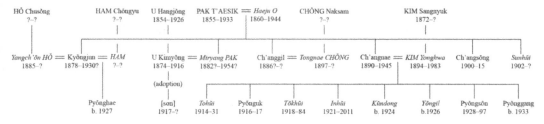

FIGURE 6.2 The junior line: Pak T'aesik and his descendants.

sixth rank seems rather high for a man just twenty-seven *se* in age.[54] In fact, Kyŏngjun reportedly preferred archery over reading and never attended a formal school.[55] After the Paks had settled in Puyŏ, at thirty-four *se* in 1911 Kyŏngjun began living separately from his parents—contrary to the prevalent custom according to which the eldest son would live with his parents.[56] As a widower, he married Madam Ham (n.d.), a daughter of Ham Chŏngyu (also known as Ham Ch'anhŭi, n.d.) from a local family of Sŏch'ŏn, and the couple had two sons.[57] The fact that this was Madam Ham's second marriage and she brought with her a girl from her previous marriage suggests that either Kyŏngjun's parents in particular could not have been happy about this marriage or they maintained a flexible attitude toward marriage and women. Kyŏngjun did not live long enough to see his new children grow up. He reportedly died after becoming sick from eating dog meat stew on a hot summer day around 1930, when his elder son was only a few years old.[58]

On T'aesik's second son Pak Ch'anggil, we have some information suggesting meanings of divorce, which was a rare practice at the time. All that we know for sure about him is that on March 5, 1919, he and his wife, Madam Tongnae Chŏng (1897–n.d.), agreed on divorce. Her father, Chŏng Naksam (n.d.), who was from a local family, refused to accept her back into his household, presumably considering her a shame to the family from a more traditional Confucian perspective; perhaps driven by his Christian faith, T'aesik set up a separate residence for her.[59] The couple is not known to have had any children, and none of the surviving Paks remembers hearing anything about Ch'anggil, which makes one wonder if there was something about the couple that was shameful or traumatic to the extent that the family no longer discussed them after the divorce. Interestingly, a person of the same name and roughly the right age appears as an officer of the World Friends

Group (Seudan), a special mobile propaganda team of the Korean Communist Party (Koryŏ Kongsandang), in Japanese Consul-General of Jiandao Suzuki Yōtarō's classified report (March 26, 1924) on anti-Japanese Korean activities in Manchuria—received by Minister of Foreign Affairs Matsui Keishirō (April 7, 1924).[60] Given that the divorce took place during the heat of the March First Movement, one could wonder if T'aesik's son Ch'anggil took the drastic action of leaving behind everything and going to Manchuria or Russia to join an anti-Japanese resistance movement—as did many known Korean independence activists on the outbreak of the March First Movement. If the documented World Friends Group officer is indeed T'aesik's second son, then it may have been participation in communist anti-Japanese activity that made him someone whom it was better for the family to forget during the remainder of the colonial era, when the Government-General was especially harsh in suppressing leftist activities.

Pak Ch'angnae: Unhappy to Serve, Unable to Resist

Much more concrete information is available about Ch'anggil's younger brother and T'aesik's third son, Pak Ch'angnae, whose training for a career as an educator spanned the years when the Korean Empire became a Japanese colony. Born in 1890 in what is now northern Sŏsomun subdistrict in Seoul, he was fifteen or sixteen *se* when the family fled Seoul for rural Puyŏ. In March 1909, Ch'angnae was one of 100 admitted into the three-year "main course" (*ponkwa*) track of Seoul Normal School (Hansŏng Sabŏm Hakkyo), founded in 1895 as Korea's first institution providing systematic modern education (Photograph 6.1). At the time Ch'angnae entered the school, its official mission was to train teachers for ordinary schools.[61] Although Korea had been a Japanese protectorate since 1905, so far I have not uncovered any evidence suggesting that the institution had become overtly pro-Japanese in inclination.[62] Given the admission requirements, Ch'angnae himself had presumably graduated from an ordinary school, and perhaps even an high ordinary school as many of his classmates had. Instruction time per week was thirty-four hours for the students, and subjects included "self cultivation" (*susin*), education, Korean, literary Chinese, Japanese, history, geography, mathematics, physics-chemistry, "drawing" (*tohwa*), gym, music, agriculture, commerce, and artisanry. Accommodated in a dormitory, the students

PHOTOGRAPH 6.1 Seoul Normal School (date unknown). Source: Sŏul T'ŭkpyŏlsi-Sa P'yŏnch'an Wiwŏnhoe, *Sajin ŭro ponŭn Sŏul*, vol. 1, p. 223. Reprinted with the permission of Sŏul T'ŭkpyŏlsi-Sa P'yŏnch'an Wiwŏnhoe.

received clothing, meal stipends, and spending money. The enrollees in the three-year course were required to serve as teachers at ordinary schools for at least six years after graduation.[63] In November 1911, the Government-General merged the school with Kyŏngsŏng High Ordinary School (Kyŏngsŏng Kodŭng Pot'ong Hakkyo) and continued the teacher training program through a Provisional Teaching Staff Training Institute (Imsi Kyowŏn Yangsŏngso).[64] In February 1912, Ch'angnae, along with sixty-one other students, completed the program as a member of the Institute's first graduating class.[65]

Ch'angnae's accomplishment was significant. Subsequent careers of Ch'angnae and other graduates of the Teaching Staff Training Institute show that as members of a small elite of Koreans with modern education, they had the potential to rise high in colonial society.[66] As of 1910, just 110,800 out of about 13 million Koreans (0.9 percent) were enrolled in a formal school, excluding traditional village schools (*sŏdang*).[67] And as of 1912, Ch'angnae was one of a paltry 1,472 public ordinary schoolteachers in Korea, among

PHOTOGRAPH 6.2 Hongju Public Ordinary School (Hongju Kongnip Pot'ong Hakkyo) teachers and students on the commencement day (March 1913). Author's personal possession. The third man from left in the first row is Pak Ch'angnae who at the time was 24 *se* in age and teaching at the school. Including Ch'angnae, all four Korean teachers, seated in the row, are wearing Korean dress, *hanbok*, rather than the military-style uniform that was the norm for all public school teachers of Japanese ethnicity at the time. The bearded, uniformed man in the middle of the row, Komatsu Kaneyoshi, was the official vice-principal and de facto principal. Beginning his teaching career in Korea's Cheju Island in 1909, Komatsu was one of colonial Korea's increasing number of Japanese residents who would total some 700,000 by 1940.

whom were 1,076 Koreans and 396 Japanese.[68] Out of the 62 members of the class of 1912, three appear among the 4,776 individuals in the aforementioned *Dictionary of Pro-Japanese Collaborators*.[69]

Ch'angnae is not on the pro-Japanese collaborator list, and his life and career as a frustrated public ordinary school teacher (*hundo*) and civil servant of the Japanese colonial state partially explain why. Unlike many other

PHOTOGRAPH 6.3 Pak Ch'angnae at 27 *se* (1916).
Author's personal possession. Unlike the 1913
photograph wherein only the Japanese teachers wore
military-style uniforms and swords, here Ch'angnae
is dressed likewise. Pursuing the "cultural policy"
(*bunka seiji*, 1919–31) as a concession to Koreans after
the March First Movement, the Japanese would do
away with military uniforms for teachers in Korea.

members of his class who achieved administrative positions in the colonial
government's education-related organs or committees, Ch'angnae's career
as a civil servant did not extend beyond that of a schoolteacher, and as
soon as he became eligible for a pension in 1929 he quit.[70] From 1912 until
then, he taught at eight public schools in three provinces, namely South
Ch'ungch'ŏng, Hwanghae, and Kyŏnggi (Photographs 6.2, 6.3).[71] From

time to time throughout his career as a public school teacher, Ch'angnae expressed his anti-Japanese sentiment. In fact, in April 1924, while walking home after drinking heavily, he picked a fight with a police officer (incidentally a Pak).[72] Sometimes, in the late 1930s and the 1940s, when he drank he got into shouting matches over the wall with his neighbor, Mun Seyŏng (1888–n.d.), who chided Ch'angnae for teaching the Japanese-dictated curriculum to the young while Mun himself was busy compiling a massive Korean language dictionary.[73] Ch'angnae certainly had things to say, but he evidently stayed clear of any overtly anti-Japanese activity. Post-1945 Korean celebrations and depictions of the 1919 March First Movement, for example, may give one an impression that most Koreans had participated—including someone especially strong-willed and resentful toward the colonial rule such as Ch'angnae. None of the surviving children has heard of their father's involvement in any anti-Japanese activity, and I have not uncovered any substantiating document either. One surviving daughter, though, conjectures that her father had nationalistic aspirations, as she remembers her father once muttering: "Had my parents not married me off so early, I would not be here [going about] like this."[74]

As was true for most Koreans, Ch'angnae complied, in February 1940, with the Name Order of 1939 (Ordinance 19) that required all Koreans to adopt a Japanese-style "family name." By August 1940, about 82 percent of Koreans had reported their new names, and those who had not were ordered to do so as soon as possible or risk not receiving government-administered service items ranging from postal mail to school enrollment to food rations.[75] Given the circumstances, Koreans tried to adopt Japanese-style family names that reflected the meaning or the history of their original Korean surname and ancestral seat; it seems that many Paks changed their surname to Arai (Ko. Sinjŏng, literally "new well," "well of Silla") to reflect the legend according to which six village chiefs washed the baby they had just found, Pak Hyŏkkŏse, at a well named Najŏng.[76] According to the story, Pak grew fast as a wise boy, and at age twelve he was elevated by the six leaders as the ruler of Silla.[77] This story evidently did not impress Ch'angnae, though, as he chose the surname Mieyama (Ko. Samgangsan, literally "three rivers and mountains"), an acronym for "samch'ŏl-li kŭmsu kangsan" (literally "3,000 i of mountains and rivers beautiful as if embroidered on silk"), which was a euphemistic name for Korea. The Japanese found the name nice in both pronunciation and surface meaning, while the Koreans praised Ch'angnae as a patriot.[78] Ch'angnae adopted as his personal name Heiji, literally meaning governance through peace and used not uncommonly among the Japanese.[79] Now Mieyama Heiji, Ch'angnae let all of his children choose their own Japanese given names, except for the youngest two, who were just eleven and six *se* at the time.[80]

Though not overtly challenging the colonial authority, Ch'angnae associated with Korean nationalists, especially Cho Pyŏngok (pen name Yusŏk, 1894–1960) and Sin Ikhŭi (pen name Haegong, 1892–1956). Especially during the final years of colonial rule, when the only way for Korean nationalists to not compromise their nationalist credentials was to lie low, Cho and Sin indeed kept a low profile. During this time Ch'angnae maintained close relations with both, often drinking with them.[81] What the two men had in common with Ch'angnae was membership in roughly the same age group of educated, Christian Koreans from either Kyŏnggi or Ch'ungch'ŏng province and reputations as nationalistic "manly persons" (*hoin*).[82] Sin hailed from an aristocratic Disciple (*Soron*)-faction family of high standing known for examination graduates and government officials, was Catholic, and spent time outside Korea during the final years of Japanese colonial rule. Cho, a closer friend of Ch'angnae, was wandering around looking for gold mines at the time.[83] Hailing from Ch'ŏnan, not far from Asan, where Ch'angnae was teaching at the time of the March First Movement demonstrations, Cho's family background was virtually no different from that of a commoner, not at all that of a provincial aristocrat.[84] Despite his apparently low-status antecedents, however, Cho, like Sin, differed from Ch'angnae in being independently wealthy, enough to study abroad, and associated more overtly with one nationalistic movement or another, both in and outside Korea.

Much of the information on Ch'angnae's life and career derive from his surviving children by wife Kim Yonghwa (1894–1983), a Naju Kim who came from either a local functionary or a wealthy commoner family. In January 1911, while still a student, Ch'angnae married Yonghwa, whose father, Kim Sangnyuk (1872–n.d.), was a wealthy businessman from Kunsan, one of Imperial Korea's treaty ports.[85] A landlord owning rice hulling factories as well as running a construction business, Kim reportedly was impressed enough by the young man with a modern education to betroth to him his daughter.[86] Kim's origins seem to have been undistinguished in that so far I have not found the father of any of his wives or those of his patrilineal ancestors in a genealogy.

After a two-year gap in his teaching career, in April 1915 Ch'angnae took up a teaching post far away in Hwanghae province, and his four-year sojourn there until 1919 created tension between him and his parents. Especially as an elder celebrating his age of sixty *se*, T'aesik and Madam Haeju O did not like having their son and daughter-in-law living so far away.[87] They also missed their only grandson, Pak Pyŏnguk (1916–17), whose given name, meaning "distinguishing and rising," owed itself to T'aesik, who initiated the use of the ideograph *pyŏng* (Ch. *bing*, bright, distinguished), for his grandsons. In either April or May 1917, Ch'angnae and Yonghwa traveled from Hwanghae province to Inch'ŏn, where they dropped off four-month-old Pyŏnguk at the mansion of U Kimyŏng, to whom Ch'angnae's sister was a concubine. At the time, the U household was mourning the death of the mother of Kimyŏng. Before anyone could take the boy to Kunsan as planned, he caught typhoid and died.[88]

The loss of the son, as well as the birth of a second daughter at the end of 1918, seems to have prompted the couple to move closer to home. Thus it was that in April 1919 Ch'angnae took up a teaching post in Asan, South Ch'ungch'ŏng province, about 60 kilometers north-northeast of Puyŏ, though this assignment closer to home did not last long. Available records show not only that Ch'angnae did not teach there beyond the 1919–20 school year but that for at least two years, until April 1922, he was not holding any position in the colonial government.[89] This gap allows some room for speculating on his role during the eventful weeks following the March First Movement, though as noted, no known document or testimony suggests that Ch'angnae was in any way involved. Given that he was a civil servant, as well as a husband, and a father with a four-year-old daughter and a baby girl at home, these facts themselves—rather than any involvement in anti-Japanese activity—probably were the reason he took some time off from 1920 to 1922.

Ch'angnae's assignment in April 1922 to a school in Kyŏnggi province ushered in an eight-year period of greater stability. Moving from Yongin (1922–23) to Suwŏn (1923–25) to Kap'yŏng (1925–30), he found his assignments becoming longer and longer. Perhaps he benefited from the subsequent efforts of the colonial government to treat Koreans better.[90] As of 1928, Ch'angnae and Yonghwa had five daughters and a son, born in that year—that is, ten years after the couple lost their first son.[91] Although, according to his children's recollections, the happiest time for the family was when they were living in Kap'yŏng, located about 50 kilometers northeast of Seoul, Ch'angnae continued to harbor resentment toward the Japanese. I have found no evidence indicating that the aforementioned scuffle, in Suwŏn, with a police officer had compromised his career prospects, but as soon as he attained eligibility for severance pay in 1930, Ch'angnae concluded his teaching career.[92]

After an unsuccessful business venture in Kunsan, in 1932 Ch'angnae again took up a teaching position—his final job—at Sinmyŏng School (Sinmyŏng Hakkyo) in Seoul (Photograph 6.4).[93] Along with better-known various Chinmyŏng and Sungmyŏng schools, Sinmyŏng was a private institution founded and controlled by the family of former Imperial Consort Sunhŏn (also known as Imperial Consort Ŏm, 1854–1911), a concubine of the Kwangmu emperor and the mother of Imperial Prince Yŏng (1897–1970), who was heir apparent to his elder half-brother, the Yunghŭi emperor. Sinmyŏng provided education to those who had been deprived of normal educational opportunities, including many adults, and it offered night classes, although in 1939 the colonial government finally recognized it as a public ordinary school, meaning that the school and its staff such as Ch'angnae were subjected to increasingly heavy-handed Japanese policies of the time.[94] Principal Yu Yŏngnyŏl (1871–n.d.), who probably was a member of the prominent *chungin* Hanyang Yu lineage and married to a former palace lady, was a negligent manager, and in effect Ch'angnae ran the school on Yu's behalf.[95] Before long, Ch'angnae became the vice-principal, the position he held until his death in April 1945.[96]

Ch'angnae's Legacy to Modern Korea: The Daughters

Ch'angnae's eldest daughter, Pak Tohŭi (1914–31), born in Puyŏ, typifies a new generation of Korean girls receiving the best available modern education, though her studies were cut short by her untimely death at sixteen. On the recommendation of a family acquaintance, Sin Albet'ŭ, who was a prominent educator and women's movement activist at the time, Ch'angnae and Yonghwa sent Tohŭi off to study in Seoul at the famed Sungmyŏng Girls High Ordinary School (Sungmyŏng Yŏja Kodŭng Pot'ong Hakkyo)—originally founded in 1906 as Myŏngsin Girls School (Myŏngsin Yŏ Hakkyo)—one of the many private schools founded and maintained by the natal family of Imperial Consort Sunhŏn. Whenever Tohŭi visited home in Kunsan from Seoul, she got to ride in the rickshaw from the harbor while the younger siblings joyfully ran after her.[97] Clearly she was the pride and the future of the family as she was the best educated of the Paks at the time. While hospitalized for typhoid at the Medical Center of Kyŏngsŏng Medical College (Kyŏngsŏng Ŭihak Chŏnmun Hakkyo, presently Seoul National University's College of Medicine), in May 1931

PHOTOGRAPH 6.4 Pak Ch'angnae in his 50s (ca. 1944). Author's personal possession. He is wearing the *kokuminfuku* (Ko. *kungminbok*) propagated during the wartime by the colonial government.

Tohŭi suffered and died when mistakenly treated with another gas instead of oxygen.[98]

Also born in Puyŏ, Ch'angnae's second daughter, Pak Tŏkhŭi (1918–84) received a formal education that was more practical in orientation than that of her older sister. After ordinary school, she studied midwifery, which, though the number of practitioners was increasing during the colonial period, still was not attracting enough recruits.[99] In a clear reflection of the decision of parents unshackled by a conservative notion of what a daughter of a good family should study (if she should study at all), the training endowed her with a useful skill that not only helped other women during their critical hours but also brought home additional income.[100] Toward the end of the colonial era, her parents married her to Yi Chongch'un (1914–2006), a Kwangju Yi from a wealthy local functionary family of the Chŏlla region.[101] Like many of his kinsmen, he received practical education early and became a professional, working as a judicial scrivener. The couple had two sons and a daughter, all during wartime.[102]

Tŏkhŭi's younger sister, Pak Inhŭi (1921–2011), got her formal education with greater difficulty, though this did not hold her back from avid reading. Born in Puyŏ, Inhŭi had to transfer twice as a student: from Kap'yŏng Public Ordinary School (Kap'yŏng Kongnip Pot'ong Hakkyo) to Kunsan First Public Ordinary School (Kunsan Cheil Kongnip Pot'ong Hakkyo) in 1930, and then from the latter to Tŏksu Public Ordinary School (Tŏksu Kongnip Pot'ong Hakkyo) in 1932. In fact, it was only with some difficulty, and a tribute to their determination, that she was educated, that her parents were able to enroll her at Tŏksu, as the nearest public ordinary school in the neighborhood of Ch'angnae's faculty residence on Sinmyŏng School campus was full. When the parents turned to Tŏksu, the grade in which Inhŭi had to enroll was full, and they settled for enrolling her one grade lower.[103]

As was true for most young Korean students like her, Inhŭi had no choice but to adjust to the cultural assimilation policies of the colonial government, beginning in the 1930s. In September 1935, the Government-General of Korea instructed provincial governors to make sure that all school personnel—principals, teachers, and students—attended ceremonies at Shinto shrines. With its expanding war effort on the continent, the Japanese authorities maintained that these ceremonies were more about patriotic celebrations or national rites than a religious act.[104] Inhŭi, her siblings, and her friends did not think much of this new duty; in fact as children, she and her classmates simply could not help giggling during the ceremonies.[105] Then in March 1938, the colonial government in effect banned the use of Korean in instruction.[106] When asked what this actually meant for any Korean student caught speaking in Korean, Inhŭi explained with a chuckle that usually the punishment was to clean the bathroom. In 1940, Inhŭi became Mieyama Hagiko (given name literally meaning "bush clover child"), in accordance with the new name-change requirement. Though certainly complying with the new assimilation policies of the colonial government, her father was telling her and her siblings, in and out of school, to stay away from those openly criticizing the Japanese as well as those who went out of their way to flatter the Japanese. Beyond ordinary school, Inhŭi's parents had no means to continue her formal education, but she continued to study on her own through her teenage years, and among the siblings she was most fond of reading (Photograph 6.5). She recalls how hard it was at first, when Korea was liberated, to suddenly read the newspapers in Korean—a kind of recollection that the educated elderly are not supposed to share so readily in public in Korea today.[107] Toward the end of the colonial era, she married Cho Ilche, who came from a Seoul family that had had some members working in the government of Imperial Korea.[108]

Among Inhŭi's sisters, Pak Kŭndong (b. 1924), born in Suwŏn, Kyŏnggi province, attained the highest level of formal education thanks to the greater financial stability that her parents had achieved by the mid-1930s. Unlike her elder sisters, she received an obviously boyish name from her parents, who by then were eager for a boy after four girls following the death of their first son. While growing up, Kŭndong disliked her name.[109] Literally meaning "rooted in the East," it seems to have expressed Ch'angnae's wish for a child who, from the Orient, would make a name for herself. Just as her elder sister Tohŭi had done earlier, Kŭndong continued her study beyond ordinary school. She studied at the prestigious Ewha Girls High School (Ihwa Kodŭng Yŏ Hakkyo).[110] The school traced its history back to an American Methodist missionary-founded girls school (1886) on which King Kojong had bestowed the name "Ihwa," but as with all other schools in colonial Korea, of course it had to abide by the dictates of the Government-General. The curriculum at the time reflected a popular shift among private girls schools from an emphasis on being a "wise mother and good wife" (hyŏnmo yangch'ŏ) to becoming a "new woman" (sin yŏsŏng) with her own vocation—though clearly the Japanese state's take on issues of women's status from 1910 to 1945 was hardly of unilineal progression. Moreover, as modern girls who were so not just in terms of how they donned short hair, wore Western dresses, and pursued hobbies that for most Koreans at the time were very Western such as ice skating, tennis, and dancing, many Ewha girls lived and worked in a way that today's more mainstream South Korean public discourse would consider "radical."[111]

Kŭndong's younger sister, and Ch'angnae and Yonghwa's fifth daughter, Pak Yŏngil (b. 1926), born in Kap'yŏng, Kyŏnggi province, could not

PHOTOGRAPH 6.5 Kim Yonghwa, Pak Pyŏnggang, Pak Inhŭi, and a neighborhood woman (clockwise; 1936). Author's personal possession. While visiting the Paks, the woman suggested that they go get a picture taken at a photo studio, and they did.

study beyond ordinary school though the family found her the cleverest of the siblings. When she completed her study at Ch'ŏngun Public Ordinary School (Ch'ŏngun Kongnip Pot'ong Hakkyo) in the neighborhood of her father's faculty housing on Sinmyŏng School campus, her parents had no choice but to discontinue her schooling as they had to save resources for her younger brother, who was just one year away from graduating from ordinary school.[112] Discontinued schooling did not stop her from enjoying books. In fact, in 1940, when Ch'angnae asked all his daughters to choose a Japanese given name, the fourteen-year-old Yŏngil chose Sachiko (meaning "joyful child"), the name of one of the pretty characters in a teenager's storybook she was reading.[113]

Not Meant to Be: Future Citizens of the Japanese Empire

Joyful over the arrival of a second grandson, Pak Pyŏngsŏn (1928–97), T'aesik gave him a name literally meaning "distinguishing Chosŏn (Korea)." He enrolled in Maedong Public Ordinary School (Maedong Kongnip Pot'ong Hakkyo), the status of which, in 1938, the colonial government changed from public ordinary school (Ja. *kōritsu futsū gakkō*, Ko. *kongnip pot'ong hakkyo*) to elementary school (Ja. *shō gakkō*, Ko. *so hakkyo*) according to the "Japan and Korea as a single body" (*Nai-Sen ittai*) ideology geared toward more fully assimilating the Koreans into the Japanese mainstream. In effect, the name change was supposed to allow the Koreans to shed the old names revealing their inferior status and at least assume a more Japanese appearance.[114] Even without this change, Pyŏngsŏn was in an educational environment strongly influenced by his Japanese classmates, who made up the majority of the students. After finishing at what was now Maedong Elementary School, he studied at the well-regarded Kyŏnggi Provincial First-Class Commercial School (Kyŏnggi Torip Kapchong Sangŏp Hakkyo), present Kyŏnggi Commercial High School (Kyŏnggi Sangŏp Kodŭng Hakkyo). Founded in 1923, this school, too, had a student body that was predominantly Japanese.[115] Perhaps mindful of Pyŏngsŏn's rather strong personality, in 1940 Ch'angnae chose for him a Japanese name, Shigeru, meaning "luxuriant" or "flourishing."[116] In fact, during the final phase of the Pacific War (1941–45), the boy, now Mieyama Shigeru, vigorously challenged his father's observation that the end was near. He insisted that the Imperial Army was putting up a valiant struggle and would prevail in the end.[117] Around the time of his father's death in the spring of 1945, he entered Posŏng College (Posŏng Chŏnmun Hakkyo), presently Korea University, majoring in economics.[118]

Born in 1933, Pak Pyŏnggang, the youngest child and third son of Ch'angnae and Yonghwa (then respectively forty-four *se* and forty *se*), received primary schooling geared toward more fully assimilating Koreans into the Japanese mainstream.[119] He attended Ch'ŏngun Citizens' School

(Ch'ŏngun Kungmin Hakkyo, formerly Ch'ŏngun Public Ordinary School), as had his sister Yŏngil, who was seven years older.[120] In April 1941 the school became Ch'ŏngun Citizens' School following the Citizens' School Ordinance of 1941, which aimed explicitly to fashion national subjects in time of war. Accordingly, all public elementary schools became "citizens' schools" (Ja. *kokumin gakkō*, Ko. *kungmin hakkyo*).[121] Pyŏnggang recalls how the colonial government banned the use of Korean language in schools; everything was in Japanese, though outside the classrooms kids spoke Korean.[122] Pyŏnggang got from his father a Japanese name, Hiroshi, meaning "vast," "broad," or "wide."[123]

The career of U Changch'un (1898–1959), a remote connection of the Paks, illustrates possibilities and limits of a talented colonial subject under the Japanese system.[124] Born in Japan as the son of exiled U Pŏmsŏn and his Japanese wife, Sakai Naka, Changch'un grew up as a poor, fatherless Korean after his father's assassination in 1903. Nonetheless, he obtained advanced education that allowed him to pursue a meaningful career in the field of thremmatology.[125] After completing ordinary and high ordinary schools in Hiroshima, in 1916 he entered Tokyo Imperial University's "practical studies" program in agricultural science, providing vocational training rather than formal college education. Upon graduating in 1919, he worked at the Ministry of Agriculture and Forestry's Agrarian Experiment Station; his research in thremmatology produced significant results.[126] Although Changch'un earned a doctoral degree in agricultural science (1936) from Tokyo Imperial University, the fact that he was a Korean and had not graduated from a regular university program meant promotions eluded him, until promotion to the status of first-class engineer (*Gishi*)—in effect an honorary promotion marking an early retirement, typical of educated Koreans serving Imperial Japan.[127]

Conclusion

The Japanese takeover of Korea affected the Paks and their kin differently across generations. Those who had already begun their careers long before 1910 found that the new era had little to offer them. A general sense of resignation and even a desire for salvation overcame men such as Pak T'aesik, who sought peace through Christianity as he watched his children and grandchildren brave the new world. The change was particularly hard on the next generation, who grew up as educated citizens of Imperial Korea and now found themselves, as adults, dealing with the Japanese state. None is known to have pursued any overtly anti-Japanese activity, but still the social trajectory varied from begrudging acceptance of reality, as Pak Ch'angnae went about his career as a teacher, to others who were less particular—including his cousin Pak Changhwan, who rose high in the colonial police. Ch'angnae's brother-in-law, the literary licentiate U Kimyŏng, was unable to restore the family's former glory before dying prematurely, whereas his cousin U Changch'un, living and working in Japan as a fatherless Korean, overcame hardship in becoming a renowned scientist. Born and educated during the colonial era, the next generation of Paks such as the children of Ch'angnae had no choice but to live and grow up within the system, which increasingly sought to assimilate Koreans culturally. The children certainly were not in a position to fuss over the Government-General of Korea's requirements that Koreans participate in Shinto shrine ceremonies, use only Japanese in classrooms, adopt a Japanese name, and learn to be good subjects of the Japanese empire, especially as taught at the new citizens schools.

Although this study considers a Korean family defined by patrilineal descent, we have examined women's roles beyond linking families through marriage. The stories of Pak T'aesik's daughters, daughters-in-law, and granddaughters enable us to consider various issues, including education, hypergamy, concubinage, and motherhood. Compared to millions of other Koreans of their gender at the time, arguably the Pak women fared better in a world where pursuing modernity in the sense of Western civilization was a concern of many educated, urban Koreans. T'aesik's daughters married men of wealth or higher social status, whereas the granddaughters grew up attending modern schools, wearing Western clothes, enjoying ice-skating in the winter, and playing tennis. All the same, they were not immune to anguish stemming from the pressure to produce an heir, husbands who brought home concubines, prodigal adopted sons, the hardships of the Second World War, and the sacrifices necessary when limited family resources had to be devoted to educating a brother.

Epilogue

FOR ALMOST TWO GENERATIONS, JAPANESE COLONIAL RULE unleashed forces that broke up old Korean social collectives and introduced opportunities for individuals to assume new identities. By 1945, on the eve of liberation, the Pak lineage no longer formed a cohesive kin group and individual Paks had to negotiate a society undergoing rapid transformation. Those with colonial socioeconomic capital maintained it at the risk of suffering vengeful retribution. Others simply struggled to survive, especially in the turbulent years following national liberation and the Korean War. In general, many Paks found ways to get ahead in the context of South Korea's economic take-off in the 1960s, although securing a stable middle-class livelihood—in Korea or abroad—took decades.[1] The story of the Paks told here provides a personal perspective on the social changes in Korea's modern history, but it also reveals important detail on the varied genealogical practices of the descendants of specialist *chungin* post-1945 and the overall significance to historians of studying *chungin*, especially in terms of historical agency.

The evident breakup of the Pak family as a socioeconomically and geographically cohesive kin group reflects the phases that Korean society has undergone vis-à-vis perceptions of descent and status. In particular, the post-1945 saga of the descendants of specialist *chungin* clearly reflects this. Although some invented traditions of a more illustrious family history, the majority stopped participating in genealogy compilation. Still others have kept records just for record's sake, no longer putting any stock in the social value of genealogies.

Free of old status anxiety, some descendants of Seoul *chungin*, such as the Ch'ŏllyŏng Hyŏn living in America, have continued to participate in genealogy compilations, especially stressing their modern-era achievements.[2] Evidently viewing genealogy as a more status-neutral record of family history, the 2001 edition of the Hyŏn genealogy includes details regarding the technical specialist careers of *chungin* members, but the manner in which one member, Hyŏn Sun (1878–1968), and his descendants are recorded is particularly noteworthy. Hyŏn was a Methodist minister, independence activist, and founder of an American branch of his family; one of his children, David Hyun (b. 1917), founder of the Korean-American Coalition in Los Angeles, became a noted architect whose renowned creations include the Japanese Village Plaza in Los Angeles's Little Tokyo.[3] The modern genealogy records all the American members with the kind of detail not commonly found in Korean genealogies. In addition to their educational and career credentials, we find their Western given names written in the Korean alphabet, not Chinese ideographs, and the names of non-Korean spouses are also included.[4]

Other descendants of *chungin* who continue participating in genealogy compilation seem to have been inspired to focus on nationally celebrated ancestors instead; a specialist-*chungin* Kyŏngju Kim lineage is a case in point. Arguably the most famous member of the lineage is Kim Pŏmu (baptized as Thomas, 1751–87), officially Korea's first Catholic martyr. Hailing from a family of interpreters, Kim underwent interrogation and torture in 1785 for his faith and died in 1787 from the lingering trauma.[5] A 1989 edition of the Kyŏngju Kim genealogy records his descendants in detail, including information that reveals their *chungin* status.[6] It appears that the unique place their famous ancestor came to occupy in the history of Christianity in Korea has helped them maintain interest in updating their genealogies.

The descendants of *chungin* not famous enough for wider recognition have shown varied attitudes toward genealogy, as have the Paks. Since 1945, some descendants of the *chungin* Paks have continued to participate in genealogy compilations; others have not. None lived in North Korea, where the communist government introduced revolutionary change, but in the South the chaos of the immediate aftermath of liberation, the Korean War, ongoing urbanization, rapid industrialization, and concomitant social dislocation demanded diligence and courage—virtues that at the time seemed more suited toward the future than the past. The Paks have lost the memory of their family's precolonial past, but the subsequent story remains familiar as the members can recount it without need for a genealogy. Moreover, their experience illustrates what old status hierarchy and genealogy meant to the Paks.

In the last few decades, the senior-line Paks from the rural counties of South Ch'ungch'ŏng province became acclimated to a more conservative culture wherein genealogies still mattered. Unlike their Seoul-based junior-line kinsmen who stopped bothering, the members of the senior line continued to get themselves recorded in updated editions of Pak genealogy. Both the 1924 and 1998 editions of the Miryang Pak genealogy for this branch record all members of the senior line while leaving out the entire junior line. Besides dates of birth and death, courtesy names, and grave locations, some entries record the significant achievements of individuals.[7] Evidently, the senior-line Paks have valued genealogy as a record of family history, as have other descendants of nineteenth-century *chungin* who continue to participate in genealogy compilations.

In contrast, the story of the junior line shows both neglect toward genealogy compilation and a desire to possess written records. When asked in 1992 why the family had lost records, the lineage heir, Pak Pyŏnghae (b. 1927), offered two seemingly contradictory explanations that nevertheless suggest a lack of care or respect for genealogy. According to one, his grandfather Pak T'aesik had to abandon the record when fleeing Seoul in 1905.[8] A second explanation, reportedly from his now-deceased mother, Madam Ham, relates that the family disposed of a multivolume set of genealogical records after it got damaged by "rain water leaking through the roof."[9] Regardless of the truth, Pyŏnghae found it hard to bear others looking down on his family for having no genealogy.[10] In the 1980s, he brought home a two-volume genealogy that recorded his grandfather, Pak T'aesik, as a posthumously adopted heir of a local Miryang Pak who had died a century earlier.[11] His cousins in Seoul were unappreciative of this service, finding faults in the newly acquired written genealogy.[12]

Various aspects of the discourse on genealogies in contemporary Korea allow us to think about the importance of studying *chungin* in Korean history. The historiography of pre-1910 Korea has privileged the elite and the aristocracy, and one looks in vain for a *longue durée* history of a nonaristocratic family.[13] The general lack of a more objective history of the majority of the population clearly amounts to ignoring a large part of Korea's past. The demise of late Chosŏn status hierarchy, lingering status anxieties, a relatively sudden shift in the instrument of literacy from classical Chinese to vernacular Korean script (and, for a brief period, Japanese), a modern education system, urbanization, and industrialization have all contributed to the contemporary phenomenon wherein, other than those of aristocratic descent, most Koreans command little knowledge of their actual pre-twentieth-century ancestors. What has emerged in its place is a discourse of family history bounded by early modern master narratives emphasizing royal and aristocratic ancestors of various descent groups identified by a surname and an ancestral seat designation.

Even professional historians studying Korea have not yet narrated the kind of multigenerational history of, say, a peasant family that one can find in other fields.[14] In the 1970s, *minjung*, or people-centered, historiography began stressing ordinary people as the true subjects of history rather than elites, but in spite of their awareness of the use of power relations within Confucian society *minjung* thinkers have offered little critique of the pre-modern model of social and kinship relations.[15] The seemingly heightened awareness of a need for histories that examine all actors has not yet produced a significant body of stories highlighting nonaristocratic families during Korea's transition to modernity. An ever-increasing number of primary sources continue to be translated, reprinted, and converted into searchable databases, but large collections of early modern household registration documents, mostly in Japan, still await a systematic effort toward data digitization and analysis.[16]

Moreover, many contemporary sources on historical Korean personalities give the impression that the normative mode of existence in early modern Korea was that of an aristocrat. Not only do famous individuals (especially intellectuals) remain favorite subjects of research among scholars, but biographical dictionaries and databases—featuring mostly aristocrats—treat nonelites differently.[17] For instance, one such database mentions little about O Kyŏngsŏk's career as an interpreter in terms of the technical specialist ranks and offices that he held but concentrates instead on his significance as a leading early advocate of reform and modernization. In contrast, the entry on his contemporary, Pak Yongdae (1849–n.d.), an aristocratic scholar-official known mainly for supervising the compilation of a government-commissioned encyclopedia, provides all the minutiae of his bureaucratic career.[18] Even more remarkable is an otherwise informative online biographical entry for an eminent Chinese language scholar of *chungin* status, Ch'oe Sejin (1465?–1552), describing his background as "poor and lowly" (*hanmi*),[19] a description that uncritically replicates that given in a sixteenth-century obituary notice prepared by aristocratic court historians.[20]

The manner in which present-day Korean society views its past personalities in conjunction with status hinders a fuller appreciation of diverse human experiences and historical agency. Many may contend that genealogies have no place in a modern society, but such a position seems to assume that genealogy by definition is elitist or feudal.[21] Rather than throwing the baby out with the bathwater, historians can more actively engage the public in promoting a more status-neutral discussion of family records and histories. One approach may be to demonstrate more concrete personal links and continuities between nonaristocratic actors in Korean history and their modern-day descendants by telling more nonelite stories of human interest. Certainly in the case of specialist *chungin*, many of their descendants seem to have found much to be proud of in reflecting on why their ancestors generally welcomed radical change. Eventually, an emerging concept of new family history might allow the majority of Koreans to appreciate the part that their ancestors from all walks of life played in the birth of modern Korea.

Character List

alsŏngsi　謁聖試
An Hansŏng　安漢成
An Kyŏngsu　安駉壽
Andong Kim　安東金
Andong Kwŏn　安東權
Ansan　安山
Ansŏng　安城
Anŭi　安義
Anŭi Kim　安義金
Arai　新井
Asahi　朝日
Asan　牙山

Beijing　北京
bing　炳
bunka seiji　文化政治

ch'abu　車夫
ch'ajang　車匠
Ch'ambong　參奉
Ch'amnyŏnggwan　參領官
Ch'amsŏgwan　參書官

ch'ang　昌
Ch'angdŏk　昌德
ch'angjŏng　倉正
Ch'angnyŏng　昌寧
Ch'angnyŏng Cho　昌寧曺
Ch'angnyŏng Sŏng　昌寧成
Ch'angwŏn Kong　昌原孔
Ch'anin　贊人
ch'anmuwŏn　贊務員
ch'ea kunjik　遞兒軍職
ch'eajik　遞兒職
Ch'in'gun Changwiyŏng Udae 親軍壯
　　衛營右隊
Ch'in'gun Chwayŏng Ch'ogwan 親軍
　　左營哨官
Ch'inil inmyŏng sajŏn　親日人名事典
Ch'oe Huch'an　崔厚賛
Ch'oe Sangnyun　崔尙崙
Ch'oe Sejin　崔世珍
Ch'ojŏng　楚亭
ch'ŏk　尺
Ch'ŏllyŏng Hyŏn　川寧玄

Ch'ŏmji Chungch'ubusa 僉知中樞府事

Ch'ŏmjŏlchesa 僉節制使

Ch'ŏmjŏng 僉正

ch'ŏn 賤

Ch'ŏnan 天安

Ch'ŏndogyo 天道敎

Ch'ŏngdam 清潭

Ch'ŏnggye 清溪

Ch'ŏngjaegong 清齋公

Ch'ŏngju Han 清州韓

Ch'ŏngp'ung Kim 清風金

Ch'ŏngun Kongnip Pot'ong Hakkyo 清雲公立普通學校

Ch'ŏngun Kungmin Hakkyo 清雲國民學校

Ch'ŏngyang 青陽

Ch'ongyungch'ŏng 摠戎廳

ch'ŏp 妾

Ch'owang 草旺

ch'ujŭng 追贈

Ch'ungch'ŏng 忠清

Ch'ungju 忠州

Ch'ungnam Chŏp'o Chusik Hoesa 忠南紵布株式會社

Ch'ungnam Hŭngsan Chusik Hoesa 忠南興産株式會社

Ch'ungnyŏng 祝靈

Ch'usŏk 秋夕

Chamsil 蠶室

chang 昌

changgyo 將校

changin 匠人

changjŏk 帳籍

changmugwan 掌務官

Changnye 掌隷

Changnyewŏn 掌隷院

chapchik 雜職

Cheju 濟州

Chesŏngbo 諸姓譜

chi 枝

Chido 知道

Chigugwan 知彀官

chigyŏk 職役

Chiksan 稷山

chin 鎭

Chinju Chŏng 晋州鄭

Chinju Kang 晋州姜

Chinmyŏng 進明

chinsa 進士

Chinwidae 鎭衛隊

Chipsa 執事

chisangjŏn 紙床塵

Cho Ilche 趙一濟

Cho Pyŏngok 趙炳玉

Cho Toro 趙道魯

Cho Un 趙雲

Cho Yŏngha 趙寧夏

Cho Yuin 曹由仁

chŏk chongson 嫡宗孫

chŏkcha 嫡子

chokpo 族譜

Chŏlch'ung Changgun 折衝將軍

Chŏlla 全羅

chŏn 錢

chŏn Pusayong 前副司勇

Chŏn Sŭngjo 全承祖

Chŏng 正

chŏng 鼎

chŏng 町

Chŏng Ch'ungŏn 鄭忠彦

Chŏng Kŏbok 鄭巨福

Chŏng Naksam　鄭樂三
Chŏng Pyŏngha　鄭秉夏
Chŏng Sinmin　鄭信民
Chŏng Sisul　丁時述
Chŏng Talsun　鄭達順
Chŏng Yagyong　丁若鏞
Chongbusi　宗簿寺
chŏngjik　正職
Chŏngjo　正祖
Chongno　鍾路
Chŏngnyŏnggwan　正領官
chongson　宗孫
Chŏngsŏn-bang　貞善防
Chŏnhwakwa　電話課
Chŏnju Yi　全州李
Chŏnun'guk　轉運局
Chōsen Ginkō　朝鮮銀行
Chōsen Shokushan Ginkō　朝鮮殖
　産銀行
Chosŏn　朝鮮
chuhyŏn'gun　州縣軍
Chuksan　竹山
chun　俊
Chung　中
chung　中
Chung-bu　中部
Chung-ch'on　中村
Chungch'uwŏn Ŭigwan　中樞院議
　官
Chunghwa　中和
chungin　中人
Chungin naeryŏk chi yakko　中人來歷
　之略考
chungsugi　重修記
chungsun　中旬
chungyun　中尹

Chusa　主事
chwayun　佐尹

ding　鼎

Edo　江戶

Gishi　技士

ha mijŏn　下米廛
Hadong Chŏng　河東鄭
Haegong　海公
Haegwan Kamnisŏ　海關監理署
Haeju　海州
Haeju Kim　海州金
Haeju O　海州吳
hallyang　閑良
Ham Ch'anhŭi　咸燦喜
Ham Chŏngyu　咸正酉
Hamyŏl Namgung　咸悅南宮
Han (river)　漢
Han (dynasty)　漢
Han Man'gŭn　韓萬根
hanbok　韓服
*Han'guk yŏktae inmul chonghap
chŏngbo sisŭt'em*　한국역대인물종합
　정보시스템
Hanho Nonggong Ŭnhaeng　漢湖
　農工銀行
hanmi　寒微
Hansan　韓山
Hansŏng　漢城
Hansŏng Chŏn'gi Hoesa　漢城電氣
　會社
Hansŏng Nonggong Ŭnhaeng
　漢城農工銀行

Hansŏng Sabŏm Hakkyo　漢城師
　範學校
Hansŏng Ŭnhaeng　漢城銀行
Hanyang Yu　漢陽劉
Hiroshima　廣島
Hŏ Chusŏng　許住成
Hŏ Hŭp　許洽
Hŏ Imsŏng　許任成
hoejang　會長
hojang　戶長
Hong Kong　香港
Hong Kyŏngnae　洪景來
Hong Sunmok　洪淳穆
Hongju　洪州
Hongju Kongnip Pot'ong Hakkyo
　洪州公立普通學校
Hongsan　鴻山
Hŏnjŏng Yŏn'guhoe　憲政研究會
Howich'ŏng　扈衛廳
huan　煥
Hŭijŏng　熙政
Hullyŏn Togam　訓鍊都監
Hullyŏndae　訓鍊隊
Hullyŏnwŏn　訓鍊院
hundo　訓導
Hŭngsŏn Taewŏn'gun　興宣大院君
hwan　煥
Hwang Hyŏn　黃玹
Hwanghae　黃海
Hwangju　黃州
Hwanjae　瓛齋
Hwasŏng　華城
Hwasu　花水
Hwasun Ch'oe　和順崔
hwawŏn　畵員
hyang　鄉
hyanggyo　鄉校

hyangni　鄉吏
Hyangwŏn　香遠
hyangyak　鄉約
Hyegyŏng　惠慶
hyŏn　賢
hyŏn　縣
Hyŏn Hakku　玄學垢
Hyŏn Hyangun　玄鄉運
Hyŏn Sŏngmun　玄錫文
Hyŏn Sun　玄楯
Hyŏn Ŭn　玄㵦
Hyŏn'gam　縣監
Hyŏngjo　刑曹
Hyŏnjong　顯宗
hyŏnmo yangch'ŏ　賢母良妻
Hyŏnnae　縣內

i　二
i (distance unit)　里
i (provincial subdistrict)　里
Ich'ŏn　利川
Ihwa Kodŭng Yŏ Hakkyo　梨花高
　等女學校
Ijo P'ansŏ　吏曹判書
Ilsan　一山
Imch'ŏn　林川
Imo　壬午
Imsi Kyowŏn Yangsŏngso　臨時敎
　員養成所
Inch'ŏn　仁川
Indong Chang　仁同張
Inhyŏn　仁顯
Ipchŏng-dong　笠井洞
Isŭp　肄習
Iunsa　利運社

Jiandao　間島

Jin 金

jing 景

jinshi 進士

jun 俊

juren 舉人

k'an 칸

Kabo 甲午

kach'ul 加出

Kaebyŏk 開闢

Kaehwa sasang 開化思想

Kaehwa-dang 開化黨

Kaesŏng 開城

Kajwap'yo 家坐表

Kamdong Tangsang 監董堂上

Kamdonggwan 監董官

kamgwan 監官

Kamni 監理

kamsa 監事

Kangnŭng Yu 江陵劉

Kangwŏn 江原

kansawŏn 幹事員

Kap'yŏng 加平

Kap'yŏng Kongnip Pot'ong Hakkyo
  加平公立普通學校

Kapsin 甲申

Kasŏn Taebu 嘉善大夫

Kaya 伽倻

Keijō 京城

ki 氣

kigwan 記官

Kiho Hŭnghakhoe 畿湖興學會

Kim Ch'angyun 金昌允

Kim Chinhwan 金晉桓

Kim Chonggu 金鍾九

Kim Chŏnghyŏn 金鼎鉉

Kim Chungbyŏk 金重璧

Kim Chungjin 金重鎮

Kim Hakku 金鶴九

Kim Hangno 金學魯

Kim Hŭigyun 金憙均

Kim Ingnam 金翼南

Kim Kisŏk 金箕錫

Kim Kyŏngbok 金景福

Kim Kyuhong 金奎弘

Kim Kyusik 金奎植

Kim Munsik 金文植

Kim Ohŭng 金五興

Kim Oryong 金五龍

Kim Pŏmu 金範禹

Kim Ponggyu 金奉圭

Kim Pyŏngsi 金炳始

Kim Sangil 金尙逸

Kim Sangnyuk 金尙六

Kim Seman 金世萬

Kim Sŏnghan 金宬漢

Kim Sŏngji 金聖之

Kim Sŏngsu 金性洙

Kim Tonggwan 金東觀

Kim Yonghwa 金容和

Kimhae 金海

Kimhae Kim 金海金

Kimje 金堤

kisaeng 妓生

Ko Yŏnggŭn 高永根

Koch'ang 高敞

Koguryŏ 高句麗

Kojong 高宗

Kojong Ŏjin Tosa Togam ŭigwe
  高宗御眞圖寫都監儀軌

kokumin gakkō 國民學校

kokuminfuku 國民服

Komatsu Kaneyoshi 小松兼吉

Kŏmnyul 檢律

Kong　孔

Kong Sŭngt'ak　孔承鐸

Kongjo Ch'amŭi　工曹參議

Kongju　公州

kongnip pot'ong hakkyo　公立普通學校

kongsin　功臣

kōritsu futsū gakkō　公立普通學校

Koryŏ　高麗

Koryŏ Kongsandang　高麗共産黨

Koyang　高陽

ku　區

Kukch'ae Posang Undong　國債報償運動

Kŭm　錦

Kŭmsan　錦山

Kŭmwiyŏng　禁衛營

kun　郡

Kun'guk Kimuch'ŏ　軍國機務處

kun'gwan　軍官

kun'gyo　軍校

kunbyŏng　軍兵

kungjang　宮匠

kungmin hakkyo　國民學校

kungminbok　國民服

Kungnae-bu　宮內府

Kunjagam　軍資監

Kunsan　群山

Kunsan Cheil Kongnip Pot' ong Hakkyo　群山第一公立普通學校

Kunsu　郡守

Kwanghaegun　光海君

Kwangju　廣州

Kwangju Yi　廣州李

Kwangmu　光武

Kwangt'ongsa　廣通社

kye　契

Kye-dong　桂洞

Kyemyŏng Kurakpu　啓明俱樂部

Kyŏmsabok　兼司僕

kyŏng　景

kyŏng　慶

Kyŏngch'algwan　警察官

kyŏnggang　京江

Kyŏnggi　京畿

Kyŏnggi Sangŏp Kodŭng Hakkyo　京畿商業高等學校

Kyŏnggi Torip Kapchong Sangŏp Hakkyo　京畿道立甲種商業學校

Kyŏnggi-do　京畿道

Kyŏnghyo-jŏn　景孝

Kyŏngju　慶州

Kyŏngju Ch'oe　慶州崔

Kyŏngmo　景慕

Kyŏngmyŏng　景明

Kyŏngsang　慶尚

Kyŏngsŏng　京城

Kyŏngsŏng Kodŭng Pot'ong Hakkyo　京城高等普通學校

Kyŏngsŏng Pangjik Chusik Hoesa　京城紡織株式會社

Kyŏngsŏng Sangŏp Hoeŭiso　京城商業會議所

Kyŏngsŏng Ŭihak Chŏnmun Hakkyo　京城醫學傳門學校

Kyŏngun　慶運

kyŏngwi　警衛

Kyoryŏn'gwan　敎鍊官

kyosaeng　校生

kyowi　校尉

Kyujanggak　奎章閣

Kyujŏnggong　糾正公

Kyunyŏk samok　均役事目

mabyŏng　馬兵
Maech'ŏn　梅泉
Maech'ŏn yarok　梅泉野錄
Maedong Kongnip Pot'ong Hakkyo
　梅洞公立普通學校
mama　媽媽
Man'gyŏng　萬頃
manho　萬戶
Mansŏng taedongbo　萬姓大同譜
Map'o　麻浦
marŭm　마름
Matsui Keishirō　松井慶四郎
Meiji　明治
Mieyama　三江山
Mieyama Hagiko　三江山萩子
Mieyama Heiji　三江山平治
Mieyama Hiroshi　三江山弘
Mieyama Sachiko　三江山幸子
Mieyama Shigeru　三江山茂
Milsŏng　密城
Milsŏng Taegun　密城大君
Min Chino　閔鎭五
Min Kyŏmho　閔謙鎬
Min Kyuho　閔奎鎬
Min Sangsun　閔常淳
Min T'aeho　閔泰鎬
Min Yŏngch'ŏl　閔泳喆
Min Yŏnghwi　閔泳徽
Min Yŏngjun　閔泳駿
Min Yujung　閔維重
Ming　明
Minjok Munje Yŏn'guso　民族問題
　研究所
Minjŏkpŏp　民籍法
minjung　民衆
Miryang Pak　密陽朴
Miryang Pak-ssi sebo　密陽朴氏世譜

Miyang　美陽
Mokp'o　木浦
Muan　務安
mudang　巫堂
Mukchŏng-dong　墨井洞
mukwa　武科
Mun Seyŏng　文世榮
Munhwa Yu　文化柳
munkwa　文科
munoe mijŏn　門外米廛
murokkwan　無祿官
Muwi Tot'ongsa　武衛都統使
Muwiso　武衛所
Muwiyŏng　武衛營
Muye pyŏlgam　武藝別監
myŏn　面
Myŏng　命
myŏng　命
Myŏnghye Kongjubang　明惠公主房
Myŏngsin Yŏ Hakkyo　明新女學校
Myŏngsŏng　明成

Naesamch'ŏng　內三廳
naet'angjŏn　內帑錢
Nagan Kim　樂安金
Nagan O　樂安吳
Nai-Sen ittai　內鮮一體
Najŏng　羅井
Naju Chŏng　羅州鄭
Naju Kim　羅州金
Namgung Chin　南宮鎭
Namgung Ŏk　南宮檍
Namhan　南漢
Namin　南人
Namp'yŏng Cho　南平曺
Namwŏn Yang　南原梁
nangch'ŏng　郎廳

Nanjing 南京
Nippon Yūsen Kabushiki Kaisha
　日本郵船株式会社
Nodong Kongje 勞動共濟
nokkwan 祿官
noksa 祿事
nononghoe 勞農會
Noron 老論
Nowŏn 蘆原
Nŭnggok 陵谷
Nŭngsŏng Ku 綾城具

o 五
O Kyŏngsŏk 吳慶錫
O Sech'ang 吳世昌
O Sigyŏng 吳時璟
O Susik 吳秀植
O Tojŏng 吳道貞
O Ŭnghyŏn 吳膺賢
ŏbyu 業儒
Odŏk 五德
Okch'ŏn 沃川
Okch'ŏn Chŏn 沃川全
okchŏng 獄正
Oksan 玉山
Ŏm 嚴
Onyang 溫陽
Onyang Pang 溫陽方
Oso 吾所
Owi 五衛
Owijang 五衛將
Ŏyŏnggun 御營軍

p'a 派
P'aeng Hanju 彭翰周
P'aeng Tŭktae 彭得大
P'ap'yŏng 坡平

p'okto 暴徒
p'un 뜐
P'unggyŏng 豊慶
p'yŏng 坪
P'yŏngan 平安
P'yŏngsan Sin 平山申
P'yŏngt'aek 平澤
P'yŏngyang 平壤
Paech'ŏn 白川
paejong inwŏn 陪從人員
paejong taesin 陪從大臣
Paeksŏk 白石
Pak Ch'anggil 朴昌吉
Pak Ch'angnae 朴昌來
Pak Chaesin 朴在信
Pak Changhwan 朴章煥
Pak Chega 朴齊家
Pak Chibŏn 朴枝蕃
Pak Chihan 朴枝漢
Pak Chihyŏn 朴枝玄
Pak Chijae 朴枝材
Pak Chinsik 朴震植
Pak Chisŏng 朴枝盛
Pak Chiyŏng 朴枝英
Pak Chonghwan 朴宗煥
Pak Chu 朴胄
Pak Chun'gi 朴準基
Pak Chungsan 朴仲山
Pak Hyŏkkŏse 朴赫居世
Pak Hyŏn'gyŏng 朴賢慶
Pak Inhŭi 朴仁姬
Pak Isu 朴二壽
Pak Kiin 朴起仁
Pak Kŭndong 朴根東
Pak Kyŏngjun 朴慶俊
Pak Kyŏngmu 朴景茂
Pak Kyŏnguk 朴景郁

Pak Kyuhwan　朴奎煥

Pak Kyusu　朴珪壽

Pak Man'gi　朴萬基

Pak Manju　朴萬柱

Pak Minhwan　朴玟煥

Pak Myŏnghwan　朴明煥

Pak Myŏngŏp　朴命業

Pak Ŏnch'im　朴彦忱

Pak Pyŏnggang　朴炳康

Pak Pyŏnghae　朴炳海

Pak Pyŏngsŏn　朴炳鮮

Pak Pyŏnguk　朴炳旭

Pak Samsu　朴三壽

Pak Sangdŭk　朴尙得

Pak Sasu　朴四壽

Pak Simmun　朴審問

Pak Sun'gang　朴順江

Pak Sŭngjik　朴承稷

Pak Sŭngyŏng　朴昇英

Pak Sunhŭi　朴順姬

Pak T'aesik　朴泰植

Pak Taedŭk　朴大得

Pak Tohŭi　朴道姬

Pak Tŏkhŭi　朴德姬

Pak Tŏkhwa　朴德華

Pak Tongsu　朴東壽

Pak Ŭijun　朴儀俊

Pak Ŭn'gyŏng　朴恩慶

Pak Wŏn'gyŏng　朴元慶

Pak Yongdae　朴容大

Pak Yŏngho (son of Chu)　朴永浩

Pak Yŏngho (son of Yusin)　朴永浩

Pak Yŏngil　朴英一

Pak Yŏngnok　朴永錄

Pak Yŏngsŏk　朴永錫

Pak Yunsik　朴潤植

Pak Yusin　朴有信

palgiin　發起人

pang　防

Pang Chin'gi　方震夔

Pang Chŏnghwan　方定煥

Pang Hanch'ŏl　方漢喆

Pang Handŏk　方漢德

Pang Kyech'ang　方繼昌

Pang Munyŏng　方文榮

Pang Seyang　方世讓

Pang Ujŏng　方禹鼎

Pibyŏnsa tŭngnok　備邊司謄錄

pido　匪徒

piryu　匪類

Pisŏwŏn　秘書院

poin　保人

Pojinjae　寶晉齋

pon'gwan　本貫

Pongsa　奉事

ponkwa　本科

Pŏpchŏn　法典

pŏpkwan　法官

Poryŏng　保寧

Posŏng Chŏnmun Hakkyo　普成專門學校

pu　部

Pu Wiryŏm　夫尉廉

puhoejang　副會長

Puhogun　副護軍

puin　夫人

Puk-ch'on　北村

p'un　分

Pun Sijong　分侍從

Puram-sa　佛巖寺

Pusa　府使

Pusan　釜山

Pusayong　副司勇

Puyŏ　扶餘

Puyun 府尹
pyŏlchang 別將
pyŏlchŏng 別正
Pyŏlgigun 別技軍
Pyŏlmadae 別馬隊
Pyŏlmusa 別武士
pyŏng 炳
pyŏngjŏng 兵正

Qing 清
qing 慶

Sa 四
sa 史
Sado 思悼
sadon 查頓
Saemunan 새문안
saengwŏn-chinsa si 生員進士試
Sagwa 司果
sahak 邪學
sajagwan 寫字官
sajang 私匠
Sajik 司直
Sajŏng 司正
Sakai Naka 酒井仲
Sam 三
sama 司馬
samch'ŏl-li kŭmsu kangsan
三千里錦繡江山
Samgangsan 三江山
Samhwa 三和
samil che 三日製
sang 尙
sang mijŏn 上米廛
sanjik 散職
sanjik 山職
Sap'an Wiwŏn 查辦委員

saryŏng 使令
Sayak 司鑰
Sayŏgwŏn 司譯院
Sayong 司勇
se 歲
Segŏmjŏng 洗劍亭
Seja Igwisa 世子翊衛司
Sejong sillok 世宗實錄
Seoul 서울
Seudan 世友團
shan 善
shang 尙
shō gakkō 小學校
si 市
sik 植
silchik 實職
Silla 新羅
Sillok 實錄
sillyang yŏkch'ŏn 身良役賤
Sin Albet'ŭ 申알베트
Sin Hŏn 申櫶
Sin Ikhŭi 申翼熙
sin yŏsŏng 新女性
Sinjŏng 新井
Sinmyŏng Hakkyo 新明學校
sinsa 申巳
Sirhak 實學
Siwidae 侍衛隊
sŏ 署
sŏ 庶
sŏ 壻
Sŏ Chaep'il 徐載弼
Sŏ Chonghwi 徐宗徽
So Chunghwa 小中華
so hakkyo 小學校
Sŏ Myŏngu 徐命祐
Sŏch'ŏn 舒川

Sŏdae-mun 西大門
Sŏdaemun 西大門
sŏdang 書堂
Sŏgang mijŏn 西江米廛
Sŏgigwan 書記官
sogo 束伍
Sŏgyŏng 西京
Sŏjŏng ilgi 西征日記
sŏk 石
Sŏksŏng 石城
sŏn 善
sŏn 善
Sŏn'gonggam 繕工監
Sŏngjin 城津
Sŏngwŏllok 姓源錄
Sŏnhwa 宣化
Sŏnjo 宣祖
Sŏnjŏn'gwan 宣傳官
Sŏnmu kun'gwan 選武軍官
sŏnyŏ 庶女
sŏŏl 庶孽
Sop'a 小波
sŏri 胥吏
Soron 少論
Sŏso-mun 西小門
Sŏsomun 西小門
sŏwŏn 書院
Ssijok wŏllyu 氏族源流
Such'im 水砧
sudŏk 水德
sugun 水軍
Sujong mugwan 隨從武官
Sukchong 肅宗
sulla pijang 巡邏裨將
Sumundong-gye 水門洞契
sun'gŏm 巡檢
Sŭng 丞

sŭngjŏk 承嫡
Sŭngjŏngwŏn ilgi 承政院日記
Sŭngmunwŏn 承文院
Sungmyŏng 淑明
Sungmyŏng Yŏja Kodŭng Pot'ong
    Hakkyo 淑明女子高等普通學校
Sunhŏn 純獻
Sunhŭng An 順興安
Sunjo 純祖
Sunjong 純宗
suryŏng 守令
susin 修身
Suwŏn 水原
Suzuki Yōtarō 鈴木要太郎

T'ae 泰
T'aegŭk 太極
T'aegŭk Hakhoe 太極學會
T'aegŭk hakpo 太極學報
T'aengniji 擇里志
t'ogwan 土官
T'ongdŏngnang 通德郎
T'onggong 通共
T'ongjŏng Taebu 通政大夫
T'ongni Kimu Amun 統理機務衙門
T'ongsinsa 通信使
T'ongun 通雲
Tae Chosŏn Chŏma Chesa Chusik
    Hoesa 大朝鮮苧麻製絲株式會社
Taech'i 大致
taech'ŏng 大廳
Taedaejang 大隊長
Taedongpŏp 大同法
Taegu 大邱
Taegu Sŏ 大邱徐
Taehan Ch'ŏnil Ŭnhaeng 大韓天
    一銀行

Taehan Chaganghoe 大韓自强會
Taehan Cheguk 大韓帝國
Taehan Hyŏphoe 大韓協會

Taejang 大狀
taejŏng 隊正
taenyŏn'gun 待年軍
taesang 大相
Taiping 太平
Tang 唐
tangha 堂下
Tanyang 丹陽
Tanyang U 丹陽禹
Tasan 茶山
to 道
Tŏgwŏn 德源
Tŏgyu 德裕
tohwa 圖畵
tojang 導掌
Tŏksu 德水
Tŏksu Kongnip Pot'ong Hakkyo
　德水公立普通學校
Tokugawa 德川
Tokyo 東京
tong 洞
Tonga ilbo 東亞日報
Tongdae-mun 東大門
Tonghak 東學
Tongji Chungch'ubusa 同知中樞府
　事
Tongnae Chŏng 東萊鄭
Tongnip Hyŏphoe 獨立協會
Tongnip sinmun 獨立新聞
Tongnipkwan 獨立館
toryŏng 都領
Tosa 都事
Tsushima 對馬島

Tŭkchin'gwan 特進官

U 禹
U Ch'anggi 禹昌基
U Ch'angjae 禹昌在
U Changch'un 禹長春
U Chisŏn 禹止善
U Hangjŏng 禹恒鼎
U Hangsŏn 禹恒善
U Hŭiyŏng 禹憙英
U Kimyŏng 禹夔命
U Kŭmbong 禹金鳳
U Kyŏngmyŏng 禹敬命
U Kyŏngsŏn 禹慶善
U Maengsŏn 禹孟善
U Murip 禹武立
U Myŏngjŏn 禹命傳
U Pŏmsŏn 禹範善
U T'aehyŏng 禹泰亨
U T'aewŏn 禹泰元
U Tŏgun 禹德運
U Tŏgwŏn 禹德遠
Uhu 虞侯
ŭigwe 儀軌
Ŭisŏng Kim 義城金
Ŭmjuk 陰竹
ŭmsŏ 蔭敍
Ŭnjin 恩津
uri 郵吏
Urimwi 羽林衛
Usŏn 藕船

wangdo 王道
Wanggol 왕골
wiwŏn 委員
wŏn 圓
wŏnjŏk 原籍

wŏnjong kongsin 原從功臣

Wŏnsan 元山

wŏnyŏk 員役

wu 五

xian 賢

yang 良

yang 兩

Yang Cheha 양제하

Yang Chuha 梁柱夏

yangban 兩班

Yangch'ŏn Hŏ 陽川許

Yanghwa 良化

Yesan 禮山

Yi 李

Yi Ch'aeyŏn 李采淵

Yi Chihyŏn 李智賢

Yi Chongch'un 李鍾春

Yi Chunghwan 李重煥

Yi Haegon 李海坤

Yi Haesuk 李海淑

Yi Hakkyun 李學均

Yi Hŭngmu 李興懋

Yi Ilho 李一浩

Yi Injwa 李麟佐

Yi Kŭnbae 李根培

Yi Kyŏngha 李景夏

Yi Namsu 李南洙

Yi Sangjŏk 李尚迪

Yi Sunsin 李舜臣

Yi Suyong 李秀鎔

Yi T'aegyŏng 李太京

yŏbu 女夫

Yŏhŭng Min 驪興閔

Yŏng 英

yŏng 永

yong 永

Yonggang P'aeng 龍岡彭

Yongin 龍仁

Yŏngjang 營將

Yŏngjo 英祖

Yŏngmae 亦梅

Yŏngŭijŏng 領議政

Yongyangwi 龍驤衛

Yŏnsan 連山

Yu Honggi 劉鴻基

Yu Yŏnghŭi 劉永喜

Yu Yŏngnyŏl 劉永烈

yuhak 幼學

yuhyŏp 遊俠

Yukpang 六房

Yulhak Pyŏlche 律學別提

yulkwa 律科

Yun Ch'iho 尹致昊

Yun Hyojŏng 尹孝定

Yun Kyusŏp 尹奎爕

Yunghŭi 隆熙

yusaengan 儒生案

Yusŏk 維石

Yu-ssi taedongbo 劉氏大同譜

Zhaoshangju 招商局

zhen 鎮

zhi 植

zhi 枝

Zhou 周

Notes

Prologue

1. As discussed in Chapter 1, a coupling of a surname and an ancestral seat designation has historically denoted a particular patrilineal descent group, which, by the early modern era (ca. 1500–ca. 1880), crystallized into a detailed pedigree showing elite descent. Well before the official emancipation of slavery in 1894, the overall population of Koreans who were most likely not to have a surname, the slaves, had begun declining sharply in the late eighteenth century, although contributing factors are not well understood. See Palais, *Confucian Statecraft and Korean Institutions*, 251. In the extant household registration documents dated between 1896 and 1907, I see not a single case of a male without a surname. Catalogued as *"Kankoku koseki seisatsu,"* the original set, in 165 bound volumes (*ch'aek*), is at Kyōto Daigaku Sōgō Hakubutsukan. I consulted the microfilm copy at Langson Library (Microfilm M 000797), University of California, Irvine. Every citation in this book refers to the document as simply *hojŏk* (household registration) and gives year, household head's name, and address.

2. Literally meaning "two orders," the term *yangban* originally referred to incumbent civil and military officials of the Koryŏ period (918–1392). By the early part of the Chosŏn period (1392–1910), if not even earlier, *yangban* designated the aristocracy in the sense of an ascriptive status one could only inherit rather than achieve. Song Chunho, *Chosŏn sahoesa yŏn'gu*, 171–80; Wagner, "The Korean Chokpo as a Historical Source," 1–3; and Palais, *Politics and Policy in Traditional Korea*, 6–9.

3. Younger North Koreans tend to not know their ancestral seats, though older citizens do. Among the latter, they generally do not have a detailed knowledge of any particular branch affiliation, but some speak of descent from or connection to a historically famous personality known by the same surname–ancestral seat combination. This situation reflects the official ideology of the North Korean state denouncing

"feudal" customs. Especially since the 1990s, as the North Korean state put more effort into excavating and displaying archeological and historical artifacts, more citizens seem to have become aware of the concepts of ancestral seat and genealogy (*chokpo*). For example, in 1992, when the government undertook various excavation projects in Kaesŏng, the capital of the Koryŏ dynasty, Wang Chisŏng, an elderly resident ostensibly descended from the Koryŏ royal family, reportedly began showing his children an old genealogy (dated 1905) that his family had kept for decades. The son, who until then had known nothing about his ancestry, thinks his father apparently never felt the need to display such a feudal artifact under the socialist system. He recalls that before dying two years later, his father told him and the rest of the family much about their ancestors—instilling in them a strong pride in their roots. Kim Chiyŏng, "Sahoe chuŭi to chabon chuŭi to anin, Nam-Puk habŭipŏp ŭro unyŏngdoel t'ongil kukka ŭi yet sudo," accessed June 8, 2011, http://www.minjog21.com/news/read.php?idxno=264.

4. The increasing number of such couples, however, prompted the government to allow every few years a window period during which they could register their marriages as well as their children. In July 1997, the constitutional court ruled that the legal prohibition did not agree with the constitution (though it was not unconstitutional) and stipulated that the law shall expire, if not amended, by January 1, 1999. *Tonga ilbo*, July 16, 1997. Because of heated debate between the supporters and critics of the old prohibition, however, only in March 2005 was the legislature able to pass a revised set of civil laws (effective January 2008) reflecting the ruling. *Tonga ilbo*, March 4, 2005.

5. For years in the United States, I have taught a course on modernity in East Asia. For the course, I conduct an informal survey on how many students have ever met their more distant cousins. Whether raised in East Asia or in the United States, students of East Asian patrilineal descent are far less likely to have met such cousins than the students of Western European patrilineal descent. Not knowing much about the more recent history of one's family arguably reflects the degree of institutional discontinuity that separates contemporary, postcolonial Korea from premodern, or precolonial, Korea. The rapid, late industrialization and urbanization processes have broken up traditional kinship groups not just through migrations of the members but also because of the widely varying social trajectories they took up. Lett, *In Pursuit of Status*, 223.

6. I based this observation on the students of Korean descent that I have taught in Korean history courses since 1998. Typically, I have the students ask their parents or grandparents whether they have heard anything about any family member's involvement in the March First Movement.

7. Chapter 1 discusses the history of the term *chungin*.

8. For an example of English-language discussion highlighting prominent *chungin* as modernizers and pro-Japanese collaborators, see Kyung Moon Hwang, *Beyond Birth*, 106–60.

9. As discussed in Chapter 6, since the late nineteenth century a majority of specialist *chungin* and their descendants have turned their backs on the culture of genealogy compilation.

10. Eugene Y. Park, "Old Status Trappings in a New World," 173–78.

11. Representative reference material is *Han'guk minjok munhwa taebaekkwa sajŏn* (hereafter *HMMTS*). Compiled by the Academy of Korean Studies, this twenty-seven-volume encyclopedia of Korean culture features probably the largest number of entries on Korean persons.

12. Park, "Old Status Trappings in a New World," 168, 178–79.

13. Ibid., 157–60. Also, Chapter 6 discusses these patterns in further detail.

14. Chungang Ilbosa, *Sŏngssi ŭi kohyang* (hereafter *SK*), 1418.

15. Han Yŏngu, *Tasi ch'annŭn uri yŏksa*, 412.

16. Representative studies include Han Yŏngu, "Chosŏn hugi 'chungin' e taehayŏ," 66–89; Cho Sŏngyun, "Chosŏn hugi Sŏul chiyŏk chungin seryŏk ŭi sŏngjang kwa han'gye," 235–49; Kim Yangsu, "Chosŏn hugi sahoe pyŏndong kwa chŏnmunjik chungin ŭi hwaltong," 174–80; Yi Namhŭi, "Chosŏn sidae (1498–1894) chapkwa ipkyŏkcha ŭi chillo wa kŭ ch'ui," 241–72; and Song Mano, "1851 nyŏn ŭi chungin t'ongch'ŏng undong kwa Chosŏn hugi chungin ch'ŭng ŭi tonghyang," 133–60.

17. Examples include Kim Yangsu, "Chosŏn hugi yŏkkwan kamun ŭi yŏn'gu," 97–151; Son Sukkyŏng, ed., *Chungin Kim Pŏmu kamun kwa kŭdŭl ŭi munsŏ*; and Kim Tuhŏn, "Chosŏn hugi chungin ŭi sŏryu mit ch'ŏp e taehan ch'abyŏl," 33–66.

18. They include Kang Myŏnggwan, "Chosŏn hugi kyŏng ajŏn sahoe ŭi pyŏnhwa wa yŏhang munhak," 109–48; Chŏng Husu, *Chosŏn hugi chungin munhak yŏn'gu*; and Chŏng Okcha, *Chosŏn hugi chungin munhwa yŏn'gu*.

19. For example, see Yi Hunsang, "Chosŏn hugi ŭi hyangni wa kŭndae ihu idŭl ŭi chinch'ul," 244–74; and Kyung Moon Hwang, *Beyond Birth*, 106–60.

20. Overall, modern scholarship on Korean history has stressed the agency of—roughly in the following order—the Korean nation, rising new socioeconomic forces, the masses or the "*minjung*," women, and ethnocultural minorities. Exemplary works are too numerous to cite. Three representative studies are Sin Ch'aeho, *Chosŏn saron*; Paek Namun, *Chosŏn sahoe kyŏngjesa*; and Yi Kibaek, *Han'guksa sillon*.

21. Park, "Old Status Trappings in a New World," 176–77.

22. For a recent English-language presentation of this observation, see Kyung Moon Hwang, *Beyond Birth*, 107–17.

23. This assessment often centers around three prominent leaders of nonaristocratic backgrounds. They are Yun Ch'iho (pen name Chwaong, 1865–1945), descended from an illegitimate son of an aristocratic official; Ch'oe Namsŏn (1890–1957), from a specialist *chungin* family; and Yi Kwangsu (1892–n.d.), who hailed from a northwestern regional elite family. For a recent English-language discussion, see Kyung Moon Hwang, *Beyond Birth*, 74–75, 147–51, 248–49.

CHAPTER 1

1. T'onggyech'ŏng, "Ch'ong chosa in'gu (2000): sŏngssi, pon'gwan," *Kukka t'onggye p'ot'ŏl,* accessed June 8, 2012, http://kosis.kr/abroad/abroad_01List.jsp.

2. Ibid.

3. For a South Korean newspaper report on the phenomenon, see *Chosŏn ilbo,* November 29, 2000.

4. Eponymous ancestors of most of the Paks, most of the ostensibly Silla royal descent Kims, most of the supposedly Kaya royal descent Kims, and all the Chŏnju Yi respectively are King Kyŏngmyŏng (Pak Sŭngyŏng, r. 917–23), King Kyŏngsun (Kim Pu, r. 927–35), Kim Sangjwa (fl. early tenth century), and Yi Kŭnghyu (fl. tenth century). *SK,* 165–66, 226–27, 641, 742. No reliable primary source, however, links a tenth-century individual of the surname Pak, Kim, or Yi to any of the four individuals.

5. A South Korean individual using a more common surname–ancestral seat combination is less likely to find himself or a recent ancestor in the genealogy of the descent group in which he ostensibly belongs. Thus, for example, in the case of the Miryang Pak, the second largest descent group (population 3,031,478 in 2000) in South Korea, roughly just 13 percent appear in known Miryang Pak genealogies, whereas the Muns, numbering some 420,000 in 2000, report that about 170,000 (42 percent) appear in the Mun genealogy. I estimated the Miryang Pak figure of 13 percent on the basis of the fact that the descent group's largest segment, the Kyujŏnggong branch (*p'a*), which allegedly accounts for 70 to 80 percent of all Miryang Pak recorded in a genealogy, produced a sixteen-volume genealogy of its members in 1981, and the estimated number of individuals recorded in the set was no more than 200,000. *Miryang Pak-ssi Kyujŏnggong-p'a taedongbo* (1980), 1.256, "Pal." In comparison, eleven other segments of the Miryang Pak are much smaller in population, as is clearly suggested by the size of individual genealogy sets. The Mun figure is according to their website, which offers a searchable genealogy database. In sum, in South Korea the percentage of people who actually can find themselves in their respective descent group genealogy is somewhere between 10 and 50 percent. T'onggyech'ŏng; and Mun Pyŏngdal, "Chokpo kŏmsaek," *Namp'yŏng Mun-ssi chŏnja taedongbo menyu,* accessed June 8, 2012, http://www.moonsi.com.

6. I offer pro bono service to anyone seeking a more professional analysis of a Korean genealogy. Of all the contemporary Korean genealogies that I have examined over the years, I find that roughly half of them present claims that contradict early twentieth-century or older editions.

7. For a discussion of a surname having an association with a particular Y-chromosome type defined by certain markers, see Sykes, "Surnames and the Y Chromosome," 1417–18. On Y chromosomes of Jewish men of priestly tradition, see Skorecki et al., "Y Chromosomes of Jewish Priests," 32; Thomas et al., "Origins of Old Testament Priests," 138–39; and Boster, Hudson, and Gaulin, "High Paternity

Certainties of Jewish Priests," 967–70. Studies show that in terms of direct male descent, multiple haplogroups are found among modern Korean men, including 25–40 percent who share a common haplotype, O3-M122, with about 55 to 65 percent of Chinese males and roughly 15 to 25 percent of Japanese men. The O3-M122 haplogroup derives from a mutation that took place between ten thousand and thirty thousand years ago in southern or southwestern China, and the spread of rice cultivation seems linked to the rapid increase and expansion of the descendant population. Bing Su et al., "Y-Chromosome Evidence for a Northward Migration of Modern Humans into Eastern Asia During the Last Ice Age," 1718–24; Wook Kim et al., "Y Chromosome DNA Variation in East Asian Populations and Its Potential for Inferring the Peopling of Korea," 75–83; Underhill et al., "The Phylogeography of Y Chromosome Binary Haplotypes and the Origins of Modern Human Populations," 43–62; Hong Shi et al., "Y-Chromosome Evidence of Southern Origin of the East Asian-Specific Haplogroup O3-M122," 408–19; Seung-Bum Hong et al., "Y-chromosome Haplogroup O3-M122 Variation in East Asia and Its Implications for the Peopling of Korea," 1–8; Jin et al., "Y-chromosome Haplogroup C Lineage and Implications for Population History of Korea," 253–59; and Jin, Tyler-Smith, and Kim, "The Peopling of Korea Revealed by Analyses of Mitochondrial DNA and Y-Chromosomal Markers," 1–8.

8. For a discussion of cross-class pursuit of status from the seventeenth to the nineteenth century as evident in military examination rosters, see Eugene Y. Park, *Between Dreams and Reality*, 153.

9. Yi Sugŏn, *Han'guk chungse sahoesa yŏn'gu*, 60–69. Besides passing the examination that even the aristocracy began to hold in higher regard over protection or "shadow privilege" appointments (*ŭmsŏ*), functionaries continued to enter officialdom through far less prestigious functionary or clerical positions in the central government. Regardless of their origins, though, the families producing central officials for generations constituted the aristocracy. Duncan, *The Origins of the Chosŏn Dynasty*, 52–86. For classic studies on the Koryŏ protection appointment system, see Pak Yong-un, *Koryŏ sidae ŭmsŏje wa kwagŏje yŏn'gu*; and Kim Yongsŏn, *Koryŏ ŭmsŏ chedo yŏn'gu*.

10. Duncan, *Origins of the Chosŏn Dynasty*, 31–32, 53, 144.

11. Deuchler, *The Confucian Transformation of Korea*, 53.

12. Duncan, *Origins of the Chosŏn Dynasty*, 155, 190–91.

13. Between 1383 and 1390, the government made the local functionaries who had somehow acquired an office resume their hereditary obligations and made it difficult for them to take the examination without satisfying very narrowly defined rank and documentation criteria. *Koryŏsa* 75.48b–49a. I have yet to encounter a single case where a family of clearly nonaristocratic status as of the late fourteenth century somehow joined the aristocracy through an examination degree, a court rank, or an office.

14. I based the following discussion on Deuchler, *Confucian Transformation of Korea*, 207–30, 232–36, 267–73; and Peterson, *Korean Adoption and Inheritance*, 20–21.

15. The following discussion is based on Wagner, "Two Early Genealogies and Women's Status in Early Yi Dynasty Korea," 28–30; Peterson, *Korean Adoption and Inheritance*, 104–6, 163–64, 189–90; and *HMMTS*, s.v. "Andong Kwŏn-ssi Sŏnghwabo" [The Chenghua era-edition Andong Kwŏn genealogy].

16. The following discussion is based on Kawashima, "Lineage Elite and Bureaucracy in Early Yi to Mid-Yi Dynasty Korea," 8–17; Wagner, "Two Early Genealogies," 26–31; Peterson, *Korean Adoption and Inheritance*, 7; and *HMMTS*, s.v. "Kajŏngbo" [The Jiajing era-edition genealogy].

17. Wagner, "Two Early Genealogies," 26–28; and Peterson, *Korean Adoption and Inheritance*, 160–62.

18. *Ssijok wŏllyu*, 260, 668–69.

19. Haboush, *A Heritage of Kings*, 23–24; and Haboush, "Constructing the Center," 62–81.

20. Yi Sugŏn, *Han'guk chungse sahoesa yŏn'gu*, 21–33.

21. Song Ch'ansik, "Chokpo ŭi kanhaeng," 50–66; and Paek Sŭngjong, "Wijo chokpo ŭi yuhaeng," 67–85.

22. Park, *Between Dreams and Reality*, 132–41.

23. Song Chunho, *Chosŏn sahoesa yŏn'gu*, 84–88; and Yi Hunsang, "19 segi Chŏlla-do Koch'ang ŭi hyangni segye wa Sin Chaehyo," 247.

24. This was certainly the case with the Paks, as discussed in Chapter 3.

25. Song Chunho, *Chosŏn sahoesa yŏn'gu*, 32; and Yi Sugŏn, *Han'guk chungse sahoesa yŏn'gu*, 32.

26. Yi Sŏngmu, "Chosŏn ch'ogi ŭi kisulgwan kwa kŭ chiwi," 193–229; and Han Yŏngu, "Chosŏn hugi 'chungin' e taehayŏ," 72–79.

27. *Sejong sillok*, 148.1a–155.17b. On the concept of indigenous surnames, see Yi Sugŏn, *Han'guk chungse sahoesa yŏn'gu*, 34–39.

28. Hyŏn Ŭn, *Chungin naeryŏk chi yakko*, as cited in *HMMTS*, s.v. "Chungin" [*Chungin*].

29. *HMMTS*, s.v. "Chungin."

30. Chŏng Yagyong, "Kajwap'yo," as cited in *HMMTS*, s.v. "Chungin."

31. Chŏng Yagyong, *Kyunyŏk samok*, as cited in *HMMTS*, s.v. "Chungin."

32. Hwang Hyŏn, *Maech'ŏn yarok*, 1a.40–41; and Yi Chunghwan, *T'aengniji*, as cited in *HMMTS*, s.v. "Chungin."

33. *HMMTS*, s.v. "Chungin."

34. *HMMTS*, s.v. "Ch'eajik" [Temporary stipend posts].

35. *HMMTS*, s.v. "Hanp'um sŏyongpŏp" [Law of appointment according to rank limit].

36. Yi Sŏngmu, "Chosŏn chŏn'gi chungin ch'ŭng ŭi sŏngnip munje," 34–36; Kim Yangsu, "Chosŏn hugi sahoe pyŏndong kwa chŏnmunjik chungin ŭi hwaltong," 175–78; and *HMMTS*, s.v. "Hanp'um sŏyongpŏp."

37. *HMMTS*, s.v. "Hyangni" [Local functionary].

38. *HMMTS*, s.v. "Changgyo" [Military officer].

39. This is the farthest I can push back in time in terms of a documented usage of "Miryang" as the ancestral seat by a member of the family, Pak Chaesin (1797–n.d.), discussed in Chapter 3. He appears as a Miryang Pak in the sources recording his son-in-law, Kong Sŭngt'ak (1833–n.d.), as a jurist examination passer (1859). Han'gukhak Chungang Yŏn'guwŏn, "Kong Sŭngt'ak," *Han'guk yŏktae inmul chonghap chŏngbo sisŭt'em*, accessed June 8, 2012, http://people.aks.ac.kr/index.aks.

40. For an example of this story as told in a surname reference work, see *SK*, 740.

41. T'onggyech'ŏng.

42. Ibid.

43. Pak Chongjae, "Silla p'al taegun punbong hŏgu sŏl e taehan koch'al," *Pan-nam Pak-ssi homp'eiji*, accessed December 19, 2011, http://www.bannampark.org/park01_12.htm.

44. *Ssijok wŏllyu*, 141–48, 179.

45. For example, see *Miryang Pak-ssi sebo*, 8b; Miryang *Pak-ssi Kyujŏnggong-p'a sebo*, 1.65a; and *Miryang Pak-ssi Ch'ŏngjaegong che samja Sajikkong p'abo*, 1.17–21.

46. *Miryang Pak-ssi Kyujŏnggong-p'a sebo*, 1.65a; and *Miryang Pak-ssi Ch'ŏngjaegong che samja Sajikkong p'abo*, 1.17–21.

47. *Miryang Pak-ssi chokpo*, 1.42, 6.33–34; and *Miryang Pak-ssi Kyujŏnggong-p'a taedongbo* (1980), 1.285–86, 15.449–56.

48. Wagner, "Korean Chokpo as a Historical Source," 5.

49. Chŏng Haeŭn, "Pyŏngja Horan sigi kun'gong myŏnch'ŏnin ŭi mukwa kŭpche wa sinbun pyŏnhwa," 72–99.

50. *Chŏngch'uk chŏngsi mun-mukwa pangmok*, "Mukwa pangmok," 1b, 3a; *Injo sillok*, 34.60a, 35.24a, 35.31a; and Im Inmuk, *Mukwa ch'ongyo*, 2.39b. Unless a specific source is cited, all military examination passer-related statistics throughout this study derive from my unpublished database (a Microsoft Access file) of 35,053 degree holders. Since 1996, I have been collecting information on them from various primary sources such as military examination rosters, *Veritable Records* (*Sillok*), military examination graduate genealogies (*mubo*), local gazetteers, and local *yangban* registers. Among the passers of the 1637 examination, a majority of whom were slave soldiers, was a junior fourth military rank holder, O Cheryang (1608–n.d.), whose descendants went on to constitute the prominent *chungin* Haeju O family, famous for modern reform movement leaders such as O Kyŏngsŏk (pen name Yŏngmae, 1831–79) and his son, O Sech'ang (pen name Wich'ang, 1864–1953). Chapter 3 discusses the father at some length.

51. *Miryang Pak-ssi Kyujŏnggong-p'a sebo*, 1.65a.

52. Ibid.

53. The oldest ostensibly comprehensive Sunhŭng An genealogy that I consulted is the *Sunhŭng An-ssi chokpo*, compiled in 1783.

54. Unfortunately the record is least complete for the earlier Chosŏn period. On the extent to which extant licentiate rosters are complete, see Ch'oe Chinok, *Chosŏn sidae saengwŏn-chinsa yŏn'gu*, 21–23.

55. The two offices are mentioned on *Miryang Pak-ssi Kyujŏnggong-p'a sebo*, 1.65a.

56. Ibid., 1.65a.

57. Also, the latest edition of the ostensibly comprehensive Ch'ŏngju Han gene-alogy is now searchable through a database, "Ch'ŏngju Han-ssi int'ŏnet chokpo," *Ch'ŏngju Han-Ssi Chungang Chongch'inhoe*, accessed May 1, 2011, http://www.cheongjuhan.net.

58. *Miryang Pak-ssi Kyujŏnggong-p'a sebo*, 1.65a.

59. Ibid., 1.65a.

60. *Naju Chŏng-ssi taedongbo*, 1.1–3, 5–7, 2.324–28.

61. *Miryang Pak-ssi Kyujŏnggong-p'a sebo*, 1.65a.

62. Ibid., 1.65a.

63. *Sarŭng Togam ŭigwe*, 215a.

64. Kiin's wife and father-in-law appear on *Miryang Pak-ssi Kyujŏnggong-p'a sebo*, 1.65a.

65. *Sŏngwŏllok*, 102–3; and *Chŏnju Yi-ssi Changch'ŏn-gun p'abo*, 1.42–46.

66. *Sŭngjŏngwŏn ilgi*, 202.88a (1667.6.23), 203.18a (1667.7.12), "Wŏnmun charyo kŏmsaek," *Sŏul Taehakkyo Kyujanggak Han'gukhak Yŏn'guwŏn*, accessed May 7, 2012, http://kyujanggak.snu.ac.kr.

67. Im Sŏnbin, "Ko munsŏ rŭl t'onghae pon Chosŏn hugi Chiksan hyanggyo ŭi unyŏng silt'ae," 133–54.

68. This uncatalogued three-volume document is at the Land and Housing Museum (T'oji Chut'aek Pangmulgwan) in Sŏngnam, Kyŏnggi-do. The first volume, covering the year 1679, records 632; the second volume, covering 1697, records 1,767; and the third volume, recording 1,479 soldiers, is missing the part of the front cover where the year would have been indicated. *Han'gyŏre*, November 4, 2007. My contact person at the museum, who asked not to be quoted, confirmed that none of the individuals I was searching for appeared in the source. December 1, 2007.

69. Palais, *Confucian Statecraft and Korean Institutions*, 88–91.

70. *Tonga ilbo*, March 12, 2008.

71. Quinones, "The Prerequisites for Power in Late Yi Korea," 144–47; and Quinones, "Military Officials of Yi Korea," 697–700.

CHAPTER 2

1. For a recent discussion of limited commercialization and urbanization in eighteenth-century Korea, see Yi Hŏnch'ang, "Kŭndae kyŏngje sŏngjang ŭi kiban hyŏngsŏng-gi rosŏ 18 segi Chosŏn ŭi sŏngch'wi wa kŭ han'gye," 103–11.

2. The following discussion on late Chosŏn commerce is based on Palais, *Confucian Statecraft and Korean Institutions*, 778–80, 812–14; and Paek Sŭngch'ŏl (Baek Seung-ch'ol), "The Development of Local Markets and the Establishment of a New Circulation System in Late Chosŏn Society," 152–62.

3. Paek Sŭngch'ŏl, *Chosŏn hugi sangŏpsa yŏn'gu*, 259–302.

4. Park, *Between Dreams and Reality*, 154–58.

5. It is likely that the *yangban*-commoner distinction was clear to most people in the society. Especially from the aristocracy's vantage point, there was nothing a

non-*yangban* could do to make himself into one. Even commoners, to whom purchased ranks and offices may have been more awe-inspiring, would have been hard pressed to believe that the acquisition of such trappings by their own kind meant elevation to *yangban* status. Park, *Between Dreams and Reality*, 158–68.

6. *Sŏngwŏllok*, 861, 866.

7. For a brief discussion on invented traditions, see Hobsbawm, "Introduction: Inventing Tradition," 1–9.

8. Eugene Y. Park, "Imagined Connections in Early Modern Korea, 1600–1894," 19–23.

9. Yi Sugŏn, *Yŏngnam sarim-p'a ŭi hyŏngsŏng*, 3–4.

10. On the Namp'yong Cho (and eventually the Ch'angnyŏng Cho) of Kimhae, see *Kimhae hyangan kŭp Kimhae ŭpchi chŏryak*, 16b–17a; and *Ch'angnyŏng Cho-ssi Sijunggong p'abo* 1:4–6, 26–27.

11. Cho Kang (1622–67) and his son, Cho Iryang (1641–99), both of whom passed the military examination in the seventeenth century, appear in extant military examination rosters as Namp'yŏng Cho. Eighteenth-century documents, though, begin to record Namp'yŏng Cho men as Ch'angnyŏng Cho, including their wives' natal family genealogies and examination rosters. Interestingly, a distant Seoul kinsman of the Kimhae lineage members appear in his early seventeenth-century licentiate examination roster as a Namwŏn Cho, whereas an eighteenth-century member of the Kimhae lineage appears in his wife's genealogy as a Ch'angwŏn Cho. Perhaps the two cases reflect the lineage's transition-phase descent group designation, changing from Namp'yŏng to Namwŏn to Ch'angwŏn to Ch'angnyŏng.

12. *Chŏngjo sillok*, 39.27a.

13. *Sejong sillok*, 149.10b, 150.30a, 151.25a. For recent, in-depth discussions of a specialist *chungin* line making such a claim, see Kenneth R. Robinson, "The Chinese Ancestors in a Korean Descent Group's Genealogies," 89–114; and Kenneth R. Robinson, "Yi Hoe and His Korean Ancestors in T'aean Yi Genealogies," 221–50.

14. *Chŏngjo sillok*, 23.52a, 25.7b.

15. *Yŏyudang chŏnsŏ*, 9.25a.

16. The court stipulated privileges for the minor meritorious subjects' descendants, according to social status. O Kapkyun, "Punmu Kongsin e taehan punsŏkchŏk yŏn'gu," 317–18. For a recent English-language discussion of what motivated nonelite participation, see Jackson, "The 1728 Musillan Rebellion: Resources and the Fifth-Columnists," 39–41.

17. *Yangmu wŏnjong kongsin nokkwŏn*, 61b; and Ch'oe Sŭnghŭi, "Chosŏn hugi wŏnjong kongsin nokhun kwa sinbunje tongyo," 152–53.

18. For a recent English-language overview of the rebellion, see Jackson, 9–16.

19. The posthumous honor is recorded on *Miryang Pak-ssi Kyujŏnggong-p'a sebo*, 13.11a.

20. Ibid., 13.11a.

21. Ibid., 1.65a, 13.11a.

22. Ibid., 13.11a.

23. Ibid., 13.11a–b.

24. *Miryang Pak-ssi Ch'ŏngjaegong che samja Sajikkong p'abo*, 1.243.

25. Kim Tuhŏn, 45–47.

26. *Kyŏnggi-do Ŭmjuk-kun sojae changt'o: Chang Sŏkkyu chech'ul tosŏ munjŏk ryu*, Kyujanggak-assigned document number 2 (prepared in 1759); and *Miryang Pak-ssi Kyujŏnggong-p'a sebo*, 13.11a. In general in late Chosŏn Korea, adoption was more pronounced among aristocratic and *chungin* families than it was among those of lower social status. See Cho Sŏngyun and Cho Ŭn, "Hanmal ŭi kajok kwa sinbun," 128.

27. *Miryang Pak-ssi Kyujŏnggong-p'a sebo*, 13.11a.

28. See Chapters 3, 4, and 5.

29. See Chapters 3 and 4.

30. Pak Kŭndong, interviews by author, Seoul, South Korea, June 1, 1992; and telephone interview by author, Ansŏng, South Korea, September 13, 2004.

31. Park, *Between Dreams and Reality*, 76–78.

32. The *chungin* Miryang Pak descent lines other than that descended from Pak Chisŏng appear on *Sŏngwŏllok*, 436–99.

33. *Miryang Pak-ssi Kyujŏnggong-p'a sebo*, 13.11a–b.

34. Ibid., 13.11b.

35. *Ŭiyŏkchu p'alsebo*, 3.4b; and *Chŏnju Yi-ssi Changch'ŏn-gun p'abo*, 1.227, 2.582.

36. *Miryang Pak-ssi Kyujŏnggong-p'a sebo*, 13.11b.

37. Ibid., 13.11a.

38. Ibid., 13.11a.

39. *Miryang Pak-ssi Kyujŏnggong-p'a sebo*, 13.11a.

40. Ibid., 13.11a.

41. A massive thirteen-volume ostensibly comprehensive set, the 2006 edition Kyŏngju Ch'oe genealogy provides an index. See *Kyŏngju Ch'oe-ssi taedongbo*, vol. 13.

42. *Chungin* Kyŏngju Ch'oe lines appear on *Sŏngwŏllok*, 802–19.

43. For an English-language discussion of government sale of court ranks and office in the late Chosŏn period, see Park, *Between Dreams and Reality*, 128–32.

44. Paek Sŭngch'ŏl, *Chosŏn hugi sangŏpsa yŏn'gu*, 265–66.

45. *Miryang Pak-ssi Kyujŏnggong-p'a sebo*, 13.11a.

46. Ibid., 13.11a; and Kang Man'gil, "Kyŏnggang sangin yŏn'gu," 31. For a more general discussion of the "capital-[Han] River" merchants, see Kang Man'gil, 2–46; Pae Kyubŏm, "Kyŏnggang sangin ŭi chabon ch'ukchŏk kwajŏng kwa chŏn'gae yangsang," 50–79; Yi Uk, "Chosŏn hugi Han'gang-byŏn ŭi sangp'um kyŏngje palchŏn kwa sangŏp chŏngch'aek ŭi pyŏnhwa," 43–57; and Pak Hŭngju, "Sŏul maŭl gut ŭi yuhyŏng kwa kyet'ong," 135–36.

47. *Sŭngjŏngwŏn ilgi*, 444.166b (1708.10.11), "Wŏnmun charyo kŏmsaek," *Sŏul Taehakkyo Kyujanggak Han'gukhak Yŏn'guwŏn*, accessed May 7, 2012, http://kyujanggak.snu.ac.kr; and *Sukchong sillok*, 64.3b.

48. *Sukchong sillok*, 64.3b.

49. *HMMTS*, s.v. "Pyŏlmadae" [Special cavalryman].

50. Yi Kwangnin, "Kyŏngjuin yŏn'gu," 237; Kim Hwajin, *Han'guk ŭi p'ungt'o wa munhwa*, 209; Yi Seyŏng, "18, 19 segi kongmul sijang ŭi hyŏngsŏng kwa yut'ong kujo ŭi pyŏndong," 249; Yi Uk, "18 segi mal Sŏul sangŏpkye ŭi pyŏnhwa wa chŏngbu taech'aek," 152–53; and Cho Yŏngjun, "Chosŏn hugi yŏgaek chuin mit yŏgaek chuinkwŏn chaeron," 11, 17.

51. *Miryang Pak-ssi Kyujŏnggong-p'a sebo*, 13.11a.

52. Ibid., 13.11a; and Pak Hŭibyŏng, "Chosŏn hugi min'gan ŭi yuhyŏp sung-sang kwa yuhyŏp chŏn ŭi sŏngnip," 336, 342–43. Cho Susam (penname Ch'ujae, 1762–1849) wrote *Ch'ujae kii*, an eighteenth-century collection of feats of extraordinary individuals of nonelite social status devoting an entry to Kim Ohŭng as one of several men overcoming tigers. A modern translation of this work is available as Cho Susam, *Ch'ujae kii: 18-segi Chosŏn ŭi kiin yŏlchŏn*, translated by Hŏ Kyŏngjin (2008).

53. *Miryang Pak-ssi Kyujŏnggong-p'a sebo*, 13.11a.

54. *Kŭmwiyŏng tŭngnok*, 82.10a, 84.10a, 89.59a, 91.2b, 92.3a; and *Sŭngjŏngwŏn ilgi*, 1346.98b (1773.12.18), "Wŏnmun charyo kŏmsaek," *Sŏul Taehakkyo Kyujanggak Han'gukhak Yŏn'guwŏn*, accessed May 7, 2012, http://kyujanggak.snu.ac.kr.

55. *Kyŏnggi-do Ŭmjuk-kun sojae changt'o: Chang Sŏkkyu chech'ul tosŏ munjŏk ryu*, Kyujanggak-assigned document number 2 (prepared in 1759).

56. For a discussion of managers' social status, see Kim Yongsŏp, *Chosŏn hugi nongŏp-sa yŏn'gu*, I.397–401.

57. Pak Chunsŏng, "17, 18 segi kungbang-jŏn ŭi hwaktae wa soyu hyŏngt'ae ŭi pyŏnhwa," 261–74; Cho Yŏngjun, "Chosŏn hugi kungbang ŭi silch'e," 278–300; and Yang Sŏna, "18–19 segi tojang kyŏngyŏngji esŏ kungbang kwa tojang ŭi kwan'gye," 176–91.

58. *Yangmu wŏnjong kongsin nokkwŏn*, 9b; Yi Pyŏngdŏk, *Ŭmjuk-kun ŭpchi (Kyŏnggi-do)*, 1:10b; and *Yŏhŭng Min-ssi p'abo*, 13a–b, 23a–b.

59. *Miryang Pak-ssi Kyujŏnggong-p'a sebo*, 13.11a.

60. Ibid., 13.11a; and *HMMTS*, s.v. "Taega" [Promoting a kinsman instead of the individual actually granted a promotion].

61. Pierre Bourdieu's discussion of the possible end result of hysteresis effect and an autonom is useful for a better understanding of such credentials. In what Bourdieu describes as a hysteresis effect, status-conscious, upwardly mobile social elements can seek out diplomas or certificates that were already devalued as meaningful markers of social standing among the old elite. Such hysteresis effect is more pronounced among those further removed from the educational system and hence more likely to be attracted to devalued diplomas. Calling it "autonom," Bourdieu identifies a social realm wherein such devalued diplomas continue to enjoy high prestige. See Bourdieu, *Distinction*, 142–44.

62. *Ŏyŏngch'ŏng chungsun tŭngnok*, 2.27b, 2.84a; and *Ilsŏngnok*, 20.558.*sang* (1794.3.28). Unless noted otherwise, all *Ilsŏngnok* volume and page numbers refer to those of the hard-copy reprint edition.

63. *Miryang Pak-ssi Kyujŏnggong-p'a sebo*, 13.11a.

64. Wagner, "Two Early Genealogies and Women's Status in Early Yi Dynasty Korea," 31.

65. This is in contrast to the *Records of the Royal House* (*Sŏnwŏllok*), completed in 1681, which records all identifiable direct male descendants of the dynasty up to the time of the genealogy's compilation. In contrast, coverage of a descent line with one or more females in the intervening generations stops at the end of a particular page. One unique feature of this work is that it provides the given names of females known to the compilers at the time. For example, see 39.1b. Reprint edition is available as *Chosŏn wangjo sŏnwŏllok* (Kwangmyŏng: Minch'ang Munhwasa, 1992), 10 vols.

66. *Sŭngjŏngwŏn ilgi*, 1346.98b (1773.12.18), "Wŏnmun charyo kŏmsaek," *Sŏul Taehakkyo Kyujanggak Han'gukhak Yŏn'guwŏn*, accessed May 7, 2012, http://kyujanggak.snu.ac.kr.

67. *Kyŏnggi-do Ŭmjuk-kun sojae changt'o: Chang Sŏkkyu chech'ul tosŏ munjŏk ryu*, Kyujanggak-assigned document number 2 (prepared in 1759); and *Miryang Pak-ssi Kyujŏnggong-p'a sebo*, 13.11a.

68. A study of late nineteenth- and early twentieth-century census documents from the counties of Kyŏnggi province near Seoul shows that the Kimhae Kim and the Miryang Pak ranked first and third in population among household heads. See O Sŏng, *Han'guk kŭndae sangŏp tosi yŏn'gu*, 179. Also, the Kimhae Kim and the Miryang Pak have been the two most popular identifiers in South Korea for decades as recorded in the census surveys taken in 1960, 1985, and 2000. Ch'oe Tŏkkyo, *Han'guk sŏngssi taegwan*, 46–47, 62, 270–71, 276; *SK*, 225, 745; and T'onggyech'ŏng. It seems that the overall representation pattern among the most populous descent group designations had become more or less fixed by the end of the nineteenth century, if not much earlier.

69. *Sŭngjŏngwŏn ilgi*, 1405.37a (1777.8.24), "Wŏnmun charyo kŏmsaek," *Sŏul Taehakkyo Kyujanggak Han'gukhak Yŏn'guwŏn*, accessed May 7, 2012, http://kyujanggak.snu.ac.kr.

70. *Kyŏnggi-do Ŭmjuk-kun sojae changt'o: Chang Sŏkkyu chech'ul tosŏ munjŏk ryu*, Kyujanggak-assigned document number 2 (prepared in 1759).

71. *Kyŏnggi-do Ansan-gun Ch'osan-myŏn sojae changt'o: Yong-dong kung chech'ul tosŏ munjŏk ryu*, Kyujanggak-assigned document numbers 1 (prepared in 1752), 4 (prepared in 1757), 5 (prepared in 1745), 6 (prepared in 1753), and 7 (prepared in 1744); and *Kyŏnggi-do Ansan-gun Ch'osan-myŏn sojae changt'o: Yong-dong kung chech'ul tosŏ munjŏk ryu*, Kyujanggak-assigned document number 31 (prepared in 1761).

72. *Kyŏnggi-do Ŭmjuk-kun sojae changt'o: Chang Sŏkkyu chech'ul tosŏ munjŏk ryu*, Kyujanggak-assigned document numbers 3 (prepared in 1777) and 4 (prepared in 1791).

73. *Kyŏnggi-do Ŭmjuk-kun sojae changt'o: Chang Sŏkkyu chech'ul tosŏ munjŏk ryu*, Kyujanggak-assigned document number 10 (prepared in 1778).

74. For a brief recent discussion of the general characteristics of palace land as characterized here, see Ch'oe Yuno, *Chosŏn hugi t'oji soyu ŭi paltal kwa chijuje*, 295–97.

75. *Sŭngjŏngwŏn ilgi*, 1404.117a (1777.8.20), 1405.62a (1777.8.24), "Wŏnmun charyo kŏmsaek," *Sŏul Taehakkyo Kyujanggak Han'gukhak Yŏn'guwŏn*, accessed May 7, 2012, http://kyujanggak.snu.ac.kr.

76. Paek Sŭngch'ŏl, "Development of Local Markets," 170–74; and Ko Tonghwan (Ko Donghwan), "Development of Commerce and Commercial Policy During the Reign of King Chŏngjo," 203–6.

77. Ko Tonghwan, 201–4, 209–11.

78. *Miryang Pak-ssi Kyujŏnggong-p'a sebo*, 13.11a.

79. Ibid., 13.11a.

80. Ibid., 13.11a.

81. Ibid., 13.11a.

82. *Ch'ongyungch'ŏng tŭngnok*, 3.31a.

83. *Taegu Sŏ-ssi chokpo*, 16 (*ryŏ*) b; *Taegu Sŏ-ssi sebo*, *Pyŏng* [3].130–31; and *Miryang Pak-ssi Kyujŏnggong-p'a sebo*, 13.11a.

84. *Yangmu wŏnjong kongsin nokkwŏn*, 9b; *Taegu Sŏ-ssi chokpo*, 16 (*ryŏ*) b; *Taegu Sŏ-ssi sebo*, *Pyŏng* [3].133; and *Yŏhŭng Min-ssi p'abo*, 13a–23b.

85. *Yŏhŭng Min-ssi p'abo*, 19a.

CHAPTER 3

1. Hong Sunmin, "Chŏngch'i chiptan ŭi sŏngkyŏk," 243–45; and Kim In'gŏl, "Chosŏn hugi hyangch'on sahoe kwŏllyŏk kujo pyŏndong e taehan siron," 336–42, 346–47.

2. O Such'ang, *Chosŏn hugi P'yŏngan-do sahoe palchŏn yŏn'gu*, 252–330; and Sun Joo Kim, *Marginality and Subversion in Korea*, 26–34.

3. Kim In'gŏl, "Chosŏn hugi hyangch'on sahoe kwŏllyŏk kujo pyŏndong e taehan siron," 342–46.

4. O Such'ang, "Chuyo chŏngch'aek ŭi silsang," 653–54; and Sun Joo Kim, "Taxes, the Local Elite, and the Rural Populace in the Chinju Uprising of 1862," 1005–6, 1018–21. For an insightful English-language overview of local administration in nineteenth-century Korea, see Karlsson, *The Hong Kyŏngnae Rebellion 1811–1812*, 44–63.

5. Totman, *Pre-Industrial Korea and Japan in Environmental Perspective*, 142–46, 149–60; and Yi Uyŏn, "18-19 segi sallim hwangpyehwa wa nongŏp saengsansŏng," 32–51.

6. For an especially insightful case study on this trend, see Paek Sŭngjong, "18–19 segi Chŏlla-do esŏ ŭi sinhŭng seryŏk ŭi taedu,"1366–67.

7. Whereas recorded references to genealogical forgery issues abound for the reign of Chŏngjo (1776–1800) in such sources as the *Veritable Records*, thereafter the number noticeably decreases. Of course, assessing the nature of this change must take into account the overall less-detailed coverage of post-1800 reigns by the *Veritable Records* and overall internal socioeconomic problems for the dynasty before the impact of Western gunboat diplomacy.

8. Yi Sugŏn, *Han'guk chungse sahoesa yŏn'gu*, 32–33.

9. Ibid., 3–4.

10. Kim Yangsu, "Chosŏn hugi sahoe pyŏndong kwa chŏnmunjik chungin ŭi hwaltong," 180–263; Song Chunho, "Chosŏn sidae ŭi kwagŏ wa yangban mit yangin (2)," 113–23; and Han Yŏngu, "Chosŏn hugi 'chungin' e taehayŏ," 66, 89.

11. Kim Yangsu, "Chosŏn hugi sahoe pyŏndong kwa chŏnmunjik chungin ŭi hwaltong," 204.

12. In the case of O Ŭnghyŏn (1810–77), the father of the famous interpreter and reform advocate O Kyŏngsŏk, he even attained an honorary yet prestigious sinecure rarely given to nonaristocrats, the third minister-without-portfolio (*Chi Chungch'ubusa*), after a successful career as an interpreter. Kim Yangsu, "Chosŏn hugi sahoe pyŏndong kwa chŏnmunjik chungin ŭi hwaltong," 192.

13. Ibid., 184–90.

14. Ibid., 190.

15. Ibid., 200.

16. Yi Namhŭi, "Chosŏn hugi 'chapkwa chungin' ŭi sahoejŏk yudongsŏng," 316–21, 329–30.

17. Kim Yangsu, "Chosŏn hugi sahoe pyŏndong kwa chŏnmunjik chungin ŭi hwaltong," 173.

18. Thus in the case of the aforementioned O Ŭnghyŏn, all five of his sons, including Kyŏngsŏk, passed the interpreter examination. As was true for affluent interpreters at the time, Ŭnghyŏn set up a home school (*kasuk*) where two or three invited interpreters of the highest reputation among his colleagues taught his sons, and Kyŏngsuk passed his examination when he was just sixteen *se* in age. Ibid., 192.

19. Ibid., 176.

20. Ibid., 192.

21. Ibid., 192, 209.

22. Ibid., 206.

23. Ibid., 192–93.

24. The following overview of O Kyŏngsŏk's career is based on ibid., 193–98.

25. For example, during his visit to Beijing in 1880, Pyŏn Wŏn'gyu (1837–96), who hailed from a prominent specialist *chungin* family, met with China's Li Hongzhang (1823–1901) and ultimately conveyed to the Korean court Li's recommendation that Korea enter into a treaty relationship with the United States, commencing with the Korean-American Treaty of 1882. Ibid., 199.

26. On the formation of Pak Kyusu's Enlightenment Thought, see Son Hyŏngbu, *Pak Kyusu ŭi Kaehwa sasang yŏn'gu*, 97–126.

27. For a discussion of the rise of the Enlightenment Party, see ibid., 178–203.

28. *Miryang Pak-ssi Kyujŏnggong-p'a sebo*, 13.11a.

29. Ibid., 13.11a.

30. *HMMTS*, s.v. "Ch'eajik."

31. *Miryang Pak-ssi Kyujŏnggong-p'a sebo*, 13.11a.

32. *Hwasun Ch'oe-ssi taedong sebo*, 1.21–31; and *Miryang Pak-ssi Kyujŏnggong-p'a sebo*, 13.11a.

33. *Hwasun Ch'oe-ssi taedong sebo*, 1.21–31.

34. *Ch'ungch'ŏngnam-do Ŭnjin-Hongsan-gun sojae changt'o: Pak Myŏnghwan chech'ul tosŏ munjŏk ryu*, Kyujanggak assigned document numbers 3 (prepared in 1809), 4 (prepared in 1809), and 5 (prepared in 1810).

35. *Miryang Pak-ssi Kyujŏnggong-p'a sebo*, 13.11a; and Kang Myŏnggwan, "Chosŏn hugi Sŏul sŏngan ŭi sinbunbyŏl kŏjuji,"334–37.

36. *Miryang Pak-ssi Kyujŏnggong-p'a sebo*, 13.11a.

37. *Sŏngwŏllok*, 1002–3; *Yonggang P'aeng-ssi sebo*, 1 (8a)–2 (8b), 8 (11b)–9 (12a), 14 (14b)–15 (15a), 29 (22a)–30 (22b); and *Miryang Pak-ssi Kyujŏnggong-p'a sebo*, 13.11a.

38. *Sŏngwŏllok*, 567–68; *Haeju O-ssi taedongbo*, 1:908–9, 9.919, 9.994–1001; and *Miryang Pak-ssi Kyujŏnggong-p'a sebo*, 13.11a.

39. Ibid., 13.11a.

40. Ibid., 13.11a.

41. Ibid., 13.11a.

42. Ibid., 13.11a.

43. *Sŏngwŏllok*, 587; *Okch'ŏn Chŏn-ssi taedongbo*, 1.19–20, 1.27–31; and *Miryang Pak-ssi Kyujŏnggong-p'a sebo*, 13.11a.

44. *Miryang Pak-ssi Kyujŏnggong-p'a sebo*, 13.11a.

45. Ibid., 13.11a.

46. *Sŏngwŏllok*, 988–90; and *Miryang Pak-ssi Kyujŏnggong-p'a sebo*, 13.11a.

47. *Miryang Pak-ssi Kyujŏnggong-p'a sebo*, 13.11a.

48. *Sŏngwŏllok*, 343–47; and ibid., 13.11a.

49. Kim Yŏngmo, *Chosŏn chibaech'ŭng yŏn'gu*, 414–35; Ch'oe Chonggo, "Kaehwagi ŭi pŏphak kyoyuk kwa Han'guk pŏmnyulga ŭi hyŏngsong," 67–79; and Ch'oe Kiyŏng, "Hanmal Pŏpkwan Yangsŏngso ŭi unyŏng kwa kyoyuk," 47–49. In many cases, Ch'oe Chonggo erroneously equates an individual's ancestral seat (*pon'gwan*) as the place of birth. For a series of articles offering an informative overview of the Chosŏn legal system, including the roles of judicial aides (*Kŏmnyul*), see Kim Chae-mun, "21 segi Han'guk pŏp munhwa ŭi kukche kyŏngjaengnyŏk hyangsang ŭl wihan Han'guk chŏnt'ong pŏp munhwa ŭi kangjwa," (35), 32–53; (36), 5–27; (37), 23–35; (38), 24–36; (39), 17–34; and (40), 28–40.

50. *Sŏngwŏllok*, 935–36; *Ch'angwŏn Kong-ssi chokpo*, 1.1a–2a, 14b, 15b, 2.58b–59b; and *Miryang Pak-ssi Kyujŏnggong-p'a sebo*, 13.11a.

51. *Kongmun p'yŏnan*, 32.127b, "Wŏnmun charyo kŏmsaek," *Sŏul Taehakkyo Kyujanggak Han'gukhak Yŏn'guwŏn*, accessed April 23, 2012, http://kyujanggak.snu.ac.kr; *Kwanbo*, September 26, 1895; *Hullyŏng*, 2 (May 13, 1896), "Wŏnmun charyo kŏmsaek," *Sŏul Taehakkyo Kyujanggak Han'gukhak Yŏn'guwŏn*, accessed May 22, 2012, http://kyujanggak.snu.ac.kr; *Yŏkt'o sogwan munch'ŏp kŏan* (September 28, 1896; October 13, 1896; December 30, 1896); *Yŏkt'o sogwan munch'ŏp naean* (April 12, 1896; August 22, 1896; August 28, 1896; October 5, 1896; October 23, 1896; December 24, 1896); *Yŏkt'o sogwan sawŏn chilbo chondang* (March 22, 1896; April 17, 1896; May 11, 1896; May 17, 1896; September 21, 1896; January 2, 1898; August 12, 1898; February 27, 1899; April 1, 1899); *Yŏkt'o sogwan sawŏn hunji chondang* (February 21, 1896; March 31, 1896; May

23, 1896; September 28, 1896; March 23, 1897; April 8, 1897); and *Yŏkhunji* (August 22, 1898; March 11, 1899; April 15, 1899; November 7, 1899).

52. Ch'oe Yuno, 295–97, 300–1, 348.

53. *Miryang Pak-ssi Kyujŏnggong-p'a sebo*, 13.11a and 32.38a–b.

54. *Sŭngjŏngwŏn ilgi: Kojong*, 10.97 (124b) (1887.8.27), 11.603 (202b) (1891.4.21), 14.1148 (48b) (June 16, 1903), 14.1149 (53a–b) (June 17, 1903), 15.629 (43b)–630 (44a) (February 10, 1906); *Kajarok*, 156b; and *Kwanbo*, June 18, 1903; June 19, 1903; February 14, 1906.

55. *Kuksangsi wŏnyŏktŭng sŏngch'aek chŏngsik*, 89b. On when and how the area became a *chungin* neghborhood, see Cho Sŏngyun, "Sŏul saram ŭi sinbun punp'o wa chugŏ chiyŏk," 107–8.

56. *Miryang Pak-ssi Kyujŏnggong-p'a sebo*, 32.38a–b; and *Miryang Pak-ssi Ch'ŏngjaegong che samja Sajikkong p'abo*, 2.325. In contrast, Kim Hyoyŏng (n.d.), the husband of Yunsik's sister (n.d.) by adoption (and the natural daughter of Pak Yŏngsŏk), held a position in the central bureaucracy. The husband came from the aforementioned *chungin* Kimhae Kim lineage, from which his father-in-law's younger sister's husband had also hailed. Hyoyŏng served as the senior rector (*Tojŏng*) of the Royal House Administration. Other than this, though, we can ascertain nothing about him or his wife, though presumably the couple resided in Seoul. *Sŏngwŏllok*, 343–47; and *Miryang Pak-ssi Kyujŏnggong-p'a sebo*, 13.11a.

57. *Miryang Pak-ssi Kyujŏnggong-p'a sebo*, 13.11a and 32.39b.

58. Kim Tonggwan and Madam Ch'ŏngp'ung Kim appear on *Miryang Pak-ssi Kyujŏnggong-p'a sebo*, 32.39b.

59. *Ch'ŏngp'ung Kim-ssi sebo*, 1.1–2, 1.6–7, 1.66–67, 1.472–73, 3.366–73, 6.1–6, 6.38–40, 6.271–75, 7.444–54.

60. *Miryang Pak-ssi Kyujŏnggong-p'a sebo*, 32.39b; and *Miryang Pak-ssi Ch'ŏngjaegong che samja Sajikkong p'abo*, 2.355. Among the little we know about Chinsik is that he had a sister who married a certain Sin Myŏngguk (n.d.), a P'yŏngsan Sin. *Miryang Pak-ssi Kyujŏnggong-p'a sebo*, 13.11a.

61. *Sŭngjŏngwŏn ilgi*, 1728.76b (1794.4.11), "Wŏnmun charyo kŏmsaek," *Sŏul Taehakkyo Kyujanggak Han'gukhak Yŏn'guwŏn*, accessed May 7, 2012, http://kyujanggak.snu.ac.kr; *Ilsŏngnok*, 28.354 (1799.8.27); and *Ilsŏngnok*, 12811-457.140 (1794.4.10), 12811-576.68 (1797.8.27), 12811-645.13 (1799.8.3), "Wŏnmun charyo kŏmsaek," *Sŏul Taehakkyo Kyujanggak Han'gukhak Yŏn'guwŏn*, accessed March 24, 2012, http://kyujanggak.snu.ac.kr.

62. *HMMTS*, s.v. "Muye pyŏlgam" [Special martial arts officer].

63. For a complete illustration of the painting with identifiable individuals indicated by their names (most rank-and-file military personnel, such as Kyŏnguk, are not indicated), see Han Yŏngu, "*Panch'ado" ro ttara kanŭn Chŏngjo ŭi Hwasŏng haengch'a*, 30–94.

64. *Ilsŏngnok*, 28.354 (1799.8.27); and *Ilsŏngnok*, 12811-576.68 (1797.8.27), 12811-645.13 (1799.8.3), "Wŏnmun charyo kŏmsaek," *Sŏul Taehakkyo Kyujanggak Han'gukhak Yŏn'guwŏn*, accessed March 24, 2012, http://kyujanggak.snu.ac.kr.

65. *Sungjŏng sam kyŏngsin kyŏngkwa chŏngsi pyŏlsi mun-mukwa chŏnsi pangmok: mukwa pang*, 1a–14b; Im Inmuk, *Mukwa ch'ongyo*, 3.61b–62a; and *Chŏngjo sillok*, 52.28b, 54.1a.

66. Yu Sangp'il, *Tongsarok*, Han'guk Kojŏn Pŏnyŏgwŏn, *Han'guk kojŏn chonghap DB*, accessed March 24, 2012, http://db.itkc.or.kr/itkcdb/mainIndexIframe.jsp.

67. A classic case is the interpreter Haeju O line, especially known for O Kyŏngsŏk and O Sech'ang. See Kim Yangsu, "Chosŏn hugi sahoe pyŏndong kwa chŏnmunjik chungin ŭi hwaltong," 191–93.

68. Yu Sangp'il, *Tongsarok*, Han'guk Kojŏn Pŏnyŏgwŏn, *Han'guk kojŏn chonghap DB*; and Lewis, "A Scroll of the 1748 Korean Embassy to Japan Preserved in the British Museum," 79.

69. Chŏng Sŏngil, "Taema-do yŏkchi pingnye e ch'amgahan t'ongsinsa ilhaeng e taehayŏ," 83–84; and Toby, "Carnival of the Aliens," 423.

70. Also, the shogunate seems to have feared that militarily effete Koreans would be unable to defend the sovereignty of their country against the likes of Russia. I would like to thank an anonymous reviewer of an earlier version of this book manuscript for these insights.

71. *Sunjo sillok*, 14.50b.

72. *Ilsŏngnok*, 12813-311.62 (1812.6.9), "Wŏnmun charyo kŏmsaek," *Sŏul Taehakkyo Kyujanggak Han'gukhak Yŏn'guwŏn*, accessed May 6, 2012, http://kyujanggak.snu. ac.kr; and Sunjo sillok, 16.5a.

73. *Kŭmwiyŏng tŭngnok*, 85.61a; *Ilsŏngnok*, 12813-311.62 (1812.6.9), "Wŏnmun charyo kŏmsaek," *Sŏul Taehakkyo Kyujanggak Han'gukhak Yŏn'guwŏn*, accessed May 6, 2012, http://kyujanggak.snu.ac.kr; and Sunjo sillok, 16.5a.

74. *Chedŭngnok*, 4.90b, 4.97b.

75. *Köllŭng Sallŭng Togam ŭigwe*, 163a.

76. *HMMTS*, s.v. "Taenyŏn'gun" [Reservists].

77. *Hyomyŏng Seja Yŏn'gyŏng Myoso Togam ŭigwe*, 1.90b.

78. *Hyŏnmok Subin Changnye Togam ŭigwe*, 1.139a, 2.99b; *Hyŏnmok Subin Hwigyŏngwŏn Wŏnso Togam ŭigwe*, 2.169b; *Hyohyŏn Wanghu Kyŏngnŭng Sallŭng Togam ŭigwe*, 1.65b; *Surŭng Sallŭng Togam ŭigwe*, 1.97a, 1.104a, 1.131b, 1.212b, 2.212b, 2.218b; and *Illŭng Ch'ŏnbong Sallŭng Togam ŭigwe*, 1.110b, 1.145a, 1.201b.

79. *Hwasŏng sŏngyŏk ŭigwe* and Kim Tonguk, *18 segi kŏnch'uk sasang kwa silch'ŏn: Suwŏn-sŏng* (1996), as cited by Munhwa K'ŏnt'ench'ŭ Tatk'ŏm, "Ch'ajang," accessed October 6, 2013, http://tinyurl.com/ma8zeyf.

80. *Ilsŏngnok*, 61.457ha.

81. Ch'oe Hyosik, "Chosŏn sidae Urimwi ŭi sŏngnip kwa kŭ p'yŏnje," 170–87.

82. I would also like to thank Yi Tae-Jin (Yi T'aejin) for sharing with me (July 19, 2006) his insights on the Urimwi.

83. *Ilsŏngnok*, 61.457ha.

84. On the *chungin* Nagan O's remarkable success in interpreter examinations, see Han Migyŏng, "Nagan O-ssi yŏkkwa ipkyŏkcha kirok e taehan yŏn'gu," 426–38.

85. *Nagan O-ssi chokpo*, 1.627; and *HMMTS*, s.v. "Yi Hakkyun."

86. *Nagan O-ssi chokpo*, 1.627; and *HMMTS*, s.v. "Pojinjae."

87. *Chejŏk tŭngbon*, Pak T'aesik, 238 Odŏk-ri, Ch'unghwa-myŏn, Puyŏ-gun, Ch'ungch'ŏngnam-do; and *chejŏk tŭngbon*, Pak T'aesik, 294 Chwahong-ri, Hongsan-myŏn, Puyŏ-gun, Ch'ungch'ŏngnam-do. Whenever cited through the book, a "*chejŏk tŭngbon*" (certified copy of household registration record showing, for a given registration address, all current members as well as once-registered yet no longer current members) indicates the name of the household head (*hoju*) and the address of original registration (*ponjŏk*). Instituted by the Government-General of Korea in 1915, the Republic of Korea (South Korea) government continued to use this format to record its population until the end of 2007. At a district (*ku*, *myŏn*) office, a member of the household or a direct descendant of him or her could request a copy of the registration document, now searchable by the household head's name and the address of original registration.

88. Chu Ja Cho, interview by author, Huntington Beach, California, March 10, 1990; Pak Pyŏnghae, interview by author, Seoul, October 5, 1995; and Pak Kŭndong, telephone interview by author, Ansŏng, South Korea, September 13, 2004.

89. On the Pangs, see Chapter 4.

90. *Chejŏk tŭngbon*, Pak P'yŏngch'i, 294 Chwahong-ri, Hongsan-myŏn, Puyŏ-gun, Ch'ungch'ŏngnam-do; and Pak Yŏngil, telephone interview by author, Taejŏn, South Korea, October 4, 2004.

91. Kang Myŏnggwan, "Chosŏn hugi Sŏul sŏngan ŭi sinbunbyŏl kŏjuji," 331–40. I also thank Kim In-Geol (Kim In'gŏl) and Chu Chin-Oh (Chu Chino) for sharing with me (on July 7 and July 24, 2011, respectively) their insights on the neighborhood's social landscape.

92. *HMMTS*, s.v. "Muwiso" [Military guard agency].

93. *Sŭngjŏngwŏn ilgi: Kojong*, 6.345 (138b) (1878.5.25).

94. *Chigugwanch'ŏng ilgi* 7.189a–b, Han'gukhak Chungang Yŏn'guwŏn, *Han'gukhak Chŏnja Tosŏgwan*, accessed November 30, 2011, http://lib.aks.ac.kr/DLiWeb20/components/searchir/detail/detail.aspx?cid=104554.

95. *Chigugwanch'ŏng ilgi* 7.189b.

96. *HMMTS*, s.v. "O kunyŏng" [Five military divisions].

97. The Military Guard Agency hired T'aesik on the twenty-eighth day of the twelfth lunar month of 1880, and the agency functioned normally until the day of the Imo Military Revolt on the ninth day of the sixth lunar month of 1882. In the lunar year, month, and day format, his duty dates are as follows: 1881.2.15, 1881.2.28, 1881.3.20, 1881.4.10, 1881.4.26, 1881.8.25, 1881.9.5, 1881.9.20, 1881.9.26, 1882.1.15, 1882.1.27, 1882.3.5, 1882.3.25, 1882.4.5, 1882.4.20, 1882.4.25, 1882.5.11, 1882.5.15, 1882.5.25, 1882.5.26. *Chigugwanch'ŏng ilgi*, 8.17b–18a, 8.22b–23a, 8.33a, 8.42a–b, 8.49a, 8.72a–b, 8.77a–b, 8.83a–b, 8.89a, 9.11a–b, 9.20a–b, 9.39b–40a, 9.50b, 9.54b, 9.60b, 9.62b–63a, 9.69b, 9.71a, 9.75a–76a.

98. *Chigugwanch'ŏng ilgi*, 8.49a. Lunar calendar date of T'aesik's assumption of household-head status on his father Yŏngho's death (1881.4.11) is recorded in *chejŏk tŭngbon*, Pak T'aesik, 238 Odŏk-ri, Ch'unghwa-myŏn, Puyŏ-gun,

Ch'ungch'ŏngnam-do; and *chejŏk tŭngbon*, Pak T'aesik, 294 Chwahong-ri, Hongsan-myŏn, Puyŏ-gun, Ch'ungch'ŏngnam-do.

99. *HMMTS*, s.v. "Pyŏlmusa" [Special military officer].

100. *HMMTS*, s.v. "Pyŏlmusa".

101. *Sŭngjŏngwŏn ilgi: Kojong*, 7.812 (168a–b) (1881.12.29), 7.823 (50a–b) (1882.1.7), 7.833 (98a) (1882.1.12), 7.921 (72a–b) (1882.3.10), 7.943 (176a) (1882.3.22); and *Kojong sillok*, 19.16b.

102. *Chigugwanch'ŏng ilgi*, 9.54b; and *Sŭngjŏngwŏn ilgi: Kojong*, 7.959 (25a)–960 (26a) (1882.4.5).

103. Sources of this information are discussed below in the main text.

104. Eugene Y. Park, "Status and 'Defunct' Offices in Early Modern Korea," 748–50.

105. *Yŏnan Yi-ssi Sobugam P'ansagong-p'a taebo* (Seoul, 2002), 1.927.

106. Pak Pyŏnghae, interview by author, Seoul, October 5, 1995.

107. On T'aesik's promotion in October 1902, see Chapter 4.

108. The Qing troops hunted down and executed the ringleaders, most of whom were lower-level officers of commoner status including artillerymen. *HMMTS*, s.v. "Imo kullan" [Imo military revolt].

109. *HMMTS*, s.v. "Muwiso."

110. *Sŭngjŏngwŏn ilgi: Kojong*, 8.5 (1882.6.5).

111. Yong-ho Ch'oe, "The Kapsin Coup of 1884," 116–17.

112. Pak Ŭnsuk, *Kapsin chŏngbyŏn yŏn'gu*, 189.

113. The Tonghak rebels generally were rural commoners and poor local aristocrats with grievances toward government corruption. Young Ick Lew, "The Conservative Character of the 1894 Tonghak Peasant Uprising," 174; and *HMMTS*, s.v. "Tonghak."

114. *HMMTS*, s.v. "Sŏ Chaep'il."

115. Chŏng Haeŭn, "Chosŏn hugi mukwa kŭpcheja yŏn'gu," 9.

116. Chu Ja Cho, telephone interview by author, Chicago, September 27, 2004; Pak Kŭndong, interview by author, Taejŏn, South Korea, July 7, 2007; and Pak Yŏngil, interview by author, Taejŏn, South Korea, July 7, 2007.

117. I am unaware of any detailed study of the mortality rate of mothers giving birth. In the 1990s, though, when I was a Ph.D. student, my advisor, Edward Wagner, mentioned that occasionally one comes across, in a Korean genealogy, a Chosŏn-period entry indicating that a mother died on the day when her child was born.

118. *Chejŏk tŭngbon*, Pak T'aesik, 238 Odŏk-ri, Ch'unghwa-myŏn, Puyŏ-gun, Ch'ungch'ŏngnam-do; *chejŏk tŭngbon*, Pak T'aesik, 294 Chwahong-ri, Hongsan-myŏn, Puyŏ-gun, Ch'ungch'ŏngnam-do; and Pak Yŏngil, interview by author, Taejŏn, South Korea, July 7, 2007.

119. Pak Yŏngil, telephone interview by author, Taejŏn, South Korea, October 4, 2004.

120. *Chejŏk tŭngbon*, Pak T'aesik, 238 Odŏk-ri, Ch'unghwa-myŏn, Puyŏ-gun, Ch'ungch'ŏngnam-do; *chejŏk tŭngbon*, Pak T'aesik, 294 Chwahong-ri,

Hongsan-myŏn, Puyŏ-gun, Ch'ungch'ŏngnam-do; *chejŏk tŭngbon*, Pak Kyŏngjun, [no number] Ch'unghwa-myŏn, Odŏk-ri, Ch'ungch'ŏngnam-do; and Chu Ja Cho, telephone interview by author, Chicago, September 27, 2004. None of these documents show Pak T'aesik's elder daughter's given name, as she was born before the colonial Japanese authority instituted a new household registration system requiring all individuals born thereafter to be registered with their given names. Unless the head of the household registered such females without given names sometime thereafter or the given names are known to posterity through such other sources as oral history, the given names of most Korean females of precolonial era will remain unknown.

121. *Sŭngjŏngwŏn ilgi: Kojong*, 9.174 (119b–120b) (1885.4.21); *chejŏk tŭngbon*, Pak Kyŏngjun, [no number], Odŏk-ri, Ch'unghwa-myŏn, Puyŏ-gun, Ch'ungch'ŏngnam-do; and *Miryang Pak-ssi Kyujŏnggong-p'a sebo*, 13.11a and 32.38a–39b.

122. The male members of this generation appear on *chejŏk tŭngbon*, Pak T'aesik, 238 Odŏk-ri, Ch'unghwa-myŏn, Puyŏ-gun, Ch'ungch'ŏngnam-do; and *chejŏk tŭngbon*, Pak T'aesik, 294 Chwahong-ri, Hongsan-myŏn, Puyŏ-gun, Ch'ungch'ŏngnam-do; and *Miryang Pak-ssi Kyujŏnggong-p'a sebo*, 32.38a–39b.

123. Chu Ja Cho, telephone interview by author, Chicago, September 27, 2004.

124. Kim Yŏngbae, "Hanmal Hansŏng-bu chugŏ hyŏngt'ae ŭi sahoejŏk sŏngkyŏk," 198.

125. Pak Pyŏnghae, interview by author, Seoul, October 5, 1995; Pak Kŭndong, telephone interview by author, Ansŏng, South Korea, September 13, 2004; and Chu Ja Cho, telephone interview by author, Chicago, September 27, 2004.

126. Pak Kŭndong, interview by author, Seoul, September 13, 2004.

127. Kim Yosuk, telephone interview by author, Seoul, January 27, 1992; and Chu Ja Cho, telephone interview by author, Chicago, September 27, 2004. For general information on historical Korean currency units, see *HMMTS*, s.v. "Hwap'ye tanwi" [Currency units].

128. Pak Yŏngil, telephone interview by author, Taejŏn, South Korea, October 4, 2004.

129. Kim Yosuk, telephone interview by author, Seoul, January 27, 1992; Pak Kŭndong, telephone interview by author, Ansŏng, South Korea, September 13, 2004; Chu Ja Cho, telephone interview by author, Chicago, September 27, 2004; Pak Yŏngil, telephone interview by author, Taejŏn, South Korea, October 4, 2004; and Pak Yŏngil, interview by author, Taejŏn, South Korea, July 7, 2007.

130. Cho Sŏngyun and Cho Ŭn, 128–29.

131. Pak Yŏngil, telephone interview by author, Taejŏn, South Korea, October 4, 2004.

132. *NAVER kugŏ sajŏn*, accessed May 10, 2012, http://krdic.naver.com.

133. For a complete list of Okch'ŏn magistrates from 1776 to 1910, see Sin Hŭich'ŏl, *Oean ko*, 102–3.

134. Kim Yosuk, telephone interview by author, Seoul, January 27, 1992; and Chu Ja Cho, telephone interview by author, Chicago, September 27, 2004. How one chooses to refer to the rioters depends on the nature of his or her relationship to them. The fact

that the Paks refer to them as a "violent mob" clearly shows that, at least at the time, they were not sympathetic to the Tonghak cause. In spite of the fact that the current Korean historiography represents the Tonghak as those fighting for their country's good, in the late nineteenth and early twentieth centuries the Koreans on the other side of the conflict used various derogatory labels such as "brigands" (*pido, piryu*) for the Tonghak. Yang Chinsŏk, "Ch'ungch'ŏng chiyŏk nongmin chŏnjaeng ŭi chŏn'gae yangsang," 27. As the available information is frustratingly vague, one can only conclude that the rioters were Tonghak partisans targeting in 1894–95 those they perceived as corrupt or pro-Japanese agents of the state.

135. *Sŭngjŏngwŏn ilgi: Kojong*, 7.424 (31b)–425 (32a) (1881.3.7), 9.111 (24a) (1885.3.5), 9.512 (125b) (1886.1.26), 9.519 (154a–b) (1886.1.29), 9.553 (28b) (1886.3.6), 9.566 (93a) (1886.3.15), 9.567 (98b) (1886.3.15), 9.568 (106b) (1886.3.16), 9.576 (142a–b) (1886.3.22), 9.865 (137a) (1886.12.29), 9.886 (95a) (1887.1.21), 10.23 (29b) (1887.5.29), 10.108 (38b) (1887.9.12), 10.136 (81a) (1887.10.20), 10.431 (16a–b) (1888.8.4), 10.821 (54a–b) (1889.7.18), 11.474 (154b–155a) (1891.1.29), 11.984 (1892.2.9), 12.229 (109a) (1892.7.22), 12.891 (42b) (1894.3.7), 13.22 (102b) (1894.7.19); *Mansŏng taedongbo*, 1:170a–b, 171b, 174b; and *Andong Kim-ssi taedongbo, sup'yŏn*.201, *sup'yŏn*.205–12, 5.1–9, 5.107–8.

136. *Sŭngjŏngwŏn ilgi: Kojong*, 13.107 (11a)–108 (11b) (1894.11.3); Ch'ungbuk Palchŏn Yŏn'guwŏn, *Ch'ungch'ŏngbuk-to Tonghak Nongmin Hyŏngmyŏngsa yŏn'gu*, 15–20, 22, 153–62, 185–91; Chŏn Sunp'yo, "Okch'ŏn-Ch'ŏngsan Tonghak Nongmin Chŏnjaeng kwa Hanmal ŭibyŏng," 127–70; and Ch'ae Kilsun, "Ch'ungch'ŏngbuk-to chungnam-bu chiyŏk Tonghak hyŏngmyŏng-sa yŏn'gu," 57–58.

137. *Chŏnju Yi-ssi Changch'ŏn-gun p'abo*, 1.227.

138. *Chŏnju Yi-ssi Changch'ŏn-gun p'abo*, 2.582–83.

139. *Sŏngwŏllok*, 102–5; and *Chŏnju Yi-ssi Changch'ŏn-gun p'abo*, 1.42–47, 1.210–41, and 2.551–90.

CHAPTER 4

1. For the court's discussion of upgrading Korea's status to that of an empire, see *Sŭngjŏngwŏn ilgi: Kojong*, 13.593 (86b)–594 (91a) (October 11, 1897); and *Kojong sillok*, 35.28b–29a, 36.20a–21a.

2. For example, see Dennett, *Americans in Eastern Asia*, 466–88; and Chandra, *Imperialism, Resistance, and Reform in Late Nineteenth-Century Korea*, 24–84, 211–19. Though not discussing the Empire period per se, Palais offers a classic diagnosis of Chosŏn's inevitable structural demise. See Palais, *Politics and Policy in Traditional Korea*, 285–86. For a brief English-language overview of various perspectives on Imperial Korea, see Kim Do-hyung, "Introduction: The Nature of Reform in the Taehan Empire," 3–9

3. Duncan, "The Confucian Context of Reform," 106–7. A representative study advancing this argument in a general sense is Chu Chino, "Han'guk kŭndae kungmin kukka surip kwajŏng esŏ wangkwŏn ŭi yŏkhwal (1880–1894)," 46–67.

4. Kim Soyŏng, "Yongam-p'o sakkŏn e taehan Taehan Cheguk ŭi wigi ŭisik kwa taeŭng," 148–57; and Kim Hyŏnsuk, "Taehan Cheguk-ki T'akchi-bu komun Allekseyep'ŭ ŭi chaejŏng chŏngch'aek kwa ch'in-Rŏ hwaltong," 86–87.

5. For an argument stressing foreign pressures, rather than leadership or institutional failings, as fundamental causes for Korea's colonization, see Yi Minwŏn, *Myŏngsŏng Wanghu sihae wa Agwan p'ach'ŏn*, 251–63.

6. Yi Tae-Jin (Yi T'aejin) made this observation during a private conversation on August 3, 2001, at Seoul National University.

7. The city indeed had played past roles as the final capital of the ancient Koguryŏ kingdom (n.d.–668) and the Koryŏ dynasty's Western Capital. Interpreters of the post-Koguryŏ history of P'yŏngyang have inextricably linked the city with alleged advocates (such as the Koguryŏ successionist Myoch'ŏng, n.d.–1135, whose rebellion based in the city failed) of an alternative ideological orientation for Korea based in its northwest. This is especially true for studies on Myoch'ŏng's Rebellion in 1135–36, though he did not espouse ""Koguryŏ succession" as portrayed by a nationalist historian, Sin Ch'aeho (pen name, Tanjae, 1880–1936). Rogers, "National Consciousness in Medieval Korea," 152–66; and Breuker, *Establishing a Pluralist Society in Medieval Korea, 918–1170*, 442.

8. This is not to suggest, however, that Imperial Korea traced its historical legitimacy back to China or defined its identity within a China-centered world order. To the contrary, those who were most ardent supporters of Kwangmu Reform rejected the late Chosŏn notion of China as the Middle Kingdom. See Schmid, *Korea Between Empires, 1895–1919*, 56–60.

9. *Sŭngjŏngwŏn ilgi: Kojong*, 14.855 (81a)–856 (82b) (May 1, 1902).

10. Earlier in the 1880s, the Korean monarch's trusted foreign advisers, such as Paul Georg von Möllendorff (1847–1901) had laid the ground for a pro-Russia policy. Mun Hŭisu, "Kukchejŏk chŏnhu kwan'gye e issŏsŏ Agwan p'ach'ŏn—1895–1896," 232–52; Hŏ Tonghyŏn, "Taehan Cheguk ŭi model rŏsŏ ŭi Rŏsia," 58–61; Pae Hangsŏp, "Cho-Rŏ sugyo (1884) chŏnhu Chosŏnin ŭi Rŏsia kwan," 147–48; Kim Yunjŏng and Sŏ Ch'isang, "Kwangmu 6-nyŏn ŭi P'yŏngyang P'unggyŏng-gung ch'anggŏn kongsa e kwanhan yŏn'gu," 178–79; and Kim Chonghŏn, "Rŏsia oegyogwan Beberŭ wa Agwan p'ach'ŏn," 368–88. In 1896, the Korean military adapted the Russian model for training as well as establishing P'yŏngyang as the command headquarters for the northwestern defense troops. Cho Chaegon, "Taehan Cheguk ki kunsa chŏngch'aek kwa kunsa kigu ŭi unyŏng," 108–10; Sŏ Inhan, *Taehan Cheguk ŭi kunsa chedo*, 205–7; and Yang Sanghyŏn, "Taehan Cheguk ŭi kunje kaep'yŏn kwa kunsa yesan unyŏng," 186, 190, 199–200.

11. *Sŭngjŏngwŏn ilgi: Kojong*, 14.862 (3b–4a) (May 6, 1902).

12. *Sŭngjŏngwŏn ilgi: Kojong*, 14.866 (9a)–867 (9b) (May 10, 1902).

13. *Sŭngjŏngwŏn ilgi: Kojong*, 14.869 (22b) (May 14, 1902). This burden on the local population would prove to be so onerous that in the following year the government had to reduce the normally assessed levy by one-third. *Kojong sillok*, 43.1b–2a.

14. Kim Yunjŏng and Sŏ Ch'isang, 181–85.

15. *Kojong Ŏjin Tosa Togam ŭigwe*, 291–304.

16. *Sŭngjŏngwŏn ilgi: Kojong*, 14.991 (9a) (October 5, 1902), 14.991 (10a)–992 (16a) (October 5, 1902). A year later, on November 10, 1903, the two revered portraits were housed in the newly constructed T'aegŭk and Chunghwa halls. *Kojong sillok*, 43.49b.

17. I speak of "iconization" in the sense of an Orthodox Christian depiction of a Christian saint or an emperor (as the vicar of God) as a holy icon standing far closer to the prototype subject than a "vain image" or an idol. Eastern Christianity went through phases of debates and conflict over the meaning of images depicting a holy figure, and each had political and theological dimensions, among others. For a classic discussion, see Brown, "A Dark-Age Crisis: Aspects of the Iconoclastic Controversy," 5–34.

18. The project also resonated with the Western historical precedent of Emperor Constantine I the Great (r. 306–337) building the New Rome in Constantinople as the empire's Christian capital. American Protestant missionaries in Korea saw in the project an opportunity for the city not only to relive its past glory but also to become the Jerusalem of the Orient. Ever since the first Protestant missionaries, Presbyterian physician Horace Allen (1884), Presbyterian minister Horace G. Underwood (1885), and Methodist minister Henry G. Appenzeller (1885) legally entered Korea (though missionary activity per se was still illegal at the time), P'yŏngyang had become especially receptive to Protestantism. Han'guk Kidokkyosa Yŏn'guhoe, *Han'guk Kidokkyo ŭi yŏksa*, 185–86. By 1902, the city's enthusiasm for the newfound faith and the growing number of converts were such that the notion of Imperial Korea's new—and Christian—capital must have excited them.

19. *Kojong Ŏjin Tosa Togam ŭigwe*, 293–305.

20. *Kojong Ŏjin Tosa Togam ŭigwe*, 305–12.

21. For the list that includes Pak T'aesik, see *Kajarok*, 181b–182a; *Kwanbo*, February 14, 1903; and *Ilsŏngnok*, 12816-498.12b–15a, "Wŏnmun charyo kŏmsaek," *Sŏul Taehakkyo Kyujanggak Han'gukhak Yŏn'guwŏn*, accessed May 7, 2012, http://kyujanggak.snu.ac.kr.

22. The Japanese forced the First Korean-Japanese Agreement of February 23, 1904, upon the Korean government. The agreement guaranteed virtually free movement of Japanese troops in Korea, and by June they occupied all the major administrative, communication, and military facilities in South P'yŏngan province, among other regions.

23. Kim Yunjŏng and Sŏ Ch'isang, 185–86.

24. Such appointments appear on *Sŭngjŏngwŏn ilgi: Kojong*, 15.399 (61b–62a) (March 23, 1905), 15.404 (85a–b) (April 1, 1905).

25. This is evident in the fact that for the majority of specialist capital *chungin* descent lines, the *Record of Surname Origins* traces their ancestries back only to the fifteenth or the sixteenth century.

26. After publishing the two original volumes of the *Comprehensive Genealogy of Ten Thousand Surnames* (1931), the compilers put out a supplementary volume

recording descent lines of more questionable aristocratic standing (1933). I exclude such families from consideration here. *Mansŏng taedongbo*, 1.1a–3a; and *Sŏngwŏllok*, 1–9.

27. T'onggyech'ŏng.

28. T'onggyech'ŏng.

29. Wagner, "The Three Hundred Year History of the Haeju Kim *Chapkwa-Chungin* Lineage," 9.

30. Ibid., 7–12. In fact, a 1906 household registration document of Kim Iksŭng (1859–n.d.), a member of the *chungin* Haeju Kim line, indicates his ancestral seat as Ch'ŏngp'ung as well as recording as his adoptive father a member of a prominent *yangban* Ch'ŏngp'ung Kim line. See *hojŏk* [1906], Kim Iksŭng, 29-7 Kyo-dong, Osundŏk-kye, Kyŏnghaeng-bang, [Chung-sŏ], Hansŏng-bu. Today a small population of South Koreans still going by the Haeju Kim identity comprises at least three distinct groups (based in southwestern, northwestern, and northeastern Korea), none of which is related to the *chungin* Haeju Kim. Besides two civil examination passers, during the entire Chosŏn period the three groups produced only military examination and licentiate examination (*saengwŏn-chinsa si*) graduates but no technical examination passer. *SK*, 500–501; and Han'gukhak Chungang Yŏn'guwŏn, "Kwagŏ mit ch'wijae," *Han'guk yŏktae inmul chonghap chŏngbo sisŭt'em*, accessed November 1, 2011, http://people.aks.ac.kr/index.aks.

31. *Milsŏng Pak-ssi chokpo*, 6.26b–27b.

32. Yi Sugŏn, *Han'guk chungse sahoesa yŏn'gu*, 346–52.

33. *Sŏngwŏllok*, 464–66.

34. *Miryang Pak-ssi sebo*, 1.15a–16a. Incidentally, the 1924 Miryang Pak genealogy also records Simmun as the fifth-generation ancestor of Pak Tŏkhwa, the earliest ancestor of the reliable genealogy of the subject family of this book.

35. The roster showing Kong Sŭngt'ak as a jurist examination passer (1859) records his wife as a Miryang Pak and her three patrilineal ancestors, Pak Chaesin, Pak Kyŏngmu, and Pak Sangdŭk—the members of the senior line of our subject family.

36. Whereas the family appears in the 1924 edition genealogy of the Kyujŏnggong branch of the Miryang Pak, the earlier editions compiled in 1620 (one volume), 1662 (one volume), and 1742 (*Miryang Pak-ssi chokpo*, six volumes)—all purporting to cover the entire branch—do not include the family. All three editions are either in private possession or available through auction, and I consulted the digitized version on the web at Pak Chongsun, "Kyujŏnggong-p'a charyosil," *Miryang Pak-ssi Kyujŏnggong-p'a homp'eiji*, accessed November 7, 2007, http://gyujeong.co.kr. The 1924 edition places the family within the Kyujŏnggong branch's subbranch, the Ch'ŏngjaegong branch originating from the aforementioned Pak Simmun, but the 1873 Ch'ŏngjaegong-branch-only Miryang Pak genealogy (thirteen volumes) does not include it. The 1924 edition records the entire senior line but not other lines descended from Pak Tŏkhwa.

37. *Miryang Pak-ssi Kyujŏnggong-p'a sebo*, 1.65a.

38. I have consulted the 1620, 1662, 1742, 1873, 1924, and 1980 editions of the Kyujŏnggong-branch Miryang Pak genealogy. See *Miryang Pak-ssi chokpo*, 1.42a–b; *Miryang Pak-ssi sebo*, 8b; *Miryang Pak-ssi Kyujŏnggong-p'a sebo*, 1.65a; *Miryang*

Pak-ssi Kyujŏnggong-p'a taedongbo (1980), 1.285; *Miryang Pak-ssi Mallyŏk kyŏngsinbo*, Pak Chongsun, "Kyujŏnggong-p'a charyosil," *Miryang Pak-ssi Kyujŏnggong-p'a homp'eiji*, accessed May 13, 2012, http://gyujeong.co.kr; and *Miryang Pak-ssi Sungjŏng iminbo*, Pak Chongsun, "Kyujŏnggong-p'a charyosil," *Miryang Pak-ssi Kyujŏnggong-p'a homp'eiji*, accessed May 13, 2012, http://gyujeong.co.kr.

39. Park, *Between Dreams and Reality*, 153.

40. Chŏng Okcha, part 3, "Chosŏn hugi ŭi kisuljik chungin"; Han Yŏngu, "Chosŏn hugi 'chungin' e taehayŏ," 85–89; Han Yŏngu, "Chosŏn sidae chungin ŭi sinbun-kyegŭpchŏk sŏngkyŏk," 189–91; Chŏng Muryong, "Chosŏn-jo chungin kyech'ŭng sigo (3)," 37–60; and Song Mano, 133–60.

41. Wagner, "The Three Hundred Year History of the Haeju Kim *Chapkwa-Chungin* Lineage," 9–10.

42. *Miryang Pak-ssi Kyujŏnggong-p'a sebo*, 1.65a.

43. *Kajarok*, 181b; *Kwanbo*, February 14, 1903; *Ilsŏngnok*, 12816-498.12b–15a, "Wŏnmun charyo kŏmsaek," *Sŏul Taehakkyo Kyujanggak Han'gukhak Yŏn'guwŏn*, accessed May 7, 2012, http://kyujanggak.snu.ac.kr; and *Kojong Ŏjin Tosa Togam ŭigwe*, 309.

44. Chu Ja Cho, interview by author, Huntington Beach, Calif., March 10, 1990; and Pak Pyŏnghae, interview by author, Seoul, October 5, 1995.

45. For a relevant discussion, see Duus, *The Abacus and the Sword*, 368–76; and Duus "Economic Dimensions of Meiji Imperialism," 161–63.

46. Pak Pyŏnghae, interview by author, Seoul, October 5, 1995; and Pang Kijun, telephone interview by author, Puyŏ, South Korea, October 8, 2007.

47. These figures are according to the recorded examination passers in the genealogy. *Onyang Pang-ssi chang p'a chongbo*, 1.388, 1.455–71, 2.21–51, 4.78–119. Given that this genealogy clearly offers an incomplete coverage of the descendants of Pang Kyech'ang, as well as the fact that genealogies in general can make false claims about examination passing, the actual number of degree holders may be slightly higher—especially in the case of military examination passers including a significant percentage of the kind of socially marginalized individuals left out of genealogies.

48. *Sunjo sillok*, 15.20b–21a, 16.2a–4a; and *Onyang Pang-ssi chang p'a chongbo*, 2.25–26.

49. *HMMTS*, s.v. "Pang Ujŏng."

50. *Onyang Pang-ssi chang p'a chongbo*, 2.35, 4.90–91; Chu Chino, "1898-nyŏn Tongnip Hyŏphoe undong ŭi chudo seryŏk kwa chiji kiban," 178, 182, 186; and *HMMTS*, s.v. "Pang Handŏk."

51. *Onyang Pang-ssi chang p'a chongbo*, 2.35, 4.85; Yi Sanggŭm, *Sarang ŭi sŏnmul*, 28–30; and *HMMTS*, s.v. "Pang Chŏnghwan."

52. Park, *Between Dreams and Reality*, 157–58.

53. *Onyang Pang-ssi chang p'a chongbo*, 1.466–67, 2.42.

54. *Sŭngjŏngwŏn ilgi: Kojong*, 4.451 (3b) (1873.5.1); and *Onyang Pang-ssi chang p'a chongbo*, 1.40–41.

55. *Koyang-gun chimyŏng yuraejip*, 366–67; and *Onyang Pang-ssi taedongbo*, 2.477–78, 2.522–24. A more recent edition of the Pang genealogy, the *Onyang Pang-ssi chang p'a chongbo*, records the relocated sites in Ch'unch'ŏn. See *Onyang Pang-ssi chang p'a chongbo*, 1.466–67, 2.38–42, 4.96–107.

56. Brian Park, interview by author, Santa Ana, Calif., May 26, 2007; Brian Park, e-mail communication, June 4, 2012; Brian Park, telephone interview by author, Laguna Woods, Calif., June 17, 2012; and Kim Yosuk, interview, October 7, 2002.

57. Brian Park, interview by author, Santa Ana, Calif., May 26, 2007; Brian Park, e-mail communication, June 4, 2012; and Brian Park, telephone interview by author, Laguna Woods, Calif., June 17, 2012.

58. Pang Kijun, telephone interview by author, Puyŏ, South Korea, October 8, 2007.

59. *Chejŏk tŭngbon*, Pang Ch'anbŏm, 240 Odŏk-ri, Ch'unghwa-myŏn, Puyŏ-gun, Ch'ungch'ŏngnam-do; and Pang Kijun, telephone interview by author, Puyŏ, South Korea, October 8, 2007.

60. Pang Kijun, telephone interview by author, Puyŏ, South Korea, October 8, 2007.

61. Pak Pyŏnghae, interview by author, Seoul, October 5, 1995.

62. *Kimhae Kim-ssi sŏnwŏn taedong sebo: ch'ong p'yŏn*, 2:147–48.

63. Song Hyŏn'gang, "Ch'ungnam chibang Changno-gyo ŭi chŏllae wa suyong," 36–43. For basic biographical information on Bull, see Kim Sŭngt'ae and Pak Hyejin, *Naehan sŏn'gyosa ch'ongnam, 1884–1984*, 188.

64. "Odŏk Kyohoe yaksa," inscribed on *Odŏk Changno Kyohoe ch'angnip kinyŏmbi*; Chu Ja Cho, interview by author, Huntington Beach, Calif., March 10, 1990; and Pak Pyŏnghae, interview by author, October 5, 1995.

65. Chu Ja Cho interview by author, March 10, 1990; Pak Pyŏnghae interview by author, October 5, 1995; and Pang Kijun, telephone interview by author, Puyŏ, South Korea, October 8, 2007.

66. Chu Ja Cho interview by author, March 10, 1990; Pak Pyŏnghae interview by author, October 5, 1995; and Pak Kŭndong, telephone interview by author, Seoul, September 13, 2004.

67. As noted in Chapter 3, the stated objective of Enlightenment Thought was not Westernization per se, but in practice it entailed imitation of the West, especially various ideas and institutions that were perceived to be superior to non-Western analogues.

68. Song Hyŏn'gang, 33–35, 56–63.

69. *Chejŏk tŭngbon*, Pak T'aesik, 238 Odŏk-ri, Ch'unghwa-myŏn, Puyŏ-gun, Ch'ungch'ŏngnam-do; *chejŏk tŭngbon*, Pak T'aesik, 294 Chwahong-ri, Hongsan-myŏn, Puyŏ-gun, Ch'ungch'ŏngnam-do; *chejŏk tŭngbon*, Pak Kyŏngjun, [no number] Ch'unghwa-myŏn, Odŏk-ri, Ch'ungch'ŏngnam-do; *Yŏnan Yi-ssi sebo*, Kŏnbo, 1.1a–2a, 1.13a–b, 1.22b–23b; *Yŏnan Yi-ssi Sobugam P'ansagong-p'a taebo*, 1.617, 1.619–20, 1.927; Pak Pyŏnghae, interview by author, Seoul, October 5, 1995; Pak Kŭndong, telephone interview by author, September 13, 2004; Chu Ja Cho, telephone interview by author,

Chicago, September 27, 2004; and Pak Yŏngil, telephone interview by author, Taejŏn, South Korea, October 4, 2004.

70. Chu Ja Cho, interview by author, Huntington Beach, Calif., March 10, 1990; Pak Pyŏnghae, telephone interview by author, Seoul, January 27, 1992; Pak Pyŏnghae, interview by author, Seoul, October 5, 1995; and Pang Kijun, telephone interview by author, Puyŏ, South Korea, October 8, 2007.

71. Song Hyŏn'gang, 39, 42–43, 56–63.

72. "Odŏk Kyohoe yaksa"; Song Hyŏn'gang, 43; Chu Ja Cho, interview by author, Huntington Beach, Calif., March 10, 1990; and Pak Pyŏnghae, interview by author, Seoul, October 5, 1995.

CHAPTER 5

1. *HMMTS*, s.v. "Sadon" [Relations through marriage].

2. According to Han'guk Pogŏn Sahoe Yŏn'guwŏn, *2006-nyŏn chŏn'guk kajok pogŏn pokchi silt'ae chosa*, as reported in *Chungang ilbo*, November 13, 2007.

3. Cho Hŭisŏn and Ryu Mihyŏn, "Sarye rŭl t'onghaesŏ pon honsu kwanhaeng munje yŏn'gu," 2, 4–5, 7–12; Kim Sidŏk, "Hollye chŏnt'ong, ta pakkwin kŏt ŭn anida," 97–98; and Hong Nayŏng and Ch'oe Hyegyŏng, "Sŏul chiyŏk ŭi honsu mit yedan p'ungsok e kwanhan yŏn'gu," 211–13.

4. *Hojŏk* (1903), U Ch'anggi, 13-9 Mukchŏng-dong, Och'ŏn-gye, Hundo-bang, Nam-sŏ, Hansŏng-bu; *hojŏk* (1903), U Hangjŏng, 14-2 Mukchŏng-dong, Och'ŏn-gye, Hundo-bang, Nam-sŏ, Hansŏng-bu; *hojŏk* (1906), U Hangjŏng, 33-7 Taerip-tong, Sup'yogyo-gye, Changt'ong-bang, Chung-sŏ, Hansŏng-bu; *chejŏk tŭngbon*, U Hang-jŏng, 27 Kwanch'ŏl-tong, Kyŏngsŏng-bu, Kyŏnggi-do (218 Iptong-jŏng); *Sŏngwŏllok*, 343–47; and *Tanyang U-ssi taedongbo*, 1.479, 2.394–95, 4.412.

5. See *Ssijok wŏllyu*, 681; and *Tanyang U-ssi taedongbo*, 1.345.

6. *Tanyang U-ssi chokpo*, 1.54b.

7. For the genealogy covering the generations mentioned, see *Tanyang U-ssi tae-dongbo*, 1.345, 1.479, 2.394–95, 4.410–12. In the case of the aforementioned U Hang-jŏng, a government document once erroneously recorded him by his earlier name, "U Hangsŏn," and printed a correction. See *Chungch'uwŏn naemun*, 2.90a.

8. *Tanyang U-ssi taedongbo*, 1.345, 1.478–79.

9. U Pŏmsŏn, *P'yŏngsaeng iryŏksa*, as cited in Yun Hyojŏng, 108.

10. *Oean*, 1.19a–b; *Sŭngjŏngwŏn ilgi: Kojong*, 13.628 (78b) (November 20, 1897); and *Tanyang U-ssi taedongbo*, 1.479, 2.394–95, 4.410–12.

11. *Kwanbo*, October 12, 1898; June 14, 1899; November 17, 1899; November 28, 1899; January 28, 1900; and June 7, 1902; *Sŭngjŏngwŏn ilgi: Kojong*, 14.133 (41a) (November 15, 1899), 14.143 (89b) (November 25, 1899); and *Tanyang U-ssi taedongbo*, 4.412.

12. *Kwanbo*, June 14, 1899; and *Sŭngjŏngwŏn ilgi: Kojong*, 13.950 (179a) (December 12, 1898).

13. *Kwanbo*, November 17, 1899; and *Sŭngjŏngwŏn ilgi: Kojong*, 14.143 (89b) (November 25, 1899).

14. *Hwangsŏng sinmun*, October 10, 1898; and Chu Chino, "1898-nyŏn Tongnip Hyŏphoe undong ŭi chudo seryŏk kwa chiji kiban," 178, 201, 203.

15. See Chu Chino, "19 segi huban Kaehwa kaehyŏngnon ŭi kujo wa chŏn'gae," 91–103, 131–55, 171–221; and Chin-Oh Chu (Chu Chin-Oh), "The Independence Club's Conceptions of Nationalism and the Modern State," 72–77.

16. *Hwangsŏng sinmun*, March 27, 1907.

17. "Hoewŏn myŏngbu," 65.

18. *HMMTS*, s.v., "Taehan Hyŏphoe" [Korean association].

19. "Ponhoe kisa," 51.

20. *Hwangsŏng sinmun*, June 13, 1899.

21. *Hojŏk* (1903), U Ch'anggi, 13-9 Mukchŏng-dong, Och'ŏn-gye, Hundo-bang, Nam-sŏ, Hansŏng-bu.

22. *Taehan maeil sinbo*, January 19, 1908; and *Tongnip sinmun*, February 26, 1898. As of 1906, the size of his tile-roofed mansion was 69 *k'an*. See *hojŏk* (1906), Yi Kŭnbae, 32-6 Sorip-tong, Yusaik-kye, Changt'ong-bang, Chung-sŏ, Hansŏng-bu. In the same year, even his concubine's tile-roofed mansion was 42 *k'an* in scale. See *hojŏk* (1906), Yi Kŭnbae, 32-3 Sorip-tong, Yusaik-kye, Changt'ong-bang, Chung-sŏ, Hansŏng-bu.

23. *Hojŏk* (1903), U Ch'anggi, 13-9 Mukchŏng-dong, Och'ŏn-gye, Hundo-bang, Nam-sŏ, Hansŏng-bu.

24. *Hwangsŏng sinmun*, March 27, 1907; *chejŏk tŭngbon*, U Hangjŏng, 27 Kwan-ch'ŏl-tong, Kyŏngsŏng-bu, Kyŏnggi-do (218 Iptong-jŏng); and Pak Yŏngil, telephone interview by author, Taejŏn, South Korea, October 4, 2004.

25. *Hwangsŏng sinmun*, May 19, 1906.

26. *Hwangsŏng sinmun*, March 6, 1908; April 23, 1908; May 26, 1908; September 15, 1908; October 22, 1908; February 17, 1909; February 21, 1909; May 19, 1909; May 25, 1909; and November 30, 1909.

27. *Tongnip sinmun*, June 12, 1897. I would also like to thank Kent Davy, Barbara Wall, Frank Hoffmann, and Wayne Patterson for helping me identify the British and the Americans mentioned only by their surnames in the newspaper. E-mail from Kent Davy, May 11, 2012; Barbara Wall, May 11, 2012; Frank Hoffmann, May 11, 2012; and Wayne Patterson, May 11, 2012.

28. Incidentally, as discussed, Hangjŏng's kin by marriage, Pak T'aesik, and the latter's kinsmen had landholdings in South Ch'ungch'ŏng province's western coastal region, producing ramie fabric, though I have yet to confirm their role in this venture, if any.

29. Chŏng Yagyong, *Kyŏngse yup'yo*, 8.16b–17a, as cited in Yi Chongbŏm and Ch'oe Wŏn'gyu, ed., *Charyo Han'guk kŭnhyŏndaesa immun*, 23–24.

30. *Tongnip sinmun*, June 12, 1897.

31. *Hwangsŏng sinmun*, May 19, 1906; May 21, 1906; and June 1, 1906.

32. *Hwangsŏng sinmun*, June 3, 1906; June 4, 1906; June 5, 1906; June 6, 1906; June 7, 1906; June 8, 1906; and June 10, 1906.

33. Yi Sŭngnyŏl, *Cheguk kwa sangin*, 221–25.

34. *Maeil sinbo*, December 25, 1917; January 13, 1918; May 21, 1918; June 8, 1918; June 9, 1918; June 23, 1918; June 25, 1918; June 29, 1918; July 2, 1918; July 3, 1918; July 4, 1918; July 6, 1918; July 13, 1918; July 17, 1918; August 1, 1918; and August 20, 1918.

35. Aside from the dated argument for late Chosŏn sprouts of capitalism, currently two main arguments on the origins of Korean capitalism highlight, respectively, the Korean Empire period and the colonial era. For classic studies taking these positions, see Eckert, *Offspring of Empire*, 253–59; and Yi Sŭngnyŏl, 353–59.

36. *Sŭngjŏngwŏn ilgi: Kojong*, 11.341 (42b) (1890.11.6), 12.538 (49a) (1893.4.12); *Kojong sillok*, 30.23b; *Tanyang U-ssi taedongbo*, 1.479, 2.394–95, 4.410–12; and *HMMTS*, s.v. "Sŭngnyuk" [Rising to the sixth rank].

37. *HMMTS*, s.v. "Iunsa," "Min Yŏngjun," and "Chŏng Pyŏngha."

38. One of Qing China's "self-strengthening" experiments or institutions, the China Merchants Steamship Company was established in 1873 to transport grain on Chinese rivers and compete with foreign steamship lines. Larsen, *Tradition, Treaties, and Trade*, 206–9.

39. *HMMTS*, s.v. "Iunsa."

40. *HMMTS*, s.v. "Iunsa."

41. *HMMTS*, s.v. "Kwangt'ongsa."

42. For example in 1897, Kyŏngsŏn donated money to *The Independent*. See *Tong-nip sinmun*, April 27, 1897.

43. As of November 1907, he was the vice-principal of the famous Posŏng College (Posŏng Chŏnmun Hakkyo, precursor to present Korea University), founded in 1906 by a prominent statesman and businessman Yi Yongik (1854–1907). See *Taehan maeil sinbo*, November 14, 1907. In April 1910, Kyŏngsŏn donated supplies to the private Hŭngyŏng School (Hŭngyŏng Hakkyo) in Koyang. See *Taehan maeil sinbo*, April 17, 1910.

44. *Hojŏk* (1903), U Hangjŏng, 14-2 Mukchŏng-dong, Och'ŏn-gye, Hundo-bang, Nam-sŏ, Hansŏng-bu; and *Tanyang U-ssi taedongbo*, 1.479, 2.394–95, 4.410–12, 6.865.

45. Yun Hyojŏng, 108.

46. See Yun Hyojŏng, 108. As of 1906, Yun's concubine was living in a house an impressive 20 *k'an* in size—clearly suggesting the overall wealth of Yun himself. See *hojŏk* (1906), Yun Hyojŏng, 2 Wŏn-dong, Taesadong-gye, Kwanin-bang, Chung-sŏ, Hansŏng-bu.

47. See Yun Hyojŏng, 109–10.

48. *Sŭngjŏngwŏn ilgi: Kojong*, 6.386 (173b) (1878.6.30), 6.591 (171b) (1878.12.28), 6.976 (90a) (1879.12.21), 7.510 (57b) (1881.5.7), 8.290 (107a) (1882.12.18), 8.645 (75b) (1883.12.14), 13.65 (46b) (1894.9.11), 13.129 (26a) (1894.12.10), 13.256 (31b) (1895.11.14); and *Kojong sillok*, 32.38b–39a.

49. Yun Hyojŏng, 110–11.

50. *Sŭngjŏngwŏn ilgi: Kojong*, 9.645 (39b) (1886.5.7).

51. The following discussion of the murder of Queen Myŏngsŏng is based on Yi Minwŏn, 65–95; and Han Yŏngu, *Myŏngsŏng Hwanghu*, 42–60.

52. Yun Hyojŏng, 108–9.

53. *HMMTS*, s.v. "U Pŏmsŏn."

54. *Hojŏk* (1903), U Kyŏngmyŏng, 14-4 Mukchŏng-dong, Och'ŏn-gye, Hundo-bang, Nam-sŏ, Hansŏng-bu; *Sŏngwŏllok*, 1002–3; *Yonggang P'aeng-ssi sebo*, 1 (8a)–2 (8b), 8 (11b)–9 (12a), 11 (13a), 27 (21a); and *Tanyang U-ssi taedongbo*, 4.412.

55. For example, see *HMMTS*, s.v. "P'aeng Hanju."

56. *Kwanbo*, June 10, 1895; November 17, 1897; January 29, 1898; June 8, 1898; June 28, 1898; June 30, 1898; July 7, 1898; July 26, 1898; August 6, 1898; January 12, 1899; February 18, 1899; March 24, 1899; April 1, 1899; April 6, 1899; May 13, 1899; May 17, 1899; May 22, 1899; May 23, 1899; May 24, 1899; June 26, 1899; June 30, 1899; June 28, 1900; July 14, 1900; August 11, 1900; August 20, 1900; August 23, 1900; September 8, 1900; September 11, 1900; October 8, 1900; February 9, 1901; March 18, 1901; July 10, 1901; July 26, 1901; August 2, 1901; August 30, 1901; October 25, 1901; November 29, 1901; January 2, 1902; January 17, 1902; January 22, 1902; May 7, 1902; June 7, 1902; August 26, 1902; December 26, 1902; February 14, 1903; March 16, 1903; June 1, 1903; June 12, 1903; July 9, 1903; August 22, 1903; March 29, 1904; March 31, 1904; April 4, 1904; May 16, 1904; October 8, 1904; December 7, 1904; and March 4, 1905.

57. *Yun Ch'iho ilgi*, 5.245.

58. *Yun Ch'iho ilgi*, 5.245.

59. *Hojŏk* (1906), P'aeng Hanju, 28-4 Kwanja-dong, Sŏch'ŏnsu-gye, Changt'ongbang, Chung-sŏ, Hansŏng-bu, 1906.

60. Chu Chino, "19 segi huban Kaehwa kaehyŏngnon ŭi kujo wa chŏn'gae," 91, 97, 239.

61. "1904–5 nyŏn sakkŏn ŭi konghunja p'osang kwa myŏngdan" [Rewarding the meritorious individuals for the events of 1904–5 and the list of their names], *Nae-bu naegŏ an* 2, Kuksa P'yŏnch'an Wiwŏnhoe, *Han'guksa teit'ŏ peisŭ*, accessed April 22, 2012, http://db.history.go.kr.

62. Hwang Hyŏn, *Maech'ŏn yarok* 4.321 ("Kwangmu p'al-nyŏn kapchin: Puilcha").

63. *Kwanbo*, October 8, 1904; and "1904–5 nyŏn sakŏn ŭi konghunja p'osang kwa myŏngdan."

64. *Tonga ilbo*, June 30, 1920.

65. *Sŭngjŏngwŏn ilgi: Kojong*, 9.796 (94a–b) (1886.10.16).

66. *Sŭngjŏngwŏn ilgi: Kojong*, 11.655 (159a–160a) (1891.5.20).

67. For information on this particular licentiate examination, see Han'gukhak Chungang Yŏn'guwŏn, "Kwagŏ mit ch'wijae," *Han'guk yŏktae inmul chonghap chŏngbo sisŭt'em*, accessed November 1, 2011, http://people.aks.ac.kr/index.aks.

68. *Hojŏk* (1903), U Ch'anggi, 13-9 Mukchŏng-dong, Och'ŏn-gye, Hundo-bang, Nam-sŏ, Hansŏng-bu; and *Hwangsŏng sinmun*, March 27, 1907.

69. Pak Kŭndong, telephone interview by author, September 13, 2004; Chu Ja Cho, telephone interview by author, Chicago, September 27, 2004; and Brian Park, interview by author, Media, Pa., October 31, 2010.

70. *Kwanbo*, July 24, 1900; July 31, 1900; May 7, 1901; May 9, 1901; and July 6, 1905; and *Sŭngjŏngwŏn ilgi: Kojong*, 14.361 (85a) (July 21, 1900), 14.588 (81b) (May 5, 1901).

71. *Hwangsŏng sinmun*, March 27, 1907.

72. *Chejŏk tŭngbon*, U Hangjŏng, 27 Kwanch'ŏl-tong, Kyŏngsŏng-bu, Kyŏng-gi-do (218 Iptong-jŏng); and *Tanyang U-ssi taedongbo*, 4.412. Specialist *chungin* of late Chosŏn were at least as discriminatory toward concubines and their descendants as were their *yangban* contemporaries, if not more. Kim Tuhŏn, 63–66.

73. *Chejŏk tŭngbon*, U Hangjŏng, 27 Kwanch'ŏl-tong, Kyŏngsŏng-bu, Kyŏnggi-do (218 Iptong-jŏng).

74. Chu Ja Cho, telephone interview by author, Chicago, September 27, 2004.

75. After Kimyŏng's death, the daughter of Pak T'aesik enjoyed a comfortable life through the colonial era; "she rarely had to wet her hands for any housework." Eventually, however, Kimyŏng's posthumous adoptive son, U Chonghwa (1917–n.d.), wasted the family's fortune away. Shortly after liberation, when Korea was brimming with the hope and excitement fanned by a widespread demand for more equitable distribution of wealth, he and Pak T'aesik's daughter abandoned their mansion in Inch'ŏn amid rumors that a violent mob attacking the rich was approaching. By the eve of the Korean War, the two had lost everything, taking refuge in Pak Ch'angnae's household in Seoul. Kim Yosuk, telephone interview by author, Seoul, January 27, 1992; and Chu Ja Cho, telephone interview by author, Chicago, September 27, 2004.

76. *Hojŏk* (1903), U Kyŏngmyŏng, 14-4 Mukchŏng-dong, Och'ŏn-gye, Hun-do-bang, Nam-sŏ, Hansŏng-bu; *chejŏk tŭngbon*, U Hangjŏng, 27 Kwanch'ŏl-tong, Kyŏngsŏng-bu, Kyŏnggi-do (218 Iptong-jŏng); and *Tanyang U-ssi taedongbo*, 4.412.

77. *Kwanbo*, July 6, 1898 and August 6, 1898; and *Sŭngjŏngwŏn ilgi: Kojong*, 13.800 (53b) (July 4, 1898), 13.990 (179a) (Januay 6, 1899), 15.617 (92b) (January 19, 1906).

78. *Hwangsŏng sinmun*, March 27, 1907. As discussed above, the family's activism won enemies to such an extent that in 1899, Kyŏngmyŏng found a deliberately set explosive just outside the family mansion.

79. "Chamnok," 57.

80. *Hwangsŏng sinmun*, May 23, 1907.

81. U Kyŏngmyŏng, "Kyoyuk ŭi mokchŏk," 17–19; and U Kyŏngmyŏng, "Chiban esyŏ ŏrin aŭ kiranŏn pŏp," 37–40.

82. *Hojŏk* (1903), U Kyŏngmyŏng, 14-4 Mukchŏng-dong, Och'ŏn-gye, Hun-do-bang, Nam-sŏ, Hansŏng-bu; and *chejŏk tŭngbon*, U Hangjŏng, 27 Kwanch'ŏl-tong, Kyŏngsŏng-bu, Kyŏnggi-do (218 Iptong-jŏng). Traditionally and even today among many South Koreans, a newborn has either no given name or only a temporary name until the parents, or more commonly a naming expert (*changmyŏngga*), devise an auspicious one based on the lunar year, month, day, and time of the child's birth. In the nineteenth and early twentieth centuries, the temporary name could remain the "childhood name" (*amyŏng, aho*), which the parent used as an informal name for the child. Embodying a wish that the child live a healthy, long life, a childhood name often has an unflattering meaning (for example, a common childhood name "Kaettong"

means "dog poop") to ward off evil spirits from the child. After surviving various childhood diseases, a male receives a formal adult name upon a proper rite of passage. *HMMTS*, s.v. "Irŭm" [Name].

CHAPTER 6

1. In South Korea, the mainstream's effort to deal with collaborators shifted in nature from seeking legal justice to retroactively pursuing historical justice. The latter effort has undergone creation of a public myth of collaborating minority versus the nation and debunking the myth through denouncing countless, formerly celebrated patriots as collaborators. De Ceuster, "The Nation Exorcised," 218–26.

2. In the historiography, the issue of collaboration is virtually inseparable from a discussion of colonial modernity. Kyu Hyun Kim, "Reflections on the Problems of Colonial Modernity and 'Collaboration' in Modern Korean History," 96–106.

3. For an English-language discussion analyzing Korea's secondary status groups and highlighting their pro-Japanese collaboration, see Kyung Moon Hwang, *Beyond Birth*, 157–60, 345–49.

4. *Yu-ssi taedongbo*, 9.667–713. In this respect, the 1994 edition was no different. For a recent study overstating its case by contending that Yu's role as such is even empirically questionable, see Pak Ŭnsuk, "Yu Taech'i," 134–44.

5. *Yu-ssi taedongbo*, 9.667–713.

6. For a controversial recent study contending that Yu Taech'i was not from a capital *chungin* family, see Pak Ŭnsuk, "Yu Taech'i," 134–44.

7. *Yŏnju Hyŏn-ssi taedongbo*, 1.178–90, 2.1002–52, 6.477–574.

8. Informative discussions of the Ch'ŏllyŏng Hyŏn include Kim Hyŏnyŏng, "Chosŏn hugi chungin ŭi kagye wa kyŏngnyŏk," 105–19; Kim Yangsu, "Chosŏn chŏnhwan'gi ŭi chungin chiban hwaltong," 185–272; Kim Yŏnggyŏng, "Hanmal Sŏul chiyŏk chunginch'ŭng ŭi kŭndaehwa undong kwa hyŏnsil insik," 1–52; and Kim Yangsu, "Sŏul chungin ŭi 19 segi saenghwal," 47–92.

9. Ch'ŏn arranges statistics from the *Police Bulletin* (*Keimu ihō*) so that each genre is ranked according to the number of permits the authority granted to individual volumes during the 1920s. See Ch'ŏn Chŏnghwan, *Kŭndae ŭi ch'aek ilkki*, 171–81, 488.

10. Pang Hyosun, "Ilche sidae min'gan sŏjŏk palhaeng hwaltong ŭi kujochŏk t'ŭksŏng e kwanhan yŏn'gu," 36–37.

11. "Ajik to chokpo t'aryŏng: ŏpseja ponggŏn yusŭp" [Still harping on genealogies: let us get rid of feudal customs], *Tonga ilbo*, October 31, 1949.

12. "Tongyang sik yulli sasang ŭi pyŏnch'ŏn (sok): kajŏng yulli ŭi il tan" [The change in the Oriental-style ideology of ethics (supplement): an aspect of family ethics], *Kaebyŏk*, November 1, 1921, p. 17.

13. "Kapcha il nyŏn ch'onggwan (sok)" [Comprehensive review of the new sixty-year cycle's year one (supplement)], *Kaebyŏk*, January 1, 1925, p. 55.

14. *Tonga ilbo*, September 14, 1926.

15. "Chokpo kanhaeng ŭi yŏp'ae," *Chosŏn ilbo*, February 1, 1928.

16. Yi Hyŏnhŭi, "Hanmal chungin Kaehwa sasangga ŭi kaehyŏk undong," 65–80; Sin Yongha, "O Kyŏngsŏk ŭi Kaehwa sasang kwa Kaehwa hwaltong," 107–35; Chŏng Okcha, part 3, "Chosŏn hugi ŭi kisuljik chungin"; Yi Hyŏnhŭi, "1870 nyŏndae ŭi Kaehwa sasang kwa kŭ chudo kyech'ŭng," 107–24; Kim Kyŏngt'aek, "Hanmal chunginch'ŭng ŭi Kaehwa hwaltong kwa ch'inil Kaehwaron," 250–63; Kim Yangsu, "Chosŏn kaehang chŏnhu chungin ŭi chŏngch'i oegyo," 311–66; Kim Yŏnggyŏng, "Hanmal Sŏul chiyŏk chunginch'ŭng ŭi kŭndaehwa undong kwa hyŏnsil insik," sections 3 and 4; and Kim Hyŏnmok, "Hanmal kisuljik chungin ch'ulsin kwallyo ŭi sinbun kwa tonghyang," section 3.

17. On hegemonic discourse and power holders, see Joseph V. Femia, *Gramsci's Political Thought*, 24–26.

18. Hong Sunmin, 1.243–56; Song Chunho, *Chosŏn sahoesa yŏn'gu*, 283–84; and Park, *Between Dreams and Reality*, 117–41.

19. Pak Pyŏnghae, interview by author, Seoul, October 5, 1995; Kim Chŏngbae, interview by author, Seoul, July 15, 2001; Kim Sŏngbae, interview by author, Irvine, Calif., October 15, 2002; Pak Kŭndong, telephone interview by author, Ansŏng, South Korea, September 13, 2004; Chu Ja Cho, telephone interview by author, Chicago, September 27, 2004; Pak Yŏngil, telephone interview by author, Taejŏn, South Korea, October 4, 2004; Chu Ja Cho, interview by author, Chicago, May 27, 2007; Pak Kŭndong, interview by author, Taejŏn, South Korea, July 7, 2007; Pak Yŏngil, interview by author, Taejŏn, South Korea, July 7, 2007; Pang Kijun, telephone interview by author, Puyŏ, South Korea, September 22, 2007; Pak T'aewŏn, telephone interview by author, Seoul, July 1, 2008; and Yi Sangŏk, e-mail communication, May 12, 2009. The interviewees are direct descendants of the members of specialist *chungin* Tongju Ch'oe, Kimhae Kim, Miryang Pak, Onyang Pang, and Kyŏngju Kim families of Seoul.

20. Moskowitz, "The Creation of the Oriental Development Company," 98–102; Myers and Yamada, "Agricultural Development in the Empire," 451–52; Gragert, *Land Ownership Under Colonial Rule*, 30–35, 54–110; and Yi Sŭngnyŏl, 213–16.

21. Eckert, *Offspring of Empire*, 7–103.

22. For a reference to a military examination passer with the same name, see *Sŭngjŏngwŏn ilgi: Kojong*, 9.174 (119b–120b) (1885.4.21).

23. His submitted documents are found in *Ch'ungch'ŏngnam-do Ŭnjin-Hongsan-gun sojae changt'o: Pak Myŏnghwan chech'ul tosŏ munjŏk ryu*; and *Ch'ungch'ŏngnam-do Yesan-gun sojae changt'o: Pak Myŏnghwan chech'ul tosŏ munjŏk ryu*.

24. *Miryang Pak-ssi Kyujŏnggong-p'a sebo*, 32.38a–b.

25. *Kwanbo*, July 4, 1904; and July 5, 1904; and *Sŭngjŏngwŏn ilgi: Kojong*, 15.189 (45b) (July 1, 1904).

26. *Ch'ungch'ŏngnam-do Puyŏ-gun yangan*, 1 (*Hyŏnnae-myŏn*).44a.

27. *Ch'ungch'ŏngnam-do Puyŏ-gun yangan*, 1 (*Hyŏnnae-myŏn*).44a, 45b, 48b, 63b; *Kongmun p'yŏnan* 41, Kuksa P'yŏnch'an Wiwŏnhoe, *Han'guksa teit'ŏ peisŭ*, accessed

April 22, 2012, http://db.history.go.kr; and *Miryang Pak-ssi Kyujŏnggong-p'a sebo*, 32.39a.

28. *Hojŏk* (1906), Namgung Ŏk, 3-2 Samch'ŏng-dong, Samch'ŏngdong-gye, Chinjang-bang, Puk-sŏ, Hansŏng-bu; *chejŏk tŭngbon*, U Hangjŏng, 27 Kwanch'ŏl-tong, Kyŏngsŏng-bu, Kyŏnggi-do (218 Iptong-jŏng); *Hamyŏl Namgung-ssi chokpo*, 1.371, 2.287, 2.294–95, 2.343, 4.417, 4.419; *Mansŏng taedongbo*, 2.248a–b; and Chu Chino, "Han'guk kŭndae kungmin kukka surip kwajŏng esŏ wangkwŏn ŭi yŏkhwal (1880–1894)," 174 fn. 2, 179, 182–83, 185, 201.

29. *Miryang Pak-ssi Kyujŏnggong-p'a sebo*, 32.39a.

30. As of 1901, Kyuhwan's younger brother Pak Tuhwan (1870–1942), too, possessed land in Hyŏnnae district in Puyŏ county. The land register records his name as "Pak Ch'ilsŏng," which probably was Tuhwan's actual or informal name as distinct from "Tuhwan" as recorded in the genealogy. Ch'ungch'ŏngnam-do Puyŏ-gun yangan, 1 (Hyŏnnae-myŏn).88a. Unlike the wives of his brothers Kyuhwan and Myŏnghwan, we know little about Tuhwan's wife other than that she was Madam Ch'ungju Chi (1867–1934), the daughter of a certain Chi Kŏnyŏng (n.d.). Both she and Tuhwan were buried in Puyŏ. *Miryang Pak-ssi Kyujŏnggong-p'a sebo*, 32.39a; and *Miryang Pak-ssi Ch'ŏngjaegong che samja Sajikkong p'abo*, 2.347–48. Tuhwan's uncle, Pak Chinsik, also had two daughters, the respective husbands of whom were So Hwijŏng (n.d.) and Yi Ŭisŏl (n.d.). Other than discovering that their ancestral seats were Chinju and Hŭngyang, I have not been able to uncover any information on them. *Miryang Pak-ssi Kyujŏnggong-p'a sebo*, 32.39b.

31. *Miryang Pak-ssi Kyujŏnggong-p'a sebo*, 32.39b.

32. *Muan kunji*, 1.24a, 1.26b–27a, 1.29b, 1.31a, 1.34a, 1.37b, 1.40a, 1.43b–44b, 1.45b, 1.54a, 2.2a, 2.7b, 2.13a, 2.17a–b, 2.30a, 2.41b; *Ssijok wŏllyu*, 246; *Mansŏng taedongbo*, 1.203a; *Naju Kim-ssi taedong sebo*, 1.1–3, 1.5–7, 1.25; and *SK*, 246–47.

33. *Chōsen Sōtokufu shisei 25 shūnen kinen hyōshōsha meikan*, 622, Kuksa P'yŏnch'an Wiwŏnhoe, *Han'guksa teit'ŏ peisŭ*, accessed May 12, 2012, http://db.history. go.kr. The colonial government's stated reason for the 1909 law was to remedy the incompleteness of the old household registration survey and to clarify the social relations (kinship ties) among the population. The law understood a "family" (*ka*) as that centered around the head of the household (*hoju*) and his or her kin, and a single document was to record all the members as well as indicate how they were related to the household head. Usually recognizing the locality where the household head was residing—at the time of his or her registration according to the new law—as the place of the family's original household registration (*ponjŏk*), the system required each local police department to maintain and update all the people's registers within its jurisdiction. In July 1909 the police conducted the registration survey, and with its completion in December 1910 the new law was in effect throughout Korea. It required a household head to report within ten days of the occurrence of every major new life event such as birth, death, marriage, divorce, and adoption. Critical discussions of the People's Registration Law include Im Kyŏngt'aek, "Ilche ŭi 'kungmin' mandŭlgi," 201–4; Kyung Moon Hwang, "Citizenship, Social Equality and Government Reform,"

364–69; Yi Chŏngsŏn, "Han'guk kŭndae 'hojŏk chedo' ŭi pyŏnch'ŏn," 287–320; Yi Sŭngil, "Chosŏn Ch'ongdokpu ŭi Chosŏnin tŭngnok chedo yŏn'gu," 18–36; and Yi Sŭngil, "Chosŏn Hojŏngnyŏng chejŏng e kwanhan yŏn'gu," 40–65.

34. The positions that I have been able to confirm are the Poryŏng Police Department deputy constable (*Junsaho*, Ko. *Sunsabo*; 1912–19); the Poryŏng Police Department constable (*Junsa*, Ko. *Sunsa*; 1919–22); the Poryŏng Police Department deputy inspector (*Keibuho*, Ko. *Kyŏngbubo*; 1922–24); the Ch'ŏnan Police Department inspector (*Keibu*, Ko. *Kyŏngbu*; 1924–26); the Inch'ŏn Police Department inspector (1926–28); the Suwŏn Police Department inspector (1928–32); the Kyŏngsŏng Chongno Police Department inspector and judiciary deputy chief (*Shihōkei Jiseki*, Ko. *Sabŏpkye Ch'asŏk*; 1932–36); the Kaesŏng Police Department inspector and judiciary chief (*Shihō Shunin*, Ko. *Sabŏp Chuim*; 1936–39); the Kyŏngsŏng Yŏngdŭngp'o Police Department inspector (n.d.); the Kyŏngsŏng Pon-jŏng Police Department inspector (1939); and the Kyŏnggi Province Police superintendent (*Keishi*, Ko. *Kyŏngsi*; November 29–December 6, 1939). *Chōsen Sōtokufu kanpō*, June 7, 1933; June 20, 1933; November 29, 1938; December 5, 1939; and December 6, 1939; *Chōsen Sōtokufu shokuinroku*, Kuksa P'yŏnch'an Wiwŏnhoe, *Han'guksa teit'ŏ peisŭ*, accessed May 12, 2012, http://db.history.go.kr; and *Chōsen Sōtokufu shisei 25 shūnen kinen hyōshōsha meikan*, 622.

35. Ching-chih Chen, "Police and Community Control Systems in the Empire," 223–24; and Eckert et al., *Korea Old and New*, 259.

36. *Chōsen Sōtokufu kanpō*, June 7, 1933; June 20, 1933; November 29, 1938; December 5, 1939; and December 6, 1939; *Chōsen Sōtokufu shokuinroku*, Kuksa P'yŏnch'an Wiwŏnhoe, *Han'guksa teit'ŏ peisŭ*, accessed May 12, 2012, http://db.history.go.kr; and *Chōsen Sōtokufu shisei 25 shūnen kinen hyōshōsha meikan*, 622.

37. *Chōsen Sōtokufu shisei 25 shūnen kinen hyōshōsha meikan*, 622.

38. *Chōsen Sōtokufu kanpō*, November 29, 1938.

39. *Shina jihen kōrōsha kōseki chōsho* [Record of meritorious deeds of the heroes of the China Incident], as cited by *Ch'inil inmyŏng sajŏn*, 2.97.

40. *Chōsen Sōtokufu kanpō*, November 12, 1912; and April 12, 1915.

41. See *Ch'inil inmyŏng sajŏn*, 2.97.

42. A son, Pak Chŏnggi (1915–n.d.), followed in the footsteps of his father. As of 1952 he was a police lieutenant (*kyŏngwi*) in his home county, Puyŏ, but it is not clear when Chŏnggi entered the service. Most probably he had been serving in the colonial police for some time, given his age of thirty-eight *se* and rank as of 1952. *Taehan Min'guk chigwŏllok*, Kuksa P'yŏnch'an Wiwŏnhoe, *Han'guksa teit'ŏ peisŭ*, accessed May 13, 2012, http://db.history.go.kr; and *Miryang Pak-ssi Ch'ŏngjaegong che samja Sajikkong p'abo*, 2.362–65. If so, then he exemplifies the continuity of Korean bureaucratic personnel of the colonial era into the post-liberation period in South Korea.

43. *Miryang Pak-ssi Ch'ŏngjaegong che samja Sajikkong p'abo*, 2.325.

44. *Chōsen Sōtokufu kanpō*, January 12, 1914.

45. *Naju Kim-ssi taedong sebo*, 1.1–3, 1.5–7, 1.25, 1.139–42, 3.22–23; and *Miryang Pak-ssi Kyujŏnggong-p'a sebo*, 32.38a–b.

46. Nakamura Shirō, *Chōsen ginkō kaisha kumiai yōroku* (1927, 1929, 1931, 1933, 1935), Kuksa P'yŏnch'an Wiwŏnhoe, *Han'guksa teit'ŏ peisŭ*, accessed May 13, 2012, http://db.history.go.kr. Presumably backed by his influence among local colonial authority and community leaders, after Korea's liberation Man'gi served as the Hongsan district chief (*myŏnjang*). During the Korean War, somehow he did not flee in time to avoid capture by the advancing North Korean troops, and on August 1, 1950 he was killed by the communists, who generally targeted those perceived to be agents of the South Korean government. *Miryang Pak-ssi Ch'ŏngjaegong che samja Sajikkong p'abo*, 2.326. On a classic discussion of violence whenever one side of the conflict gained control of a town or a village during the war, see Bruce Cumings, *The Origins of the Korean War, Vol. II*, 697–705, 719–22; and Pak T'aegyun, *Han'guk Chŏnjaeng*, 320–29. Reflecting the violence and tragedy of the Korean War, the Pak genealogy records one of his sons as missing. *Miryang Pak-ssi Ch'ŏngjaegong che samja Sajikkong p'abo*, 2.326–27.

47. Chu Ja Cho, telephone interview by author, Chicago, November 14, 1990; Pak Kŭndong, telephone interview by author, Ansŏng, South Korea, September 13, 2004; Chu Ja Cho, telephone interview by author, Chicago, September 27, 2004; and Pak Yŏngil, telephone interview by author, Taejŏn, South Korea, October 4, 2004.

48. *Chejŏk tŭngbon*, Pak T'aesik, 294 Chwahong-ri, Hongsan-myŏn, Puyŏ-gun, Ch'ungch'ŏngnam-do; *chejŏk tŭngbon*, O-ssi, 294 Chwahong-ri, Hongsan-myŏn, Puyŏ-gun, Ch'ungch'ŏngnam-do; *chejŏk tŭngbon*, Pak P'yŏngch'i, 294 Chwahong-ri, Hongsan-myŏn, Puyŏ-gun, Ch'ungch'ŏngnam-do; and Kim Yosuk, interview by author, Yongin, South Korea, October 7, 2002.

49. On the dynamics of encounters between missionary women and Korean women in the course of production of the first generation of educated Korean women, see Choi, *Gender and Mission Encounters in Korea*, 13–14, 179–83.

50. Pak Yŏngil, telephone interview by author, Taejŏn, South Korea, October 4, 2004.

51. Pak Pyŏnghae, interview by author, Seoul, October 5, 1995; Pak Kŭndong, telephone interview by author, Ansŏng, South Korea, September 13, 2004; and Pak Yŏngil, telephone interview by author, Taejŏn, South Korea, October 4, 2004.

52. Chu Ja Cho, telephone interview by author, Chicago, November 14, 1990; Pak Kŭndong, interview by author, Seoul, June 1, 1992; and Pak Yŏngil, telephone interview by author, Taejŏn, South Korea, October 4, 2004.

53. *Chejŏk tŭngbon*, Pak Kyŏngjun, [no number] Ch'unghwa-myŏn, Odŏk-ri, Ch'ungch'ŏngnam-do; *Sŏngwŏllok*, 988–90; *Miryang Pak-ssi Kyujŏnggong-p'a taedongbo* (1986), 2.991; and Pak Pyŏnghae, interview by author, Seoul, October 5, 1995.

54. *Sŭngjŏngwŏn ilgi: Kojong*, 15.819 (58a) (January 27, 1907).

55. Pak Kŭndong, interview by author, Seoul, June 1, 1992.

56. Kyŏngjun's establishment of a separate household is recorded on *chejŏk tŭngbon*, Pak Kyŏngjun, [no number] Ch'unghwa-myŏn, Odŏk-ri, Ch'ungch'ŏngnam-do.

57. Pak Pyŏngsŏn, interview by author, Seoul, June 1, 1992; and Pak Pyŏnghae, interview by author, Seoul, October 5, 1995.

58. Information on Kyŏngjun's second marriage and death derives from Pak Kŭndong, interview by author, Seoul, 1, 1992.

59. *Chejŏk tŭngbon*, Pak T'aesik, 294 Chwahong-ri, Hongsan-myŏn, Puyŏ-gun, Ch'ungch'ŏngnam-do.

60. Suzuki Yōtarō, Kuksa P'yŏnch'an Wiwŏnhoe, *Han'guksa teit'ŏ peisŭ*, accessed May 26, 2012, http://db.history.go.kr.

61. No Inhwa, "Taehan Cheguk sigi ŭi Hansŏng Sabŏm Hakkyo e kwanhan yŏn'gu," 12–24; and Kim Kwanggyu, "Taehan Chegukki ch'odŭng kyowŏn ŭi yangsŏng kwa imyong," 110–23.

62. Though not adopted by the Japanese Residency-General as textbooks but still widely read by reform-minded Koreans, many books on Korean history authored by the Koreans at the time highlighted feats by the Koreans of diverse backgrounds that the authors deemed meaningful for narrating the national history. Yuh, "Rejection, Selection, and Acceptance," 89–96.

63. "Sabŏm hakkyo ryŏng" [Ordinance on teachers colleges], as reported in *Kwanbo*, August 30, 1906.

64. *Chōsen Sōtokufu kanpō*, November 13, 1911.

65. *Chōsen Sōtokufu kanpō*, May 13, 1912.

66. This is not to suggest, however, that the potential impact of Ch'angnae and his classmates arguably was as great as with, say, those who graduated from Kyŏngsŏng High Ordinary School proper, the precursor to the famed Kyŏnggi High School, and went on to hold higher-level positions in the bureaucracy or played more prominent roles in cultural or business spheres. Furukawa, "Ilche sidae ŭi chung, kodŭng kyoyuk," 51, 56; and Im Kyŏngsŏk, *Ijŏng Pak Hŏnyŏng iltaegi*, 496–97.

67. Eckert et al., *Korea Old and New*, 263.

68. Song Kyujin et al., *T'onggye ro pon Han'guk kŭnhyŏndaesa*, 353, table 2-172.

69. The three are Yi Wŏn'gyu, Yi Chaebung, and Paek Myŏnggap. See *Ch'inil inmyŏng sajŏn*, 2.209, 3.56, 3.108.

70. This explanation of the end of Ch'angnae's teaching career is offered by his daughter, who was the eldest surviving child until her death in May 2011. See Chu Ja Cho, telephone interview by author, Chicago, September 27, 2004.

71. The schools where he taught from 1912 to 1930 are Hongju Public Ordinary School (1912–13), Changyŏn Public Ordinary School (1915–17), Kangnyŏng Public Ordinary School (1917–18), Paekch'ŏn Public Ordinary School (1918–19), Asan Public Ordinary School (1919–n.d.), Sorae Public Ordinary School (1922–23), P'alt'an Public Ordinary School (1923–25), and Kap'yŏng Public Ordinary School (1925–30). See *Chōsen Sōtokufu shokuinroku*, Kuksa P'yŏnch'an Wiwŏnhoe, *Han'guksa teit'ŏ peisŭ*, accessed April 25, 2012, http://db.history. go.kr.

72. *Sidae ilbo*, April 23, 1924.

73. Chu Ja Cho, interview by author, Chicago, May 27, 2007; and Brian Park, interview by author, Chicago, May 27, 2007.

74. Chu Ja Cho, interview by author, Chicago, May 27, 2007.

75. Ku Kwangmo, "Ch'angssi kaemyŏng chŏngch'aek kwa Chosŏnin ŭi taeŭng," 32, 37–46; Yi Myŏnghwa, "Ilche hwangmin kyoyuk kwa kungmin hakkyo-je ŭi sihaeng," 323; and Ch'oe Chaesŏng, "'Ch'angssi kaemyŏng' kwa ch'inil Chosŏnin ŭi hyŏmnyŏk," 346–70.

76. One of Ch'angnae's children, Brian Park, recalls how many Pak-surnamed Koreans at the time seemingly went for the name Arai. Brian Park, interview by author, Chicago, May 27, 2007. For a study on how the Koreans responded to the Name Order, see Ku Kwangmo, 46–49.

77. *Samguk sagi*, 1.1a–b; and *Samguk yusa*, 1.1a–4a.

78. *Chejŏk tŭngbon*, Pak P'yŏngch'i, 294 Chwahong-ri, Hongsan-myŏn, Puyŏ-gun, Ch'ungch'ŏngnam-do; and Brian Park, interview by author, Chicago, May 27, 2007.

79. *Chejŏk tŭngbon*, Pak P'yŏngch'i, 294 Chwahong-ri, Hongsan-myŏn, Puyŏ-gun, Ch'ungch'ŏngnam-do; and Brian Park, interview by author, Chicago, May 27, 2007. I would like to thank Frank Chance for informing me that the given name is used rather commonly among the Japanese. Frank L. Chance, private conversation, July 21, 2011.

80. Chu Ja Cho, interview by author, Chicago, May 27, 2007; Brian Park, interview by author, Chicago, May 27, 2007; Pak Kŭndong, interview by author, Taejŏn, South Korea, July 7, 2007; and Pak Yŏngil, interview by author, July 7, 2007.

81. Chu Ja Cho, interview by author, May 27, 2007; Pak Kŭndong, interview by author, Taejŏn, South Korea, July 7, 2007; and Pak Yŏngil, interview by author, Taejŏn, South Korea, July 7, 2007.

82. I would like to thank An Jong Chol (An Chongch'ŏl) for pointing this out to me during a private conversation on July 16, 2009.

83. On Sin's ancestry, see *Mansŏng taedongbo*, 2.43b–44b, 46a, 48b. Common biographical discussions of Sin's family background refer to him and his mother as, respectively, the seventh son and the fourth wife of Chief Magistrate of Seoul (Hansŏng-bu *P'anyun*) Sin Tan (1832–1905). Tan hailed from an aristocratic lineage that was descended from the famous but ill-fated Korean commander during the Battle of Ch'ungju (1592), Sin Rip (1546–92), a lineage that produced at least twelve civil examination, thirty-four military examination, and thirty-three licentiate examination graduates. Fittingly so, his first three wives were from aristocratic families of comparable social status. In contrast, Ikhŭi's mother, Madam Tongnae Chŏng (1867–1932?), was a daughter of a local functionary of Kimhae, Kyŏngsang province. Ikhŭi's father, Tan, would have formally married Madam Chŏng only by going against the norms of elite Korean families for whom marriage was a sociopolitical institution at the time. All the same, if his previous wives had all died by the time of Ikhŭi's birth, then the situation could have allowed the son and his later hagiographers to simply regard his mother as Tan's "fourth wife." *Mansŏng taedongbo*, 2.44a–b, 46a–b, 48b; Song Chunho, *Chosŏn sahoesa yŏn'gu*, 503–4; Park, *Between Dreams and Reality*, 75;

and *HMMTS*, s.v. "Sin Ikhŭi." For details of Cho Pyŏngok's personal life during the final years of the colonial era, I thank Park Tae-Gyun (Pak T'aegyun), private conversation, July 8, 2009. An observation that Pak Ch'angnae associated more closely with Cho Pyŏngok than with Sin Ikhŭi is by Pak Kŭndong, interview by author, Taejŏn, South Korea, July 7, 2007.

84. Cho Pyŏngok, *Na ŭi hoegorok*, 23–25.

85. Actually, all the household registration documents recording Kim Yonghwa as a member of the Pak household show her ancestral seat as Kimhae instead of Naju. Also, they record her father's given name as Chaewŏn rather than Sangnyuk, which is the name of Yonghwa's father in the Naju Kim genealogy. See *chejŏk tŭngbon*, Pak T'aesik, 238 Odŏk-ri, Ch'unghwa-myŏn, Puyŏ-gun, Ch'ungch'ŏngnam-do; *chejŏk tŭngbon*, Pak T'aesik, 294 Chwahong-ri, Hongsan-myŏn, Puyŏ-gun, Ch'ungch'ŏngnam-do; *chejŏk tŭngbon*, O-ssi, 294 Chwahong-ri, Hongsan-myŏn, Puyŏ-gun, Ch'ungch'ŏngnam-do; *chejŏk tŭngbon*, Pak P'yŏngch'i, 294 Chwahong-ri, Hongsan-myŏn, Puyŏ-gun, Ch'ungch'ŏngnam-do; and *chejŏk tŭngbon*, Pak Pyŏngsŏn, 465-29 Majang-dong, Sŏngdong-gu, Sŏul-t'ŭkpyŏlsi. None of Yonghwa's surviving children has an explanation for these discrepancies, although one daughter, Pak Yŏngil, has known her maternal grandfather's brother's name as Kim Pongnyuk. Also, the Naju Kim genealogy indeed shows Pongnyuk as a younger brother of Sangnyuk. Moreover, Pak Kŭndong and Brian Pak remember meeting or hearing about some of their maternal cousins, and they appear on household registration documents as Naju Kim. See *chejŏk tŭngbon*, Kim Pongnyuk, 205 Tunyul-tong, Kunsan-si, Chŏllabuk-to; *chejŏk tŭngbon*, Kim Ch'anggwŏn, 205 Tunyul-tong, Kunsan-si, Chŏllabuk-to; *Naju Kim-ssi taedong sebo*, 1.1–3, 1.5, 1.13, 1.78–79, 2.3–4, 2.606–7; Pak Yŏngil, telephone interview by author, Taejŏn, South Korea, October 4, 2004; Pak Kŭndong, interview by author, Taejŏn, South Korea, July 7, 2007; and Brian Park, interview by author, Santa Ana, Calif., May 26, 2007.

86. Pak Yŏngil, telephone interview by author, Taejŏn, South Korea, October 4, 2004.

87. Ibid.

88. *Chejŏk tŭngbon*, Pak T'aesik, 238 Odŏk-ri, Ch'unghwa-myŏn, Puyŏ-gun, Ch'ungch'ŏngnam-do; *chejŏk tŭngbon*, Pak T'aesik, 294 Chwahong-ri, Hongsan-myŏn, Puyŏ-gun, Ch'ungch'ŏngnam-do; *chejŏk tŭngbon*, O-ssi, 294 Chwahong-ri, Hongsan-myŏn, Puyŏ-gun, Ch'ungch'ŏngnam-do; and Pak Yŏngil, telephone interview by author, Taejŏn, South Korea, October 4, 2004.

89. *Chōsen Sōtokufu shokuinroku*, Kuksa P'yŏnch'an Wiwŏnhoe, *Han'guksa teit'ŏ peisŭ*, accessed May 12, 2012, http://db.history.go.kr.

90. From 1919 to 1922, he climbed the pay scale from the tenth to the eighth official rank (*kwandŭng*), as well as receiving a jump in monthly salary from 18 *wŏn* to 60 *wŏn*. *Chōsen Sōtokufu shokuinroku*, Kuksa P'yŏnch'an Wiwŏnhoe, *Han'guksa teit'ŏ peisŭ*, accessed May 12, 2012, http://db.history.go.kr.

91. *Chejŏk tŭngbon,* Pak T'aesik, 238 Odŏk-ri, Ch'unghwa-myŏn, Puyŏ-gun, Ch'ungch'ŏngnam-do; *chejŏk tŭngbon,* Pak T'aesik, 294 Chwahong-ri, Hongsan-myŏn, Puyŏ-gun, Ch'ungch'ŏngnam-do; and *chejŏk tŭngbon,* O-ssi, 294 Chwahong-ri, Hongsan-myŏn, Puyŏ-gun, Ch'ungch'ŏngnam-do.

92. Pak Yŏngil, telephone interview by author, Taejŏn, South Korea, October 4, 2004; and Chu Ja Cho, interview by author, Chicago, May 27, 2007.

93. Using both his severance pay and a loan from his wealthy father-in-law, Kim Sangnyuk, in 1930 Ch'angnae and the family moved to Kunsan, where Kim resided and operated rice hulling factories as well as running a construction business. Ch'angnae had little luck with his own business, a rice hulling factory, and in just two months it folded. Under great financial constraint, he was also unhappy with what he regarded as his father-in-law's unwillingness to help him further. What exacerbated the feeling was that by then Kim reportedly was under the spell of a young new wife who squandered his wealth. Pak Yŏngil, telephone interview by author, Taejŏn, South Korea, October 4, 2004; and Brian Park, interview by author, Santa Ana, Calif., May 26, 2007.

94. *Tonga ilbo,* January 13, 1935; March 4, 1935; and January 9, 1939. Also, Brian Park, interview by author, Santa Ana, Calif., May 26, 2007.

95. Pak Kŭndong, telephone interview by author, Ansŏng, South Korea, September 13, 2004; and Pak Yŏngil, telephone interview by author, Taejŏn, South Korea, October 4, 2004. The school provided him with housing. Brian Park, interview by author, Santa Ana, Calif., May 26, 2007. Around this time, on learning that the minister was having an affair with a widow, Ch'angnae stopped attending the neighborhood Segŏmjŏng Church where he had been serving as a presbyter. Ch'angnae's children too had no choice but to stop going to church. Pak Kŭndong, telephone interview by author, Ansŏng, South Korea, September 13, 2004; and Pak Kŭndong, interview by author, Seoul, July 13, 2011.

96. All the same, the obvious contrast in the level of public recognition between the aforementioned Cho Pyŏngok and Sin Ikhŭi on the one hand and Ch'angnae on the other seems to have much to do with his sudden death a few months before liberation. After suffering a burn from an overheated *ondol* floor while sleeping after heavy drinking, he was admitted to the hospital of Asahi Medical School (Severance Medical College since the end of Japanese colonial rule, before merging with Yonhui College to form Yonsei University), where he came down with an infection. Seeing no hope, the hospital released him, and he died at home. Brian Park, telephone interview by author, Laguna Woods, Calif., June 1, 2011. His nationalistic associates released from the infamous Sŏdaemun Prison on liberation reportedly lamented why he could not have lived longer to do more for a now-liberated Korea. Pak Yŏngil, telephone interview by author, Taejŏn, South Korea, October 4, 2004. Since it was wartime with an acute shortage of resources, the family cremated his remains and scattered the ashes in the streams of Inwang Mountain, not too far from the house. Pak Kŭndong, interview by author, Seoul, June 1, 1992; and Brian Park, interview by author, Santa Ana, Calif., May 26, 2007.

97. Pak Kŭndong, interview by author, Taejŏn, South Korea, July 7, 2007.

98. Pak Kŭndong, interview by author, Seoul, June 1, 1992.

99. Yoo, *The Politics of Gender in Colonial Korea*, 109, 180–82.

100. Brian Park, interview by author, Santa Ana, Calif., May 26, 2007.

101. *Kwangju Yi-ssi taedongbo*, 1.3–5, 1.9–10, 1.12–13, 1.175–77, 2.1113–15, 8.888; and Brian Park, interview by author, Santa Ana, Calif., May 26, 2007. The Miryang Pak genealogy cited here erroneously records Yi Chongch'un's ancestral seat as Chŏnju.

102. *Kwangju Yi-ssi taedongbo*, 8.888. Decades later, two sons immigrated to New Zealand and Britain. Brian Park, interview by author, Santa Ana, Calif., May 26 2007.

103. Chu Ja Cho, telephone interview by author, Chicago, September 27, 2004.

104. An Chongch'ŏl, *Miguk sŏn'gyosa wa Han-Mi kwan'gye, 1931–1948*, 56–57, 59.

105. Chu Ja Cho, interview by author, ChicagoMay 27, 2007.

106. For a critical discussion of this policy in the context of the Government-General's greater effort to integrate the Koreans into the Japanese mainstream as "imperial subjects," see Yi Myŏnghwa, 319, 326.

107. Chu Ja Cho, interview by author, Chicago, May 27, 2007.

108. Wonji Aycock, private conversation, November 29, 1991; and Chu Ja Cho, interview by author, Chicago, May 27, 2007. In the late 1960s, Inhŭi's eldest child and daughter, Wonji Aycock (b. 1945), went to the United States to pursue graduate training in chemistry at Rensselaer Polytechnic Institute, where she met her future husband, a Euro-American. Later, as a naturalized U.S. citizen, she invited her parents and siblings, who also eventually became first-generation Americans. Brian Park, interview by author, Santa Ana, Calif., May 26, 2007.

109. *Chejŏk tŭngbon*, Pak T'aesik, 294 Chwahong-ri, Hongsan-myŏn, Puyŏ-gun, Ch'ungch'ŏngnam-do; *chejŏk tŭngbon*, O-ssi, 294 Chwahong-ri, Hongsan-myŏn, Puyŏ-gun, Ch'ungch'ŏngnam-do; *chejŏk tŭngbon*, Pak P'yŏngch'i, 294 Chwahong-ri, Hongsan-myŏn, Puyŏ-gun, Ch'ungch'ŏngnam-do; and Pak Kŭndong, interview by author, Taejŏn, South Korea, July 7, 2007.

110. Brian Park, interview by author, Santa Ana, Calif., May 26, 2007.

111. No Yŏnghŭi, "Ilbon sin yŏsŏngdŭl kwa pigyohae pon Na Hyesŏk ŭi sin yŏsŏnggwan kwa kŭ han'gye," 343–57; Kim Ŭnsil, "Chosŏn singminji chisigin Na Hyesŏk ŭi kŭndaesŏng ŭl chilmun handa," 148–78; Yoo, 58–94; and Choi, 145–76.

112. *Chejŏk tŭngbon*, Pak T'aesik, 294 Chwahong-ri, Hongsan-myŏn, Puyŏ-gun, Ch'ungch'ŏngnam-do; *chejŏk tŭngbon*, O-ssi, 294 Chwahong-ri, Hongsan-myŏn, Puyŏ-gun, Ch'ungch'ŏngnam-do; *chejŏk tŭngbon*, Pak P'yŏngch'i, 294 Chwahong-ri, Hongsan-myŏn, Puyŏ-gun, Ch'ungch'ŏngnam-do; Kim Yosuk, interview by author, Yongin, South Korea, October 7, 2002; Brian Park, interview by author, Santa Ana, Calif., May 26, 2007.

113. *Chejŏk tŭngbon*, Pak P'yŏngch'i, 294 Chwahong-ri, Hongsan-myŏn, Puyŏ-gun, Ch'ungch'ŏngnam-do; and Pak Yŏngil, interview by author, Taejŏn, South Korea, July 7, 2007. Decades later, a daughter, her Chinese husband, and their children migrated to Canada. Pak Yŏngil, interview by author, Taejŏn, South Korea, July 7, 2007.

114. On Pyŏngsŏn's birth and death year information, see *Chejŏk tŭngbon*, Pak T'aesik, 294 Chwahong-ri, Hongsan-myŏn, Puyŏ-gun, Ch'ungch'ŏngnam-do;

chejŏk tŭngbon, O-ssi, 294 Chwahong-ri, Hongsan-myŏn, Puyŏ-gun, Ch'ungch'ŏngnam-do; *chejŏk tŭngbon*, Pak P'yŏngch'i, 294 Chwahong-ri, Hongsan-myŏn, Puyŏ-gun, Ch'ungch'ŏngnam-do. On Japanese policies on primary education during the period of wartime mobilization, see Furukawa, "Ilche sidae ch'odŭng kyoyuk kigwan ŭi ch'wihak sanghwang," 137, 170–72; Chŏng Kyuyŏng, "Chŏnsi tongwŏn ch'eje wa singminji kyoyuk ŭi pyŏnyong," 46–56; Caprio, *Japanese Assimilation Policies in Colonial Korea, 1910–1945*, 153–61; Ch'oe Hyegyŏng, "Ilche kangchŏm-gi pot'ong hakkyo ŭi sŏllip kwa kyoyuk hwaltong," 154–60; and Yi Myŏnghwa, 318–39.

115. Brian Park, interview by author, Santa Ana, Calif., May 26, 2007.

116. *Chejŏk tŭngbon*, Pak P'yŏngch'i, 294 Chwahong-ri, Hongsan-myŏn, Puyŏ-gun, Ch'ungch'ŏngnam-do; and Brian Park, interview by author, Chicago, May 27, 2007.

117. Brian Park, interview by author, Santa Ana, Calif., May 26, 2007.

118. Brian Park, interview by author, Swarthmore, Pa., October 27, 2011. After completing his college education, Pyŏngsŏn worked as a staff member at the U.S. embassy. When the North Korean troops occupied Seoul in June 1950, the communists made their initial rounds in all the neighborhoods. While searching the Pak household, they found a Marxist book inside the briefcase of Pyŏngsŏn. They readily declared that the household was "ideologically wholesome" and moved on. Throughout the period of North Korean occupation until September, Pyŏngsŏn and his younger brother Pyŏnggang (b. 1933) did their best not to be seen by military recruiters or herded to mass rallies after attending the first few, which they found intimidating. Reacting to the overall negative experience, the whole family fled Seoul shortly before the second North Korean occupation of Seoul in January 1951. Thanks to the husband of their mother Yonghwa's cousin, a merchant ship captain, the family traveled all the way to Pusan by ship rather than enduring the tortuous walking journey more typical of millions of refugees at the time. Seeing no future in wartime Korea, Pyŏngsŏn attempted to enter Japan by hiding in the cargohold of a Japan-bound ship. His plan was to get help from his Japanese friends, but on arrival in Yokohama he was apprehended and sent back to South Korea. What the post-Korean War years had in store for him was a career, in the 1950s, as a struggling journalist and writer, accumulating wealth, thereafter, as a private investor through real estate speculation in a country of rapid economic growth. From 1985, a stroke kept him incapacitated until his death in 1997. Brian Park, interview by author, Santa Ana, Calif., May 26, 2007; and Pak Kŭndong, interview by author, Taejŏn, South Korea, July 7, 2007.

119. Actually two years before Pyŏnggang's birth, in November 1931 in Kunsan, Ch'angnae and Yonghwa had a baby girl, their sixth daughter. Following the by-then twice-used talisman of giving a boy's name to the newborn girl, this time even including the *pyŏng*-generational character, they named her Pak Pyŏngil. At just two weeks old, on December 12 the girl died at the North Chŏlla Provincial Kunsan Medical Center (Chŏllabuk-do Kunsan Ŭiryowŏn). Chejŏk tŭngbon, Pak T'aesik, 294 Chwahong-ri, Hongsan-myŏn, Puyŏ-gun,

Ch'ungch'ŏngnam-do; chejŏk tŭngbon, O-ssi, 294 Chwahong-ri, Hongsan-myŏn, Puyŏ-gun, Ch'ungch'ŏngnam-do; and chejŏk tŭngbon, Pak P'yŏngch'i, 294 Chwahong-ri, Hongsan-myŏn, Puyŏ-gun, Ch'ungch'ŏngnam-do. She was the first of two children Ch'angnae and Yonghwa would lose in less than five months while dealing with financial woes in Kunsan.

120. Brian Park, interview by author, Santa Ana, Calif., May 26, 2007. On the days of downpour, she gave him a piggyback ride home from school. Brian Park, letter to Lauren H. Park, September 12, 2008.

121. Furukawa, "Ilche sidae ch'odŭng kyoyuk kigwan ŭi ch'wihak sanghwang," 170–72; Chŏng Kyuyŏng, 56–61; Caprio, 153–61; Ch'oe Hyegyŏng, 158–60; and Yi Myŏnghwa, 318–39.

122. Brian Park, interview by author, Chicago, May 27, 2007; and Chu Ja Cho, interview by author, Chicago, May 27, 2007.

123. *Chejŏk tŭngbon*, Pak P'yŏngch'i, 294 Chwahong-ri, Hongsan-myŏn, Puyŏ-gun, Ch'ungch'ŏngnam-do; and Brian Park, interview by author, Chicago, May 27, 2007. To help support the household, Pyŏnggang intended to work after graduation, and everyone around advised that a vocational school would be his best bet—though his true aspiration was to become an artist. Accordingly, in September 1945 he entered Seoul Industrial High School (Sŏul Kongŏp Kodŭng Hakkyo). He was just a year away from graduation when the Korean War broke out in June 1950. After fleeing to Pusan with the family in December 1950, he worked at a U.S. military base as an officer's houseboy and military base kitchen helper. At one point, Pyŏnggang had to fetch bombs for American military aircraft. In April 1953, his brother Pyŏngsŏn made an arrangement through a friend who was a high school teacher so that Pyŏnggang could resume his schooling. When the South Korean government and the school wherein he was enrolled returned to Seoul, he too moved back to the capital and continued his study at the same school, graduating in the following year. Afterward, Pyŏnggang studied chemical engineering at what is now Yonsei University (1954–58) and the University of Missouri (1963–64). In the context of South Korea's rapid economic growth since the mid-1960s, he went on to pursue a two-decade-long corporate career with Hanhwa Group, one of the country's top ten conglomerates. Including overseas assignments in Tokyo (1967–70) following the Korean-Japanese Normalization Treaty of 1965, which entailed Japanese payments and loans to South Korea, and Los Angeles (1980–83), Pyŏnggang's career culminated with a position as CEO (1983–85). In 1985 he resigned on acquiring a U.S. green card, and the family settled in America, deciding that the future of its three children was brighter there. Brian Park, interview by author, Santa Ana, Calif., May 26, 2007; and Brian Park, e-mail communication, June 4, 2012.

124. For a sympathetic book-length biography in Japanese, see Tsunoda, *Waga sokoku*.

125. "The science of breeding animals and plants under domestication." *Merriam-Webster Online*, accessed April 27, 2013, http://www.merriam-webster.com/dictionary/thremmatology.

126. Beginning in 1926, his published studies initially dealt with morning glories and petunias, coming up with new breeds. Following this with research in canola genetics and thremmatology, in 1935 his scholarship reached its zenith when he completed his doctoral dissertation, which attempted a genomic analysis of the genera of the cruciferous flower family. By crossing indigenous ten-chromosome Japanese canola and nine-chromosome cabbage to produce a unique, nineteen-chromosome canola, he demonstrated that cross-species plants can exist through the doubling of the chromosomes within their cells. His findings effectively critiqued Charles Darwin's theory of evolution, according to which formation of species is due to natural selection. Also, most of his predictions as presented in his "Thremmatology of Vegetables" (1945) are now in practical application. Kim T'aeuk, "U Changch'un Paksa ŭi yŏksajŏk pijung kwa kŭ wich'i," 142; and Taehan Chibang Haengjŏng Kongjehoe P'yŏnjipsil, "Segyejŏgin yukchong hakcha U Changch'un Paksa," 106–7.

127. Taehan Chibang Haengjŏng Kongjehoe P'yŏnjipsil, 107–9; and Kim Kŭnbae, "U Changch'un ŭi Han'guk kwihwan kwa kwahak yŏn'gu," 143–45. Invited by the South Korean government, in March 1950 Changch'un moved from Japan to his fatherland, where he achieved prominence as a celebrated scientist helping the country produce its own vegetable species rather than relying on Japanese imports. Until his death in 1959, Changch'un served as the director of the Korean Agricultural Science Research Institute (Han'guk Nongŏp Kwahak Yŏn'guso) and the president of the Central Agricultural Technology Research Institute (Chungang Wŏnye Kisurwŏn). While conducting research, he also trained future thremmatologists and nursery specialists. Hard work required personal sacrifice. In order to move to South Korea, a country with which Japan would not have formal relations until 1965, he had to leave behind his mother, wife, and six children. Kim T'aeuk, 142, 144–46, 147–50; Taehan Chibang Haengjŏng Kongjehoe P'yŏnjipsil, 107–9; and Kim Kŭnbae, 150–63.

EPILOGUE

1. See Chapter 6 for detail on the post-1945 stories of some individual family members.

2. The following discussion is a revision of Park, "Old Status Trappings in a New World," 177–78.

3. *Yŏnju Hyŏn-ssi taedongbo*, 6.503–4; *HMMTS*, s.v. "Hyŏn Sun"; and "Korean-American Architect David Hyun," *Korean Slate: Things Korean and not (in Korea Town LA)*, accessed October 17, 2011, http://koreanslate.com/korean-american-archi-tect-david-hyun.html. The second source gives Hyŏn Sun's birth year as 1880 instead of 1878 as recorded in the genealogy.

4. *Yŏnju Hyŏn-ssi taedongbo*, 6.503–4.

5. *HMMTS*, s.v. "Kim Pŏmu."

6. *Kyŏngju Kim-ssi Ch'ungsŏn'gong-p'a chokpo*, 294–95, 393–97, 496–98.

7. *Miryang Pak-ssi Kyujŏnggong-p'a sebo*, 13.10b–11a, 32.38a–39b; and *Miryang Pak-ssi Ch'ŏngjaegong che samja Sajikkong p'abo*, 1.242–43, 2.325–65.

8. Pak Pyŏnghae, interview by author, Seoul, June 27, 1992.

9. Ham [given name unknown], as quoted by Pak Pyŏnghae, interview by author, Seoul, October 5, 1995.

10. Pak Pyŏnghae, interview by author, Seoul, June 27, 1992; and Pak Pyŏnghae, interview by author, Seoul, October 5, 1995.

11. *Miryang Pak-ssi Kyujŏnggong-p'a taedongbo* (1986), 2.486, 991.

12. Pak Pyŏnghae, interview by author, Seoul, October 5, 1995; and Pak Kŭndong, telephone interview by author, Ansŏng, South Korea, September 13, 2004.

13. To my knowledge, a study that comes close to achieving this is a recent monograph by Hildi Kang, *Family Lineage Records as Resource for Korean History: A Case Study of Thirty-Nine Generations of the Sinch'ŏn Kang Family (720 A.D.–1955)*, which is a critical analysis—in the manner of an exegesis—of the genealogy of her husband's patrilineal ancestors who resided in Chŏngju in northwestern Korea during much of the Chosŏn period. All the same, this study and mine are fundamentally different in scope and methodology. Her subject is the Sinch'ŏn Kang as a "family," which is a post-seventeenth-century construct that encompassed—and brought together—previously unrelated Kangs of various ancestral seats. In fact, the particular descent line that Kang examines, that is, the descendants of Kang Yunch'ung (n.d.–1359), used to be the Koksan Kang before it evidently changed (sometime in the late Chosŏn period) the ancestral seat identifier to Sinch'ŏn. See *Ssijok wŏllyu*, 726. Regardless, historians must commend Kang's study for both the research behind it, including oral history, and the resulting narrative, a multigenerational history of her husband's patrilineal ancestors, who apparently belonged to the northwestern regional elite discriminated against by the Chosŏn aristocracy.

14. The following discussion is a revision of Park, "Old Status Trappings in a New World," 178–79.

15. Duncan, "Confucian Social Values in Contemporary South Korea," 68.

16. On such collections in Japan, see Tōyō Bunko Tōhoku Ajia Kenkyūhan (Chōsen), *Nihon shozai Chōsen koseki kankei shiryō kaidai*, 342–45.

17. These tendencies are evident in the most commonly-used Korea biographical references, such as Han'guk Inmyŏng Taesajŏn P'yŏnch'ansil, *Han'guk inmyŏng taesajŏn*; *HMMTS*; and Han'gukhak Chungang Yŏn'guwŏn, *Han'guk yŏktae inmul chonghap chŏngbo sisŭt'em*.

18. *HMMTS*, s.v. "O Sech'ang" and "Pak Yongdae."

19. Kang Ch'angsŏk, "Hunmin chŏngŭm charyosil: Ch'oe Sejin (1465?–1552)," accessed December 26, 2009, http://kang.chungbuk.ac.kr/zbxe/4127.

20. *Chungjong sillok*, 97.49b. For a more critical study on Ch'oe Sejin, see Kim Wanjin, "Chungin kwa ŏnŏ saenghwal: Ch'oe Sejin ŭl chungsim ŭro."

21. Paek Sŭngjong, "Wijo chokpo ŭi yuhaeng," 67–85; and Yi Kibaek, "Chokpo wa hyŏndae sahoe," 108–17.

Works Cited

Primary Sources

Andong Kim-ssi taedongbo [Comprehensive genealogy of the Andong Kim]. 13 vols. Seoul: Andong Kim-Ssi Taedongboso, 1984.

"Chamnok" [Miscellaneous records]. *T'aegŭk hakpo* 7 (February 24, 1907): 54–60.

Ch'angnyŏng Cho-ssi Sijunggong p'abo [Genealogy of the Ch'angnyŏng Cho, Sijunggong branch]. 2 vols. Pusan: Ch'angnyŏng Cho-Ssi Sijunggong-P'a Ut'aegong Chongmunhoe, 1985.

Ch'angwŏn Kong-ssi chokpo [Genealogy of the Ch'angwŏn Kong]. 3 vols. Miryang: n.p., 1725.

Chedŭngnok [Certified records of royal ancestor worship rituals]. 7 vols. N.p.: n.p., 1786–1846.

Chejŏk tŭngbon [Certified household registers] of *hoju* [household heads]:

Kim Ch'anggwŏn. 205 Tunyul-tong, Kunsan-si, Chŏllabuk-to.

Kim Pongnyuk. 205 Tunyul-tong, Kunsan-si, Chŏllabuk-to.

O-ssi [Madam O]. 294 Chwahong-ri, Hongsan-myŏn, Puyŏ-gun, Ch'ungch'ŏngnam-do.

Pak Kyŏngjun. [No number] Ch'unghwa-myŏn, Odŏk-ri, Ch'ungch'ŏngnam-do.

Pak P'yŏngch'i. 294 Chwahong-ri, Hongsan-myŏn, Puyŏ-gun, Ch'ungch'ŏngnam-do.

Pak Pyŏngsŏn. 465-29 Majang-dong, Sŏngdong-gu, Sŏul-t'ŭkpyŏlsi.

Pak T'aesik. 238 Odŏk-ri, Ch'unghwa-myŏn, Puyŏ-gun, Ch'ungch'ŏngnam-do.

Pak T'aesik. 294 Chwahong-ri, Hongsan-myŏn, Puyŏ-gun, Ch'ungch'ŏngnam-do.

Pang Ch'anbŏm. 240 Odŏk-ri, Ch'unghwa-myŏn, Puyŏ-gun, Ch'ungch'ŏngnam-do.

U Hangjŏng. 27 Kwanch'ŏl-tong, Kyŏngsŏng-bu, Kyŏnggi-do (218 Iptong-jŏng).

Chigugwanch'ŏng ilgi [Daily records of the Palace Security Office]. 9 vols. N.p.: Muwiso, n.d. Han'gukhak Chungang Yŏn'guwŏn. *Han'gukhak Chŏnja Tosŏgwan* [Korean studies electronic library]. Accessed November 30, 2011. http://lib. aks.ac.kr/DLiWeb20/components/searchir/detail/detail.aspx?cid=104554.

Cho, Chu Ja. Interview, March 10, 1990.

———. Telephone interview, November 14, 1990.

———. Telephone interview, September 27, 2004.

———. Interview, May 27, 2007.

Cho Susam. *Ch'ujae kii: 18-segi Chosŏn ŭi kiin yŏlchŏn* [Ch'ujae's tales of wonders: biographies of peculiar personae of 18th-century Chosŏn]. Trans. Hŏ Kyŏngjin. P'aju: Sŏhae Munjip, 2008.

Chŏngch'uk chŏngsi mun-mukwa pangmok [Roster of the 1637 courtyard civil and military examinations]. N.p.: n.p., n.d. Kyujanggak Han'gukhak Yŏn'guwŏn, Sŏul Taehakkyo. Sangbaek Ko 351.306 B224mn 1637.

Chŏngjo sillok [Veritable records of King Chŏngjo]. In *Chosŏn wangjo sillok*.

"Ch'ŏngju Han-ssi int'ŏnet chokpo." [Internet genealogy of the Ch'ŏngju Han]. *Ch'ŏngju Han-Ssi Chungang Chongch'inhoe.* Accessed May 1, 2011. http://www.cheongjuhan.net.

Ch'ŏngp'ung Kim-ssi sebo. [Genealogy of the Ch'ŏngp'ung Kim]. 7 vols. Seoul: Ch'ŏngp'ung Kim-Ssi Taejonghoe, 2010.

Ch'ongyungch'ŏng tŭngnok [Certified records of the Anti-Manchu Division Command]. 3 vols. N.p.: Ch'ongyungch'ŏng, 1725–1858.

Chŏnju Yi-ssi Changch'ŏn-gun p'abo [Genealogy of the Chŏnju Yi, Changch'ŏn-gun branch]. 2 vols. Koch'ang: Yŏngmojae, 1989.

Chōsen Sōtokufu. *Chōsen Sōtokufu kanpō* [Official gazette of the Government-General of Korea]. Reprint. 142 vols. Seoul: Asea Munhwasa, 1985.

———. *Chōsen Sōtokufu shisei 25 shūnen kinen hyōshōsha meikan* [Directory of individuals honored in commemoration of the twenty-five-year anniversary of the start of administration by the Government-General of Korea]. Kyŏngsŏng: Chōsen Sōtokufu Shisei 25 Shūnen Kinen Hyōshōsha Meikan Kankōkai, 1935. Kuksa P'yŏnch'an Wiwŏnhoe. *Han'guksa teit'ŏ peisŭ* [Korean history database]. Accessed May 12, 2012. http://db.history.go.kr.

———. *Chōsen Sōtokufu shokuinroku* [Employee records of the Government-General of Korea]. Kyŏngsŏng: Chōsen Sōtokufu, 1910–43. Kuksa P'yŏnch'an Wiwŏnhoe. *Han'guksa teit'ŏ peisŭ* [Korean history database]. Accessed May 12, 2012. http://db.history.go.kr.

Chosŏn ilbo (*The Chosunilbo*).

Chosŏn wangjo sillok [Veritable records of the Chosŏn dynasty]. 48 vols. Seoul: Kuksa P'yŏnch'an Wiwŏnhoe, 1955–58.

Chosŏn wangjo sŏnwŏllok [Records of the royal house of the Chosŏn dynasty]. Reprint. 10 vols. Kwangmyŏng: Minch'ang Munhwasa, 1992.

Ch'ungch'ŏng-do changt'o munjŏk [Register of royal estates in Ch'ungch'ŏng province]. 41 vols. N.p.: Naesusa, 1909.

Ch'ungch'ŏngnam-do Ŭnjin-Hongsan-gun sojae changt'o: Pak Myŏnghwan chech'ul tosŏ munjŏk ryu [Royal estates located in Ŭnjin-Hongsan counties, South Ch'ungch'ŏng province: bound documents presented by Pak Myŏnghwan]. Vol. 13 of *Ch'ungch'ŏng-do changt'o munjŏk.*

Ch'ungch'ŏngnam-do Yesan-gun sojae changt'o: Pak Myŏnghwan chech'ul tosŏ munjŏk ryu [Royal estates located in Yesan county, South Ch'ungch'ŏng province: bound documents presented by Pak Myŏnghwan]. Vol. 27 of *Ch'ungch'ŏng-do changt'o munjŏk.*

Ch'ungch'ŏngnam-do Puyŏ-gun yangan [Land register of Puyŏ county, South Ch'ungch'ŏng province]. 16 vols. N.p.: Yangji Amun, 1901.

Chungang ilbo (*Korea JoongAng Daily*).

Chungch'uwŏn naemun [Documents from the Privy Council]. 10 vols. N.p.: Ŭijŏngbu, 1896–1910.

Chungjong sillok [Veritable records of King Chungjong]. In *Chosŏn wangjo sillok.*

Haeju O-ssi taedongbo [Comprehensive genealogy of the Haeju O]. 10 vols. Seoul: Haeju O-Ssi Taedong Chongch'inhoe, 1992.

Hamyŏl Namgung-ssi chokpo [Genealogy of the Hamyŏl Namgung]. 4 vols. Seoul: Hamyŏl Namgung-Ssi Chongch'inhoe, 1994.

Han'guk Kojŏn Pŏnyŏgwŏn. *Han'guk kojŏn chonghap DB* (*DB of Korean Classics*). http://db.itkc.or.kr/itkcdb/mainIndexIframe.jsp.

Han'gyŏre (*Hankyoreh*).

"Hoewŏn myŏngbu" [List of members]. *Taehan Hyŏphoe hoebo* 3 (June 25, 1908): 65–68.

Hojŏk [household registers] of *hoju* [household heads]:

    Kim Iksŭng. 29-7 Kyo-dong, Osundŏk-kye, Kyŏnghaeng-bang, [Chung-sŏ], Hansŏng-bu, 1906.

    Namgung Ŏk. 3-2 Samch'ŏng-dong, Samch'ŏngdong-gye, Chinjang-bang, Puk-sŏ, Hansŏng-bu, 1906.

    P'aeng Hanju. 28-4 Kwanja-dong, Sŏch'ŏnsu-gye, Changt'ong-bang, Chung-sŏ, Hansŏng-bu, 1906.

    U Ch'anggi. 13-9 Mukchŏng-dong, Och'ŏn-gye, Hundo-bang, Nam-sŏ, Hansŏng-bu, 1903.

    U Hangjŏng. 14-2 Mukchŏng-dong, Och'ŏn-gye, Hundo-bang, Nam-sŏ, Hansŏng-bu, 1903.

    U Hangjŏng. 33-7 Taerip-tong, Sup'yogyo-gye, Changt'ong-bang, Chung-sŏ, Hansŏng-bu, 1906.

    U Kyŏngmyŏng. 14-4 Mukchŏng-dong, Och'ŏn-gye, Hundo-bang, Nam-sŏ, Hansŏng-bu, 1903.

    Yi Kŭnbae. 32-3 Sorip-tong, Yusaik-kye, Changt'ong-bang, Chung-sŏ, Hansŏng-bu, 1906.

    Yi Kŭnbae. 32-6 Sorip-tong, Yusaik-kye, Changt'ong-bang, Chung-sŏ, Hansŏng-bu, 1906.

    Yun Hyojŏng. 2 Wŏn-dong, Taesadong-gye, Kwanin-bang, Chung-sŏ, Hansŏng-bu, 1906.

Hullyŏng [Directives]. 4 vols. N.p.: Kungnae-bu, 1896.

Hwang Hyŏn. *Maech'ŏn yarok* [Memoir of Maech'ŏn]. Reprint. Han'guk saryo ch'ongsŏ 1. Seoul: Kuksa P'yŏnch'an Wiwŏnhoe, 1971.

Hwangsŏng sinmun [Capital gazette].

Hwasŏng sŏngyŏk ŭigwe: sujŏng kugyŏk [Royal protocols on the construction of the Hwasŏng city walls: a revised translation]. Trans. Kim Manil, Paek Sŏnhye, Sŏ Chŏngsang, Sim Yŏnghwan, Yi Talho, Yŏm Sanggyun, and Yun Hant'aek. Suwŏn: Kyŏnggi Munhwa Chaedan, 2001.

Hwasun Ch'oe-ssi taedong sebo [Comprehensive genealogy of the Hwasun Ch'oe]. 7 vols. Taejŏn: Hwasun Ch'oe-Ssi Taedong Chongch'inhoe, 1984.

Hyohyŏn Wanghu Kyŏngnŭng Sallŭng Togam ŭigwe [Royal protocols of the unnamed new royal tomb administration for the preparation of Queen Hyohyŏn's Kyŏngnŭng]. 2 vols. N.p.: Sallŭng Togam, 1843.

Hyomyŏng Seja Yŏn'gyŏng Myoso Togam ŭigwe [Royal protocols of the administration for the preparation of Crown Prince Hyomyŏng's Yŏn'gyŏng tomb site]. 2 vols. N.p.: Myoso Togam, 1830.

Hyŏnmok Subin Changnye Togam ŭigwe [Royal protocols of the administration for the funeral of Royal Consort Hyŏnmok Subin]. 4 vols. N.p.: Yejang Togam, 1822.

Hyŏnmok Subin Hwigyŏngwŏn Wŏnso Togam ŭigwe [Royal protocols of the administration for the preparation of the tomb site of Royal Consort Hyŏnmok Subin's Hwigyŏngwŏn]. 2 vols. N.p.: Wŏnso Togam, 1822.

Illŭng Ch'ŏnbong Sallŭng Togam ŭigwe [Royal protocols of the unnamed new royal tomb administration in preparation for moving the royal remains to Illŭng [tomb of King Ikchong and Queen Sunwŏn]]. 2 vols. N.p.: Ch'ŏnbong Togam, 1856.

Ilsŏngnok [Record of daily reflection]. 2,329 vols. Seoul: Kyujanggak, 1760–1910. "Wŏnmun charyo kŏmsaek" [Original document search]. *Sŏul Taehakkyo Kyujanggak Han'gukhak Yŏn'guwŏn.* Accessed March 24, 2012, May 6, 2012, May 7, 2012. http://kyujanggak.snu.ac.kr.

Ilsŏngnok [Record of daily reflection]. Reprint. 86 vols. Seoul: Sŏul Taehakkyo Tosŏgwan, 1982–96.

Im Inmuk. *Mukwa ch'ongyo* [Essentials on the military examination]. Reprint. Seoul: Asea Munhwasa, 1974.

The Independent. See *Tongnip sinmun.*

Injo sillok [Veritable records of King Injo]. In *Chosŏn wangjo sillok.*

Kaebyŏk [Creation].

Kajarok [Record of court rank promotions]. N.p.: Nae-bu, 1905.

Kankoku koseki seisatsu [Bound volumes of Korean household registration documents]. 165 vols. Manuscript. 1896–1907. Kyōto Daigaku Sōgō Hakubutsukan.

Kim Chŏngbae. Interview, July 15, 2001.

Kim Sŏngbae. Interview, October 15, 2002.

Kim Yosuk. Telephone interview, January 27, 1992.

———. Interview, October 7, 2002.

Kimhae hyangan kŭp Kimhae ŭpchi chŏryak [The Kimhae local *yangban* register and abridged gazetteer]. Kimhae: Myŏngnyundang, 1912.

Kimhae Kim-ssi sŏnwŏn taedong sebo: ch'ong p'yŏn [Comprehensive royal genealogy of the Kimhae Kim: overview]. 2 vols. Seoul: Kimhae Kim-Ssi Sŏnwŏn Taedongboso, 2001.

Kojong Ŏjin Tosa Togam ŭigwe [Royal protocols of the administration in preparation for preparing Kojong's portrait]. Reprint. Seoul: Sŏul Taehakkyo Kyujanggak, 1996.

Kojong sillok [Veritable records of Emperor Kojong]. In *Kojong-Sunjong sillok*.

Kojong-Sunjong sillok [Veritable records of Emperor Kojong and Emperor Sunjong]. Kyŏngsŏng: Riōshoku, 1935. Reprint. 3 vols. Seoul: T'amgudang, 1986.

Kŏllŭng Sallŭng Togam ŭigwe [Royal protocols of the unnamed new royal tomb administration for the preparation of Kŏllŭng]. N.p.: Sallŭng Togam Ŭigwech'ŏng, 1821.

Kongmun p'yŏnan [Edited registers of official documents]. 99 vols. N.p.: T'akchi-bu, n.d. Kuksa P'yŏnch'an Wiwŏnhoe. *Han'guksa teit'ŏ peisŭ* [Korean history database]. Accessed April 22, 2012. http://db.history.go.kr.

Koryŏsa [History of Koryŏ]. Reprint. 3 vols. Seoul: Yŏnse Taehakkyo Tongbanghak Yŏn'guso, 1955.

Kuksa P'yŏnch'an Wiwŏnhoe. *Taehan Cheguk kwanwŏn iryŏksŏ* [Career histories of bureaucratic personnel of the Korean Empire]. Seoul: T'amgudang, 1972.

Kuksangsi wŏnyŏktŭng sŏngch'aek chŏngsik [Prescribed forms for staff personnel serving at state funerals]. N.p.: Sahŏn-bu, 1849–90.

Kŭmwiyŏng tŭngnok [Certified records of the Palace Guard Division]. 111 vols. N.p.: Kŭmwiyŏng, 1682–1883.

Kwanbo [Official gazette]. Seoul: n.p., 1894–1910. Reprint (22 vols.), Seoul: Asea Munhwasa, 1973.

Kwangju Yi-ssi taedongbo [Comprehensive genealogy of the Kwangju Yi]. 14 vols. Seoul: Kwangju Yi-Ssi Taedongbo P'yŏnch'an Wiwŏnhoe, 1988.

Kyŏnggi-do changt'o munjŏk [Register of royal estates in Kyŏnggi province]. 89 vols. N.p.: Naesusa, n.d.

Kyŏnggi-do Ansan-gun Ch'osan-myŏn sojae changt'o: Yong-dong kung chech'ul tosŏ munjŏk ryu [Royal estates located in Ch'osan district, Ansan county, Kyŏnggi province: bound documents presented by the Yong-dong royal property management agency]. Vols. 10 and 73 of *Kyŏnggi-do changt'o munjŏk*.

Kyŏnggi-do Ŭmjuk-kun sojae changt'o: Chang Sŏkkyu chech'ul tosŏ munjŏk ryu [Royal estates located in Ŭmjuk county, Kyŏnggi province: bound documents presented by Chang Sŏkkyu]. Vol. 12 of *Kyŏnggi-do changt'o munjŏk*.

Kyŏngju Ch'oe-ssi taedongbo [Comprehensive genealogy of the Kyŏngju Ch'oe]. 13 vols. Seoul: Kyŏngju Ch'oe-Ssi Ch'ong Taejonghoe Taedongbo Chunggan Wiwŏnhoe, 2006.

Kyŏngju Kim-ssi Ch'ungsŏn'gong-p'a chokpo [Genealogy of the Kyŏngju Kim, Ch'ungsŏn'gong branch]. Seoul: Kyŏngju Kim-Ssi Ch'ungsŏn'gong-P'a Chokpo P'yŏnch'an Wiwŏnhoe, 1989.

Maeil sinbo [Daily news].

Mansŏng taedongbo [Comprehensive genealogy of ten thousand surnames]. 3 vols. Kyŏngsŏng: Mansŏng Taedongbo Kanhaengso, 1931–33.

Milsŏng Pak-ssi chokpo [Genealogy of the Milsŏng Pak]. N.p.: n.p., 1869.

Miryang Pak-ssi chokpo [Genealogy of the Miryang Pak]. N.p.: n.p., 1742. 6 vols.

Miryang Pak-ssi Ch'ŏngjaegong che samja Sajikkong p'abo [Genealogy of the Miryang Pak, Sajikkong branch, descended from the third son of Lord Ch'ŏngjae]. 2 vols. Kimje: Miryang Pak-Ssi Sajikkong P'aboso, 1998.

Miryang Pak-ssi Kyujŏnggong-p'a sebo [Genealogy of the Miryang Pak, Kyujŏnggong branch]. 33 vols. Kyŏngsŏng: Miryang Pak-Ssi Kyujŏnggong-P'a Taedongboso, 1924.

Miryang Pak-ssi Kyujŏnggong-p'a taedongbo [Comprehensive genealogy of the Miryang Pak, Kyujŏnggong branch]. 16 vols. Seoul: Miryang Pak-Ssi Kyujŏnggong-P'a Taedongboso, 1980.

Miryang Pak-ssi Kyujŏnggong-p'a taedongbo [Comprehensive genealogy of the Miryang Pak, Kyujŏnggong branch]. 2 vols. Puyŏ: Pak-Ssi Kibaekkong P'aboso, 1986.

Miryang Pak-ssi Mallyŏk kyŏngsinbo [Genealogy of the Miryang Pak of 1620]. N.p.: n.p., 1620. Accessed through *Miryang Pak-ssi Kyujŏnggong-p'a homp'eiji*. http://gyujeong.co.kr/.

Miryang Pak-ssi sebo [Genealogy of the Miryang Pak]. 13 vols. Seoul: n.p., 1873.

Miryang Pak-ssi Sungjŏng iminbo [Genealogy of the Miryang Pak of 1662]. N.p.: n.p., 1662. Accessed through *Miryang Pak-ssi Kyujŏnggong-p'a homp'eiji*. http://gyujeong.co.kr/.

Muan kunji [Muan county gazetteer]. 2 vols. Muan: Muan Hyanggyo, 1923.

Mun Pyŏngdal. "Chokpo kŏmsaek" [Searching the genealogy]. *Namp'yŏng Mun-ssi chŏnja taedongbo menyu* [Contents of the comprehensive electronic genealogy of the Namp'yŏng Mun]. Accessed June 8, 2012. http://www.moonsi.com.

Nae-bu naegŏ an [Registers received by the Ministry of Interior]. 4 vols. N.p.: Naegak, n.d. Kuksa P'yŏnch'an Wiwŏnhoe. *Han'guksa teit'ŏ peisŭ* [Korean history database]. Accessed April 22, 2012. http://db.history.go.kr.

Nagan O-ssi chokpo [Genealogy of the Nagan O]. 2 vols. Kwangju: Nagan O-Ssi P'yŏnch'an Wiwŏnhoe, 1985.

Naju Chŏng-ssi taedongbo [Comprehensive genealogy of the Naju Chŏng]. 7 vols. Taejŏn: Naju Chŏng-Ssi Taedongbo P'yŏnch'an Wiwŏnhoe, 1992.

Naju Kim-ssi taedong sebo [Comprehensive genealogy of the Naju Kim]. 5 vols. Seoul: Naju Kim-Ssi Taedongbo P'yŏnch'an Wiwŏnhoe, 2001.

Nakamura Shirō. *Chōsen ginkō kaisha kumiai yōroku* [Directory of Korean banks, companies, and financial associations]. 9 vols. Kyŏngsŏng: Tōa Keizai Jihōsha, 1927–1942. Kuksa P'yŏnch'an Wiwŏnhoe. *Han'guksa teit'ŏ peisŭ* [Korean history database]. Accessed May 10, 2012. http://db.history.go.kr.

Oean [Roster of provincial officials]. 4 vols. N.p.: Oe-bu, 1906.

Okch'ŏn Chŏn-ssi [Comprehensive genealogy of the Okch'ŏn Chŏn]. 6 vols. N.p.: Okch'ŏn Chŏn-Ssi Taedongbo P'yŏnch'an Wiwŏnhoe, 1989.

Onyang Pang-ssi chang p'a chongbo [Lineage register of the Onyang Pang, chang branch]. 6 vols. Seoul: Onyang Pang-Ssi P'ansŏgong-P'a Taejonghoe, 2006.

Onyang Pang-ssi taedongbo [Comprehensive genealogy of the Onyang Pang]. 8 vols. Seoul: Onyang Pang-Ssi Hwasuhoe, 1981.

Ŏyŏngch'ŏng chungsun tŭngnok [Certified records of the Royal Division archery contest]. 2 vols. N.p.: Ŏyŏngch'ŏng, 1747–1846.

Pak Chongsun. "Kyujŏnggong-p'a charyosil" [Kyujŏnggong-branch sources]. *Miryang Pak-ssi Kyujŏnggong-p'a homp'eiji* [Homepage of the Miryang Pak, Kyujŏnggong branch]. Accessed November 7, 2007, May 13, 2012. http://gyujeong.co.kr.

Pak Kŭndong. Interview, June 1, 1992.

———. Telephone interview, September 13, 2004.

———. Interview, July 7, 2007.

———. Interview, July 13, 2011.

Pak Pyŏnghae. Interview, June 27, 1992.

———. Interview, October 5, 1995.

Pak Pyŏngsŏn. Interview, June 1, 1992.

Pak T'aewŏn. Telephone interview, July 1, 2008.

Pak Yŏngil. Telephone interview, October 4, 2004.

———. Interview, July 7, 2007.

Pang Kijun. Telephone interview, September 22, 2007.

———. Telephone interview, October 8, 2007.

Pang Ujŏng. "Sŏjŏng ilgi" [Daily records of the western campaign]. In *Sŏjŏng ilgi, Chinjung ilgi* [Daily records of the western campaign, Daily records of military encampment]. Han'guk saryo ch'ongsŏ 15. Seoul: Kuksa P'yŏnch'an Wiwŏnhoe, 1974.

Park, Brian. Interview, May 26, 2007.

———. Interview, May 27, 2007.

———. Letter to Lauren H. Park, September 12, 2008.

———. Interview, October 31, 2010.

———. Telephone interview, June 1, 2011.

———. Interview, October 27, 2011.

———. E-mail communication, June 4, 2012.

———. Telephone interview, June 17, 2012.

"Ponhoe kisa" [Proceedings of the main meeting]. *Kiho Hŭnghakhoe wŏlbo* 1 (August 25, 1908): 44–55.

Samguk sagi [History of the Three Kingdoms]. Reprinted in *Wŏnbon Samguk sagi* [History of the Three Kingdoms, original text]. Annotated by Yi Kangnae. Seoul: Han'gilsa, 1998.

Samguk yusa [Memorabilia of the Three Kingdoms]. Reprinted in *Chŏmgyo Samguk yusa* [Punctuated Memorabilia of the Three Kingdoms]. Annotated by Ch'oe Kwangsik and Pak Taejae. Seoul: Koryŏ Taehakkyo Ch'ulp'anbu, 2009.

Sarŭng Togam ŭigwe [Royal protocols of the administration for the preparation of Sarŭng]. N.p.: Pongnŭng Togam, 1698.

Sejong sillok [Veritable records of King Sejong]. In *Chosŏn wangjo sillok*.

Sidae ilbo [The time news].

Sin Hŭich'ŏl. *Oean ko* [List of provincial officials]. Reprint of handwritten manuscript. Seoul: Pogyŏng Munhwasa, 2002.

Sŏngwŏllok [Records of surname origins]. Seoul: Osŏngsa, 1985.

Ssijok wŏllyu [Origins of descent groups]. Seoul: Pogyŏng Munhwasa, 1991.

Sukchong sillok [Veritable records of King Sukchong]. In *Chosŏn wangjo sillok*.

Sungjŏng sam kyŏngsin kyŏngkwa chŏngsi pyŏlsi mun-mukwa chŏnsi pangmok: mukwa pang [Palace examination roster of the 1800 courtyard special civil-military examination: military examination roster]. N.p.: n.d. National Library of Korea. Ilsan Ko 6024-60.

Sŭngjŏngwŏn ilgi [Daily records of the Royal Secretariat]. 3,243 vols. Seoul: Sŭngjŏngwŏn, 1623–1910. "Wŏnmun charyo kŏmsaek" [Original document search]. *Sŏul Taehakkyo Kyujanggak Han'gukhak Yŏn'guwŏn*. Accessed May 7, 2012. http://kyujanggak.snu.ac.kr.

Sŭngjŏngwŏn ilgi [Daily records of the Royal Secretariat]. Reprint. 126 vols. Seoul: T'amgudang, 1987.

Sŭngjŏngwŏn ilgi: Kojong [Daily records of the Royal Secretariat: Kojong]. Reprint. 15 vols. Seoul: Kuksa P'yŏnch'an Wiwŏnhoe, 1968.

Sunhŭng An-ssi chokpo [Genealogy of the Sunhŭng An]. N.p.: n.p., 1783.

Sunjo sillok [Veritable records of King Sunjo]. In *Chosŏn wangjo sillok*.

Surŭng Sallŭng Togam ŭigwe [Royal protocols of the unnamed new royal tomb administration in preparation for Surŭng]. N.p.: Sallŭng Togam, 1846.

Suzuki Yōtarō. "Ch'oegŭn Kando mit chŏbyang chibang pullyŏng Sŏnin ŭi haengdong e kwanhan kŏn" [Matters relating to the recent actions of disgruntled Koreans in Jiandao and its vicinity], document number: Kimil che 90-ho–Kimilsu che 98-ho. March 26, 1924. In document collection, "Pullyŏng chiptan kwan'gye chapkŏn—Chosŏnin ŭi pu—chae Manju ŭi pu (38)" [Miscellaneous matters relating to disgruntled groups—section on Koreans—section on Manchuria (38)]. In *Kungnaeoe hangil undong munsŏ* [Documents on anti-Japanese resistance in and outside Korea]. Kuksa P'yŏnch'an Wiwŏnhoe. *Han'guksa teit'ŏ peisŭ* [Korean history database]. Accessed May 26, 2012. http://db.history.go.kr.

Taegu Sŏ-ssi chokpo [Genealogy of the Taegu Sŏ]. N.p.: n.p., 1736. Reprinted in *Taegu Sŏ-ssi chokpo* [Genealogy of the Taegu Sŏ]. Seoul: Taegu Sŏ-Ssi Poso, 1979.

Taegu Sŏ-ssi sebo [Genealogy of the Taegu Sŏ]. 3 vols. N.p.: Taegu Sŏ-Ssi Poso, 1979.

T'aegŭk hakpo [T'aegŭk Educational Association journal].

Taehan maeil sinbo (The Korea Daily News).

Taehan Min'guk chigwŏllok [Personnel of the Republic of Korea]. N.p.: n.p., 1952. Kuksa P'yŏnch'an Wiwŏnhoe. *Han'guksa teit'ŏ peisŭ* [Korean history database]. Accessed May 13, 2012. http://db.history.go.kr.

Tanyang U-ssi chokpo [Genealogy of the Tanyang U]. 20 vols. N.p.: n.p., 1800.

Tanyang U-ssi taedongbo [Comprehensive genealogy of the Tanyang U]. 6 vols. Taejŏn: n.p., 1966.

T'onggyech'ŏng. "Ch'ong chosa in'gu (2000): sŏngssi, pon'gwan" [Total surveyed population (2000): surname, ancestral seat]. *Kukka t'onggye p'ot'ŏl (Korean Statistical Information Service)*. Accessed June 8, 2012. http://kosis.kr/abroad/abroad_01List.jsp.

Tonga ilbo (The Dong-A Ilbo).

Tongnip sinmun (The Independent).

U Kyŏngmyŏng, trans. Original author unknown. "Kyoyuk ŭi mokchŏk" [Purposes of education]. *T'aegŭk hakpo* 10 (May 24, 1907): 17–19.

———. "Chiban esyŏ ŏrin aŭ kiranŏn pŏp" [Raising young children in a household]. *T'aegŭk hakpo* 11 (June 24, 1907): 37–40.

Ŭiyŏkchu p'alsebo [Eight-generation genealogy of physician, interpreter, and accountant examination graduates]. 3 vols. N.p.: n.p., [sometime between 1871 and 1907].

Yangmu wŏnjong kongsin nokkwŏn [Roster of Yangmu minor meritorious subjects]. N.p.: Nokhun Togam, 1728.

Yi Pyŏngdŏk. *Ŭmjuk-kun ŭpchi (Kyŏnggi-do)* [Ŭmjuk county town gazetteer (Kyŏnggi province)]. N.p.: n.p., 1899.

Yi Sangŏk. E-mail communication, May 12, 2009.

Yŏhŭng Min-ssi p'abo [Branch genealogy of the Yŏhŭng Min]. N.p.: n.p., 1925.

Yŏkhunji [Directives on postal station land]. N.p.: 8 vols. Nongsanggong-bu, 1898–1905. Kuksa P'yŏnch'an Wiwŏnhoe. *Han'guksa teit'ŏ peisŭ* [Korean history database]. Accessed May 22, 2012. http://db.history.go.kr.

Yŏkt'o sogwan munch'ŏp kŏan [Outgoing documents concerning postal station land]. 3 vols. N.p.: Nongsanggong-bu, 1895–96. Kuksa P'yŏnch'an Wiwŏnhoe. *Han'guksa teit'ŏ peisŭ* [Korean history database]. Accessed May 22, 2012. http://db.history.go.kr.

Yŏkt'o sogwan munch'ŏp naean [Incoming documents concerning postal station land]. 4 vols. N.p.: Nongsanggong-bu, 1895–96. Kuksa P'yŏnch'an Wiwŏnhoe. *Han'guksa teit'ŏ peisŭ* [Korean history database]. Accessed May 22, 2012. http://db.history.go.kr.

Yŏkt'o sogwan sawŏn chilbo chondang [Preserved stock-taker query reports concerning postal station land]. 15 vols. N.p.: Nongsanggong-bu, 1895–1903. Kuksa P'yŏnch'an Wiwŏnhoe. *Han'guksa teit'ŏ peisŭ* [Korean history database]. Accessed May 22, 2012. http://db.history.go.kr.

Yŏkt'o sogwan sawŏn hunji chondang [Preserved stock-taker directives concerning postal station land]. 7 vols. N.p.: Nongsanggong-bu, 1895–97. Kuksa P'yŏnch'an Wiwŏnhoe. *Han'guksa teit'ŏ peisŭ* [Korean history database]. Accessed May 22, 2012. http://db.history.go.kr.

Yŏnan Yi-ssi sebo [Genealogy of the Yŏnan Yi]. N.p.: n.p., 1729 preface.

Yŏnan Yi-ssi Sobugam P'ansagong-p'a taebo [Comprehensive genealogy of the Yŏnan Yi, Sobugam P'ansagong branch]. 11 vols. Seoul: Yŏnan Yi-Ssi Sobugam P'ansagong-P'a Taejonghoe, 2002.

Yonggang P'aeng-ssi sebo [Genealogy of the Yonggang P'aeng]. N.p.: n.p., 1965.

Yŏnju Hyŏn-ssi taedongbo [Comprehensive genealogy of the Yŏnju Hyŏn]. 8 vols. Taejŏn: Yŏnju Hyŏn-Ssi Taedongbo P'yŏnch'an Wiwŏnhoe, 2001.

Yŏyudang chŏnsŏ [Complete writings of Yŏyudang]. Reprinted in *Yŏyudang chŏnsŏ*. 76 volumes in 9 cases. Kyŏngsŏng: Sin Chosŏnsa, 1934–38.

Yu Sangp'il. *Tongsarok* [Record of east raft]. Han'guk Kojŏn Pŏnyŏgwŏn. *Han'guk kojŏn chonghap DB (DB of Korean Classics)*. Accessed March 24, 2012. http://db.itkc.or.kr/itkcdb/mainIndexIframe.jsp.

Yu-ssi taedongbo [Comprehensive genealogy of the Yu]. 12 vols. Seoul: Yu-Ssi Taedong Chongch'inhoe Chungang Ch'ong Ponbu, 1975.

Yun Ch'iho. *Yun Ch'iho ilgi* [Diary of Yun Ch'iho]. 11 vols. Seoul: T'amgudang, 1973–1989.

Yun Hyojŏng. *P'ungun Hanmal pisa, il myŏng, Ch'oegŭn yuksip nyŏn ŭi pirok* [A secret history of the Hanmal period, or, a secret record of the last sixty years]. Seoul: Sumunsa, 1984.

Secondary Sources

An Chongch'ŏl. *Miguk sŏn'gyosa wa Han-Mi kwan'gye, 1931–1948: kyoyuk ch'ŏlsu, chŏnsi hyŏmnyŏk, kŭrigo Mi kunjŏng* [American missionaries and Korean-American relations, 1931–1948: withdrawal from the education sector, wartime cooperation, and the American military government]. Seoul: Han'guk Kiddokkyo Yŏksa Yŏn'guso, 2010.

Baek, Seung-ch'ol. See Paek Sŭngch'ŏl.

Boster, James S., Richard R. Hudson, and Steven J. C. Gaulin. "High Paternity Certainties of Jewish Priests." *American Anthropologist* 100.4 (December 1998): 967–71.

Bourdieu, Pierre. *Distinction: A Social Critique of the Judgment of Taste*. Trans. Richard Nice. Cambridge, Mass.: Harvard University Press, 1984.

Breuker, Remko. *Establishing a Pluralist Society in Medieval Korea, 918–1170*. Leiden: Brill, 2010.

Brown, Peter. "A Dark-Age Crisis: Aspects of the Iconoclastic Controversy." *The English Historical Review* 88.346 (January 1973): 1–34.

Caprio, Mark E. *Japanese Assimilation Policies in Colonial Korea, 1910–1945*. Seattle: University of Washington Press, 2009.

Ch'ae Kilsun. "Ch'ungch'ŏngbuk-to chungnam-bu chiyŏk Tonghak hyŏngmyŏng-sa yŏn'gu" [The history of the Tonghak revolution in the south and center of North Ch'ungch'ŏng province]. *Ch'ungbukhak* 10 (2008): 49–63.

Chandra, Vipan. *Imperialism, Resistance, and Reform in Late Nineteenth-Century Korea: Enlightenment and the Independence Club*. Berkeley: Institute of East Asian Studies, University of California, Berkeley, 1988.

Chen, Ching-chih. "Police and Community Control Systems in the Empire." In *The Japanese Colonial Empire, 1895–1945*, ed. Ramon H. Myers and Mark R. Peattie, 213–39.

Ch'inil Inmyŏng Sajŏn P'yŏnch'an Wiwŏnhoe. *Ch'inil inmyŏng sajŏn* [Dictionary of pro-Japanese collaborators]. 3 vols. Seoul: Minjok Munje Yŏn'guso, 2009.

Cho Chaegon. "Taehan Cheguk ki kunsa chŏngch'aek kwa kunsa kigu ŭi unyŏng"

[The military policy and the management of military institutions during the Korean Empire period]. *Yŏksa wa hyŏnsil* 19 (1996): 100–34.

Cho Hŭisŏn and Ryu Mihyŏn. "Sarye rŭl t'onghaesŏ pon honsu kwanhaeng munje yŏn'gu" [The problems of matrimonial gift custom as seen through cases]. *Han'guk Kajŏng Kwalli Hakhoeji* 17.1 (March 1999): 179–90.

Cho Pyŏngok. *Na ŭi hoegorok* [My memoir]. Seoul: Min'gyosa, 1959.

Cho Sŏngyun. "Chosŏn hugi Sŏul chiyŏk chungin seryŏk ŭi sŏngjang kwa han'gye" [The growth of *chungin* power and its limitations in late Chosŏn Seoul]. *Yŏksa pip'yŏng* 21 (May 1993): 235–49.

———. "Sŏul saram ŭi sinbun punp'o wa chugŏ chiyŏk" [Social status distribution among Seoul residents and their residence locales]. *Yŏksa pip'yŏng* 26 (February 1994): 104–10.

———, and Cho Ŭn. "Hanmal ŭi kajok kwa sinbun: Hansŏng-bu hojŏk punsŏk" [Family and social status in the Hanmal period: an analysis of Seoul household registration records]. *Sahoe wa yŏksa* 50 (December 1996): 96–133.

Cho Yŏngjun. "Chosŏn hugi kungbang ŭi silch'e" [The nature of late Chosŏn royal estate management agencies]. *Chŏngsin munhwa yŏn'gu* 31.3 (September 2008): 273–304.

———. "Chosŏn hugi yŏgaek chuin mit yŏgaek chuinkwŏn chaeron: Kyŏnggi-Ch'ungch'ŏng changt'o munjŏk ŭi chaegusŏng ŭl t'onghayŏ" [Re-theorizing late Chosŏn coastal trade brokers and coastal trader broker rights: reconstructing Kyŏnggi and Ch'ungch'ŏng royal estate registers]. *Han'guk munhwa* 57 (March 2012): 3–24.

Ch'oe Chaesŏng. "'Ch'angssi kaemyŏng' kwa ch'inil Chosŏnin ŭi hyŏmnyŏk" [The "name change" and cooperation of pro-Japanese Koreans]. *Han'guk tongnip undongsa yŏn'gu* 37 (December 2012): 345–92.

Ch'oe Chinok. *Chosŏn sidae saengwŏn-chinsa yŏn'gu* [Studies on the Chosŏn-period classics and literary licentiates]. Seoul: Chimmundang, 1998.

Ch'oe Chonggo. "Kaehwagi ŭi pŏphak kyoyuk kwa Han'guk pŏmnyulga ŭi hyŏngsong—'Pŏpkwan Yangsŏngso' wa 'Pojŏn' ŭi kyokwa wa kyosujin ŭl chungsim ŭro" [Legal education and the formation of Korea's legal experts during the Enlightenment Period: the curriculum and faculty of the "Judicial Officer Training Institute" and "Posŏng College"]. *Sŏul Taehakkyo pŏphak* 22.1 (1982): 63–101.

Ch'oe Hyegyŏng. "Ilche kangchŏm-gi pot'ong hakkyo ŭi sŏllip kwa kyoyuk hwaltong: Kyŏnggi-do Kunp'o-si chiyŏk ŭl chungsim ŭro" [The establishment of ordinary schools and their educational activities in the period of imperial Japanese domination: a study of Kunp'o, Kyŏnggi province]. *Kyŏngju sahak* 31 (June 2010): 151–83.

Ch'oe Hyosik. "Chosŏn sidae Urimwi ŭi sŏngnip kwa kŭ p'yŏnje" [The establishment of the Chosŏn-period Winged Forest Guards and its organization]. *Tongguk sahak* 15 and 16 combined volume (1981): 169–87.

Ch'oe Kiyŏng. "Hanmal Pŏpkwan Yangsŏngso ŭi unyŏng kwa kyoyuk" [Management and education at the Judicial Officer Training Institute in the Hanmal period]. *Han'guk kŭnhyŏndaesa yŏn'gu* 16 (2001): 39–75.

Ch'oe Sŭnghŭi. "Chosŏn hugi wŏnjong kongsin nokhun kwa sinbunje tongyo" [The late Chosŏn minor meritorious subject enrollments and shake-up of the status system]. *Han'guk munhwa* 22 (1998): 113–57.

Ch'oe Tŏkkyo. *Han'guk sŏngssi taegwan* [A compendium of Korean surnames]. Seoul: Ch'angjosa, 1971.

Ch'oe, Yong-ho. "The Kapsin Coup of 1884: A Reassessment." *Korean Studies* 6 (1982): 105–24.

Ch'oe Yuno. *Chosŏn hugi t'oji soyu ŭi paltal kwa chijuje* [The landlord system and the development of land ownership in late Chosŏn]. Seoul: Hyean, 2006.

Choi, Hyaeweol. *Gender and Mission Encounters in Korea: New Women, Old Ways.* Berkeley: University of California Press, 2009.

Ch'ŏn Chŏnghwan. *Kŭndae ŭi ch'aek ilkki: tokcha ŭi t'ansaeng kwa Han'guk kŭndae munhak* [Book-reading in the modern period: the birth of readership and modern Korean literature]. Seoul: P'urŭn Yŏksa, 2003.

Chŏn Sunp'yo. "Okch'ŏn-Ch'ŏngsan Tonghak Nongmin Chŏnjaeng kwa Hanmal ŭibyŏng" [The Tonghak Peasant War in Okch'ŏn-Ch'ŏngsan and righteous armies in the Hanmal period]. *Ch'ungbuk hyangt'o munhwa* 20 (2008): 127–70.

Chŏng Haeŭn. "Pyŏngja Horan sigi kun'gong myŏnch'ŏnin ŭi mukwa kŭpche wa sinbun pyŏnhwa: 'Chŏngch'uk chŏngsi mukwa pangmok' (1637 nyŏn) ŭl chungsim ŭro" [Military examination passing and change in the social status of manumitted slaves with military merit during the Korean-Manchu War period: the "Chŏngch'uk courtyard military examination roster" (1637)]. *Chosŏn sidae sahakpo* 9 (June 1999): 71–104.

———. "Chosŏn hugi mukwa kŭpcheja yŏn'gu" [Late Chosŏn military examination passers]. Ph.D. dissertation, Han'guk Chŏngsin Munhwa Yŏn'guwŏn, 2002.

Chŏng Husu. *Chosŏn hugi chungin munhak yŏn'gu* [Late Chosŏn *chungin* literature]. Seoul: Kip'ŭn Saem, 1990.

Chŏng Kyuyŏng. "Chŏnsi tongwŏn ch'eje wa singminji kyoyuk ŭi pyŏnyong: Ilbon singminji chibaeha ŭi Han'guk kyoyuk, 1937–1945" [The wartime mobilization system and the transformation of colonial education: education in Korea under Japanese colonial rule, 1937–1945]. *Kyoyukhak yŏn'gu* 40.2 (2002): 35–64.

Chŏng Muryong. "Chosŏn-jo chungin kyech'ŭng sigo (3): t'ongch'ŏng undong ŭl chungsim ŭro" [A preliminary inquiry into the *chungin* of the Chosŏn dynasty (3): the petition movement for access to prestigious offices]. [*Kyŏngsŏng Taehakkyo*] *Nonmunjip* 13.3 (1992): 37–60.

Chŏng Okcha. *Chosŏn hugi chungin munhwa yŏn'gu* [Late Chosŏn *chungin* culture]. Seoul: Ilchisa, 2003.

Chŏng Sŏngil. "Taema-do yŏkchi pingnye e ch'amgahan t'ongsinsa ilhaeng e taehayŏ" [The Korean embassy members who participated in the 1811 diplomatic mission to Tsushima]. *Honam munhwa yŏn'gu* 20 (1991): 83–118.

Chu Chin-Oh. See Chu Chino.

Chu Chino. "19 segi huban Kaehwa kaehyŏngnon ŭi kujo wa chŏn'gae: Tongnip Hyŏphoe rŭl chungsim ŭro" [The structure and development of late 19th-century

Enlightenment reform discourse: a study of the Independence Club]. Ph.D. dissertation, Yŏnse Taehakkyo, 1995.

———. "1898-nyŏn Tongnip Hyŏphoe undong ŭi chudo seryŏk kwa chiji kiban" [The leading force and the support base of the 1898 Independence Club movement]. *Yŏksa wa hyŏnsil* 15 (March 1995): 173–208.

———. "Han'guk kŭndae kungmin kukka surip kwajŏng esŏ wangkwŏn ŭi yŏkhwal (1880–1894)" [The role of royal power during the process of establishing a modern nation-state in Korea (1880–1894)]. *Yŏksa wa hyŏnsil* 50 (December 2003): 43–69.

———. [Chu Chin-Oh]. "The Independence Club's Conceptions of Nationalism and the Modern State." In *Landlords, Peasants, and Intellectuals in Modern Korea*, ed. Pang Kie-chung and Michael D. Shin, 53–89. Ithaca: East Asia Program, Cornell University, 2005.

Chungang Ilbosa. *Sŏngssi ŭi kohyang (SK)* [Origins of surnames]. Seoul: Chungang Ilbosa, 1989.

Ch'ungbuk Palchŏn Yŏn'guwŏn. *Ch'ungch'ŏngbuk-do Tonghak Nongmin Hyŏngmyŏngsa yŏn'gu* [The history of the Tonghak Peasant Revolution in North Ch'ungch'ŏng province]. N.p.: Ch'ungbuk Palchŏn Yŏn'guwŏn, 2006.

Cumings, Bruce. *The Origins of the Korean War, Vol. II: The Roaring of the Cataract, 1947–1950.* Princeton: Princeton University Press, 1990.

De Ceuster, Koen. "The Nation Exorcised: The Historiography of Collaboration in South Korea." *Korean Studies* 25.2 (2002): 207–42.

Dennett, Tyler. *Americans in Eastern Asia: A Critical Study of the Policy of the United States with Reference to China, Japan and Korea in the 19th Century.* New York: Macmillan, 1922.

Deuchler, Martina. *The Confucian Transformation of Korea: A Study of Society and Ideology.* Cambridge, Mass.: Council on East Asian Studies, Harvard University, 1992.

Duncan, John B. "Confucian Social Values in Contemporary South Korea." In *Religion and Society in Contemporary Korea*, ed. Lewis R. Lancaster and Richard K. Payne, 49–73. Berkeley: Institute of East Asian Studies, University of California, 1997.

———. *The Origins of the Chosŏn Dynasty.* Seattle: University of Washington Press, 2000.

———. "The Confucian Context of Reform." In *Reform and Modernity in the Taehan Empire*, ed. Kim Dong-no, John B. Duncan, and Kim Do-hyung, 105–25. Seoul: Jimoondang, 2006.

Duus, Peter. "Economic Dimensions of Meiji Imperialism: The Case of Korea, 1895–1910." In *The Japanese Colonial Empire, 1895–1945*, ed. Ramon H. Myers and Mark R. Peattie, 128–71.

———. *The Abacus and the Sword: The Japanese Penetration of Korea, 1895–1910.* Berkeley: University of California Press, 1995.

Eckert, Carter J. *Offspring of Empire: The Koch'ang Kims and the Colonial Origins of Korean Capitalism, 1876–1945.* Seattle: University of Washington Press, 1991.

————. Ki-baik Lee, Young-Ick Lew, Michael Robinson, and Edward W. Wagner. *Korea Old and New: A History*. Cambridge, Mass.: Korea Institute, Harvard University, 1990.

Femia, Joseph V. *Gramsci's Political Thought: Hegemony, Consciousness, and the Revolutionary Process*. Oxford: Clarendon Press, 1981.

Furukawa Noriko. "Ilche sidae ch'odŭng kyoyuk kigwan ŭi ch'wihak sanghwang—pulch'wihak adong ŭi tasu chonjae wa pot'ong hakkyosaeng ŭi chŭngga" [Enrollment at primary education institutions during the period of Imperial Japanese rule: the existence of a considerable number of unenrolled children and increase in the number of ordinary-school students]. *Kyoyuk sahak yŏn'gu* 2–3 (1990): 136–74.

————. "Ilche sidae ŭi chung, kodŭng kyoyuk" [Secondary and higher education in the period of imperial Japanese rule]. *Kyoyuk sahak yŏn'gu* 6–7 (1996): 45–67.

Gragert, Edwin H. *Land Ownership Under Colonial Rule: Korea's Japanese Experience, 1900–1935*. Honolulu: University of Hawaii Press, 1994.

Haboush, JaHyun Kim. *A Heritage of Kings: One Man's Monarchy in the Confucian World*. New York: Columbia University Press, 1988.

————. "Constructing the Center: The Ritual Controversy and the Search for a New Identity in Seventeenth-Century Korea." In *Culture and the State in Late Chosŏn Korea*, ed. JaHyun Kim Haboush and Martina Deuchler, 46–90. Cambridge, Mass.: Harvard University Asia Center, 1999.

Han Migyŏng. "Nagan O-ssi yŏkkwa ipkyŏkcha kirok e taehan yŏn'gu" [The Nagan O interpreter examination passers]. *Sŏjihak yŏn'gu* 32 (December 2005): 419–42.

Han Yŏngu. "Chosŏn hugi 'chungin' e taehayŏ: Ch'ŏlchong-gi chungin t'ongch'ŏng undong charyo rŭl chungsim ŭro" [On the late Chosŏn "chungin": sources on the Ch'ŏlchong-period *chungin* petition movement for access to prestigious offices]. *Han'guk hakpo* 45 (December 1986): 66–89.

————. "Chosŏn sidae chungin ŭi sinbun-kyegŭpchŏk sŏngkyŏk" [Status- and class-related characteristics of the Chosŏn-period *chungin*]. *Han'guk munhwa* 9 (1988): 179–209.

————. *Tasi ch'annŭn uri yŏksa* [Our history rediscovered]. Revised edition. P'aju: Kyŏngsewŏn, 2004.

————. *Myŏngsŏng Hwanghu: cheguk ŭl irŭk'ida* [Empress Myŏngsŏng: launching the empire]. P'aju: Hyohyŏng Ch'ulp'an, 2006.

————. *"Panch'ado" ro ttara kanŭn Chŏngjo ŭi Hwasŏng haengch'a* [Following Chŏngjo's royal procession to Hwasŏng through an "illustrated marching formation"]. P'aju: Hyohyŏng Ch'ulp'an, 2007.

Han'guk Inmyŏng Taesajŏn P'yŏnch'ansil. *Han'guk inmyŏng taesajŏn* [An encyclopedia of Korean biographical dictionary]. Seoul: Sin'gu Munhwasa, 1967.

Han'guk Kidokkyosa Yŏn'guhoe. *Han'guk Kidokkyo ŭi yŏksa* [A history of Korean Christianity], vol. I. Seoul: Kidok Kyomunsa, 1989.

Han'guk Minjok Munhwa Taesajŏn P'yŏnch'anbu. *Han'guk minjok munhwa taebaekkwa sajŏn (HMMTS)* [Encyclopedia of Korean culture]. 27 vols. Sŏngnam: Han'guk Minjok Munhwa Taesajŏn P'yŏnch'anbu, 1991.

Han'guk Yŏksa Yŏn'guhoe 19 Segi Chŏngch'isa Yŏn'guban, ed. *Chosŏn chŏngch'isa (1800–1863)* [A political history of Chosŏn (1800–1863)]. 2 vols. Seoul: Ch'ŏngnyŏnsa, 1990.

Han'gukhak Chungang Yŏn'guwŏn. "Kong Sŭngt'ak" [Kong Sŭngt'ak]. *Han'guk yŏktae inmul chonghap chŏngbo sisŭt'em* [A comprehensive information system on historical Korean personalities]. Accessed June 8, 2012. http://people.aks.ac.kr/index.aks.

———. "Kwagŏ mit ch'wijae" [Government service examinations and tests]. *Han'guk yŏktae inmul chonghap chŏngbo sisŭt'em* [A comprehensive information system on historical Korean personalities]. Accessed November 1, 2011. http://people.aks.ac.kr/index.aks.

Hŏ Tonghyŏn. "Taehan Cheguk ŭi model rŏsŏ ŭi Rŏsia" [Russia as a model of the Korean Empire]. *Myŏngji Taehakkyo Kukche Han'gukhak Yŏn'guso Yŏllye Haksul Taehoe* (January 2005): 53–63.

Hobsbawm, Eric. "Introduction: Inventing Tradition." In *The Invention of Tradition*, ed. Eric Hobsbawm and Terence Ranger, 1–14. Cambridge: Cambridge University Press, 1983.

Hong Nayŏng and Ch'oe Hyegyŏng. "Sŏul chiyŏk ŭi honsu mit yedan p'ungsok e kwanhan yŏn'gu: Ilche mal put'ŏ hyŏnjae kkaji" [Matrimonial and in-law gift customs in the Seoul region: from the end of the colonial period to the present]. *Sŏulhak yŏn'gu* 17 (September 2001): 179–228.

Hong, Seung-Bum, Han-Jun Jin, Kyoung-Don Kwak, and Wook Kim. "Y-chromosome Haplogroup O3-M122 Variation in East Asia and Its Implications for the Peopling of Korea." *Korean Journal of Genetics* 28.1 (March 2006): 1–8.

Hong Sunmin. "Chŏngch'i chiptan ŭi sŏngkyŏk" [Characteristics of the political group]. In *Chosŏn chŏngch'isa (1800–1863)* [A political history of Chosŏn (1800–1863)], ed. Han'guk Yŏksa Yŏn'guhoe 19 Segi Chŏngch'isa Yŏn'guban, 1.226–256. Seoul: Ch'ŏngnyŏnsa, 1990.

Hwang, Kyung Moon. *Beyond Birth: Social Status in the Emergence of Modern Korea*. Cambridge, Mass.: Harvard University Asia Center, 2004.

———. "Citizenship, Social Equality and Government Reform: Changes in the Household Registration System in Korea, 1894–1910." *Modern Asian Studies* 38.2 (May 2004): 355–87.

Im Kyŏngsŏk. *Ijŏng Pak Hŏnyŏng iltaegi* [A biography of Ijŏng Pak Hŏnyŏng]. Seoul: Yŏksa Pip'yŏngsa, 2004.

Im Kyŏngt'aek. "Ilche ŭi 'kungmin' mandŭlgi—Minjŏkpŏp esŏ ch'angssi kaemyŏng kkaji" [The making of the "*kokumin*" by Imperial Japan—from the People's Registration Law to the name change]. *Hallim Ilbonhak* 9 (2004): 189–219.

Im Sŏnbin. "Ko munsŏ rŭl t'onghae pon Chosŏn hugi Chiksan hyanggyo ŭi unyŏng silt'ae" [Reality of Chiksan county school management in late Chosŏn as seen through old documents]. *Ko munsŏ yŏn'gu* 21 (2002): 133–54.

Jackson, Andrew David. "The 1728 Musillan Rebellion: Resources and the Fifth-Columnists." Ph.D. dissertation, University of London, 2011.

Jin, Han-Jun, Chris Tyler-Smith, and Wook Kim. "The Peopling of Korea Revealed by Analyses of Mitochondrial DNA and Y-Chromosomal Markers." *PLoS ONE* 4.1 (January 2009): 1–10.

Jin, Han-Jun, Kyoung-Don Kwak, Seung-Bum Hong, and Wook Kim. "Y-chromosome Haplogroup C Lineages and Implications for Population History of Korea." *Korean Journal of Genetics* 28.3 (September 2006): 253–59.

Kang Ch'angsŏk. "Hunmin chŏngŭm charyosil: Ch'oe Sejin (1465?–1552)" [Archive of sources on the *Hunmin chŏngŭm*: Ch'oe Sejin (1465?–1552)]. *Ch'ungbuk Taehakkyo kugŏhak kangŭi charyosil* [Korean language teaching resources, Chungbuk National University]. Accessed December 26, 2009. http://kang.chungbuk.ac.kr/zbxe/4127.

Kang, Hildi. *Family Lineage Records as a Resource for Korean History: A Case Study of Thirty-Nine Generations of the Sinch'ŏn Kang Family (720 A.D.–1955)*. Lewiston: The Edwin Mellen Press, 2007.

Kang Man'gil. "Kyŏnggang sangin yŏn'gu: Chosŏn hugi sangŏp chabon ŭi sŏngjang" [River merchants along the capital's rivers: the growth of merchant capital in late Chosŏn]. *Asea yŏn'gu* 14.2 (June 1971): 23–48.

Kang Myŏnggwan. "Chosŏn hugi kyŏng ajŏn sahoe ŭi pyŏnhwa wa yŏhang munhak" [Changes to the capital-functionary society and *yŏhang* literature in the late Chosŏn period]. *Taedong munhwa yŏn'gu* 25 (1990): 109–48.

———. "Chosŏn hugi Sŏul sŏngan ŭi sinbunbyŏl kŏjuji" [Residence areas by social status inside the city walls of late Chosŏn-period Seoul]. *Yŏksa pip'yŏng* 33 (1996): 324–45.

Karlsson, Anders. *The Hong Kyŏngnae Rebellion 1811–1812: Conflict Between Central Power and Local Society in 19th-Century Korea*. Stockholm: Institute of Oriental Languages, Stockholm University, 2000.

Kawashima, Fujiya. "Lineage Elite and Bureaucracy in Early Yi to Mid-Yi Dynasty Korea." *Occasional Papers on Korea* 5 (1977): 8–19.

Kim Chaemun. "21 segi Han'guk pŏp munhwa ŭi kukche kyŏngjaengnyŏk hyangsang ŭl wihan Han'guk chŏnt'ong pŏp munhwa ŭi kangjwa: Han'guk chŏnt'ong pŏp ŭi chŏngsin kwa pŏp ch'egye (35)—sabŏp sasang, iron: pŏmnyul chŏnmunjik kongmuwŏn sin'gyu imyong, ŏmmu p'yŏngka—kŏmnyul, suryŏng, kamsa rŭl chungsim ŭro" [Lectures on traditional Korean legal culture for improving the international competitiveness of Korean legal culture in the 21st century: the spirit and legal system of traditional Korean laws (35)—legal ideology, theory: appointment, duties, and evaluation of bureaucratic experts on legal statutes—judicial aides, county magistrates, and provincial governors]. *Sabŏp haengjŏng* 43.6 (2002): 32–53.

———. "21 segi Han'guk pŏp munhwa ŭi kukche kyŏngjaengnyŏk hyangsang ŭl wihan Han'guk chŏnt'ong pŏp munhwa ŭi kangjwa: Han'guk chŏnt'ong pŏp ŭi chŏngsin kwa pŏp ch'egye (36)—sabŏp sasang, iron: pŏmnyul chŏnmunjik kongmuwŏn p'yŏngkahu sŭngjin, p'ajik, chaeimyong, p'osang, ch'ŏbŏl—kŏmnyul, suryŏng, kamsa rŭl chungsim ŭro" [Lectures on traditional Korean legal culture for improving the international competitiveness of Korean legal culture in the 21st century: the spirit and legal system of traditional Korean laws (36)—legal ideology, theory: post-evaluation promotion, dismissal, re-appointment, incentives, and the disciplining of bureaucratic experts on legal statutes—judicial aides, county magistrates, and provincial governors]. *Sabŏp haengjŏng* 43.7 (2002): 5–27.

———. "21 segi Han'guk pŏp munhwa ŭi kukche kyŏngjaengnyŏk hyangsang ŭl wihan Han'guk chŏnt'ong pŏp munhwa ŭi kangjwa: Han'guk chŏnt'ong pŏp ŭi chŏngsin kwa pŏp ch'egye (37)—sabŏp sasang, iron: pŏmnyul chŏnmunjik (p'an, kŏmsa tŭng) kongmuwŏn ŭi imgi—kŏmnyul, suryŏng, kamsa rŭl chungsim ŭro" [Lectures on traditional Korean legal culture for improving the international competitiveness of Korean legal culture in the 21st century: the spirit and legal system of traditional Korean laws (37)—legal ideology, theory: service terms of bureaucratic experts (judges and prosecutors) on legal statutes—judicial aides, county magistrates, and provincial governors]. *Sabŏp haengjŏng* 43.8 (2002): 23–35.

———. "21 segi Han'guk pŏp munhwa ŭi kukche kyŏngjaengnyŏk hyangsang ŭl wihan Han'guk chŏnt'ong pŏp munhwa ŭi kangjwa: Han'guk chŏnt'ong pŏp ŭi chŏngsin kwa pŏp ch'egye (38)—sabŏp sasang, iron: pŏmnyul chŏnmunjik (p'an, kŏmsa tŭng) kongmuwŏn ŭi imgi—kŏmnyul, suryŏng, kamsa rŭl chungsim ŭro" [Lectures on traditional Korean legal culture for improving the international competitiveness of Korean legal culture in the 21st century: the spirit and legal system of traditional Korean laws (38)—legal ideology, theory: service terms of bureaucratic experts (judges and prosecutors) on legal statutes—judicial aides, county magistrates, and provincial governors]. *Sabŏp haengjŏng* 43.9 (2002): 24–36.

———. "21 segi Han'guk pŏp munhwa ŭi kukche kyŏngjaengnyŏk hyangsang ŭl wihan Han'guk chŏnt'ong pŏp munhwa ŭi kangjwa: Han'guk chŏnt'ong pŏp ŭi chŏngsin kwa pŏp ch'egye (39)—sabŏp sasang, chaep'an iron: pŏmnyul chŏnmunjik kongmuwŏn (2)—yulkwa e hapkyŏkhan kŏmnyul tŭng ŭi ch'ou wa kaesŏnch'aek" [Lectures on traditional Korean legal culture for improving the international competitiveness of Korean legal culture in the 21st century: the spirit and legal system of traditional Korean laws (39)—legal ideology, trial theory: bureaucratic experts on legal statutes (2)—the treatment of statute examination-passer judicial aides and improvement policies]. *Sabŏp haengjŏng* 43.10 (2002): 17–34.

———. "21 segi Han'guk pŏp munhwa ŭi kukche kyŏngjaengnyŏk hyangsang ŭl wihan Han'guk chŏnt'ong pŏp munhwa ŭi kangjwa: Han'guk chŏnt'ong pŏp ŭi chŏngsin kwa pŏp ch'egye (40)—sabŏp sasang, chaep'an iron: pŏmnyul chŏnmunjik kongmuwŏn (3)—kŏmnyul, suryŏng, kamsa tŭng ŭi ch'ŏbŏl" [Lectures on traditional Korean legal culture for improving the international competitiveness of Korean legal culture in the 21st century: the spirit and legal system of traditional Korean laws (40)—legal ideology, trial theory: bureaucratic experts on legal statutes (3)—disciplining judicial aides, county magistrates, and provincial governors]. *Sabŏp haengjŏng* 43.11 (2002): 28–40.

Kim Chiyŏng. "Sahoe chuŭi to chabon chuŭi to anin, Nam-Puk habŭipŏp ŭro unyŏngdoel t'ongil kukka ŭi yet sudo: Kaesŏng kongŏp chigu ro tallinŭn

Kaesŏng saramdŭl" [Neither socialist nor capitalist, administering the former capital of the united nation through laws agreed upon by the South and the North: Kaesŏng people rush to the Kaesŏng industrial district]. *Minjok 21* 25 (April 1, 2003). Accessed June 8, 2011. http://www.minjog21.com/news/read. php?idxno=264.

Kim Chonghŏn. "Rŏsia oegyogwan Beberŭ wa Agwan p'ach'ŏn" [The Russian diplomat Weber and the royal plight to the Russian legation]. *Yŏksa pip'yŏng* 86 (2009): 365–94.

Kim Do-hyung. "Introduction: The Nature of Reform in the Taehan Empire." In *Reform and Modernity in the Taehan Empire*, ed. Kim Dong-no, John B. Duncan, and Kim Do-hyung, 1–34. Seoul: Jimoondang, 2006.

Kim Dong-no, John B. Duncan, and Kim Do-hyung, eds. *Reform and Modernity in the Taehan Empire*. Seoul: Jimoondang, 2006.

Kim Hwajin. *Han'guk ŭi p'ungt'o wa munhwa* [Korea's natural features and culture]. Seoul: Ŭryu Mun'go, 1973.

Kim Hyŏnmok. "Hanmal kisuljik chungin ch'ulsin kwallyo ŭi sinbun kwa tonghyang" [Social status and trajectories of specialist *chungin*-background bureaucrats in the Hanmal period]. *Kuksagwan nonch'ong* 89 (2000): 151–74.

Kim Hyŏnsuk. "Taehan Cheguk-ki T'akchi-bu komun Allekseyep'ŭ ŭi chaejŏng chŏngch'aek kwa ch'in-Rŏ hwaltong" [Revenue policies and pro-Russian activities of the Adviser to the Ministry of Finance Alexeiev during the Korean Empire period]. *Han'guk kŭnhyŏndaesa yŏn'gu* 45 (December 2008): 80–113.

Kim Hyŏnyŏng. "Chosŏn hugi chungin ŭi kagye wa kyŏngnyŏk: yŏkkwan Ch'ŏllyŏng Hyŏn-ssi ka ko munsŏ ŭi punsŏk" [Family lineage and the careers of late Chosŏn *chungin*: an analysis of old documents of the interpreter Ch'ŏllyŏng Hyŏn family]. *Han'guk munhwa* 8 (December 1987): 103–34.

Kim In'gŏl. "Chosŏn hugi hyangch'on sahoe kwŏllyŏk kujo pyŏndong e taehan siron" [A preliminary discussion of the structure of power and its change in late Chosŏn local society]. *Han'guk saron* 19 (1988): 313–53.

Kim Kŭnbae. "U Changch'un ŭi Han'guk kwihwan kwa kwahak yŏn'gu" [U Changch'un's return to Korea and scientific research]. *Han'guk kwahaksa hakhoeji* 26.2 (2004): 139–64.

Kim Kwanggyu. "Taehan Chegukki ch'odŭng kyowŏn ŭi yangsŏng kwa imyong" [The training and employment of primary education staff during the Korean Empire period]. *Yŏksa kyoyuk* 119 (September 2011): 91–126.

Kim Kyŏngt'aek. "Hanmal chunginch'ŭng ŭi Kaehwa hwaltong kwa ch'inil Kaehwaron: O Sech'ang ŭi hwaltong ŭl chungsim ŭro" [The reform activities of the *chungin* stratum and pro-Japanese Enlightenment discourse in the Hanmal period: the activities of O Sech'ang]. *Yŏksa pip'yŏng* 21 (1993): 250–63.

Kim, Kyu Hyun. "Reflections on the Problems of Colonial Modernity and 'Collaboration' in Modern Korean History." *Journal of International and Area Studies* 11.3 (2004): 95–111.

Kim Sidŏk. "Hollye chŏnt'ong, ta pakkwin kŏt ŭn anida" [Wedding ritual traditions, not everything has changed]. *Silch'ŏn minsokhak sae ch'aek* 3 (September 2001): 81–102.

Kim Soyŏng. "Yongam-p'o sakkŏn e taehan Taehan Cheguk ŭi wigi ŭisik kwa taeŭng" [The Korean Empire's sense of crisis and response to the Yongam-p'o Incident]. *Han'guk kŭnhyŏndaesa yŏn'gu* 31 (December 2004): 131–71.

Kim, Sun Joo. *Marginality and Subversion in Korea: The Hong Kyŏngnae Rebellion of 1812.* Seattle: University of Washington Press, 2007.

———. "Taxes, the Local Elite, and the Rural Populace in the Chinju Uprising of 1862." *Journal of Asian Studies* 66.4 (November 2007): 993–1027.

Kim Sŭngt'ae and Pak Hyejin. *Naehan sŏn'gyosa ch'ongnam, 1884–1984* [An overview of missionaries who came to Korea, 1884–1984]. Revised edition. Seoul: Han'guk Kidokkyo Yŏksa Yŏn'guso, 1996.

Kim T'aeuk. "U Changch'un Paksa ŭi yŏksajŏk pijung kwa kŭ wich'i" [Dr. U Changch'un's presence and position in history]. *Nongch'on kyŏngje* 8.1 (1985): 141–51.

Kim Tuhŏn. "Chosŏn hugi chungin ŭi sŏryu mit ch'ŏp e taehan ch'abyŏl: Ubong Kim, Hanyang Yu, Chŏngŭp Yi chungin kagye rŭl chungsim ŭro" [*Chungin* discrimination against concubines and their descendants in late Chosŏn: the Ubong Kim, Hanyang Yu, and Chŏngŭp Yi *chungin* lines]. *Chosŏn sidae sahakpo* 13 (2000): 33–66.

Kim Ŭnsil. "Chosŏn singminji chisigin Na Hyesŏk ŭi kŭndaesŏng ŭl chilmun handa" [Questioning the modernity of Na Hyesŏk, an intellectual in colonial Korea]. *Han'guk yŏsŏnghak* 24.2 (June 2008): 147–86.

Kim Wanjin. "Chungin kwa ŏnŏ saenghwal: Ch'oe Sejin ŭl chungsim ŭro" [The *chung-in* and the everyday life of language: Ch'oe Sejin]. *Chindan hakpo* 77 (1994): 73–92.

Kim, Wook, Dong Jik Shin, Shinji Harihara, and Yung Jin Kim. "Y Chromosome DNA Variation in East Asian Populations and Its Potential for Inferring the Peopling of Korea." *Journal of Human Genetics* 45 (2000): 76–83.

Kim Yangsu. "Chosŏn hugi yŏkkwan kamun ŭi yŏn'gu: Kim Chinam, Kim Kyŏngmun tŭng Ubong Kim-ssi kagye rŭl chungsim ŭro" [A study of a late Chosŏn interpreter family: Kim Chinam, Kim Kyŏngmun, and the Ubong Kim descent line]. *Paeksan hakpo* 32 (1985): 97–151.

———. "Chosŏn chŏnhwan'gi ŭi chungin chiban hwaltong: Hyŏn Tŏgyun, Hyŏn Ch'ae, Hyŏn Sun tŭng Ch'ŏllyŏng Hyŏn-ssi yŏkkwan kagye rŭl chungsim ŭro" [The activities of a *chungin* family during the Chosŏn transition era: the interpreter Ch'ŏllyŏng Hyŏn line of Hyŏn Tŏgyun, Hyŏn Ch'ae, and Hyŏn Sun]. *Tongbang hakchi* 102 (1998): 185–272.

———. "Chosŏn hugi sahoe pyŏndong kwa chŏnmunjik chungin ŭi hwaltong: yŏkkwan, ŭigwan, ŭmyanggwan, yulgwan, sanwŏn, hwawŏn, agin tŭng kwa kwallyŏn hayŏ" [Late Chosŏn social change and the activities of specialist *chungin*: government interpreters, physicians, astronomers, jurists, accountants, painters, and musicians]. In *Han'guk kŭndae ihaenggi chungin yŏn'gu* [The *chungin* during

Korea's modern transition], ed. Yŏnse Taehakkyo Kukhak Yŏn'guwŏn, 171–300. Seoul: Sinsŏwŏn, 1999.

———. "Chosŏn kaehang chŏnhu chungin ŭi chŏngch'i oegyo: yŏkkwan Pyŏn Wŏn'gyu tŭng ŭi Tongbuga mit Miguk kwa ŭi hwaltong ŭl chungsim ŭro" [The statecraft and foreign policies of the chungin before and during the Open Ports Period: the activities of interpreter Pyŏn Wŏn'gyu vis-à-vis East Asia and the United States]. Sirhak sasang yŏn'gu 12 (1999): 311–66.

———. "Sŏul chungin ŭi 19 segi saenghwal: Ch'ŏllyŏng Hyŏn-ssi yŏkkwan T'ak ŭi ilgi rŭl chungsim ŭro" [The daily life of Seoul chungin in the 19th century: the diary of the Ch'ŏllyŏng Hyŏn interpreter T'ak]. Ch'ŏngjudae Inmun kwahak nonjip 26 (2003): 47–92.

Kim Yŏngbae. "Hanmal Hansŏng-bu chugŏ hyŏngt'ae ŭi sahoejŏk sŏngkyŏk: hojŏk charyo ŭi punsŏk ŭl chungsim ŭro" [Social characteristics of forms of residence in Seoul in the Hanmal period: an analysis of household registration records]. Taehan Kŏnch'uk Hakhoe nonmunjip 7.2 (April 1991): 189–98.

Kim Yŏnggyŏng. "Hanmal Sŏul chiyŏk chunginch'ŭng ŭi kŭndaehwa undong kwa hyŏnsil insik: yŏkkwan Ch'ŏllyŏng Hyŏn-ssi ka rŭl chungsim ŭro" [The modernization movement among the Seoul chungin and their outlook in the Hanmal period: the interpreter Ch'ŏllyŏng Hyŏn family]. Hangnim 20 (1999): 1–52.

Kim Yŏngmo. Chosŏn chibaech'ŭng yŏn'gu [The Chosŏn ruling stratum]. Seoul: Ilchogak, 1977.

Kim Yongsŏn. Koryŏ ŭmsŏ chedo yŏn'gu [The Koryŏ protected appointment system]. Seoul: Han'guk Yŏn'guwŏn, 1987.

Kim Yongsŏp. Chosŏn hugi nongŏp-sa yŏn'gu [Late Chosŏn agrarian history]. Volume I, Nongch'on kyŏngje-sahoe pyŏndong [Socioeconomic change for farming villages]. Expanded edition. Seoul: Chisik Sanŏpsa, 1995.

Kim Yunjŏng and Sŏ Ch'isang. "Kwangmu 6-nyŏn ŭi P'yŏngyang P'unggyŏng-gung ch'anggŏn kongsa e kwanhan yŏn'gu" [The construction of P'unggyŏng Palace in P'yŏngyang in the 6th year of the Kwangmu era]. Taehan Kŏnch'uk Hakhoe nonmunjip (September 2009) 25.9: 177–86.

Ko Donghwan. See Ko Tonghwan.

Ko Tonghwan [Ko Donghwan]. "Development of Commerce and Commercial Policy During the Reign of King Chŏngjo." Korea Journal 40.4 (Winter 2000): 203–26.

"Korean-American Architect David Hyun." Korean Slate: Things Korean and not (in Korea Town LA). Accessed October 17, 2011. http://koreanslate.com/korean-american-architect-david-hyun.html.

Koyang-gun chimyŏng yuraejip [Origins of place names in Koyang county]. Koyang: Koyang Munhwawŏn, 1991.

Ku Kwangmo. "Ch'angssi kaemyŏng chŏngch'aek kwa Chosŏnin ŭi taeŭng" [The name-change policy and Korean responses]. Kukche chŏngch'i nonch'ong 45.4 (December 2005): 31–53.

Larsen, Kirk W. Tradition, Treaties, and Trade: Qing Imperialism and Chosŏn Korea, 1850–1910. Cambridge, Mass.: Harvard University Asia Center, 2008.

Lett, Denise Potrezeba. *In Pursuit of Status: The Making of South Korea's "New" Urban Middle Class.* Cambridge, Mass.: Harvard University Asia Center, 2002.

Lew, Young Ick. "The Conservative Character of the 1894 Tonghak Peasant Uprising: A Reappraisal with Emphasis on Chŏn Pong-jun's Background and Motivation." *Journal of Korean Studies* 7 (1990): 149–80.

Lewis, James B. "A Scroll of the 1748 Korean Embassy to Japan Preserved in the British Museum." *Acta Koreana* 13.1 (June 2010): 51–88.

Merriam-Webster Online. Accessed April 27, 2013. http://www.merriam-webster.com/dictionary/thremmatology.

Moskowitz, Karl. "The Creation of the Oriental Development Company: Japanese Illusions Meet Korean Reality." *Occasional Papers on Korea* 2 (March 1974): 73–109.

Mun Hŭisu. "Kukchejŏk chŏnhu kwan'gye e issŏsŏ Agwan p'ach'ŏn—1895–1896" [The royal flight to the Russian legation in the context of what had preceded and followed vis-à-vis international relations—1895–1896]. *Han'guk chŏngch'i oegyosa nonch'ong* 18 (1998): 231–55.

Munhwa K'ŏnt'ench'ŭ Tatk'ŏm. "Ch'ajang" [Cartwright]. *Hwasŏng ŭigwe* [Royal protocols for Hwasŏng]. Accessed October 6, 2013. http://tinyurl.com/ma8zeyf.

Myers, Ramon H., and Mark R. Peattie, eds. *The Japanese Colonial Empire, 1895–1945.* Princeton: Princeton University Press, 1984.

———, and Yamada Saburo. "Agricultural Development in the Empire." In *The Japanese Colonial Empire, 1895–1945,* ed. Ramon H. Myers and Mark R. Peattie, 420–52.

NAVER kugŏ sajŏn [NAVER Korean language dictionary]. Accessed May 10, 2012. http://krdic.naver.com.

No Inhwa. "Taehan Cheguk sigi ŭi Hansŏng Sabŏm Hakkyo e kwanhan yŏn'gu" [Seoul Normal School in the Korean Empire period]. *Ihwa sahak yŏn'gu* 16 (1985): 12–24.

No Yŏnghŭi. "Ilbon sin yŏsŏngdŭl kwa pigyohae pon Na Hyesŏk ŭi sin yŏsŏnggwan kwa kŭ han'gye" [Na Hyesŏk's perspective on new women and its limitations as compared to Japanese new women]. *Irŏ Ilmunhak yŏn'gu* 32 (1998): 341–62.

O Kapkyun. "Punmu Kongsin e taehan punsŏkchŏk yŏn'gu" [An analytical study of Punmu Meritorious Subjects]. *Ch'ŏngju Kyoyuk Taehak nonmunjip* 21 (1985): 297–320.

O Sŏng. *Han'guk kŭndae sangŏp tosi yŏn'gu* [Commercial cities in modern Korea]. Seoul: Kukhak Charyowŏn, 1998.

O Such'ang. "Chuyo chŏngch'aek ŭi silsang" [The reality of major policies]. In *Chosŏn chŏngch'isa.* In *Chosŏn chŏngch'isa (1800–1863)* [A political history of Chosŏn (1800–1863)], ed. Han'guk Yŏksa Yŏn'guhoe 19 Segi Chŏngch'isa Yŏn'guban, 2.634–85. Seoul: Ch'ŏngnyŏnsa, 1990.

———. *Chosŏn hugi P'yŏngan-do sahoe palchŏn yŏn'gu* [The social development of P'yŏngan Province in the late Chosŏn period]. Seoul: Ilchogak, 2002.

"Odŏk Kyohoe yaksa" [A brief history of Odŏk Church]. Inscribed on *Odŏk Changno Kyohoe ch'angnip kinyŏmbi* [Stele in commemoration of the founding of Odŏk

Presbyterian Church]. Erected in Odŏk-ri, Ch'unghwa-myŏn, Puyŏ-gun, Ch'ungch'ŏngnam-do, 2006.

Pae Hangsŏp. "Cho-Rŏ sugyo (1884) chŏnhu Chosŏnin ŭi Rŏsia kwan" [Korean perspectives on Russia around the time of the establishment of Korean-Russian relations (1884)]. *Yŏksa hakpo* 194 (2007): 127–60.

Pae Kyubŏm. "Kyŏnggang sangin ŭi chabon ch'ukchŏk kwajŏng kwa chŏn'gae yangsang" [Capital-(Han) River merchants' process of capital accumulation and aspects of development]. *Han'guk ŭi minsok kwa munhwa* 9 (2004): 49–81.

Paek Namun. *Chosŏn sahoe kyŏngjesa* [A socioeconomic history of Korea]. Tōkyō: Kaizōsha, 1933.

Paek Sŭngch'ŏl [Baek Seung-ch'ol]. "The Development of Local Markets and the Establishment of a New Circulation System in Late Chosŏn Society." *Seoul Journal of Korean Studies* 12 (1999): 152–76.

———. *Chosŏn hugi sangŏpsa yŏn'gu: sangŏp non, sangŏp chŏngch'aek* [The history of commerce in the late Chosŏn period: discussions on commerce, commercial policies]. Seoul: Hyean, 2000.

Paek Sŭngjong. "18–19 segi Chŏlla-do esŏ ŭi sinhŭng seryŏk ŭi taedu: T'aein-hyŏn Kohyŏllae-myŏn ŭi sŏryu" [The emergence of new forces in Chŏlla province in the 18–19th centuries: members of illegitimate-son descent lines of Kohyŏllae district, T'aein county]. In *Yi Kibaek Sŏnsaeng kohŭi kinyŏm Han'guk sahak nonch'ong* [Essays in commemoration of Mr. Yi Kibaek's seventieth birthday], ed. Yi Kibaek Sŏnsaeng Kohŭi Kinyŏm Han'guk Sahak Nonch'ong Kanhaeng Wiwŏnhoe, 2.1339–67. Seoul: Ilchogak, 1994.

———. "Wijo chokpo ŭi yuhaeng" [The popularity of fabricated genealogies]. *Han'guksa simin kangjwa* 24 (February 1999): 67–85.

Pak Chongjae. "Silla p'al taegun punbong hŏgu sŏl e taehan koch'al" [An inquiry on the fabricated theory on the enfeoffment of eight Silla princes]. *Pannam Pak-ssi homp'eiji* [The Pannam Pak homepage]. Accessed December 19, 2011. http://www.bannampark.org/park01_12.htm.

Pak Chunsŏng. "17, 18 segi kungbang-jŏn ŭi hwaktae wa soyu hyŏngt'ae ŭi pyŏnhwa" [The expansion of royal estate land and its changing ownership in the 17th and 18th centuries]. *Han'guk saron* 11 (1984): 185–278.

Pak Hŭibyŏng. "Chosŏn hugi min'gan ŭi yuhyŏp sungsang kwa yuhyŏp chŏn ŭi sŏngnip" [The veneration of errant fighters and the establishment of their biographies among the ordinary people of the late Chosŏn period]. *Han'guk Han munhak yŏn'gu* 9 and 10 combined (1988): 301–52.

Pak Hŭngju. "Sŏul maŭl gut ŭi yuhyŏng kwa kyet'ong" [Types and transmissions of shamanistic village performances in Seoul]. *Han'guk musokhak* 12 (August 2006): 119–75.

Pak T'aegyun. *Han'guk Chŏnjaeng: kkŭnnaji anŭn chŏnjaeng, kkŭnnaya hal chŏnjaeng* [The Korean War: the war that has not ended, the war that must end]. Seoul: Ch'aek kwa Hamkke, 2005.

Pak Ŭnsuk. *Kapsin chŏngbyŏn yŏn'gu: Chosŏn ŭi kŭndaejŏk kaehyŏk kusang kwa min-*

jung ŭi insik [The Kapsin Coup: modern reformist visions and the people's perceptions in Korea]. Seoul: Yŏksa Pip'yŏngsa, 2005.

———. "Yu Taech'i: chungin kŭndaehwa chuyŏk non i naŭn oryu" [Yu Taech'i: a fallacy from the theory of *chungin*-led modernization]. *Naeil ŭl yŏnŭn yŏksa* 28 (2007): 134–44.

Pak Yongun. *Koryŏ sidae ŭmsŏje wa kwagŏje yŏn'gu* [The system of protected appointments and government service examinations in the Koryŏ period]. Seoul: Ilchisa, 1990.

Palais, James B. *Politics and Policy in Traditional Korea*. Cambridge, Mass.: Harvard University Asia Center, 1991.

———. *Confucian Statecraft and Korean Institutions: Yu Hyŏngwŏn and the Late Chosŏn Dynasty*. Seattle: University of Washington Press, 1996.

Pang Hyosun. "Ilche sidae min'gan sŏjŏk palhaeng hwaltong ŭi kujochŏk t'ŭksŏng e kwanhan yŏn'gu" [The structural characteristics of private publishing activity during the Japanese colonial period]. Ph.D. dissertation, Ihwa Yŏja Taehakkyo, 2001.

Park, Eugene Y. *Between Dreams and Reality: The Military Examination in Late Chosŏn Korea, 1600–1894*. Cambridge, Mass.: Harvard University Asia Center, 2007.

———. "Status and 'Defunct' Offices in Early Modern Korea: The Case of Five Guards Generals (Owijang), 1864–1910." *Journal of Social History* 40.3 (March 2008): 737–57.

———. "Imagined Connections in Early Modern Korea, 1600–1894: Representations of Northern Elite Miryang Pak Lineages in Genealogies." *Seoul Journal of Korean Studies* 21.1 (June 2008): 1–27.

———. "Old Status Trappings in a New World: The 'Middle People' (*Chungin*) and Genealogies in Modern Korea." *Journal of Family History* 38.2 (April 2013): 166–87.

Peterson, Mark A. *Korean Adoption and Inheritance: Case Studies in the Creation of a Classic Confucian Society*. Ithaca: East Asia Program, Cornell University, 1996.

Quinones, C. Kenneth. "The Prerequisites for Power in Late Yi Korea: 1864–1894." Ph.D. dissertation, Harvard University, 1975.

———. "Military Officials of Yi Korea: 1864–1910." In *Che 1-Hoe Han'gukhak Kukche Haksul Hoeŭi nonmunjip* [Papers of the First International Conference on Korean Studies], 691–700. Sŏngnam: Han'guk Chŏngsin Munhwa Yŏn'guwŏn, 1980.

Robinson, Kenneth R. "The Chinese Ancestors in a Korean Descent Group's Genealogies." *Journal of Korean Studies* 13.1 (Fall 2008): 89–114.

———. "Yi Hoe and His Korean Ancestors in T'aean Yi Genealogies." *Seoul Journal of Korean Studies* 21.2 (December 2008): 221–50.

Rogers, Michael. "National Consciousness in Medieval Korea: The Impact of Liao and Chin on Koryŏ." In *China Among Equals: The Middle Kingdom and Its Neighbors, 10th–14th Centuries*, ed. Morris Rossabi, 151–72. Berkeley: University of California Press, 1983.

Schmid, Andre. *Korea Between Empires, 1895–1919*. New York: Columbia University Press, 2002.

Shi, Hong, Yong-li Dong, Bo Wen, Chun-Jie Xiao, Peter A. Underhill, Pei-dong Shen, Renajit Chakraborty, Li Jin, and Bing Su. "Y-Chromosome Evidence of Southern Origin of the East Asian-Specific Haplogroup O3-M122." *American Journal of Human Genetics* 77 (2005): 408–19.

Sin Ch'aeho. *Chosŏn saron: Sin Ch'aeho yugo* [A history of Korea: the writings of Sin Ch'aeho]. Seoul: Kwanghan Sŏrim, 1946.

Sin Yongha. "O Kyŏngsŏk ŭi Kaehwa sasang kwa Kaehwa hwaltong" [O Kyŏngsŏk's Enlightenment Thought and the Enlightenment Movement]. *Yŏksa hakpo* 107 (1985): 107–35.

Skorecki, Karl, Sara Selig, Shraga Blazer, Robert Bradman, Neil Bradman, P. J. Waburton, Monica Ismajlowicz, and Michael F. Hammer. "Y Chromosomes of Jewish Priests." *Nature* 385.6611 (January 2, 1997): 32.

Sŏ Inhan. *Taehan Cheguk ŭi kunsa chedo* [The military institutions of the Korean Empire]. Seoul: Hyean, 2000.

Son Hyŏngbu. *Pak Kyusu ŭi Kaehwa sasang yŏn'gu* [A study on Pak Kyusu's Enlightenment Thought]. Seoul: Ilchogak, 1997.

Son Sukkyŏng, ed. *Chungin Kim Pŏmu kamun kwa kŭdŭl ŭi munsŏ* [The *chungin* Kim Pŏmu family and their documents]. Pusan: Pusan Kyogu Sun'gyoja Hyŏnyang Wiwŏnhoe, 1992.

Song Ch'ansik. "Chokpo ŭi kanhaeng" [Compilation of genealogies]. *Han'guksa simin kangjwa* 24 (February 1999): 50–66.

Song Chunho. "Chosŏn sidae ŭi kwagŏ wa yangban mit yangin (2): munkwa wa saengwŏn-chinsasi rŭl chungsim ŭro hayŏ" [The examination system, aristocracy, and commoners in the Chosŏn period (2): the civil examination and the classics-literary licentiate examinations]. *Yŏksa hakpo* 69 (March 1976): 103–35.

———. *Chosŏn sahoesa yŏn'gu: Chosŏn sahoe ŭi kujo wa sŏngkyŏk mit kŭ pyŏnch'ŏn e kwanhan yŏn'gu* [Studies in Chosŏn social history: the structure, characteristics, and change of Chosŏn society]. Seoul: Ilchogak, 1987.

Song Hyŏn'gang. "Ch'ungnam chibang Changno-gyo ŭi chŏllae wa suyong" [Introduction and acceptance of Presbyterianism in the Ch'ungnam region]. *Han'guk Kidokkyo wa yŏksa* 17 (August 2002): 29–64.

Song Kyujin, Pyŏn Ŭnjin, Kim Yunhŭi, and Kim Sŭngŭn. *T'onggye ro pon Han'guk kŭnhyŏndaesa* [Modern Korean history through statistics]. Seoul: Ayŏn Ch'ulp'anbu, 2004.

Song Mano. "1851 nyŏn ŭi chungin t'ongch'ŏng undong kwa Chosŏn hugi chungin ch'ŭng ŭi tonghyang" [The 1851 *chungin* petition movement for access to prestigious offices and the trajectories of the late Chosŏn *chungin* stratum]. *Chŏnju sahak* 8 (2001): 133–60.

Sŏul T'ŭkpyŏlsi-Sa P'yŏnch'an Wiwŏnhoe. *Sajin ŭro ponŭn Sŏul* [A history of Seoul through photographs], vol. 1: *Kaehang ihu Sŏul ŭi kŭndaehwa wa kŭ siryŏn (1876–*

1910) [Modernization of Seoul and its ordeal since the opening of ports (1876–1910)]. Seoul: Sŏul T'ŭkpyŏlsi-Sa P'yŏnch'an Wiwŏnhoe, 2002.

Su, Bing, Junhua Xiao, Peter Underhill, Ranjan Deka, Weiling Zhang, Joshua Akey, Wei Huang, Di Shen, Daru Lu, Jingchun Luo, Jiayou Chu, Jiazhen Tan, Peidong Shen, Ron Davis, Luca Cavalli-Sforza, Ranajit Chakraborty, Momiao Xiong, Ruofu Du, Peter Oefner, Zhu Chen, and Li Jin. "Y-Chromosome Evidence for a Northward Migration of Modern Humans into Eastern Asia During the Last Ice Age." *American Journal of Human Genetics* 65 (1999): 1718–24.

Sykes, Bryan. "Surnames and the Y Chromosome." *American Journal of Human Genetics* 66 (2000): 1417–19.

Taehan Chibang Haengjŏng Kongjehoe P'yŏnjipsil. "Segyejŏgin yukchong hakcha U Changch'un Paksa" [Dr. U Changch'un, a world-class thremmatologist]. *Chibang haengjŏng* 41.462 (1992): 105–11.

Thomas, Mark G., Karl Skorecki, Haim Ben-Amid, Tudor Parfitt, Neil Bradman, and David B. Goldstein. "Origins of Old Testament Priests." *Nature* 394.6689 (July 9, 1998): 138–40.

Toby, Ronald P. "Carnival of the Aliens: Korean Embassies in Edo-Period Art and Popular Culture." *Monumenta Nipponica* 41.4 (Winter 1986): 415–56.

Totman, Conrad. *Pre-Industrial Korea and Japan in Environmental Perspective.* Leiden: Brill, 2004.

Tōyō Bunko Tōhoku Ajia Kenkyūhan (Chōsen). *Nihon shozai Chōsen koseki kankei shiryō kaidai* [A bibliographical guide to the Korean household registration-related documents in Japan]. Tokyo: Tōyō Bunko, 2004.

Tsunoda Fusako. *Waga sokoku: U hakase no unmei no tane* [My fatherland: the seeds of Dr. U Changch'un's destinity]. Tokyo: Shinchosha, 1990.

Underhill, P. A., G. Passarino, A. A. Lin, P. Shen, M. Mirazoun Lahr, R. A. Foley, P. J. Oefner, and L. L. Cavalli-Sforza. "The Phylogeography of Y Chromosome Binary Haplotypes and the Origins of Modern Human Populations." *American Journal of Human Genetics* 65 (2001): 43–62.

Wagner, Edward W. "The Korean Chokpo as a Historical Source." In *Studies in Asian Genealogy,* ed. Spencer J. Palmer, 141–52. Provo: Brigham Young University Press, 1972.

———. "Two Early Genealogies and Women's Status in Early Yi Dynasty Korea." In *Korean Women: View from the Inner Room,* ed. Laurel Kendall and Mark Peterson, 23–32. New Haven: East Rock Press, 1983.

———. "The Three Hundred Year History of the Haeju Kim *Chapkwa-Chungin* Lineage." In *Song Chunho Kyosu chŏngnyŏn kinyŏm nonch'ong pyŏlswae* [Essays in commemoration of Professor Song Chunho's retirement, offprint], ed. Song Chunho Kyosu Chŏngnyŏn Kinyŏm Nonch'ong Kanhaeng Wiwŏnhoe, 1–22. Chŏnju: Song Chunho Kyosu Chŏngnyŏn Kinyŏm Nonch'ong Kanhaeng Wiwŏnhoe, 1987.

Yang Chinsŏk. "Ch'ungch'ŏng chiyŏk nongmin chŏnjaeng ŭi chŏn'gae yangsang"

[The development and aspects of peasant warfare in the Ch'ŭngch'ŏng region]. *Paekche munhwa* 23 (1994): 21–40.

Yang Sanghyŏn. "Taehan Cheguk ŭi kunje kaep'yŏn kwa kunsa yesan unyŏng" [The Korean Empire's reorganization of military system and management of military budget]. *Yŏksa wa kyŏnggye* 61 (2006): 179–212.

Yang Sŏna. "18-19 segi tojang kyŏngyŏngji esŏ kungbang kwa tojang ŭi kwan'gye" [Relations between royal estate management agencies and local estate managers in the 18th and 19th centuries]. *Han'gukhak yŏn'gu* 36 (March 2011): 167–96.

Yi Chongbŏm and Ch'oe Wŏn'gyu, eds. *Charyo Han'guk kŭnhyŏndaesa immun* [A source-based introduction to the modern and contemporary history of Korea]. Seoul: Hyean, 1995.

Yi Chŏngsŏn. "Han'guk kŭndae 'hojŏk chedo' ŭi pyŏnch'ŏn—'Minjŏkpŏp' ŭi pŏpchejŏk t'ŭkching ŭl chungsim ŭro" [Changes to the modern Korean "household registration system"—legal characteristics of the "People's Registration Law"]. *Han'guk saron* 55 (2009): 275–328.

Yi Hŏnch'ang. "Kŭndae kyŏngje sŏngjang ŭi kiban hyŏngsŏng-gi rosŏ 18 segi Chosŏn ŭi sŏngch'wi wa kŭ han'gye" [The accomplishments and limitations of 18th-century Chosŏn as the formative period of modern economic growth]. *Yŏksa hakpo* 213 (March 2012): 97–126.

Yi Hunsang. "Chosŏn hugi ŭi hyangni wa kŭndae ihu idŭl ŭi chinch'ul: chungjae ellittŭ ŭi tamnon kwa kŭ kwigyŏl" [Late Chosŏn local functionaries and their advancement in the modern era: the discourse of a mediating elite and its effect]. *Yŏksa hakpo* 141 (1994): 244–74.

———. "19 segi Chŏlla-do Koch'ang ŭi hyangni segye wa Sin Chaehyo: Sin Chaehyo kamun sojang ko munsŏ charyo rŭl t'onghayŏ pon Sin Chaehyo ŭi sahoe chiwi wa p'ansori ŭi palchŏn I" [Sin Chaehyo and the world of the local functionaries in 19th-century Koch'ang, Chŏlla Province: Sin Chaehyo's social status and the development of *p'ansori* as seen through old documents in the Sin Chaehyo family possession, I]. *Ko munsŏ yŏn'gu* 26 (2005): 235–90.

Yi Hyŏnhŭi. "Hanmal chungin Kaehwa sasangga ŭi kaehyŏk undong: ŭisik kaehyŏk undong ŭi sigak" [The *chungin* Enlightenment thinkers' reform movement in the Hanmal period: the perspective of the movement to reform thought]. *Sahak yon'gu* 34 (1982): 65–80.

———. "1870 nyŏndae ŭi Kaehwa sasang kwa kŭ chudo kyech'ŭng: chunginch'ŭng ŭi Kaehwa sasang kwa kŭ ponjil" [Enlightenment Thought and the social stratum of Enlightenment leaders in the 1870s: the fundamental nature of *chungin* Enlightenment Thought]. *Han'guk sasang* 21 (1989): 107–24.

Yi Kibaek. *Han'guksa sillon* [A new history of Korea]. Revised edition. Seoul: Ilchogak, 1990.

———. "Chokpo wa hyŏndae sahoe" [Genealogy and contemporary society]. *Han'guksa simin kangjwa* 24 (February 1999): 108–17.

Yi Kwangnin. "Kyŏngjuin yŏn'gu" [A study of capital-resident agents from local offices]. *Inmun kwahak* 7 (1962): 237–68.

Yi Minwŏn. *Myŏngsŏng Wanghu sihae wa Agwan p'ach'ŏn: Han'guk ŭl tullŏssan Rŏ-Il kaltŭng* [The murder of Queen Myŏngsŏng and King Kojong's flight to Russian legation: the Russo-Japanese conflict surrounding Korea]. Seoul: Kukhak Charyowŏn, 2002.

Yi Myŏnghwa. "Ilche hwangmin kyoyuk kwa kungmin hakkyo-je ŭi sihaeng" [The Japanese empire's education for imperial subjects and the enactment of the citizens' school system]. *Han'guk tongnip undongsa yŏn'gu* 35 (April 2010): 315–48.

Yi Namhŭi. "Chosŏn sidae (1498–1894) chapkwa ipkyŏkcha ŭi chillo wa kŭ ch'ui: 'Chapkwa pangmok' teit'ŏbeisŭ punsŏk ŭl chungsim ŭro" [Technical examination passers' post-degree careers and their patterns in the Chosŏn period (1498–1894): an analysis of the "technical examination roster" database]. In *Chosŏn sidae ŭi sahoe wa sasang* [Chosŏn society and ideology], ed. Chosŏn Sahoe Yŏn'guhoe, 241–72. Seoul: Chosŏn Sahoe Yŏn'guhoe, 1998.

———. "Chosŏn hugi 'chapkwa chungin' ŭi sahoejŏk yudongsŏng" [Social mobility of late Chosŏn "technical-examination *chungin*"]. In *Han'guk kŭndae ihaenggi chungin yŏn'gu* [The *chungin* during Korea's modern transition], ed. Yŏnse Taehakkyo Kukhak Yŏn'guwŏn, 301–38. Seoul: Sinsŏwŏn, 1999.

Yi Sanggŭm. *Sarang ŭi sŏnmul: Sop'a Pang Chŏnghwan ŭi saengae* [A gift of love: the life of Sop'a Pang Chŏnghwan]. Seoul: Hallim Ch'ulp'ansa, 2005.

Yi Seyŏng. "18, 19 segi kongmul sijang ŭi hyŏngsŏng kwa yut'ong kujo ŭi pyŏndong" [The formation of grain markets and changes in the structure of distribution networks in the 18th and 19th centuries]. *Han'guk saron* 9 (1983): 185–254.

Yi Sŏngmu. "Chosŏn ch'ogi ŭi kisulgwan kwa kŭ chiwi: chungin ch'ŭng ŭi sŏngnip munje rŭl chungsim ŭro" [Technical-specialist officials and their status in the early Chosŏn period: issues in the formation of the *chungin* stratum]. In *Hyeam Yu Hongnyŏl Paksa hwagap kinyŏm nonch'ong* [Essays in celebration of Hyeam Dr. Yu Hongnyŏl's sixtieth birthday], ed. Hyeam Yu Hongnyŏl Paksa Hwagap Kinyŏm Saŏp Wiwŏnhoe, 193–229. Seoul: T'amgudang, 1971.

———. "Chosŏn chŏn'gi chungin ch'ŭng ŭi sŏngnip munje" [Issues in the formation of the *chungin* stratum in the early Chosŏn period]. *Tongyanghak* 8 (1978): 272–84.

Yi Sugŏn. *Yŏngnam sarim-p'a ŭi hyŏngsŏng* [The formation of the Yŏngnam *sarim*]. Kyŏngsan, Kyŏngsangbuk-to: Yŏngnam Taehakkyo Minjok Munhwa Yŏn'guso, 1979.

———. *Han'guk chungse sahoesa yŏn'gu* [The social history of medieval Korea]. Seoul: Ilchogak, 1984.

Yi Sŭngil. "Chosŏn Ch'ongdokpu ŭi Chosŏnin tŭngnok chedo yŏn'gu—1910-nyŏndae minjŏk kwa kŏju tŭngnokpu ŭi tŭngnok tanwi ŭi pyŏnhwa rŭl chungsim ŭro" [The Government-General of Korea's system of registering Koreans—changes in the unit of registration for family and residential registration records in the 1910s]. *Sahoe wa yŏksa* 67 (June 2005): 6–40.

———. "Chosŏn Hojŏngnyŏng chejŏng e kwanhan yŏn'gu" [The enactment of the Ordinance on Korean Household Registration]. *Pŏpsahak yŏn'gu* 32 (October 2005): 37–68.

Yi Sŭngnyŏl. *Cheguk kwa sangin: Sŏul-Kaesŏng-Inch'ŏn chiyŏk chabon'gadŭl kwa Han'guk purŭjua ŭi kiwŏn, 1896–1945* [Merchants and empire: the capitalists of Seoul, Kaesŏng, and Inch'ŏn regions, and the origins of the Korean bourgeoisie, 1896–1945]. Seoul: Yŏksa Pip'yŏngsa, 2007.

Yi Uk. "18 segi mal Sŏul sangŏpkye ŭi pyŏnhwa wa chŏngbu taech'aek" [Changes in Seoul commercial networks and government policies in the late 18th century]. *Yŏksa hakpo* 142 (1994): 129–73.

———. "Chosŏn hugi Han'gang-byŏn ŭi sangp'um kyŏngje palchŏn kwa sangŏp chŏngch'aek ŭi pyŏnhwa" [The development of a mercantile economy on the Han River banks and changes in commercial policies in the late Chosŏn period]. *Sŏulhak yŏn'gu* 24 (March 2005): 31–61.

Yi Uyŏn. "18-19 segi sallim hwangpyehwa wa nongŏp saengsansŏng" [Deforestation and agricultural productivity in the 18th and 19th centuries]. *Kyŏngje sahak* 34 (2003): 31–57.

Yŏnse Taehakkyo Kukhak Yŏn'guwŏn, ed. *Han'guk kŭndae ihaenggi chungin yŏn'gu* [The *chungin* during Korea's modern transition]. Seoul: Tosŏ Ch'ulp'an Sinsŏwŏn, 1999.

Yoo, Theodore Jun. *The Politics of Gender in Colonial Korea: Education, Labor, and Health, 1910–1945*. Berkeley: University of California Press, 2008.

Yuh, Leighanne. "Rejection, Selection, and Acceptance: Early Modern Korean Education and Identity (Re)Construction, 1895–1910." In *Reform and Modernity in the Taehan Empire*, ed. Kim Dong-no, John B. Duncan, and Kim Do-hyung, 73–104. Seoul: Jimoondang, 2006.

Index